GOD IS A PICKLE

Recipes and Stories for Preserving the Seasons

A Culinary Journey Through the Czech Republic

gestalten

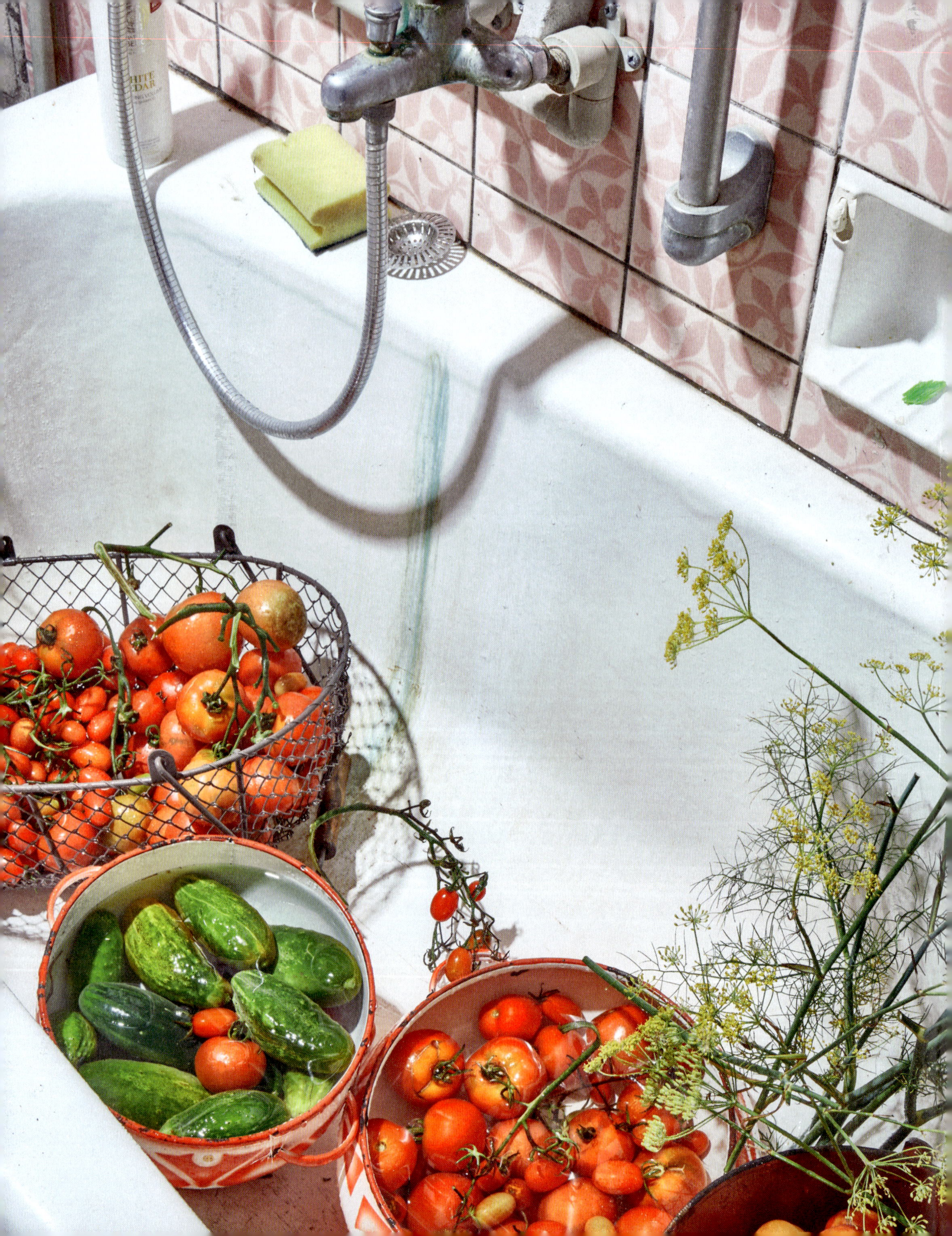

USEFUL FACTS ABOUT PRESERVING

RECIPES AND STORIES FOR PRESERVING THE SEASONS

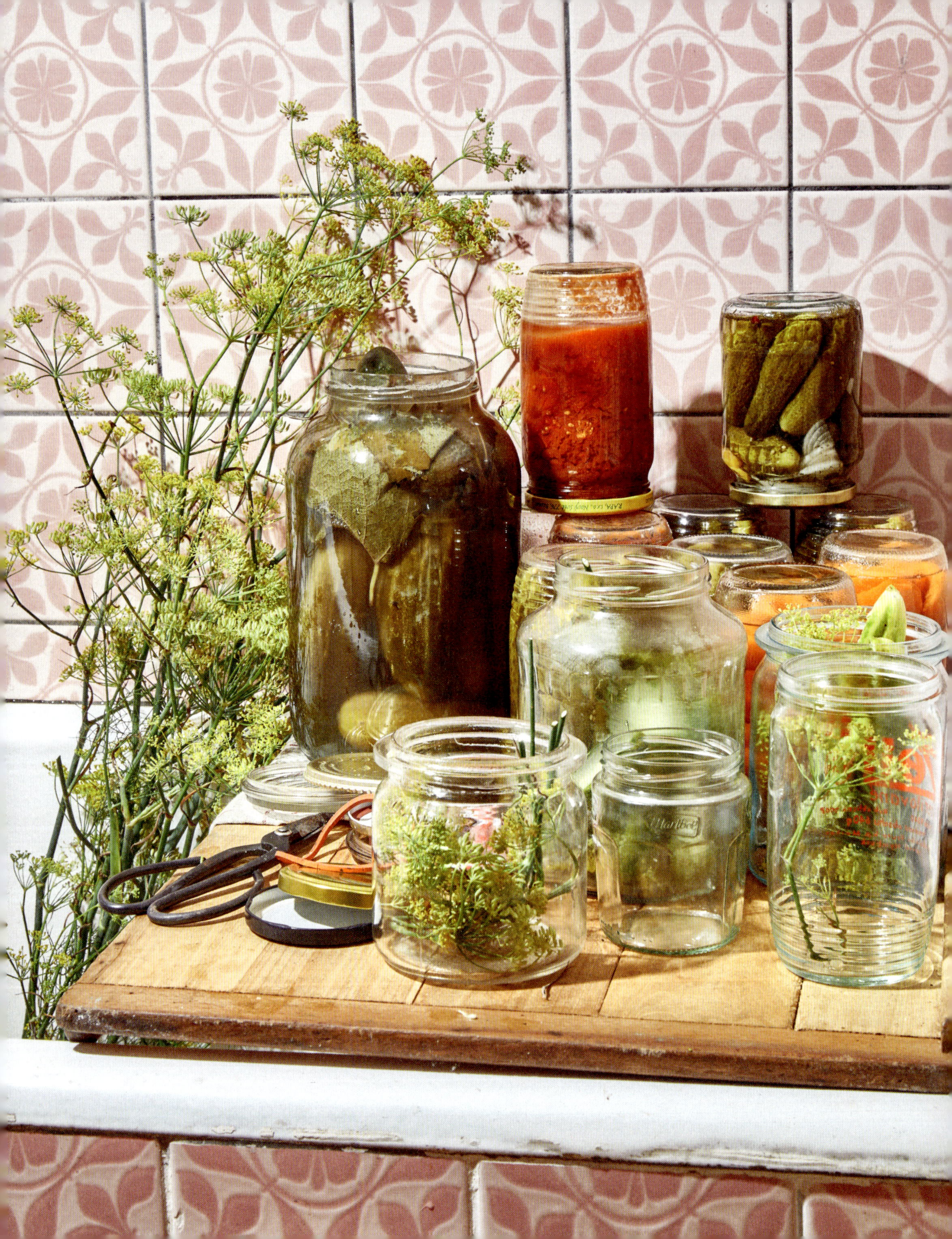

God, Bless the Pickles! Why Do Czechs Believe in Preserves?

In the Czech Republic, faith doesn't smell of incense—it smells of apricot preserves.

While people in other countries head to church on Sunday mornings, many Czechs prefer to stand in their kitchens, wooden spoon in hand, surrounded by sugar, jars, and a mountain of cucumbers that are about to become something that lasts longer than most beliefs ever do.

The Czech Republic has long ranked among the most secular nations on the earth. Two-thirds of its people have no religious affiliation—and yet belief here is alive and well, only of a different kind. Czech faith has little to do with the Bible and everything to do with yellowing, dog-eared recipe notebooks passed down from one generation to the next. Between handwritten directions for plum butter and pickled cucumbers lies more spirituality than meets the eye.

Czech kitchens aren't for preaching but for preserving. While others build altars, Czechs stack jars: cherry compote, plum jam, sauerkraut, and pickles. The pantry is the temple, canning is the ritual, and the process repeats itself year after year.

The title of this book, *God Is a Pickle,* may sound like a joke, but it's really a love letter to a country that has learned to find the sacred in the everyday.

How Czechs found their faith

Religion and the Czech lands have never had an easy relationship. As far back as in the Middle Ages, people here struggled with the idea that someone up above should decide what they believe in. Maybe that's because of their rebellious streak. Or because centuries went by in which they watched power disguise itself as an ideology.

In the fifteenth century, a priest named Jan Hus stood up to the Catholic Church, condemning its wealth, its corruption, and its love of spectacle. He preached honesty instead of pomp, Czech instead of Latin—and he paid for this with his life. His movement, the Hussites, gave rise to Europe's first great Reformation. Although they were eventually defeated by force, their message endured: faith cannot be decreed. It must be found within.

What followed was centuries of religious turmoil. After the Protestant Bohemian estates were crushed by the Catholic Hapsburgs at the Battle of White Mountain in 1620, Catholicism was reinstated as the official religion. Those who refused were silenced, converted, or driven out. Religion became something best left unspoken.

The Enlightenment of the eighteenth century brought reason, but also control. Emperor Joseph II curtailed the Church's influence and closed monasteries, but at the same time the state's authority grew. People learned to distrust institutions, whether sacred or secular.

By the end of the eighteenth century, they began to look elsewhere for meaning: to the concept of nationalism. Not God, but language, culture, and community became the symbols for belonging. These were a kind of substitute faith, with poems instead of prayers and folk songs instead of psalms. From that emancipation spirit arose the First Czechoslovak Republic in 1918, founded on education and pragmatism instead of religion.

While religion gradually lost its former significance in the Czech lands over the centuries, a true turning point in the secularization of society came in 1948 with the rise of the Communist regime. It began to suppress faith as an opponent of Marxist-Leninist ideology in a deliberate and systematic way. The state took control over everything related to spiritual life: priests and believers were persecuted and tried in political trials, church schools were closed, church property was nationalized, and artistic creation with spiritual themes was censored.

Faith became a private matter, which people practiced quietly and in secret, if at all. The forty years of repression caused a break in spiritual continuity; entire generations grew up without contact with religious tradition. Although churches were able to freely redevelop after the fall of communism in 1989, people often did not feel the need to return. A deeply rooted general distrust of institutions remained in society, and the majority of the population remained indifferent regarding religious affiliation. Religion never again returned to the center of public life and attention.

A hobby born of necessity

Long before refrigerators and supermarkets, the ancient Slavs knew how to preserve the taste of summer. Drying, salting, pickling, fermenting—these were the art of survival. No supplies meant no food in winter; nothing in the cellar meant nothing for dinner. And so everyday life in the Czech lands have long smelled of vinegar, sugar, and adventure.

When the first glass jars with rubber seals appeared in stores in the nineteenth century, it felt almost like a small miracle. Suddenly, whatever the garden produced could be kept for months—and be colorful, sweet, sour, and long-lasting. Recipes filled magazines, calendars, and women's journals: jams, compotes, syrups, mixed pickles. Preserving wasn't a luxury, but it was still an act of pride. A well-stocked pantry was proof that you had life under control.

Preserving took on a new meaning. In the 1950s through the 1980s, the Communist state was all-powerful, but the store shelves were often bare. Bananas? A rarity. Coffee? Only if you knew the right people. Meat? If you were lucky. Trade was nationalized, the range of goods was limited, and what little that was available was often rationed.

At this time, traveling abroad freely was impossible, and leisure activities were limited. Citizens satisfied their desire to escape the gray monotony of everyday life, at least, with a regular Friday exodus from the cities to their cottages. They spent their weekends and all their free time at these rural retreats—cottages (called *chata* or *chalupa*) became symbols of freedom, peace, and, not least, do-it-yourself projects. People repaired their homes by hand, tended their gardens, and grew fruit and vegetables, which they then preserved in jars. Because recipes had to be adapted to the ingredients available, creative products often emerged: zucchini pickled like pineapple, fake figs made from tomatoes as an inexpensive substitute for exotic fruit, blended jams (when there wasn't enough of one type of fruit, everything was combined), or even apple honey (an affordable alternative to real honey). Cellars were filled with dozens or even hundreds of jars of preserves each year.

Preserving was a survival strategy, but also a quiet form of control. While the state regulated everything, at least what stood in your cellar was truly yours. And anyone who ever looked at a perfectly ordered row of jars felt something socialism could never give them: pride.

Canning as part of identity

Religion has been pushed out of the Czech public sphere, but that doesn't mean that people have stopped believing. Faith hasn't disappeared, it's just changed form—most Czechs today don't believe in the traditional sense of the word, instead finding meaning in secular rituals. And one of them is canning.

It has long since outgrown its image as a relic from the old rigid regime. Preserving represents a ritual, a piece of family history, a quiet act of resistance against a world that never slows down. It means taking your time—something that almost feels revolutionary today. Compote is an iconic Czech dessert after a leisurely Sunday lunch and also a quiet protest against the sterile consumerist hustle.

Nearly every Czech knows the feeling: the clink of glass, the hiss as the lid opens, that satisfying pop when the jar seals as it cools. It's almost magical. Maybe because it brings back the nostalgia of a carefree childhood and summer holidays spent at grandparents'. Maybe because it brings order to a world that keeps changing. When you're canning, everything makes sense: slice, layer, fill, done.

And that's the beauty of it. While politics, prices, and the state of the world keep shifting, there's always something simmering on the stove, such as jam and compote, or pickles patiently waiting in brine to be eaten. Canning is a secular prayer. A quiet, sticky form of hope. In that peculiar and fascinating tradition—standing in the kitchen over hot jars in the summer, trying to capture the taste of the season in a form that will survive the winter—there is something deeply spiritual.

Almost every family has its own recipes, handwritten in old notebooks stained with syrup and sugar. They're passed down like secret formulas. Some people may never set foot in a church, but they know exactly when "canning day" comes around. There is more than fruit or vegetables and vinegar in those jars. There's lots of loving care. Memories. A certain rhythm. A feeling that whispers everything has its time. The harvest, fall, winter. And one day, spring again.

Today, preserving is back in style. Foodies post their colorful jars on Instagram, top chefs serve homemade pickles, and hipsters in Prague and Brno are rediscovering the craft, only now with tattoos instead of aprons. While canning is booming worldwide now, it's the countries of the former Eastern Bloc that have had this age-old method of preservation in their blood for generations—and, willingly or not, have perfected it. In the Czech Republic, canning is not just a culinary technique—it is part of the national identity. It even shows up in the language: if you get into a tricky situation or find yourself in trouble, people say that "you've really canned yourself." And when your mind feels overloaded or you can't find a solution to a problem, you have a "canned head."

Whether in the countryside or the city, it all comes down to the same thing: canning has a soothing effect. It creates connections. It gives you the sense of belonging to a cycle. You're not just preserving fruit—you're preserving memories. And maybe that's the true essence of this Czech faith: keeping what's good.

Between the divine and ordinary

God Is a Pickle initially sounds like a bar-room joke after the third beer. But behind this little provocation lies a whole universe: Czech history, humor, and the art of coping.

In the Czech Republic, irony isn't mockery but a way of enduring. After centuries of being denied the right to decide for themselves, people here have learned not to take life too seriously. You smile even when there's little to smile about. You make a joke before someone else makes one at your expense. Irony is a shield, a safety valve—and sometimes a quiet rebellion.

Maybe that's why Czechs have such a knack for canning. It's down-to-earth, unpretentious, honest. You don't need a sermon to understand it; you just need a little patience, love, and time. And to behold a row of clean, gleaming jars filled with the work of an entire summer is to sense a kind of peace that no religion could describe better.

Czechs today don't believe in dogma but believe in what they can make themselves: in craftsmanship, in community, in those small rituals that give meaning in a world that never stands still. In a country that's learned to distrust institutions, people prefer to put their faith in the things they can hold in their own hands—such as a jar lid that makes a soft click when the seal takes hold.

Canning has carried Czech people through crises. It's been a necessity, a hobby, a love, an obsession. And, by now, it's part of their identity. A jar of compote here is more than dessert. It's a reminder of stability, of grandmothers with patience, of summers that were meant to last forever.

So, when someone says "God is a pickle," it isn't blasphemy. It is said with a twinkle in the eye, perhaps even as a kind of prayer. A hymn to those who've learned to preserve the good things, even when the world outside has gone mad.

Because in the end, preserving—like faith—is about hope. Hope that winter will pass and that the light will return. And that somewhere in the cellar, a jar is waiting to remind us that all good things return. At some point, the summer will come round again.

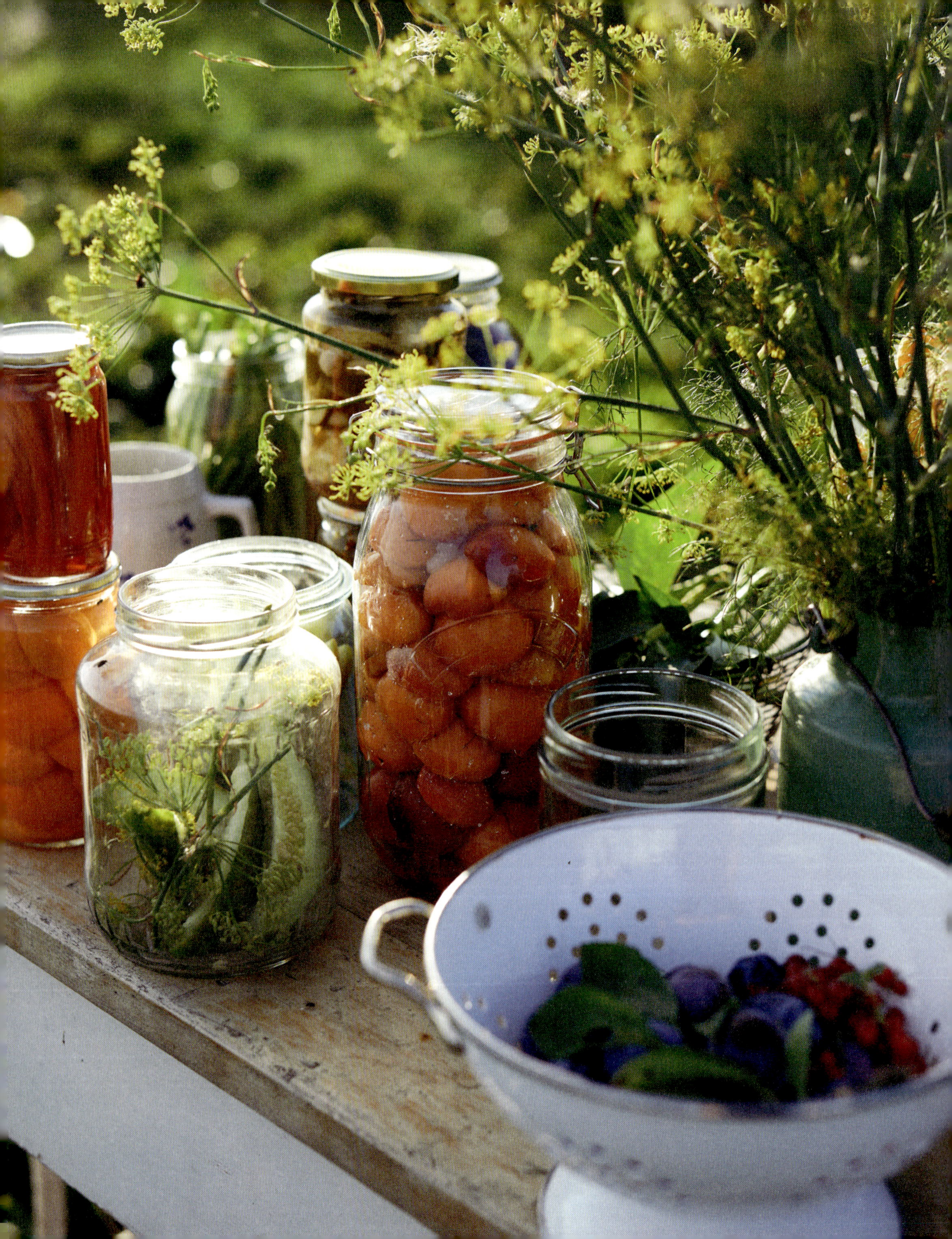

The Home Canning Process

Canning isn't rocket science, but you should follow certain procedures and rules to ensure that the freshly picked produce that goes into your jars lasts through winter.

Which fruit and vegetables are suitable for canning?

Not every fruit and vegetable can be canned. Structure and ripeness are important, and the best ones to choose are produce grown in your own garden or sourced from local organic farmers.

- For compotes: Ripe but firm fruit that contains little water holds its shape best. Whole fruit and vegetables (such as plums, raspberries, and cherries) or larger pieces (such as peaches, pears, and pumpkin/winter squash) also work well.
- Very ripe, soft fruit is better suited to making sauces and purees, jams, jellies, and fruit spreads, because they break down easily when cooked. Fruit that contains large amounts of pectin (such as apples, citrus fruit, apricots, currants, and gooseberries) provide the desired gel-like structure. Less ripe fruit also contains more pectin.
- Fruit with a higher sugar content that can be cooked for a long time without losing its typical flavor (such as apples, pears, and plums) is suitable for fruit butters and chutneys.
- For syrups, juices, and vinegars, use ripe, succulent fruit with an intense flavor and easy-to-extract juice (such as strawberries, raspberries, blackberries, blueberries, and sour cherries). You can also add aromatic herbs, such as lemon balm, mint, thyme, rosemary, and sage.
- Firm, crunchy fruit and vegetables with a fine skin should be used for pickling and fermenting, because they will keep their shape.
- Herbs and leafy vegetables are suitable for pestos and infused oils. These include basil, parsley, arugula (rocket), and wild garlic.
- Note: All rotten or moldy fruit and vegetables must be discarded, or the preserved goods will quickly spoil.

Equipment

You don't need professional equipment for canning and pickling at home. You'll find many of the required items in most households:

- Canning jars and intact, well-sealing lids
- Large saucepans and pots with lids

- Bowls, strainers, and clean dishcloths
- Oven mitts, kitchen scale, and measuring cups and spoons
- Stainless steel ladle and wide funnel
- Adhesive labels

Here are some additional items to make life easier:

- Probe thermometer: To check that the temperature is correct when sterilizing the jars or processing preserves.
- Jar lifter: To assist in taking the canning jars out of boiling water.
- Canning rack: To separate the jars from the bottom of the pot and keep the jars from touching each other, thereby preventing the glass from shattering.

Sterilizing canning jars

Cleanliness is all important when canning and pickling. Jars and lids should always be rinsed and cleaned in hot water before use, because a high water temperature will kill unwanted bacteria. All utensils used for canning should also be thoroughly cleaned.

Proven sterilization methods:

1) Boiling in water
- Clean the jars and lids with dish soap in hot water; scrub the threads thoroughly.
- Line the bottom of a large, deep pot with a dishcloth (tea towel) to keep the jars from cracking.
- Arrange the washed jars and lids, spaced apart, on the cloth.
- Cover them with water, bring slowly to a boil, and let simmer for at least 10 minutes.
- Using a clean jar lifter, take out the jars and lids and drain on a clean dishcloth.

2) Sterilizing in the oven
- Place the washed jars with the opening facing upward, spaced apart, in a deep baking pan or roasting pan filled with water (about 1 inch/3 cm). Place in an oven heated to 265 °F (130 °C/Gas Mark ¾) for 10 to 20 minutes.
- Sterilize the lids separately in a pot of boiling water; this is because the seals can be damaged by the high oven temperature.
- Drain the jars and lids on a clean dishcloth.

3) Sterilizing in the dishwasher
- Arrange the jars and lids in an empty dishwasher and run it at the highest possible temperature (at least 160 °F/70 °C) without detergent.
- While not a full sterilization, this is sufficient for jams and compotes to be consumed within 1 to 2 weeks.

Further tips:

- Clean hands are essential.
- Handle sterilized canning jars by the body of the jar, not by the thread, to avoid transferring bacteria or other unwanted microorganisms onto the lids. You should use a jar lifter to place the jars on a clean work surface.
- Don't dry sterilized containers and closures. Let the residual water air dry.
- Never taste preserves directly from the cooking spoon during the preparation process! Always use a clean spoon.
- Check canning jars carefully before use; they must be free of any cracks, chips, or other damage. You should purchase new lids for each season, because the threads will no longer seal reliably after prolonged use.
- Set a timer when sterilizing! The sterilized jars must be allowed to dry before filling, but they should still be warm when used to prevent any thermal shock that will cause the glass to shatter. Using warm jars will also help the formation of negative pressure as the jar and its contents cool, creating a vacuum that will pull the lid inward for a better seal.

Step-by-step canning

After sterilizing the jars, it's time to get canning (sometimes called bottling or processing). If the preserves need to mature before consumption or you plan to store them for more than 1 to 2 weeks, the filled sterilized jars must be further processed (canned). To do this, the filled and tightly closed jars should be heated to a higher temperature in a water bath for a certain time and then slowly cooled down again. This will kill bacteria and seal the jar airtight, extending the shelf life of the contents. For a smooth canning process, use jars of the same size.

There are several ways to can food:

1) In a water bath canner
Anyone who cans food often or in large batches should consider purchasing an automatic electric water bath

canner. It has a precise temperature gauge, a timer, and large capacity, and it ensures that the jars are evenly heated. Simply place the filled jars in the pot, select the appropriate program, and keep an eye on the thermometer. The pot does the rest.

2) In a cooking pot

Place a dishcloth (tea towel) or a canning rack on the bottom of a large, deep pot. This will prevent the jars from touching and shattering as they are sterilized. Then place the filled, tightly closed jars on the cloth or rack. Add enough warm water to reach at least halfway up the sides of the jars, but the jars can also be submerged. Heat slowly to 185 to 195 °F (85–90 °C) and keep the temperature steady for 15 to 35 minutes (the larger the jar, the more time it will need; see below). Finally, remove the jars from the pot—do this carefully, because they will be very hot.

Standard values for water bath canning:

Less ripe and firmer produce	
Canning jars 32 ounces (700 ml)	30 to 35 minutes (185 °F/85 °C)
Canning jars 16 ounces (500 ml) or smaller	20 to 25 minutes (185 °F/85 °C)
Riper and softer produce	
Canning jars 32 ounces (700 ml)	20 minutes (185 °F/85 °C)
Canning jars 16 ounces (500 ml) or smaller	15 minutes (185 °F/85 °C)

3) In the oven

Preheat the oven to 350 °F (180 °C/Gas Mark 4) in static mode using upper and lower heat or 325 °F (160 °C/Gas Mark 3) in convection (fan-assisted) mode. Line a baking pan or roasting pan with a dishcloth (tea towel) and place the filled, tightly closed preserving jars on top, spaced apart to keep them from touching each other or the edge of the pan. Fill the pan with ¾ to 1¼ inches (2–4 cm) of water. Reduce the oven temperature to 250 °F (120 °C/Gas Mark ½) for a static oven or 210 °F (100 °C/Gas Mark ¼) if a convection oven. Place the pan in the oven. Can small jars (volume less than 8 ounces/200 ml) in the oven for 15 minutes, medium jars (8 to 16 ounces/250–450 ml) for 20 minutes, and large jars (16 ounces/500 ml and larger) for 25 to 30 minutes. The time will also depend on the firmness and size of the fruit or vegetables. Leave smaller and softer ones (such as currants, cherries, and apricots) in the oven for a shorter time, and firmer and larger ones (such as cucumbers and mushrooms) for a little longer (at least 45 minutes). After canning, turn off the oven and leave the jars inside for another 30 minutes before taking them out.

4) In the dishwasher

Place the filled, tightly closed jars with the lids facing up in the dishwasher and set to a rinse cycle at the highest possible temperature (160 °F/70 °C and above). There must be no other dishes or detergent in the dishwasher when canning!

5) Filling jars with boiling hot contents

For jams, marmalades, fruit butters, ketchups, and syrups with a higher sugar content that have already been heated for a longer time during processing, you can simply put them into warm sterilized jars or bottles while boiling hot. Then close the jars tightly, place them upside down, and let cool. This will create a vacuum that seals the lid tightly. However, anything to be stored outside of the refrigerator for a longer period (several weeks) must undergo additional canning in a water bath.

Regardless of the canning method you use, the jars should be stood on a dry dishcloth (tea towel), preferably upside down, to let them cool completely at room temperature. As the contents of the jars shrink over time, a vacuum will be created inside. Finally, check that the lids are airtight—they must not be loose, bulging, or buckle under pressure.

Correct storage

Before the jars go into the pantry, label each one with its contents and the date of processing.

Store the canned preserves in a cool, dark, and dry place, which will allow it to keep for several months or even years. However, prolonged storage can lead to changes in the color, taste, aroma, and consistency of canned food. For this reason, ideally, it should be consumed within two years.

Before use, always check that the lid is on tight and the contents have not been affected by mold. After opening, use only a clean utensil to take the food out of the jar. Opened jars should be stored in the refrigerator and their contents used as quickly as possible.

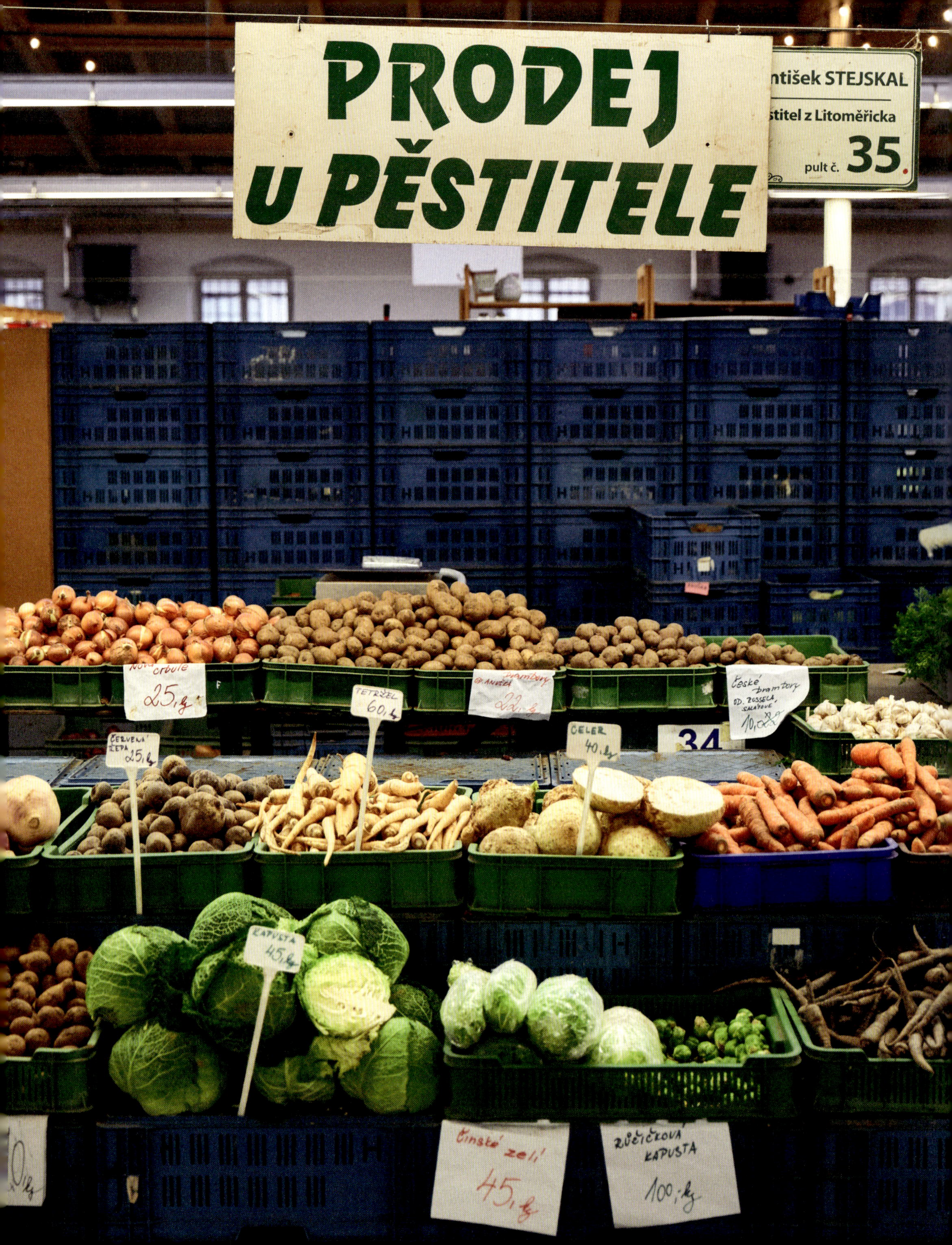
PRODEJ
U PĚSTITELE
ntišek STEJSKAL
stitel z Litoměřicka
pult č. 35
PETRŽEL
CELER
KAPUSTA
34
Čínské zelí

Typical Ingredients of Czech Cuisine

Czech cuisine, also known as Bohemian cuisine, has developed its very own style over the centuries. Because the Czech Republic lies between Central and Eastern Europe, its food has received overlapping German, Austrian, Slovakian, Hungarian, and even Polish and Jewish influences. The result is hearty, filling, and down-to-earth food with a touch of elegance. However, the essence of this cuisine still consists of regional and seasonal ingredients and recipes passed down from generation to generation. Although its dishes mainly come from a peasant tradition, it has been refined by the incorporation of creations made for the middle class and aristocracy. Today, the Czech culinary scene features a crossover of home cooking and gourmet vibes—and while it may be rustic, it is never boring.

Flour

Nothing works in Czech cuisine without flour. It is required for dozens of traditional dishes, reflecting the country's strong baking tradition. Flour is ubiquitous, appearing in staples such as bread, dumplings, cakes, and rolls. While versatile, neutral-tasting wheat flour is the primary choice, there is also a long tradition of using dark rye flour. High in fiber, rye flour is favored in cooler regions, giving sourdough bread and gingerbread a characteristic slightly sour taste.

Unlike many other cuisines, Czech recipes distinguish flours mainly by the degree of grain milling:

- *Hladká* (smooth flour used for delicate pastries, yeast-based baked goods, crepes and pancakes, cookies, sponge cakes, or roux).
- *Polohrubá* (semi-coarse flour for bundt cakes and pourable batters).
- *Hrubá* (coarse flour for dumplings, gnocchi or streusel).

Abroad, it is often not easy to find exact equivalents for these Czech flours.

- Smooth flour is closest to all-purpose, plain, pastry, cake or Italian "00" flour.
- To replicate semi-coarse flour, simply mix the smooth and coarse alternatives in a 1:1 ratio.
- Coarse flour can be substituted with wheat semolina.

Note: The closest substitutes for Czech *hladká* flour are pastry flour or Italian "00", both having a similarly low protein content for a tender dough.

All-purpose (plain) flour is a common substitute despite its higher protein making the dough denser. It is slightly stronger than *hladká*, while cake flour has the lowest protein and results in an even softer, finer texture, even softer than Czech *hladká* flour.

Yeast

Fresh yeast (also called compressed or cake yeast) is standard in the Czech Republic, especially for yeasted doughs. It usually comes in a 1½-ounce (42-gram) cake. Unlike instant yeast, which is mixed directly into the flour, fresh yeast is typically activated (proofed) first—simply crumble it into a little lukewarm milk, add 1 teaspoon each of sugar and flour, mix gently, and let it rise (the mixture will start to foam after a few minutes). The proofed yeast is then combined with the remaining ingredients and the dough kneaded.

If fresh yeast is not available (try asking for it at your local bakery, dairy department in a larger supermarket, or in Czech, Slovak, or Polish grocery stores), instant yeast can be used—but remember that you cannot substitute fresh yeast with instant yeast in a 1:1 ratio. Instant yeast is generally about 1.5 times stronger, so use roughly one-third less. As a general equivalent, about 1 (7-g) envelope, or 2¼ teaspoons, of instant yeast can replace a ⅔ ounce (19 g) cake of fresh yeast. If you are using active dry yeast, it should be dissolved in water or milk before being incorporated into the dry ingredients.

Fruit and vegetables

Authentic Czech cooking is typically seasonal and regional, which is why the country's cuisine mainly draws from fruit that ripens in gardens, orchards, and forests during their season. Apples and pears are essential for strudel, cakes, and compotes. Plums are crucial for *povidla* (plum butter) used in *buchty* rolls, and distilled into the popular Moravian fruit brandy, *slivovice* (slivovitz). Cherries and sour cherries are used in compotes, *bublanina* cakes, and sauces. Peaches and apricots feature in desserts, sweet dumplings, and jams. Berries, such as currants, gooseberries, blueberries, raspberries, blackberries, and strawberries, are used in crumb cakes, preserves, and syrups.

The Czech Republic has a mild continental climate with relatively high rainfall, warm summers, and cold winters, and the vegetables grown and used here reflect this. In recipes, the varieties most commonly used are those that can be stored for the colder months. Along with garlic and onions, the foundation of the Czech cuisine is root vegetables (carrots, celery and parsley roots, parsnips), which tolerate temperature fluctuations well and can grow even outside greenhouses. White (similar to green), red, and savoy cabbage varieties are commonly used. The lacto-fermentation of cabbage has a long tradition in the Czech Republic. And, of course, fiery hot and highly aromatic horseradish is a must. This perennial "miracle root" needs little attention and practically grows by itself, which is why horseradish can often be found growing along country roads. Horseradish is considered to reflect the rough and tough character of Czech's rural areas. In summer and fall, tomatoes, bell peppers, zucchini (courgettes), beans, peas, and cauliflower mainly feature on Czech menus.

Potatoes

Potatoes have been an indispensable part of the Czech diet since the eighteenth century, when they were quickly embraced by both the middle classes and the rural population, and not only because of their versatility. In addition to individual varieties, there are three main ways to distinguish them:

- A (salad potatoes)—mainly waxy potatoes that don't fall apart when cooked, they are ideal for salads, boiled in their skins, and used in gratin dishes.
- B (potatoes for side dishes)—the most common way potatoes are used and where slightly floury potatoes are truly all-rounders.
- C (mealy/floury potatoes)—these potatoes have the highest starch content and cook easily, meaning that they are particularly suitable for doughs, potato flatbreads, dumplings, and for making mashed potatoes and purees.

Wild mushrooms

Mushroom picking is almost a national sport in the Czech Republic. In fall, whole families go out to fill their baskets. Mushrooms, which can be found almost everywhere in the Czech Republic, are particularly popular because they are intensely flavorsome and filling. Among the different ways they can be prepared, mushrooms can be fried, dried, pickled, and used as a meat substitute during Lent. Even today, some types of mushrooms in the Czech Republic, such as the blusher mushroom (which shouldn't be picked unless you're sure you can identify it!), are still referred to as "meat mushrooms."

Herbs

Herbs, both cultivated and wild, also take pride of place in Czech cooking, as well as folk medicine. Food tastes only half as good if the traditional herbs—parsley, chives, thyme, dill, lovage, and young nettle—are missing.

Caraway seeds

Caraway (*Carum carvi*) is one of the oldest and most widely used of Czech spices. For centuries, it was commonly available even in poorer households, unlike imported spices. Many soups and meat dishes are seasoned with caraway, and it is used in baking bread and pastries, often in combination with salt and garlic. Just don't confuse it with its relative, cumin (*Cuminum cyminum*)—although the whole seeds look similar, the difference in taste is striking.

Poppy seeds

Poppies have been cultivated in the Czech Republic since at least the Middle Ages. They stand for wealth, fertility, and luck and also feature prominently in fairy tales and many customs. For example, poppy seeds can be found in pastries made to celebrate weddings and harvests. The Czech Republic is one of the world's largest producers of edible poppy seeds, so it stands to reason that poppy seeds should be used as an ingredient throughout the country. Ground poppy seeds are most commonly used as a filling for cakes, pastries, and desserts. Freshly ground poppy seeds tur rancid quickly, so it is recommended to grind them just before use.

Quark

Fresh cheese, which used to be traditionally homemade from farm milk, boasts a slightly sour, creamy flavor. It is inexpensive, nutritious, and widely available. Offering various fat contents and textures—from smooth and soft to crumbly and even hard—it works well in both sweet and savory dishes.

Abroad, equivalents include quark, farmer cheese, or curd cheese, though none fully match its texture. A creamy substitute is full-fat Greek yogurt mixed with lemon juice and drained overnight.

Beer

No other country drinks more beer than the Czech Republic, with consumption in 2024 at almost 34 gallons (128 liters) per capita. The art of brewing has a rich, more than a thousand-year-old tradition here, and high-quality beers are still brewed in many places. Beer is simply part of everyday life. It is drunk at lunch and dinner, and at celebrations. It is often cheaper than water, and it is also a cooking ingredient, naturally. It is used for deglazing when pan-frying or stewing meat and as an ingredient in marinades, batters, bread dough, sweet pastries, and even ice cream. Czechs are rightly proud of their beer and consider it part of their cultural heritage.

Meat

Meat is an integral part of traditional Bohemian and Moravian cuisine. Historically, meat consumption was an event, reserved for holidays and feasts—especially the winter animal slaughter—because it provided an important source of energy for hard work. This legacy means that, for many, meat is still considered part of a "proper" lunch, although there is a modern trend toward simpler, meat-free dishes. The most common meats are pork, beef, and poultry, sometimes supplemented by rabbit and carp. A wide variety of sausages and deli meats are also essential, including salami, ham, smoked bacon, fresh and cooked sausages, head cheese, blood sausages (*jelita*), and liver sausages (*jitrnice*). All made with love.

Notes on the recipes in the book

Baking times and temperatures: The specified temperatures and cooking times given apply to conventional electric ovens. Times will vary for ovens with a convection (fan-assisted) mode or gas ovens. Toward the end of the recommended baking or cooking time, you should keep a close eye on the dish in the oven to ensure it doesn't burn.

Canning: The recipes indicate the number of canning jars required and their volume. However, this is only a guide. The number of jars required may vary depending on the size and ripeness of the fruit, the juice released during canning process, etc. Therefore, it's always good to have at least an extra jar ready.

Don't forget to sterilize: Only use thoroughly sterilized jars. For a longer shelf life, the contents of the jar should be preserved by canning in a water bath. Mushrooms must always be canned!

Without preservatives: This book deals with traditional preserving methods without the addition of preservatives. Therefore, no gelling (jam) sugar or sulfites are used to improve the consistency of canned foods, extend their shelf life, or protect them from mold, bacteria, and yeast infestation. For this reason, homemade preserves generally require thorough heating during the canning process as a precaution.

How about fermentation? When fermenting, a fermentation weight is a helpful tool to keep the fruits and vegetables in the containers in place instead of floating to the surface. Regardless of whether you use a special fermentation weight made of ceramic or a stone, a plate, or a glass, it should always be boiled (sterilized) beforehand.

Desserts: In the Czech Republic, dessert isn't just a secondary course but a main course in its own right, both in everyday life and on festive occasions. Even school cafeterias serve complete meals, such as *buchty* rolls with milk, once a week.

The recipes in this book were tested with Czech ingredients. Using foreign alternatives may alter the final appearance or taste. For the most authentic results, seek out Czech, Slovak, or Polish grocery stores (common in large cities).

Online community groups are just as helpful. They often provide advice on where to buy basic ingredients, including typical local dairy products, popular sweet treats, and beverages online. Some Czech associations also arrange specialty deliveries for members.

And the most important thing: Recipes are not laws. If you can't find parsley root, use carrots. No allspice (mixed spiced)? Use pepper. The main thing is that cooking should be fun!

Dobrou chuť! (Enjoy your meal!)

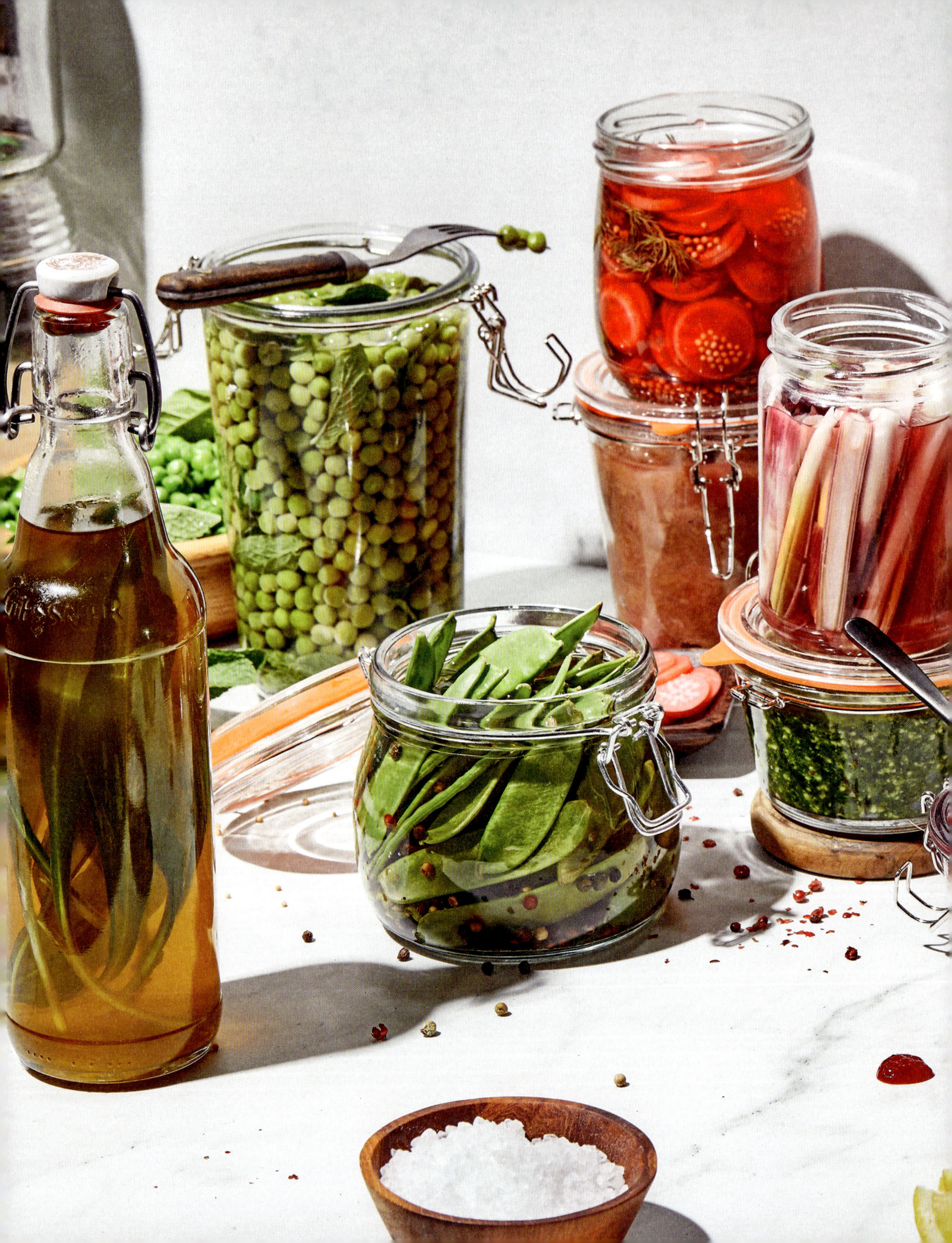

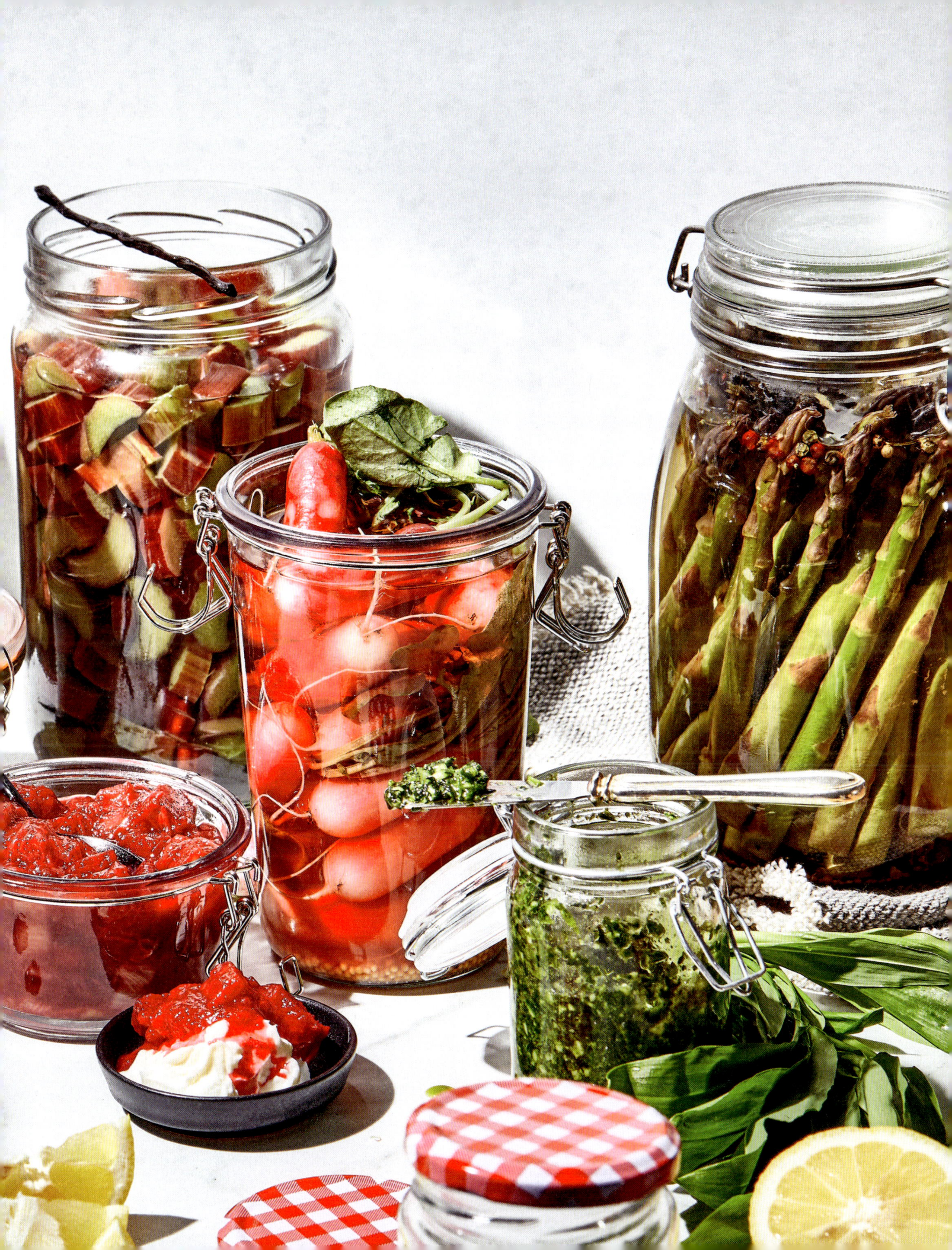

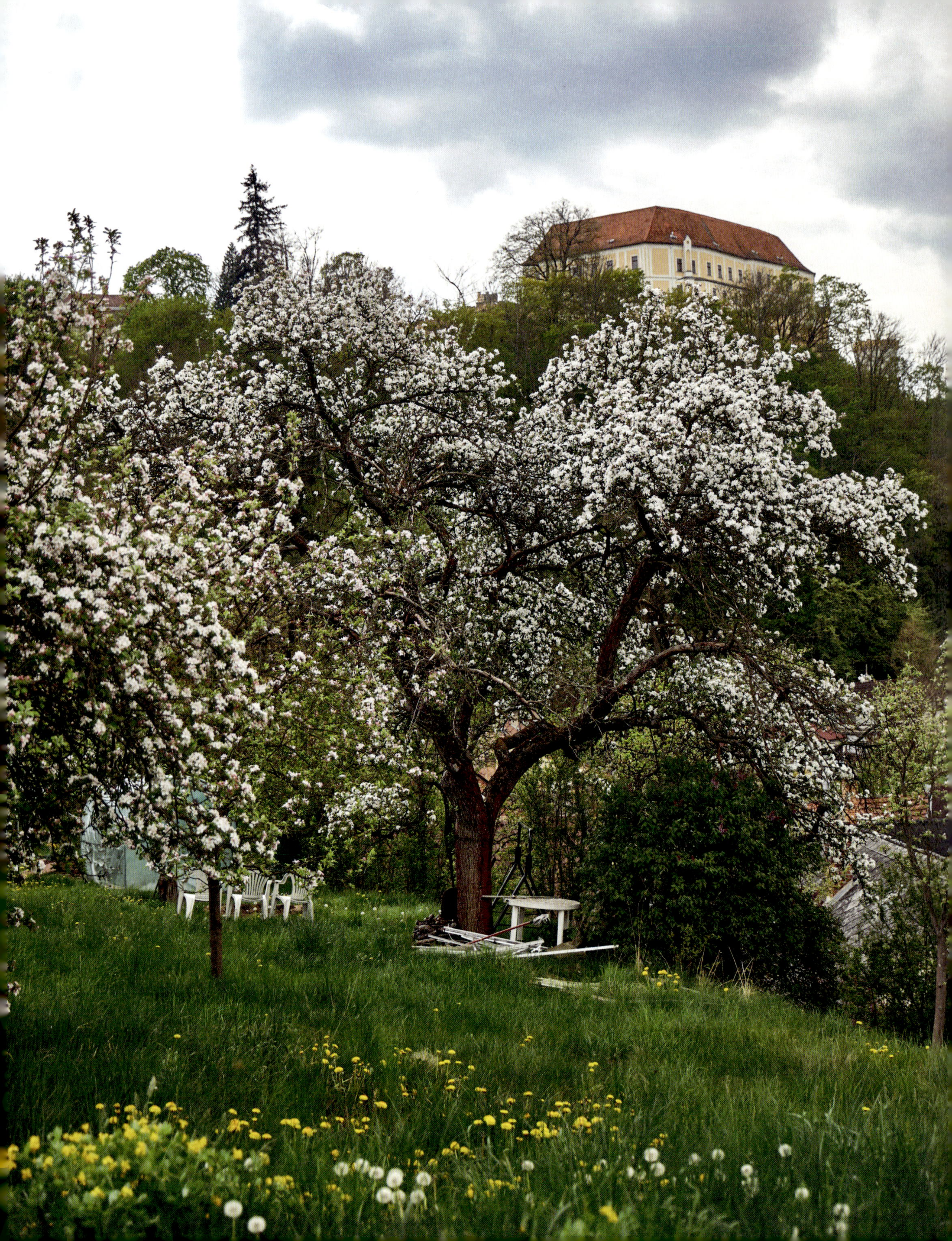

SPRING

Jedna vlaštovka jaro nedělá.

One swallow does not make a spring.

Energy Tapped from the Trees

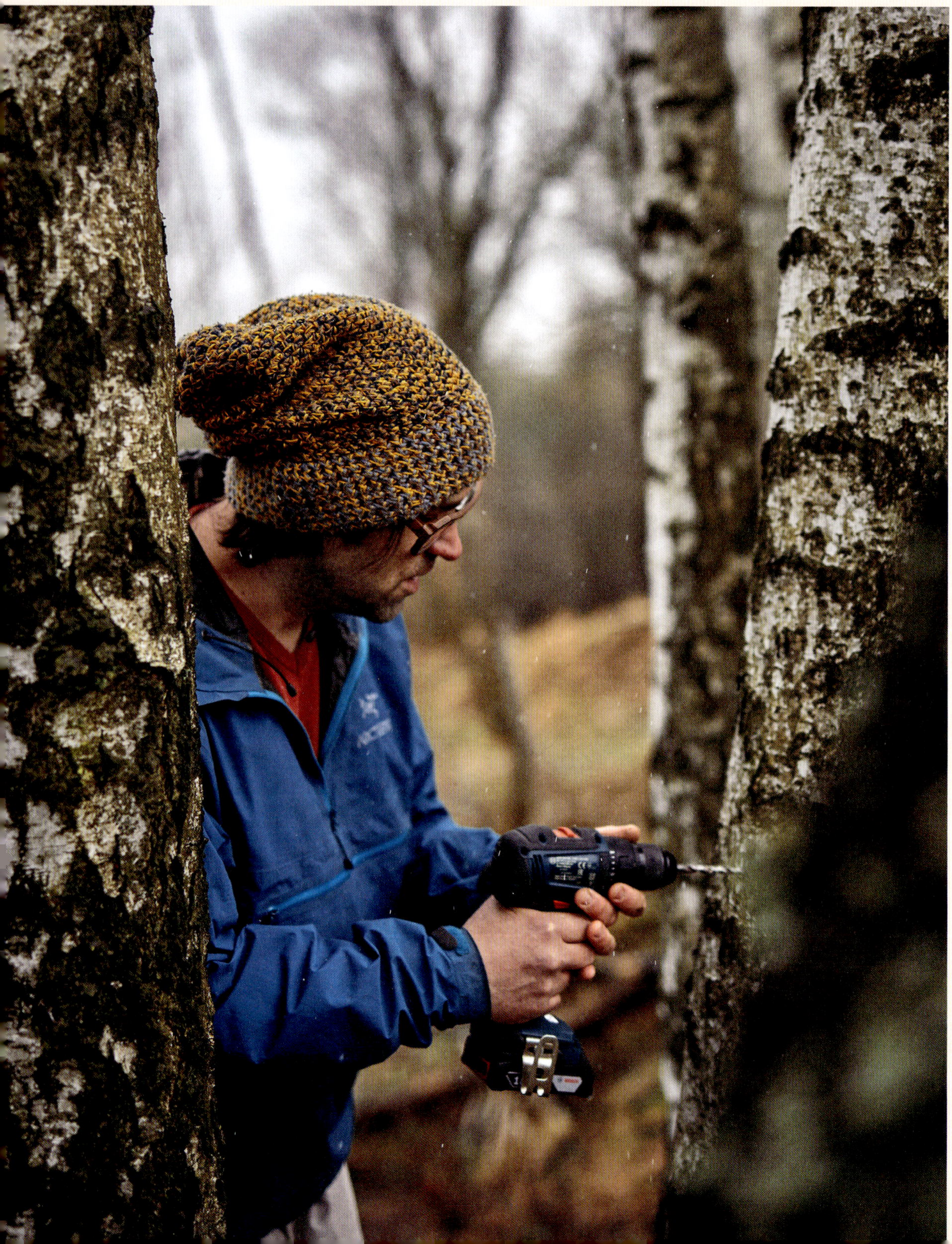

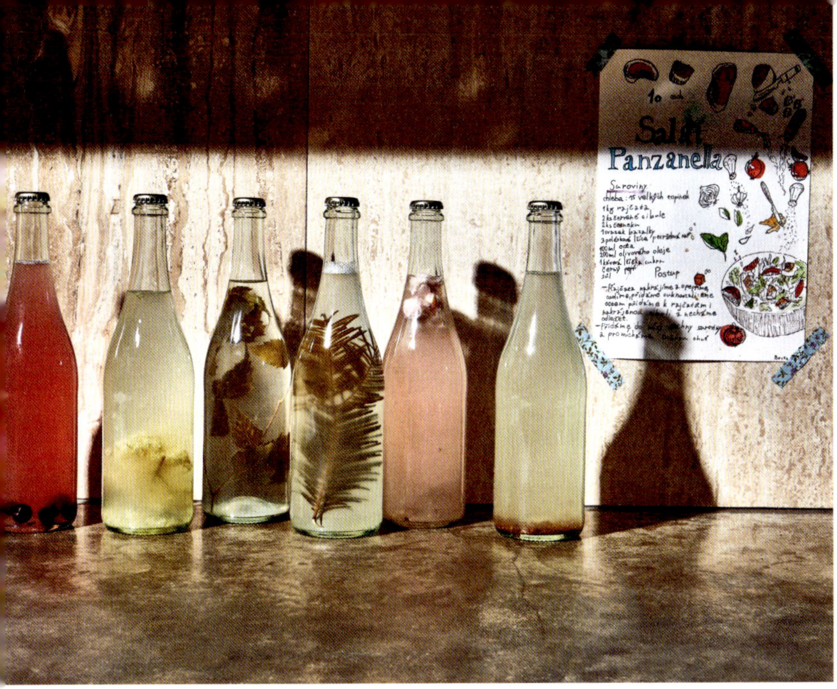

In the Vysočina region, Jan Klimeš rediscovered birch sap and transformed it into Euforia—a pure, fermented drink that awakens both the body and the mind.

Active, multitalented, and fueled by passion—these words describe Jan Klimeš in a nutshell. By profession, he restores paper and old books; he also creates distinctive lamps and notebooks. A few years ago, he and his architect wife, Naďa, left Prague behind for the Vysočina region, where together they transformed a dilapidated barn into a welcoming home. For Jan—or Honza, as his friends call him—the move from the bustle of the Czech capital to the peace and quiet of the countryside proved to be a turning point.

From his glass-walled studio overlooking meadows and orchards, nature is on full view from every side—and this view gradually stirred his curiosity. Seeing a cluster of birches nearby, he remembered a documentary showing how their trunks could be tapped. "I'd always wanted to taste birch sap. People in the Nordic countries drink it all the time. Here, finally, was my chance!"

He drilled into a tree, and out came a stream of cool, clear liquid. "Birch has long symbolized purity and new beginnings. I'll never forget the feeling of taking that first sip," Jan recalls. Birch sap is a fleeting gift of spring, available for only a few weeks before the first leaves unfurl. Collecting it demands care: The trees must never be overtapped, and once the season ends, the opening has to be sealed.

With its slightly sweet and refreshing taste, for centuries the sap has been prized in folk medicine for its benefits. Rich in minerals, antioxidants, and vitamins, it is valued for its detoxifying and anti-inflammatory effects. It lifts the mood, calms, and gently releases tension. Almost miraculously, it seems to renew not just the body, but the soul as well, quietly preparing us for the arrival of spring. Today, it even appears on the menus of modern restaurants. For lovers of handmade, unsweetened, alcohol-free beverages, birch sap is a revelation. "When I drink it regularly, I feel great. I have more energy, I want to get things done," says Honza. It was these feelings that gave his brand its name: Euforia.

Jan has been fermenting his hand-collected sap ever since. He refuses to add sugar or synthetic coloring, letting nature flow straight into the bottle instead, along with sprigs of fir, wild cherries, tea, grape skins, caraway, even poppy seeds. The result? An unfiltered, sparkling drink, tangy on the tongue, and free of preservatives or artificial flavorings. Each bottle is a small work of art, beautiful to look at and even better to taste.

"Opening a bottle of Euforia is like uncorking a bottle of wine. You savor it with the same sense of occasion. The only difference is that you don't wake up with a headache the next morning ..."

And that's how birch sap tapped in a little hilly village in Europe has found its way into the world. Cheers!

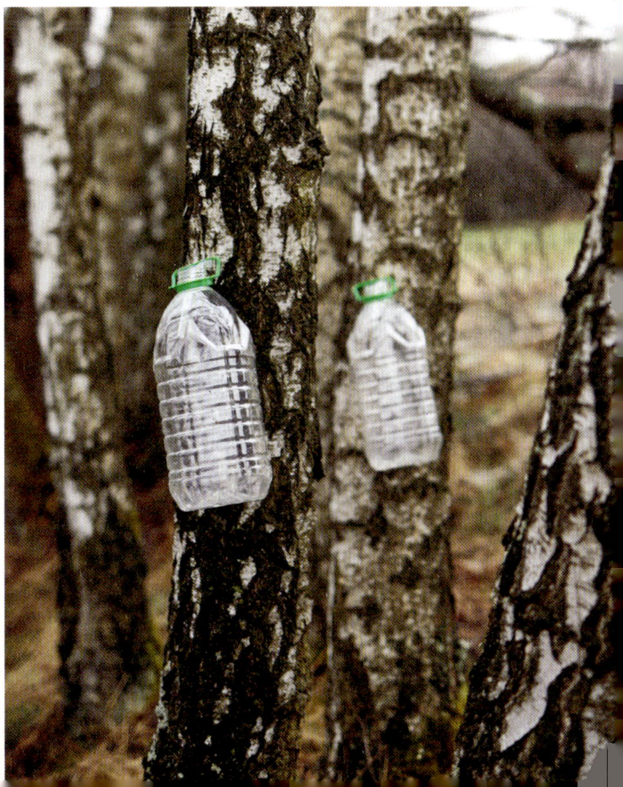

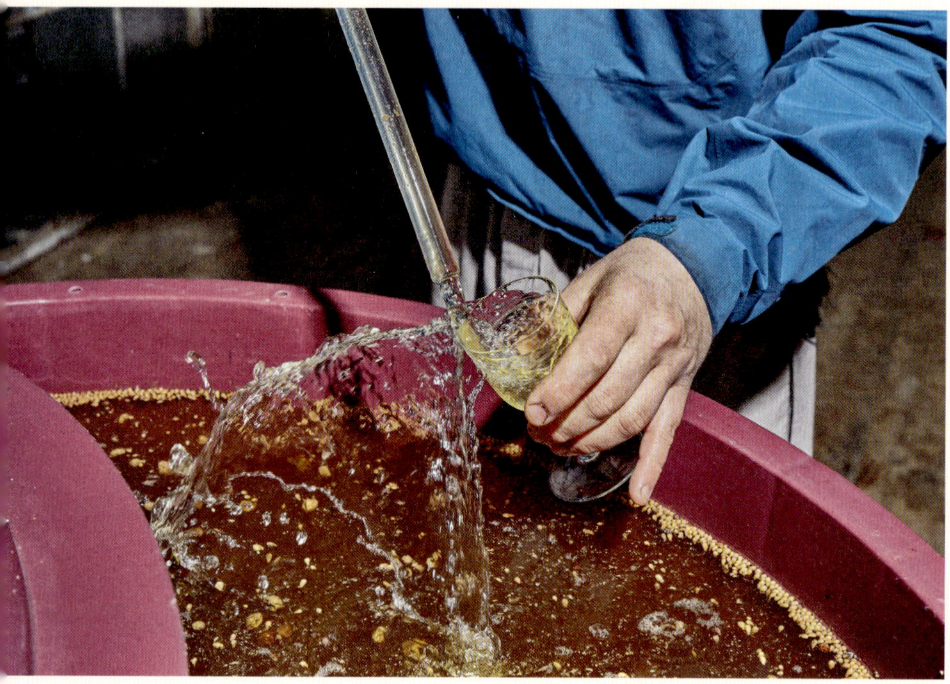

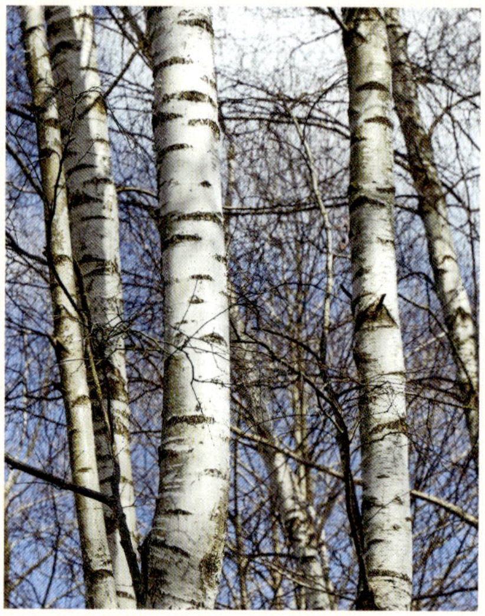

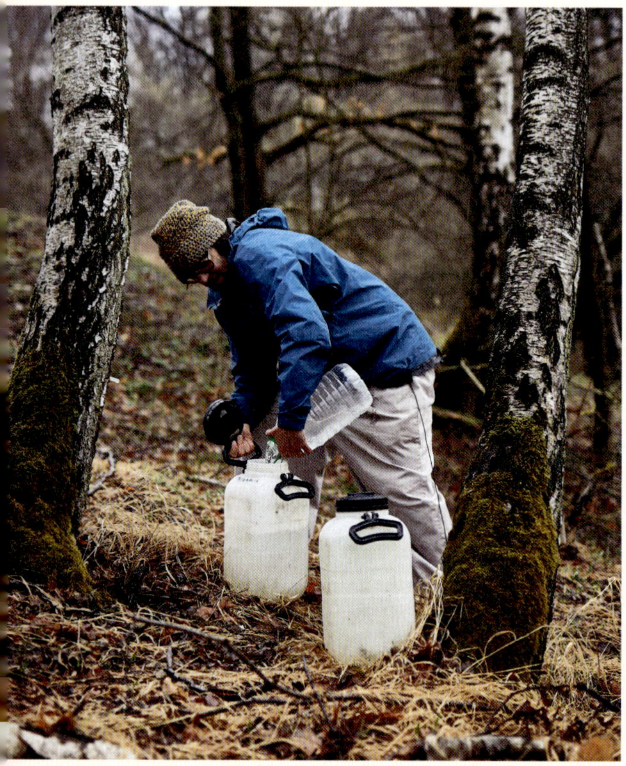

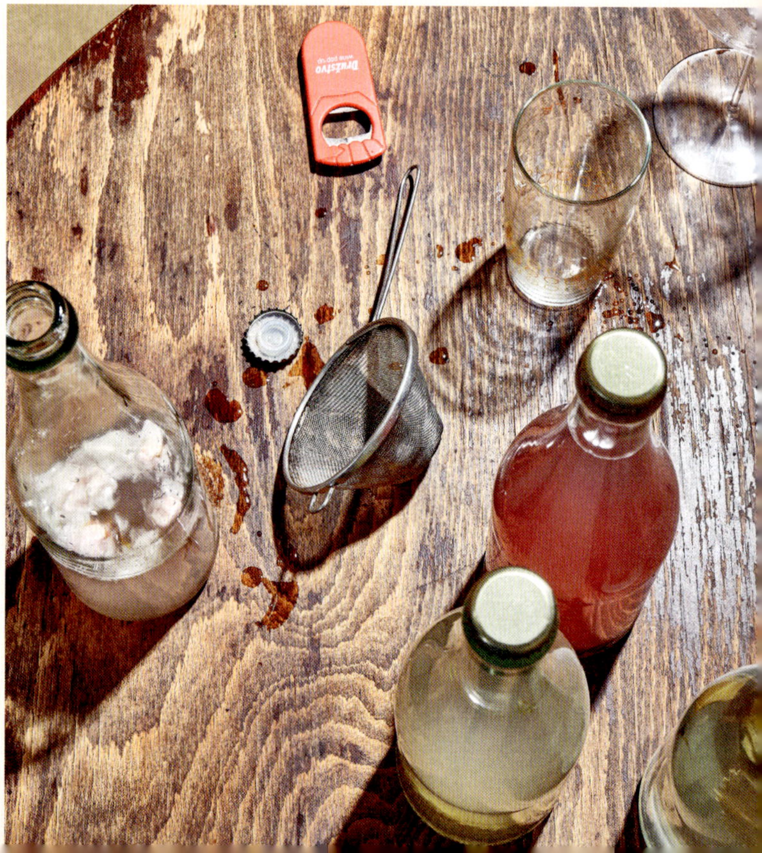

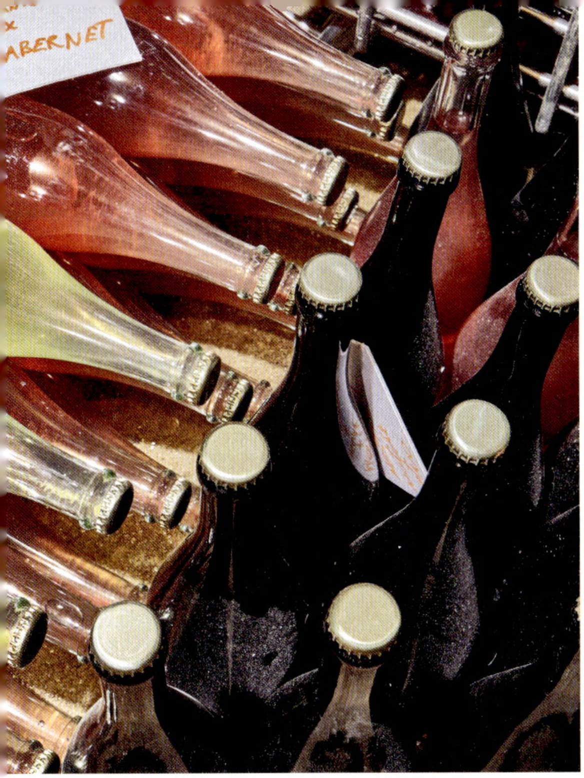

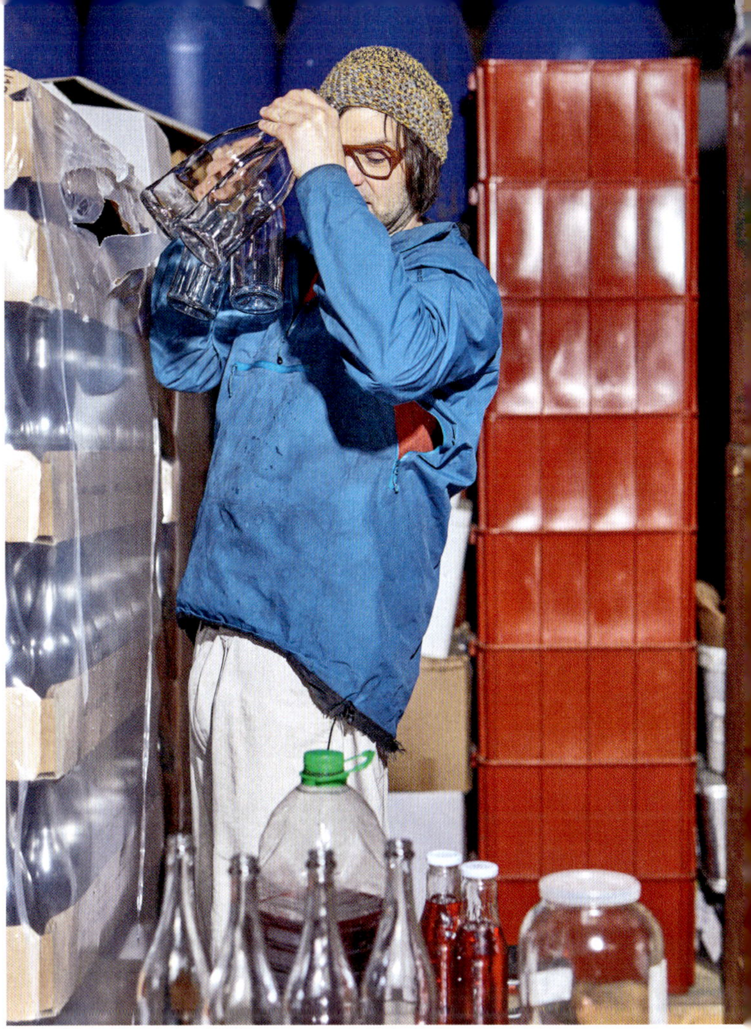

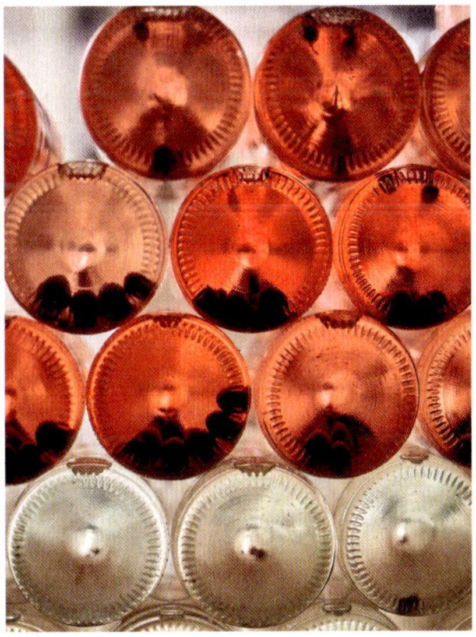

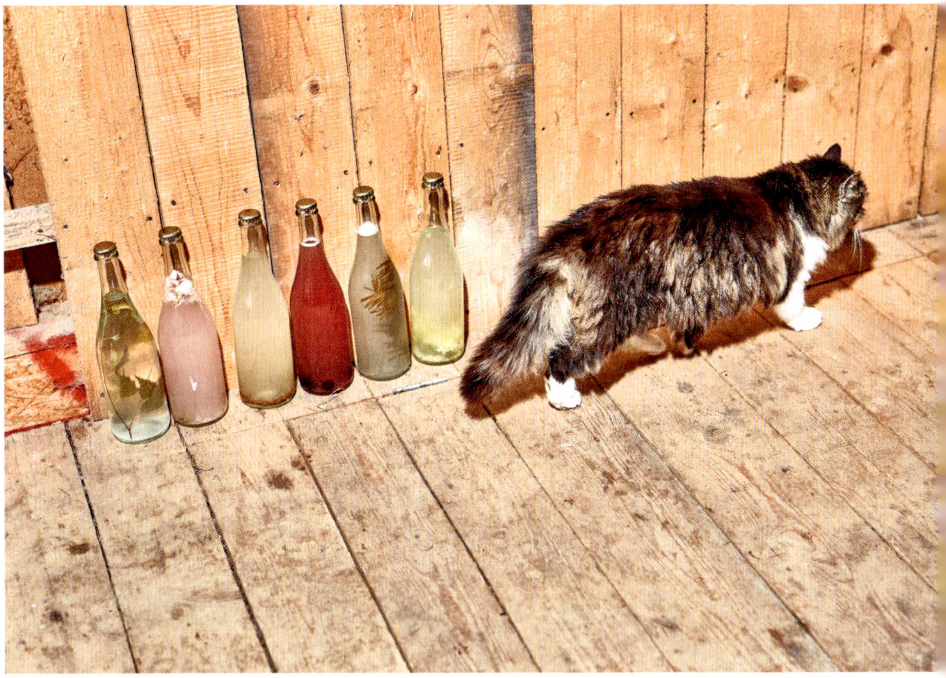

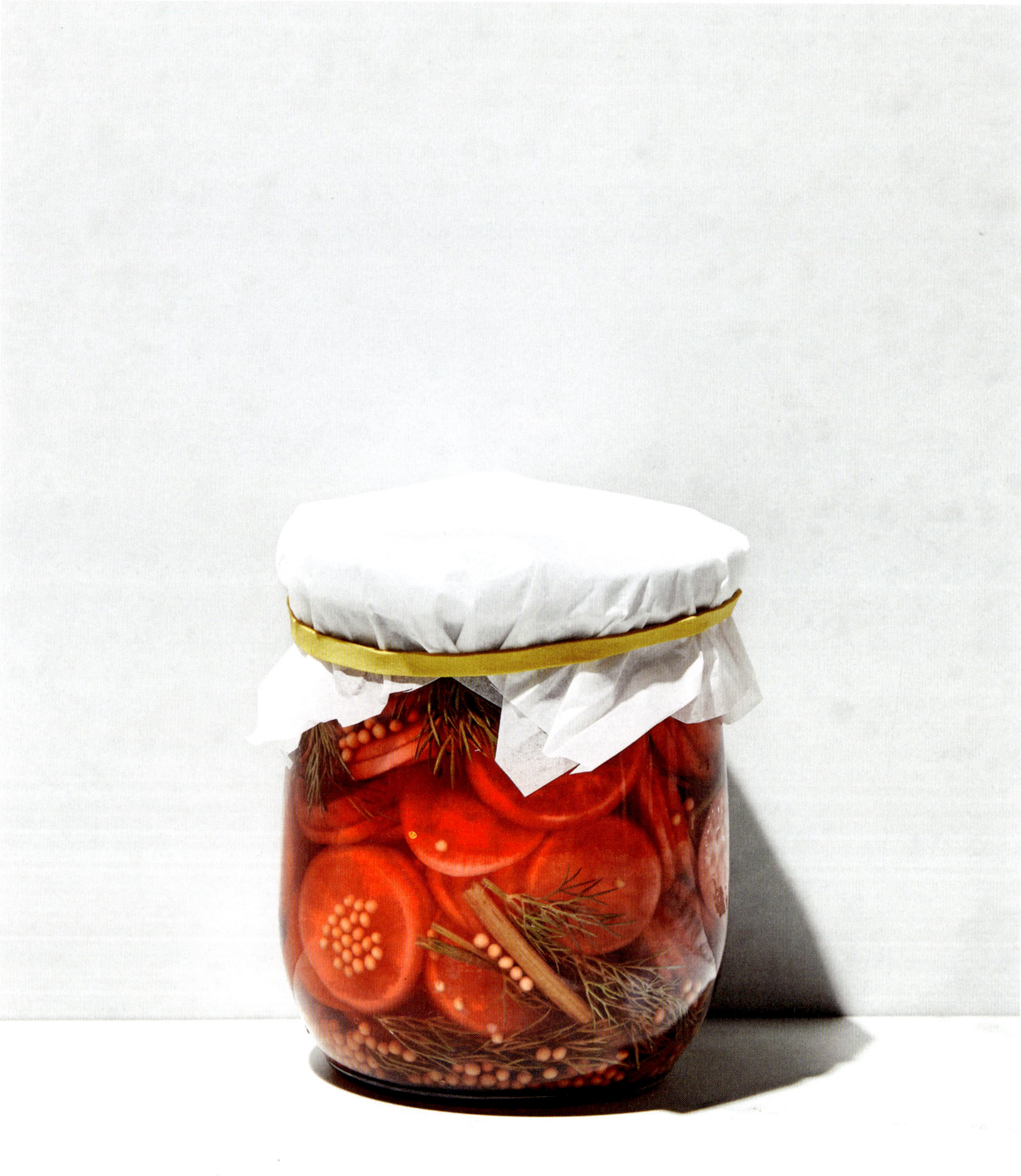

Fermented Radish Slices with Dill

For 2 canning jars (16 ounces / 400 ml each)

Ingredients

2 cups (500 ml) water

1½ teaspoons (10 g) salt

2 to 3 bunches radishes (14 ounces to 1¼ pounds / 400–600 g)

2 sprigs of fresh dill

2 teaspoons mustard seeds

To make the brine, put the water into a saucepan, bring to a boil, and let cool completely. Mix in the salt until fully dissolved.

Wash the radishes well and trim off the roots and greens (leafy tops). Wash the dill and shake dry. Using a mandoline slicer, thinly slice the radishes into rounds and layer the slices tightly in the sterilized canning jars, alternating with the mustard seeds and small dill fronds. Don't pack the jars all the way to the rim; leave at least 1¼ inches (3 cm) between the radishes and the lid.

Pour the brine over the radish slices until completely covered in the liquid. If the radish slices float to the surface, use a sterilized fermentation weight to keep them in place. Leave a space of about ¾ inch (2 cm) between the liquid and rim of the jar to allow space for the gas bubbles that form a foam on the surface during the fermentation process.

Close the jars with their lids but without tightening. Place the filled jars on a baking sheet or tray and let ferment at room temperature (preferably at 65 to 70 °F / 18–21 °C) in a dark place for 4 to 7 days. The exact fermentation time will vary depending on the temperature of the room (a warmer temperature speeds up the fermentation process). Regularly check and taste the contents of the jars with a clean fork.

As soon as no more gas bubbles form in the jar or the foam disappears, the initially cloudy liquid will become a little clearer and turn pink. The pickled radishes should now have a tart and slightly spicy flavor.

Take out the weight if using, close the jar lids tightly, and refrigerate. You can enjoy the fermented radishes immediately, but they will also keep for several weeks in the refrigerator.

Tips Because fermented radishes stimulate digestion, they make an excellent accompaniment for more substantial dishes, such as fatty cuts of meat.

You can use the leftover liquid from the jar as a salad dressing.

Sweet-and-Sour Pickled Radishes with Coriander Seeds

For 1 large canning jar (32 ounces / 800 ml)

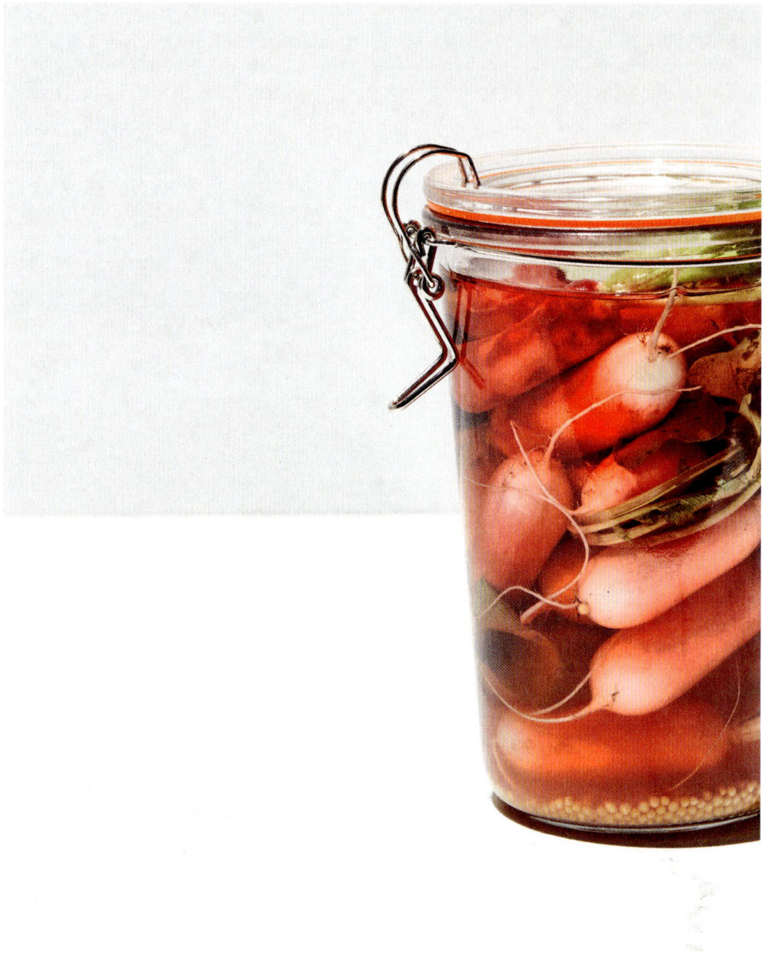

Ingredients

1 cup (250 ml) water

½ cup (125 ml) distilled white vinegar

3 ½ tablespoons (40 g) granulated sugar

½ teaspoon salt

1 teaspoon coriander seeds

1 teaspoon peppercorns

2 bay leaves

2 bunches of radishes
(about 14 ounces / 400 g)

To make the pickling liquid, add the water and vinegar to a saucepan, then mix in the sugar, salt peppercorns, and bay leaves. Bring to a boil and let simmer for about 5 minutes. Remove from the heat.

Wash the radishes thoroughly; if the leaves are in a good condition and clean, you can leave them on. Arrange the whole radishes in layers inside the jar and pour in the hot liquid until everything is completely covered. Close the jar tightly and let cool at room temperature. Store in a cool place away from light. Pickle the radishes for at least 5 days before eating.

Fermented Asparagus with Pink Peppercorns

For 1 large canning jar (128 ounces / 1 l)

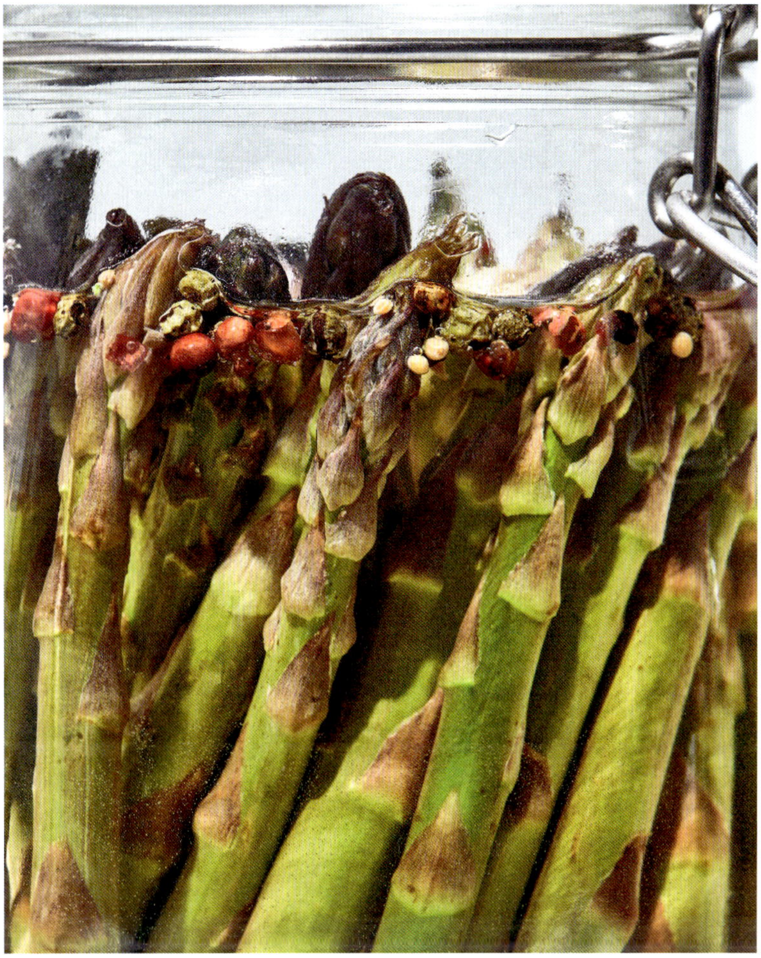

Ingredients

3 cups (750 ml) water

2 ½ teaspoons (15 g) salt

1 bunch of asparagus spears

1 teaspoon pink peppercorns

1 teaspoon mustard seeds

½ tsp allspice berries

To make the brine, put the water into a saucepan, bring to a boil, and let cool completely. Mix in the salt until fully dissolved.

Wash the asparagus spears well and trim off the woody ends. Arrange the asparagus spears in layers inside the sterilized jar and add the spices. Pour in the brine until the asparagus is completely covered in the liquid. If the asparagus spears float to the surface, use a sterilized fermentation weight to keep them in place. Leave a space of about ¾ inch (2 cm) between the liquid and rim of the jar to allow room for the gas bubbles that form a foam on the surface during the fermentation process.

Close the jar with its lid but without tightening. Place the jar in a shallow bowl and let the vegetable ferment at room temperature (preferably 65 to 70 °F / 18–21 °C) in a dark place for 5 to 9 days. The exact fermentation time will vary depending on the temperature of the room (a warmer temperature speeds up the fermentation process). Check the contents of the jar regularly. The asparagus is ready when no more gas bubbles form in the jar or the foam disappears.

Take out the weight if using, close the jar lid tightly, and refrigerate. You can use the fermented asparagus immediately, but it will also keep for several weeks in the refrigerator.

Tip There's no need to cook fermented asparagus. While tasting best on its own, it makes a quick and delicious accompaniment for many different dishes.

Salad with Wild Spring Herbs and Ferments

Serves 2

Ingredients

3 handfuls of baby greens (see tips)

1 handful of wild spring herbs (see tips)

1 handful of peas, shelled, or snow peas (mangetout)

1 carrot (preferably an early variety)

2 tablespoons Fermented Radish Slices (see p. 25)

5 tablespoons olive oil

2 tablespoons lemon juice

1 teaspoon honey

Salt and freshly ground black pepper

Wash the greens and herbs, shake dry, and coarsely chop them. Mix them with the peas in a large bowl. Peel the carrot, slice it into ribbons using a vegetable peeler, and add together with the fermented radish to the salad bowl.

Make the dressing by whisking the oil, lemon juice, and honey in a small bowl until smooth and creamy. Season with salt and pepper. Don't forget to taste the dressing before use.

Pour the dressing over the salad and toss well. Serve immediately.

Tips You can use baby spinach, arugula (rocket), lamb's lettuce (corn salad), sorrel, or any combination of these.

Spring is the ideal season for using wild herbs to add fresh flavors to your meals, so take full advantage. Depending on what is available where you live, these include daisy greens and flowers, goutweed, stinging nettles, garlic mustard, and tender dandelion greens, among others. If you love garlic, you can also use wild garlic leaves—freshly chopped, to infuse the olive oil (see p. 41), or in Wild Garlic Pesto (see p. 40).

Instead of lemon juice for the dressing, you can also use the Fermented Radish Slices brine out of the jar, which adds a pleasantly tangy acidity.

Prepare the salad as a light, complete meal—sprinkle in a small handful of your favourite nuts or seeds, crumble some sheep or goat cheese on top, and serve with a piece of whole-grain bread.

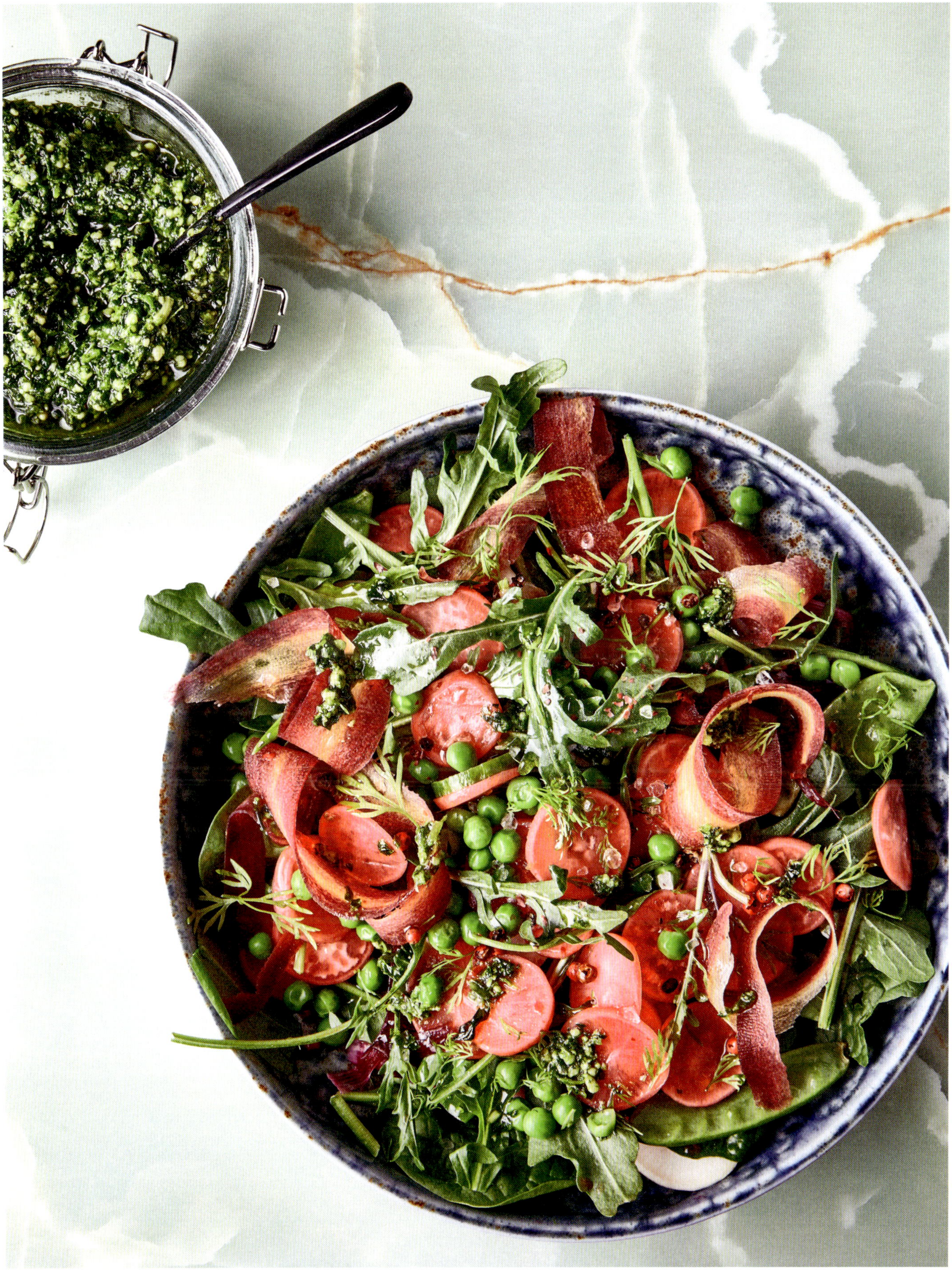

Pickled Scallions with Honey

For 1 canning jar (16 ounces / 500 ml)

Ingredients

2 to 3 bunches scallions (7 ¾ to 10 ½ ounces / 220–300 g)

1 cup (250 ml) distilled white vinegar

scant ½ cup (100 ml) water

2 ½ tablespoons (50 g) honey

1 teaspoon salt

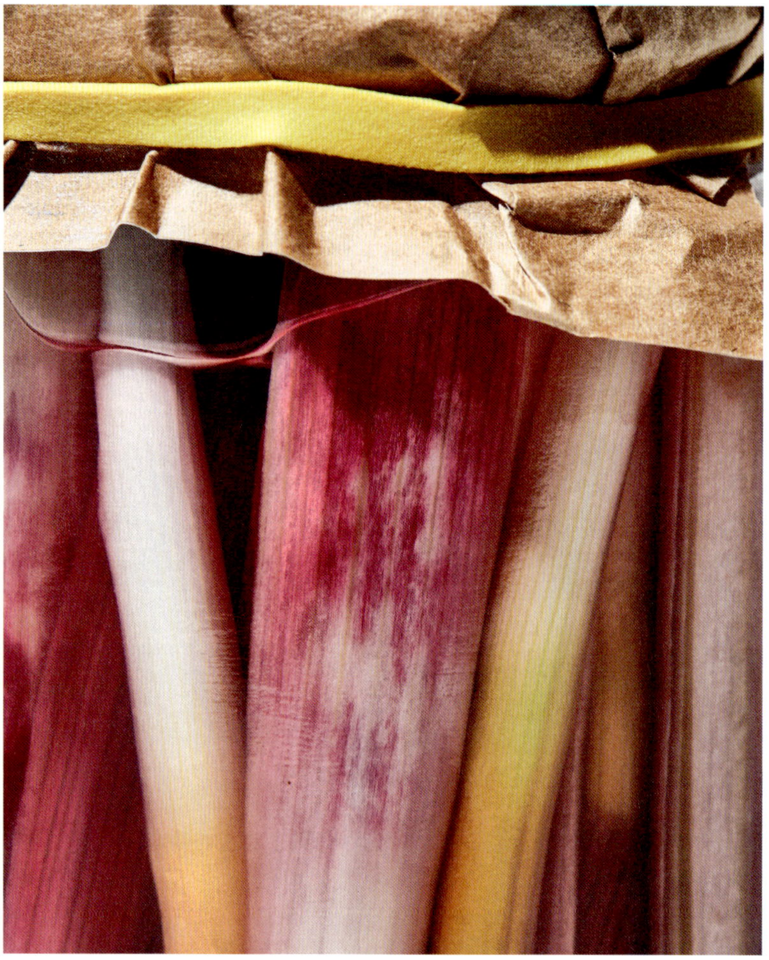

Wash the scallions, remove any wilted or damaged parts, and cut off all the green parts. (Reserve the green parts for other uses—store them in the refrigerator wrapped in a damp cloth.) Arrange the white parts tightly packed in a sterilized canning jar.

Mix the distilled white vinegar, water, honey, and salt in a saucepan. Bring to a boil and let simmer over low heat for 3 minutes. Remove the pickling liquid from the heat and let cool slightly.

Pour the hot liquid over the scallions, covering them completely in the liquid. Close the jar tightly, let cool completely, and refrigerate. Pickle the scallions for at least a few hours. Once the jar is opened, the pickled scallions should be used within a week.

Tips You can add a pinch of crushed red pepper (chili) flakes, a few peppercorns, and fennel or coriander seeds to the scallions for a more intense and spicy flavor.

Pickled scallions are great with sausages, ham, and cheese, as well as sandwiches and salads. Chopped into small pieces, they give a simple scrambled egg an added kick.

Fermented Snow Peas

For 1 canning jar (16 ounces/500 ml)

Ingredients

1 cup (250 ml) water

1 teaspoon (5 g) salt

3 cups (200 g) snow peas (mangetout)

1 teaspoon rainbow peppercorns

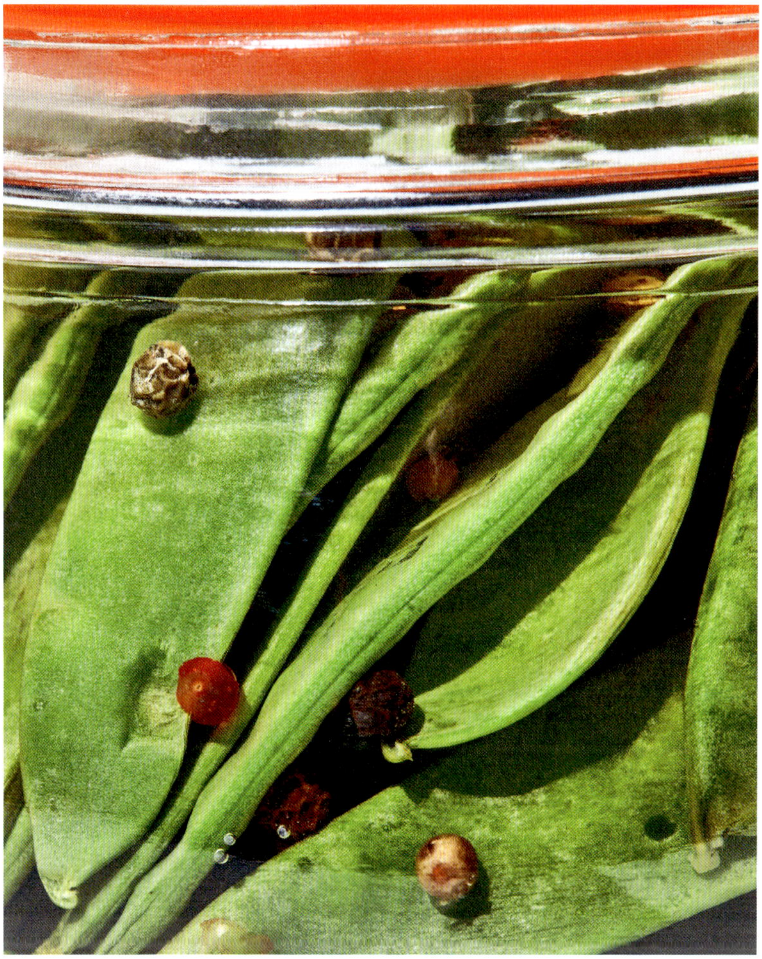

To make the brine, put the water into a saucepan, bring to a boil, and let cool. Mix in the salt until fully dissolved.

Wash the snow peas well and trim off both ends. Arrange the snow peas and peppercorns in a sterilized canning jar without filling it all the way to the rim. Leave at least 1¼ inches (3 cm) between the snow peas and the lid.

Pour the salt solution over the snow peas, covering them completely in the liquid. If the snow peas float to the surface, use a sterilized fermentation weight to keep them in place. Leave a space of about ¾ inch (2 cm) between the liquid and rim of the jar to allow room for the gas bubbles that form a foam on the surface during the fermentation process.

Close the jar with its lid but without tightening. Place the jar in a deep tray and let the vegetable ferment at room temperature (preferably 65 to 70 °F/18–21 °C) in a dark place for 4 to 7 days. The exact fermentation time will vary depending on the temperature of the room (a warmer temperature speeds up the fermentation process). Regularly check and taste the contents of the jars with a clean fork. The snow peas are ready when no more gas bubbles form in the jar or the foam disappears. They should now have a pleasantly tart and spicy flavor.

Take out the weight if using, close the jar lid tightly, and refrigerate. You can use the fermented snow peas immediately, but they will also keep for several weeks in the refrigerator.

Tip Jazz up the next spring salad you make with these crunchy fermented snow peas.

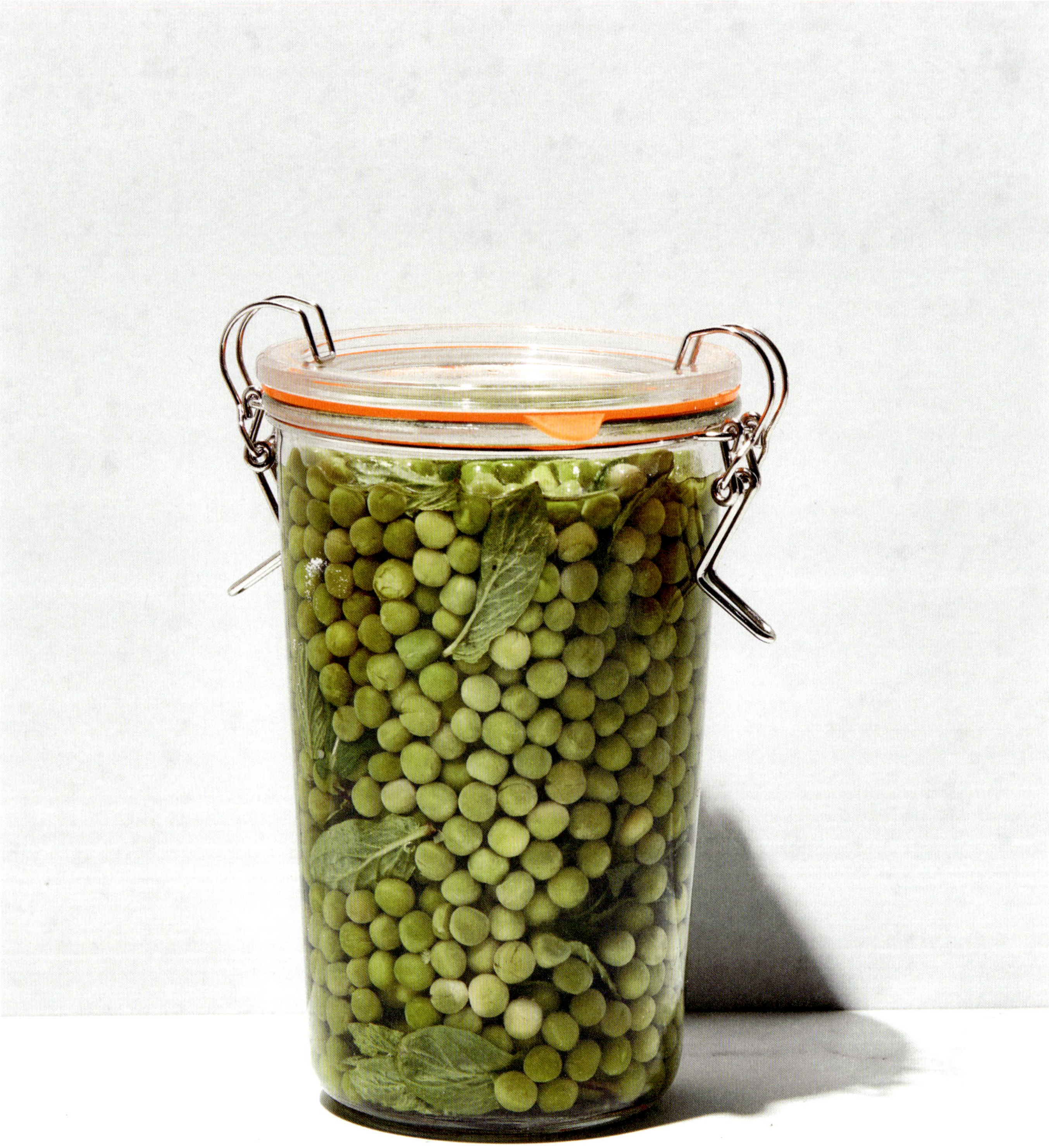

Minted Pickled Peas

For 4 canning jars (8 ounces / 200 ml each)

Ingredients

1½ cups (350 ml) apple cider vinegar

⅓ cup (80 ml) water

2½ tablespoons (30 g) granulated sugar

1 teaspoon salt

3½ cups (500 g) freshly shelled peas

1 large sprig of fresh mint

To make the pickling liquid, add the vinegar and water to a saucepan and mix in the sugar and salt. Put over medium heat and gently bring to a boil. Stir from time to time until the sugar and salt dissolve completely. As soon as the liquid begins to boil, remove from the heat and let cool.

In the meantime, divide the peas among the sterilized canning jars. Wash the mint, shake dry, and pluck the leaves. Then push mint leaves between the peas.

Pour the pickling liquid over the peas. If bubbles form between the peas, tap the open jars on the work surface or stir the contents of the jars with a clean fork. The peas should be completely covered by the liquid without floating to the surface.

Close the jars tightly. Because of the liquid's higher salt and vinegar content, there's no need to can the peas. Simply store in a cool, dark place. The peas should be pickled for at least 2 weeks before eating.

Tips You can add extra flavors to the pickled peas by adding a piece of ginger, some chopped chili pepper, or a few peppercorns.

Mint-infused pickled peas make a great accompaniment for lamb and add a beautiful flavor to salads and to the Fresh Herb and Minted Pea Frittata (see p. 34).

Fresh Herb and Minted Pea Frittata

Serves 4

Ingredients

1 onion

1 handful of wild garlic or spinach leaves

1 handful of wild spring herbs (see tips)

8 eggs

3 ½ tablespoons (50 ml) milk

Salt and freshly ground black pepper

1 tablespoon olive oil

⅓ cup (50 g) Minted Pickled Peas (see p. 33)

3 ½ ounces (100 g) sheep cheese, crumbled

Preheat the oven to 400 °F top/bottom heat (200 °C/Gas Mark 6).

Peel, halve, and thinly slice the onion. Wash the wild garlic or spinach leaves and spring herbs, pat dry, and coarsely chop. In a bowl, beat the eggs with the milk, then season with salt and pepper.

Heat the oil in a medium oven-safe skillet or frying pan and cook the onion until translucent. Add the wild garlic or spinach and cook until a little wilted. Add the herbs, followed by the beaten eggs, and stir in the peas and cheese. Cook over medium heat for about 5 minutes, until the eggs begin to set and the edges start to pull away from the sides of the pan.

Transfer the pan to the top oven shelf. Bake the frittata for 5 to 7 minutes, until the top turns golden. Carefully remove the pan from the oven using a dishcloth or oven mitt—the handle of the pan will be very hot. Arrange the finished frittata on a plate and cut into serving-size pieces. Sprinkle with fresh herbs and serve together with more pickled peas, if you want.

Tips If you have only a large skillet, reduce the frying and baking time a little or add more eggs. If you have only a small one, you can simply reduce the number of eggs. Once in the pan, the egg and herb mixture should always have a depth of at least ¾ inch (2 cm).

A frittata is easy to make and easy to change up. Adjust the ingredients according to the season or personal taste, or simply use leftovers from the refrigerator. Try this recipe using fresh or cooked vegetables, bacon, different types of cheese, leftover chicken, and/or boiled potatoes cut into small pieces.

Spring herbs you can use include tender nettles, ground elder, and ground ivy leaves.

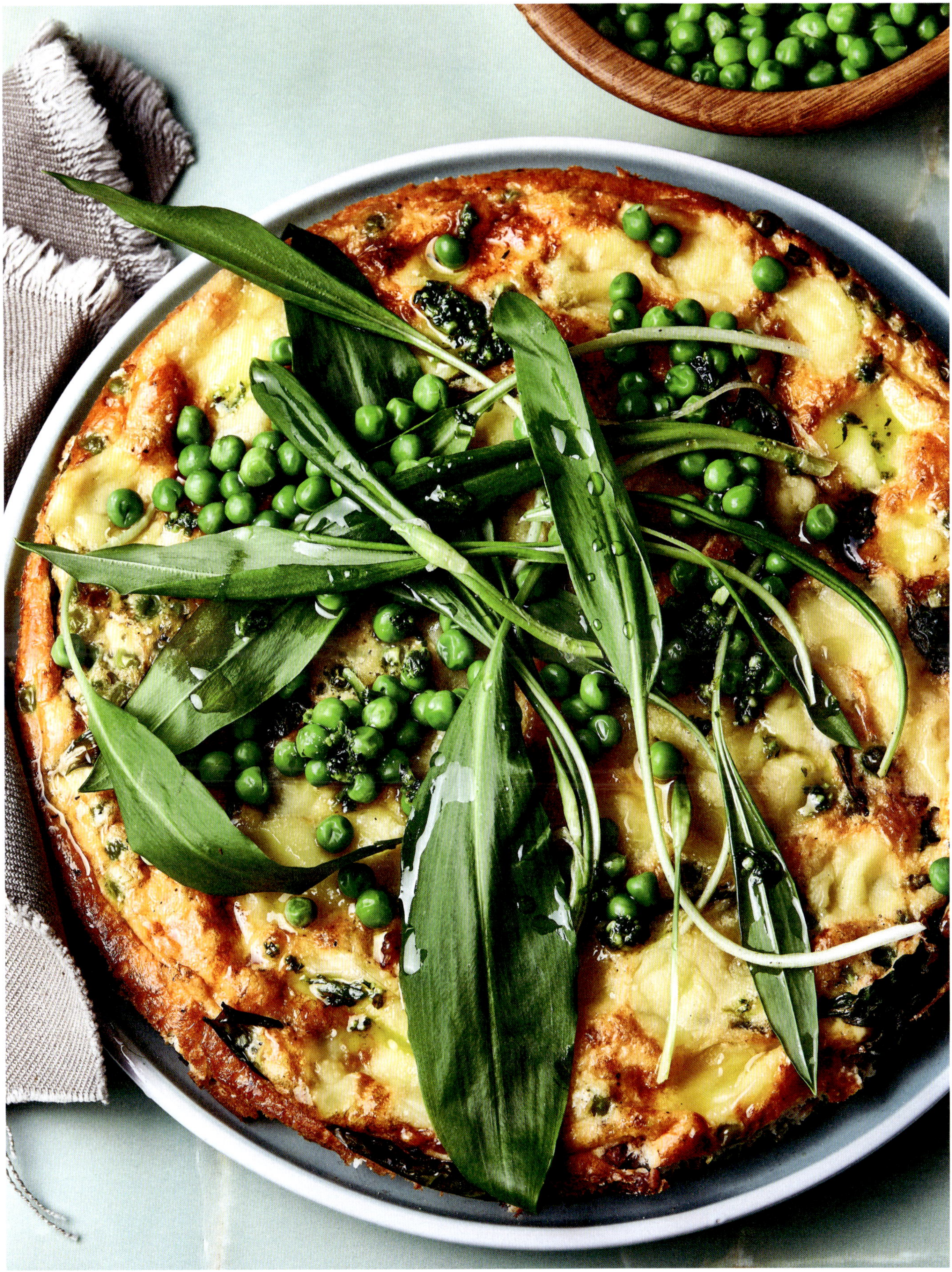

Wild Foraging: A Life-Fueling Passion

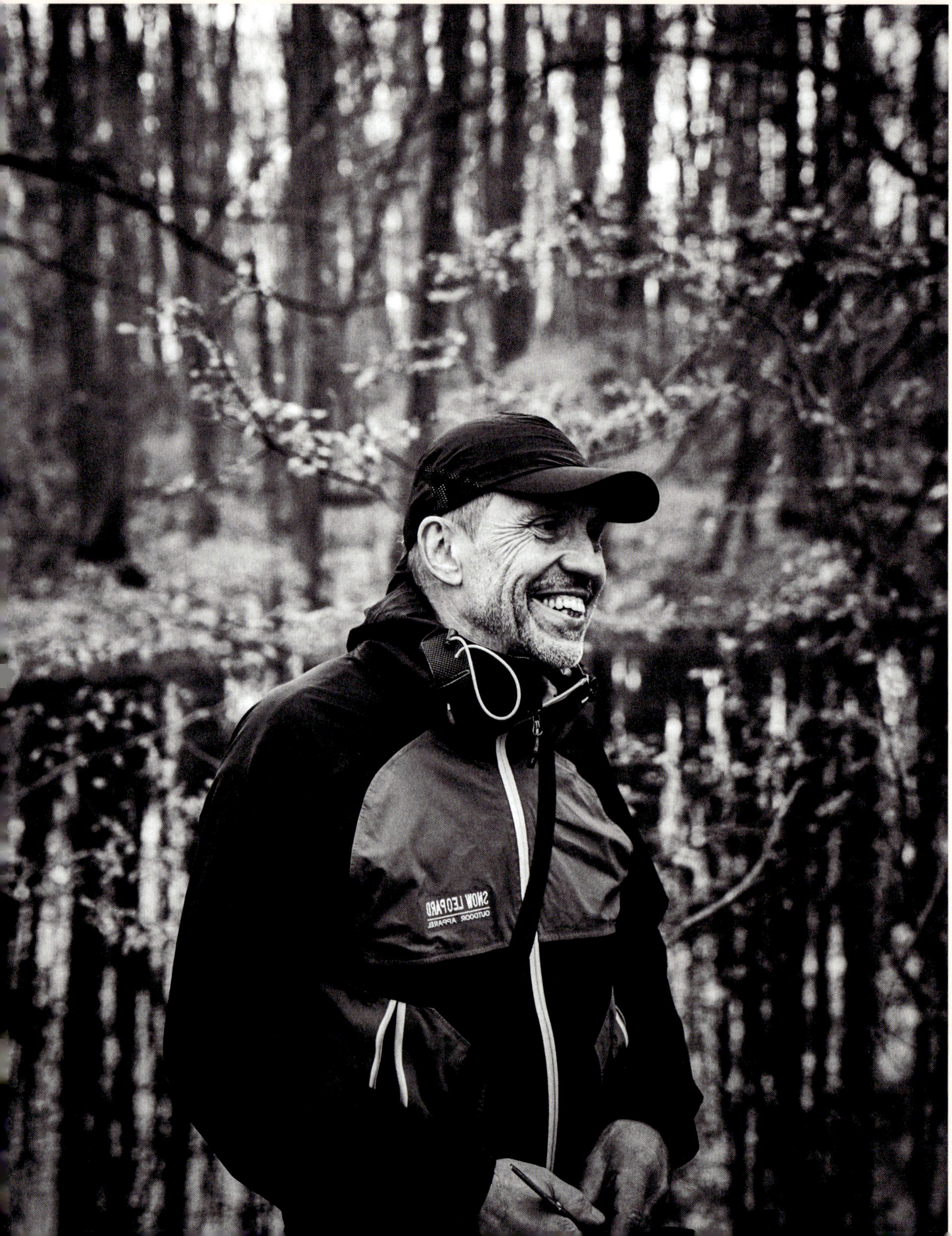

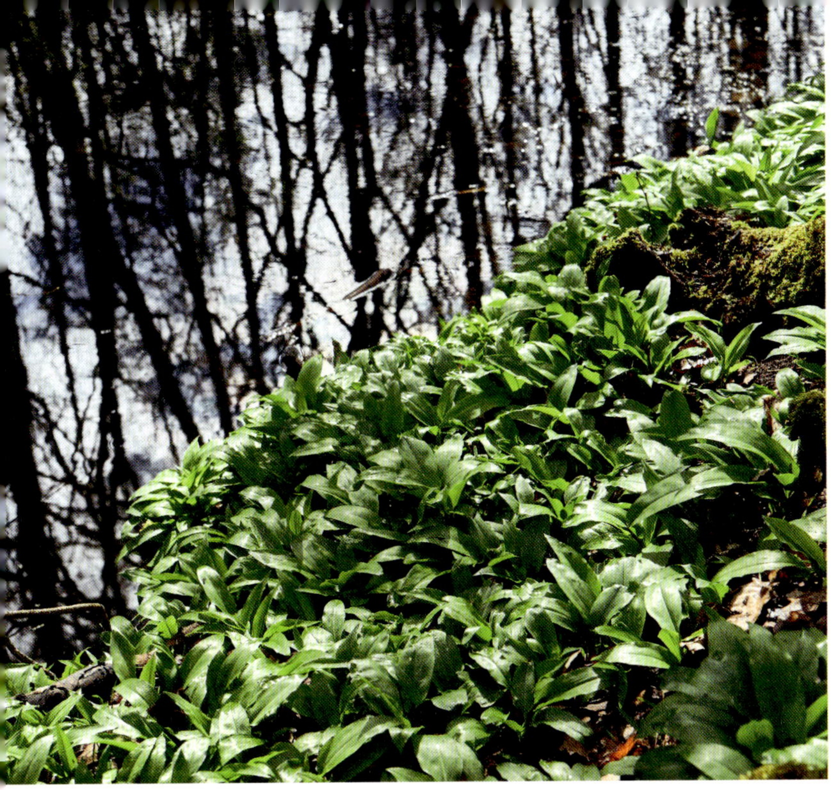

Wild herbs and overlooked fruit cast their spell on Tomáš long ago. Over time, he's become something of a legend among Czech chefs: the go-to man for free-range foraging. You'll find him out in nature year-round, picking what the land offers at that particular moment. Always gently, never greedily. He speaks of gratitude the way others speak of seasoning—something essential, to be applied with care.

Like generations before him, Tomáš fills his pantry with what he's gathered: jars of preserves that bring summer into the kitchen on a cold winter day. "That's how you can keep eating locally, even in February," he says. His shelves hold the familiar—cucumbers, plum compotes— and the unexpected. Poplar buds pickled in miso, dandelion chutney quince jam. Each jar is a little adventure of its own.

When spring arrives, you'll find him in the forests near the Elbe, bending low over the first shoots of wild garlic. "Cut it above ground, don't pull up the roots!" he calls out. It's advice worth remembering the next time you find a patch of wild garlic, or any other treasure growing freely in the woods: take only what you need, leave the rest, and cook with a little appreciation.

Thanks to Tomáš Reisinger, a seasoned chef and enthusiastic forager, long-overlooked herbs and fruit are making their way back onto Czech plates.

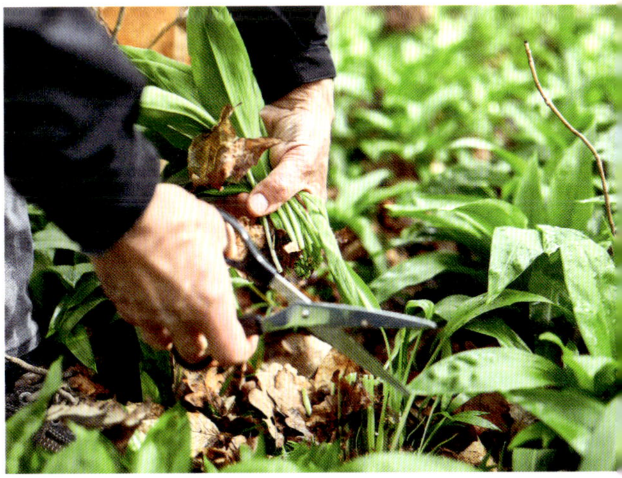

Tomáš Reisinger cooks like someone who listens to the forest. A professional chef by training and a wild-food enthusiast by instinct, he moves easily between the kitchen and the meadow, the restaurant and the riverbank.

He learned his craft first at Prague's InterContinental Hotel, then at the legendary Alcron, and later during fifteen years in Austria, where he loves its slower, more natural rhythm of cooking. "In Austria, even back then, people cook mostly with local ingredients and using wild herbs and fruit. When I came back home, it saddened me that Czech restaurants weren't open to that idea yet," he says.

Today, that's changing—and Tomáš has had a lot to do with this. After returning to the Czech Republic, he helped create the restaurants Na Jitrách in Samice, Eska in Prague, and Thir in Tábor. What really excites him is the moment when a handful of foraged berries or a sprig of wild thyme finds its way into a dish. "For me, good cooking means working with what's growing right now," he says. "Fortunately, the last decade has brought huge changes. Nordic cuisine has had a big influence—the Scandinavians have no fear of pickling fruit that others ignore."

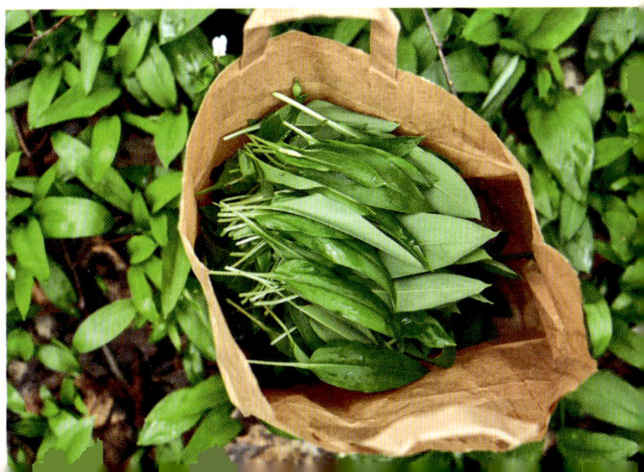

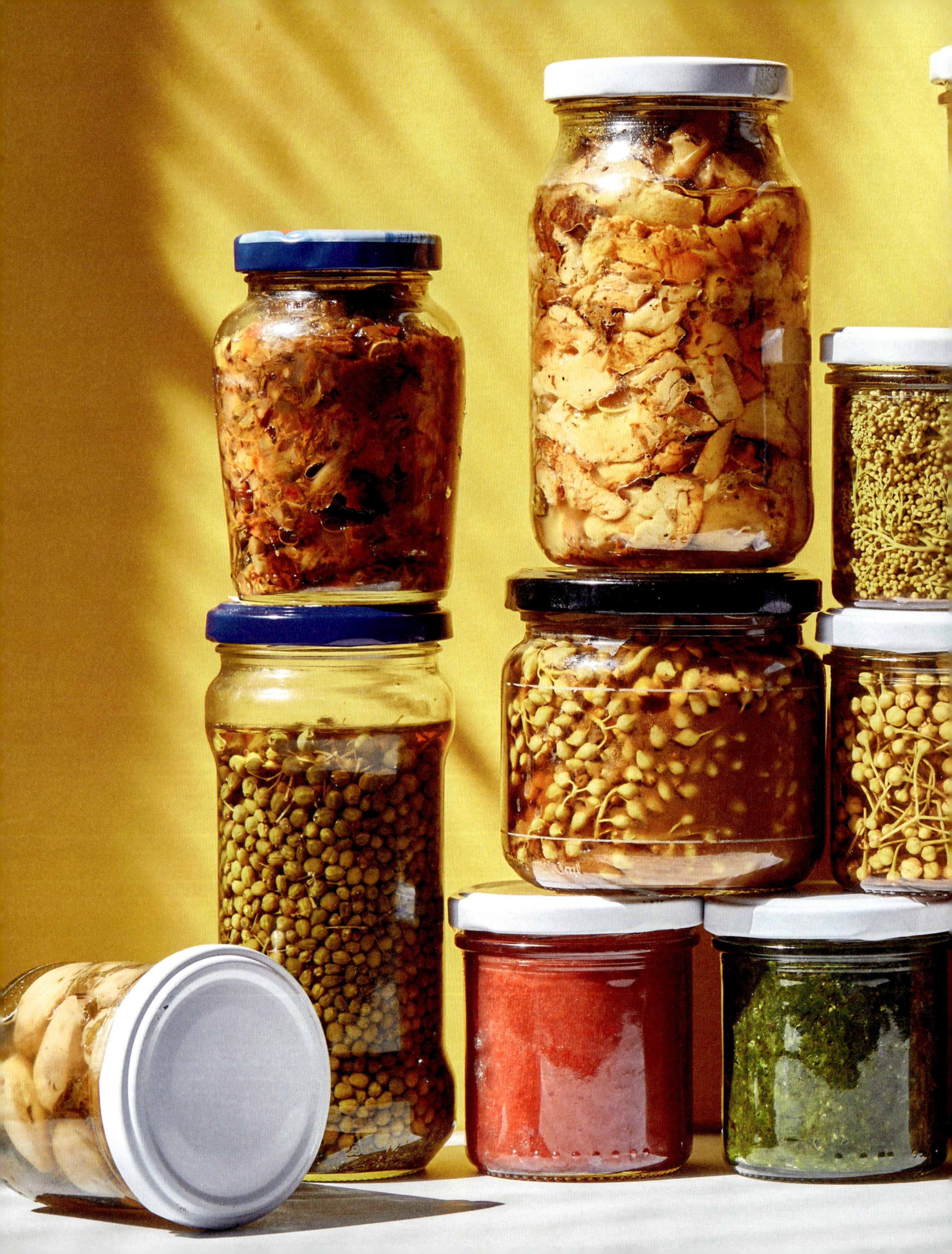

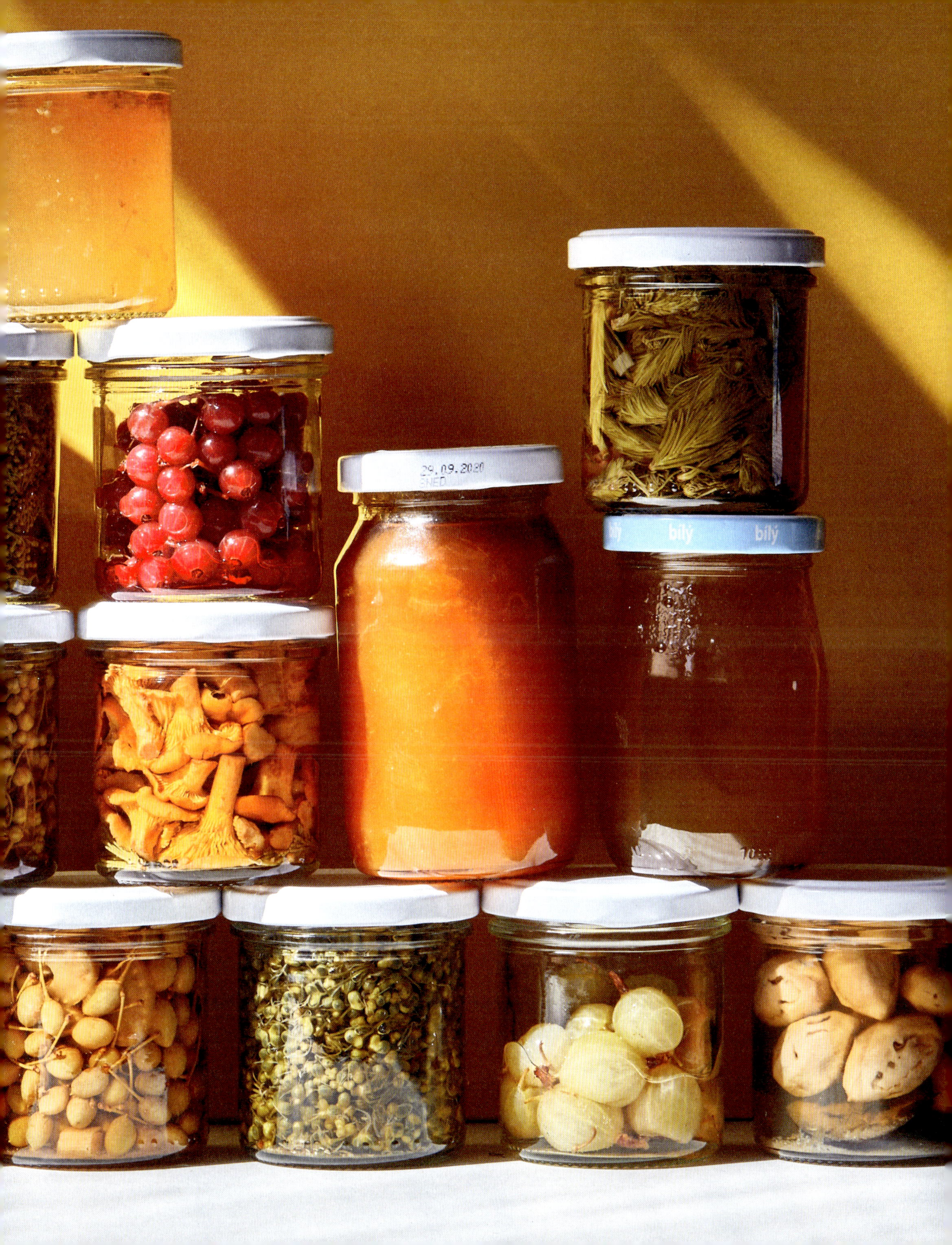
29.09.2020
bílý
bílý

Wild Garlic Pesto

For 2 or 3 small canning jars (4 ounces/150 ml each)

Ingredients

4 cups (200 g) wild garlic leaves

½ cup (60 g) pine nuts or walnuts

1¾ ounces (50 g) Parmesan cheese

Salt and freshly ground black pepper

⅔ cup (150 ml) olive oil

Juice of ½ lemon

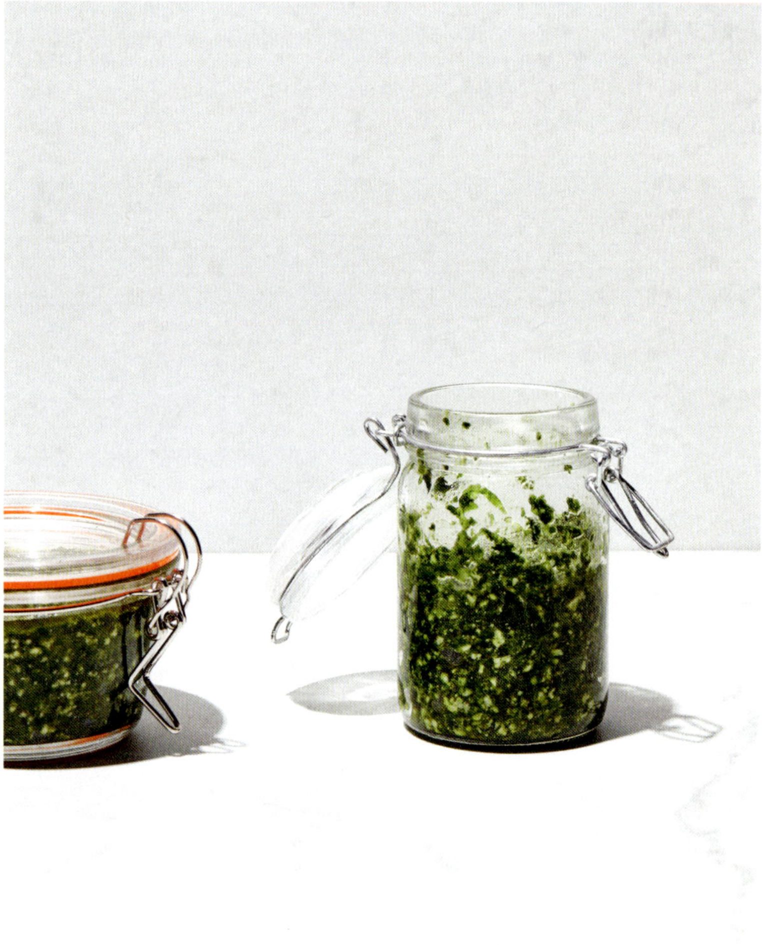

Wash the wild garlic leaves under cold running water and carefully pat dry. Coarsely chop the leaves and place in a blender.

Toast the nuts in a dry skillet or frying pan. Pine nuts are quick to burn, so watch them closely. Toast until fragrant, then transfer to a bowl and let cool. Finely grate the cheese.

Add the nuts and grated cheese to the wild garlic in the blender. Season with salt and pepper and drizzle with a little oil. Pulse until the mixture is coarsely chopped. Add the remaining oil and continue to blend until the pesto has the desired consistency. Finally, season to taste with lemon juice, salt, and pepper.

Tips You can also make this pesto using a mortar and pestle, but it will have a coarser texture.

Wild garlic pesto is wonderful for pasta dishes and as an accompaniment for roasted or grilled meats. You can add it to the dressing for a vegetable salad (see p. 28) or use it to make Yeast Knots with Wild Garlic Filling (see p. 42). It also gives yogurt- or mayonnaise-based dips a pleasantly spicy taste.

If you won't be using your homemade pesto immediately, transfer it to an airtight jar and cover the surface with a little olive oil. Refrigerated, the pesto will keep for a week.

Olive Oil Infused with Wild Garlic

For 1 bottle (16 ounces/500 ml)

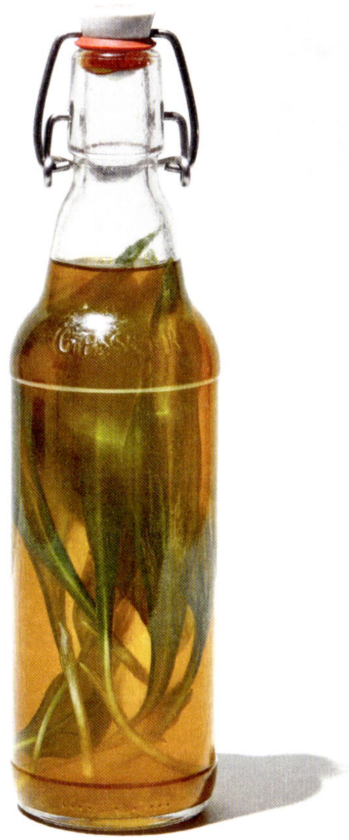

Ingredients

1 handful wild garlic leaves

2 cups (500 ml) extra virgin olive oil

Wash the wild garlic leaves under cold running water and carefully pat dry. Either leave the leaves whole or cut them into small pieces. Put the leaves into a sterilized bottle and add the oil. Close the jar and refrigerate.

Let the wild garlic infuse in the oil for about 3 weeks, then bring to room temperature and strain through a strainer or sieve. Transfer the wild garlic oil to a glass bottle and use immediately or store in a cool, dark place.

Tips The wild garlic season, one of the most popular spring herbs, is very short. However, by macerating the herbs in oil, you can enjoy their fresh flavor all year round.

Instead of straining, the wild garlic leaves can be blended together with the oil to make a rich and highly aromatic herb oil. This oil is perfect for enhancing the flavor of different dishes, and also adds a splash of color to the plate.

Wild garlic oil is extremely versatile and can be used in both hot or cold dishes, including white fish, salads, risottos, and cream soups (see p. 218).

Yeast Knots with Wild Garlic Filling

Makes about 20 knots

Ingredients

1¼ cups (300 ml) water

2¼ teaspoons (7 g) active dry (fast-action dried) yeast

1 tablespoon granulated sugar

4 cups (500 g) all-purpose (plain) flour or Italian "00" flour, plus extra for dusting

1 teaspoon salt

5 tablespoons olive oil

½ to ¾ cup (150–200 g) Wild Garlic Pesto (see p. 40)

In a saucepan, heat the water until lukewarm, then stir in the yeast and sugar. Let stand for a few minutes. Sift the flour into a large bowl and mix in the salt. Add the activated yeast mixture to the flour, followed by the oil. Using a wooden spoon or in a food processor, carefully mix everything together to form a dough, then knead for at least 10 minutes until the dough is smooth and supple. It should come away easily from the sides of the bowl. Cover the bowl with a clean dishcloth. Rest the dough in a warm place for about 1 hour, until doubled in volume (the warmer the temperature, the faster the dough will rise).

In the meantime, line 2 baking sheets with parchment (baking) paper.

Transfer the dough to a floured work surface and roll out into a large rectangle about 15½ by 19½ inches (40×50 cm). Drain off and collect the excess oil from the surface of the pesto. Spread the pesto on the right side over two-thirds of the pastry rectangle. Fold the left third of the rectangle over the middle third (over half of the pesto-covered surface). Then fold the right third over the top, as if folding a letter, and carefully roll out the pesto-filled rectangle a bit. Using a pizza cutter, cut the dough into strips about ¾ inch (2 cm) wide.

To shape each knot, first hold one end of a dough strip in one hand and twist it several times with the other. Next, while continuing to hold the end of the dough strip between your thumb and index finger, loosely wrap the rest of the strip two times around your fingers and then tuck the free end under the newly formed knot. Don't worry if the oil in the pesto filling leaks out as you shape the knots. It will prevent the rolls (buns) from burning as they bake.

Arrange the pesto knots spaced apart on the baking sheets and let rise for about 15 minutes. Preheat the oven to 375 °F top/bottom heat (190 °C/Gas Mark 5). Bake the rolls in the oven for 12 to 15 minutes, until golden. Let cool completely, then serve immediately.

Tips For a crunchy effect, sprinkle the pesto knots with chopped nuts or mixed seeds before baking.

Reserve the oil drained from the surface of the pesto for another use.

For added flavor, mix fresh spring herbs—for example, chives, basil, cilantro, parsley, and lovage—into the dough.

If you find the dough difficult to work with the first time, make the dough the evening before and let it rise overnight in the refrigerator. This will make it a little firmer and much easier to shape. It will also make the rolls even lighter and fluffier. You can also let the filled dough rest in the refrigerator for 1 hour after folding, before rolling it out, cutting it into strips, and shaping.

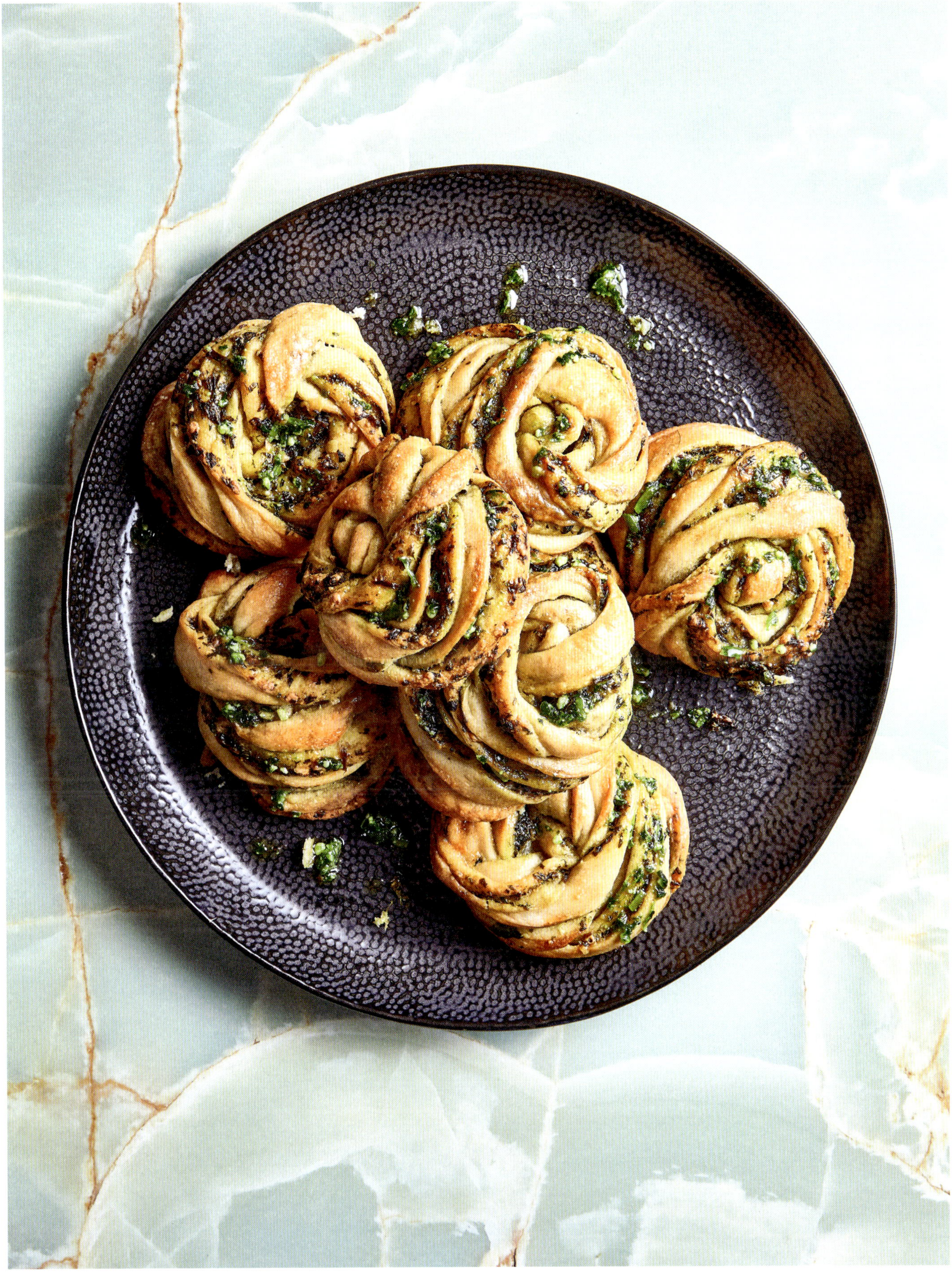

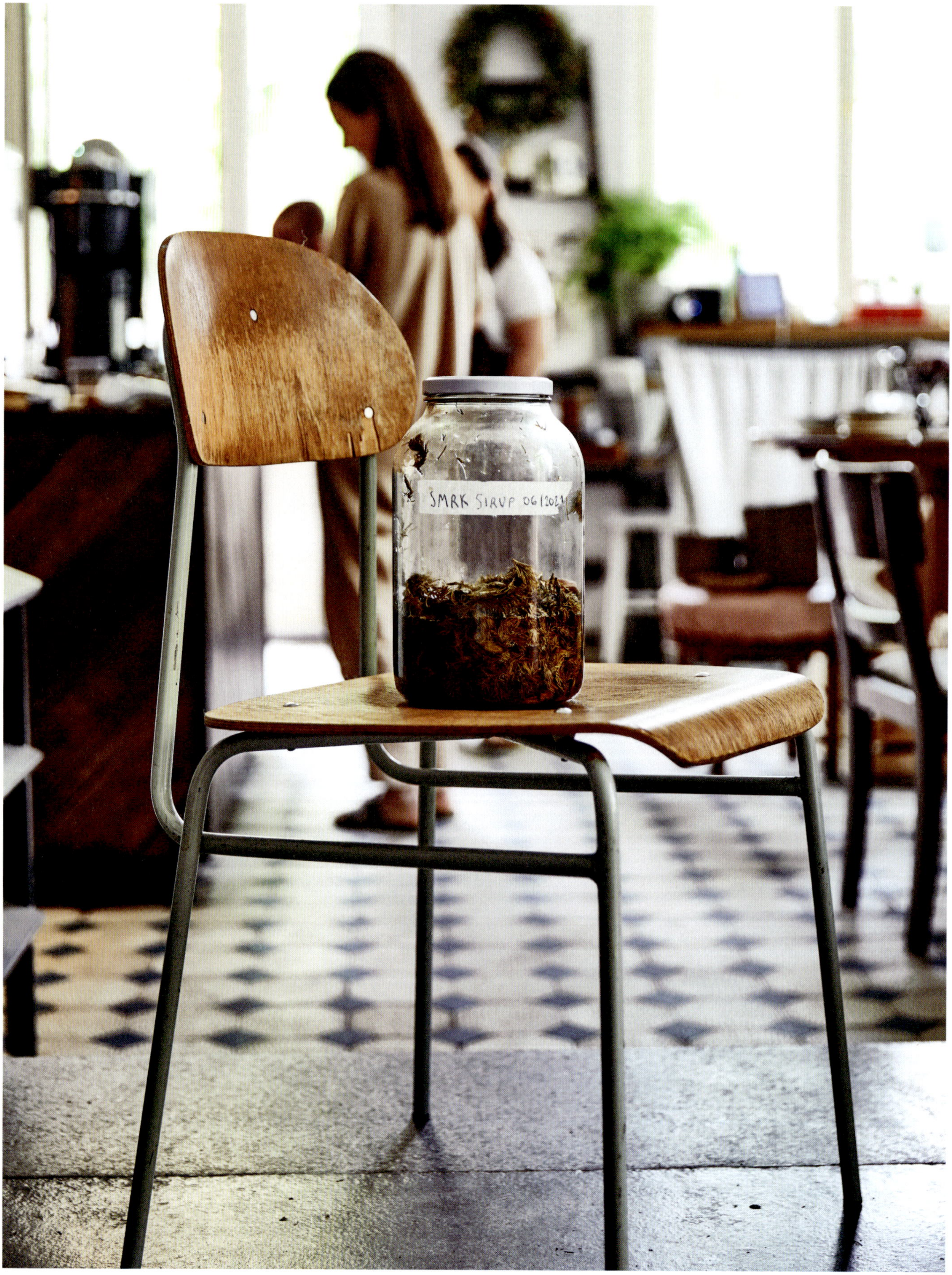
SMRK SIRUP 06/2021

Spruce Tip Syrup

For 1 or 2 large canning jars (64 ounces / 3–5 l)

Ingredients

Young spruce tips

Cane sugar

2 organic lemons

Wash the spruce tips well under cold running water and carefully pat dry. Wash and slice 2 lemons (prepare more lemons later, if necessary).

Line the bottom of a large sterilized canning jar with a wide opening with a layer of spruce tips about 2 inches (5 cm) thick and press well to compact. Cover the spruce tips with a layer of sugar about ½ inch (1 cm) thick and top with 2 lemon slices. Repeat the process until the entire jar is filled. The top layer should only consist of sugar. (Repeat if using a second jar.)

Close the jar(s) tightly and place it in a sunny position, such as a windowsill. Let the spruce tips infuse for about 3 weeks until a thick, dark syrup is produced. If there is less sunlight, it may take a little longer for the sugar to dissolve and the spruce tips to release their sap. If you like your syrup very sweet, taste the syrup as the spruce tips infuse using a clean teaspoon and add a little more sugar, if necessary.

Strain the syrup through a fine-mesh strainer or sieve and pour it into smaller sterilized glass bottles. Store in a cool, dark place. (Store it this way even after opening).

Tips To make this syrup, only pick very young spruce tips that are light green and still soft and flexible, not prickly. Mid-May is the ideal time for picking spruce tips. Note: Only pick a few young tips at a time from each tree to avoid harming the tree.

The aromatic spruce tip syrup can be used to make a refreshing drink in spring or on hot summer days by diluting 1 to 2 teaspoons of syrup with water and serving with a few ice cubes. The syrup protects against colds in fall and winter, because it contains a lot of vitamin C, as well as many valuable plant compounds. It has anti-inflammatory properties and is a natural expectorant that clears the respiratory tract.

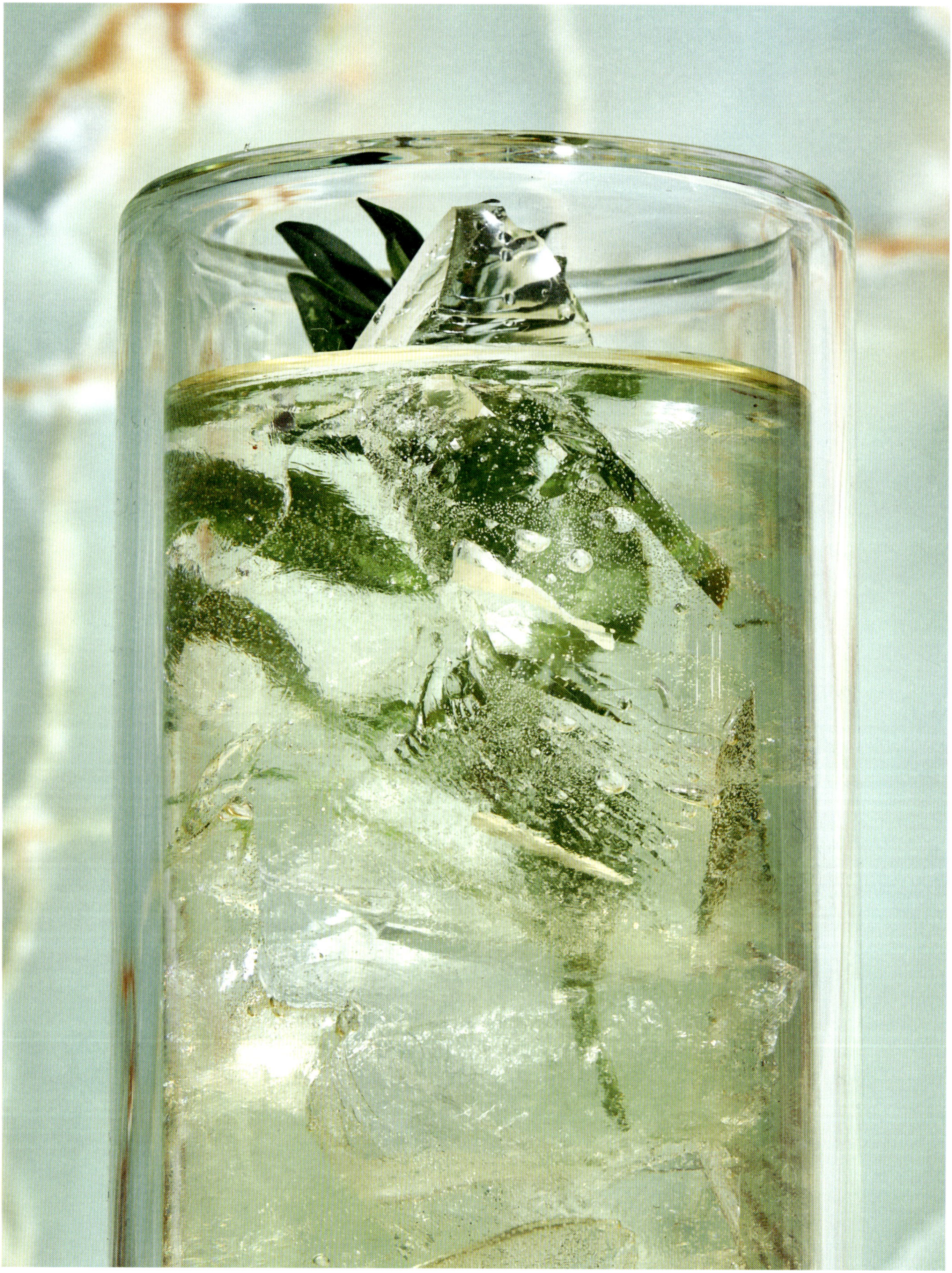

Elderflower Syrup

For 6 bottles (16 ounces / 500 ml each)

Ingredients

8 ½ cups (2 l) water

2 organic lemons

40 elderflower blossoms

⅓ cup (70 g) citric acid

10 cups (2 kg) granulated sugar

Bring the water to a boil in a large pot and let cool completely. In the meantime, wash the lemons in hot water, pat dry, and cut into slices. Carefully shake the elderflower blossoms over the work surface and spread out the flowers, which will let any insects hidden among them crawl out.

Dissolve the citric acid in the cooled water and add the lemon slices. Add the elderflowers to the pot, cover with a lid or a clean dishcloth (tea towel), and let it stand in a cool, dark place. Let infuse for 24 hours.

Filter the mixture through cheesecloth (muslin) or a clean dishcloth into a second pot. Add the sugar and place the pot over medium heat, stirring until the sugar dissolves. Using a large spoon, skim off any foam forming on the surface. When the liquid comes to a gentle simmer, remove from the heat and let cool slightly. Pour the warm syrup into sterilized and previously warmed glass bottles. Close the bottles, let cool, and refrigerate.

To use, dilute the syrup with water and enjoy.

Tips When picking elderflowers, avoid any trees growing near roads, industrial areas, or dusty paths. If organic lemons are unavailable, wash conventional lemons in hot water, then peel and slice.

You can add vodka or another clean-tasting, high-proof liquor (spirit) to the syrup before sealing the bottles. This will keep it from spoiling quickly.

For a hint of freshness, add a sprig of fresh mint to the water with the elderflowers.

Dilute the syrup with cold, sparkling mineral water and serve with ice cubes in summer.

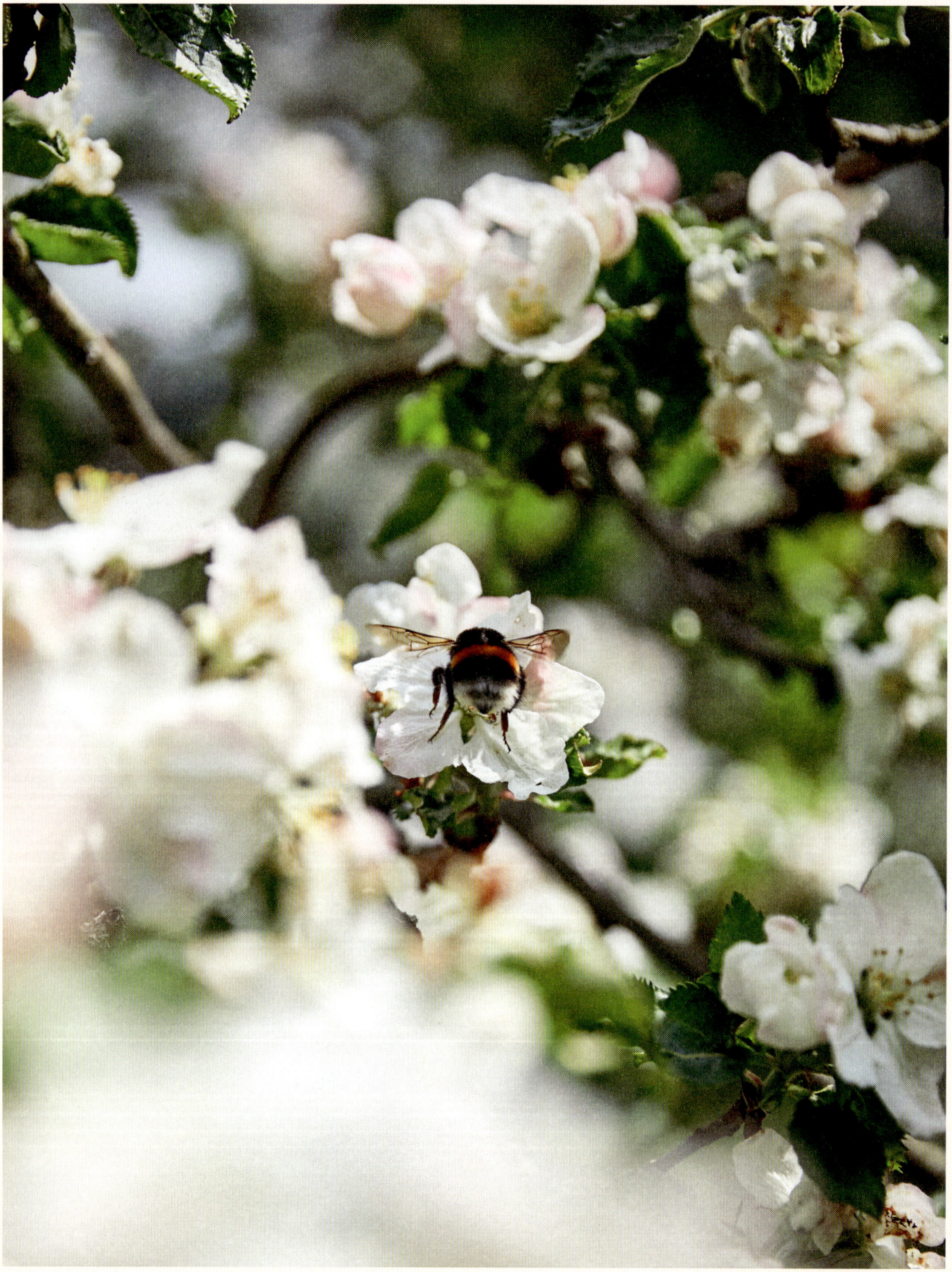

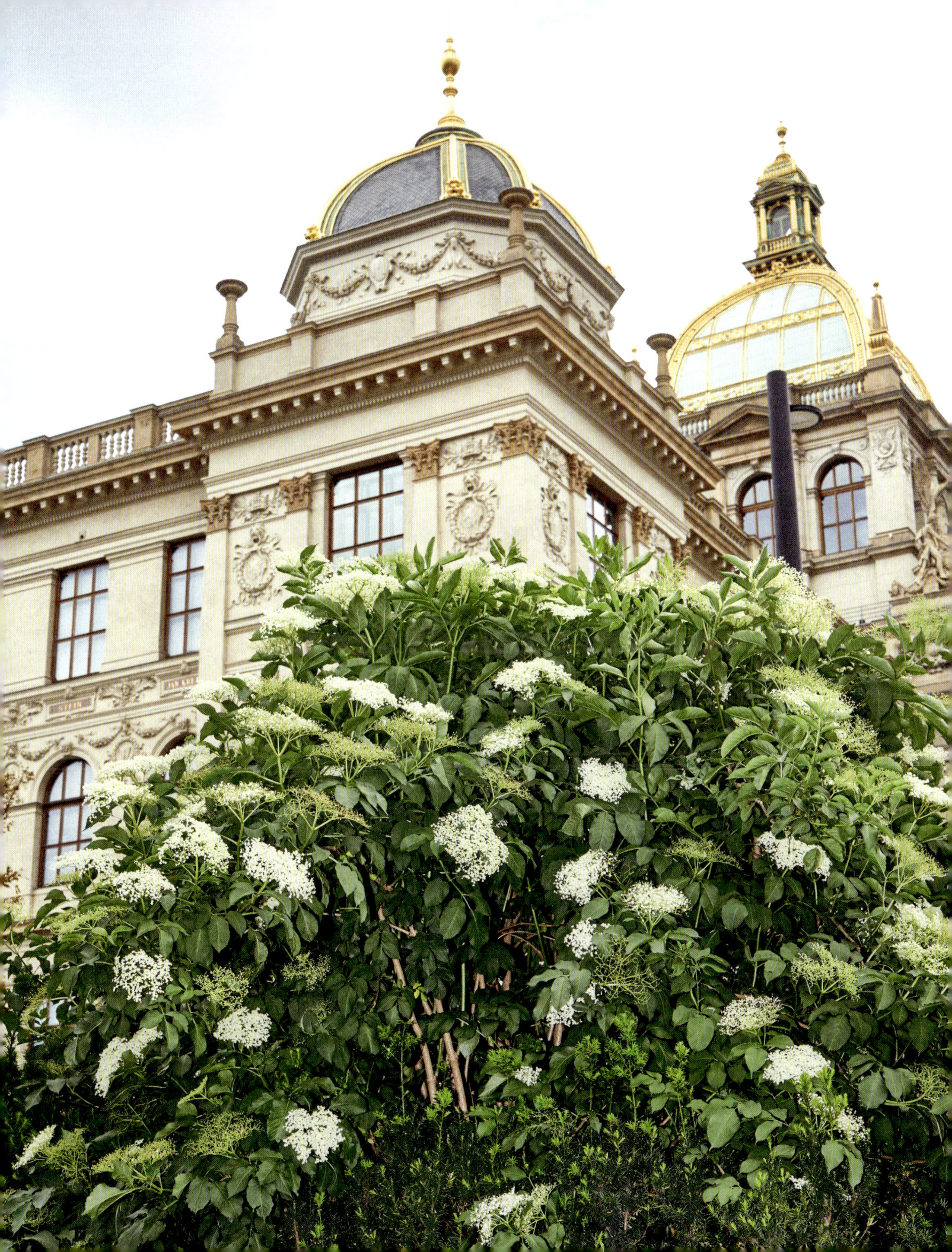

From Intuition to Innovation on the Plates

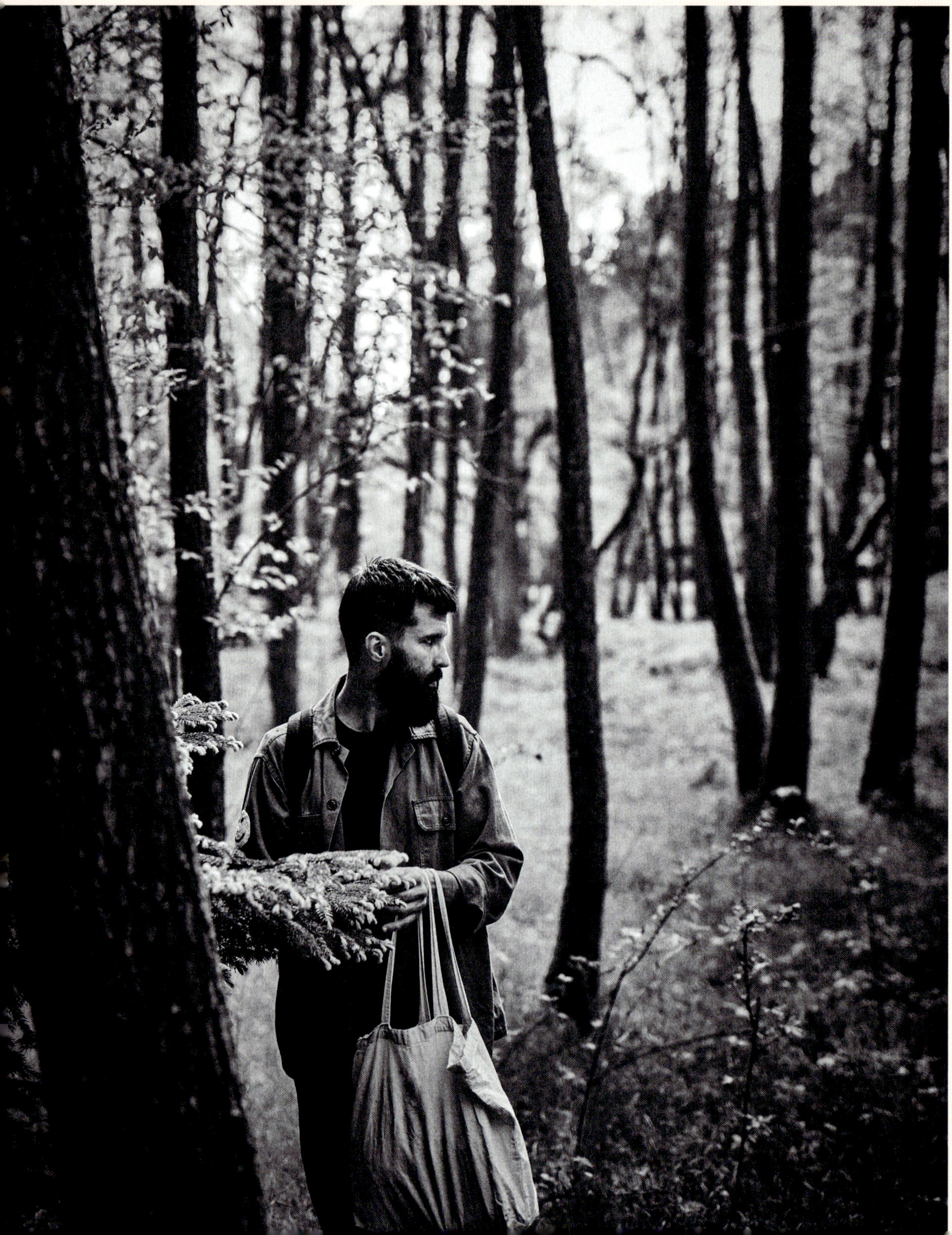

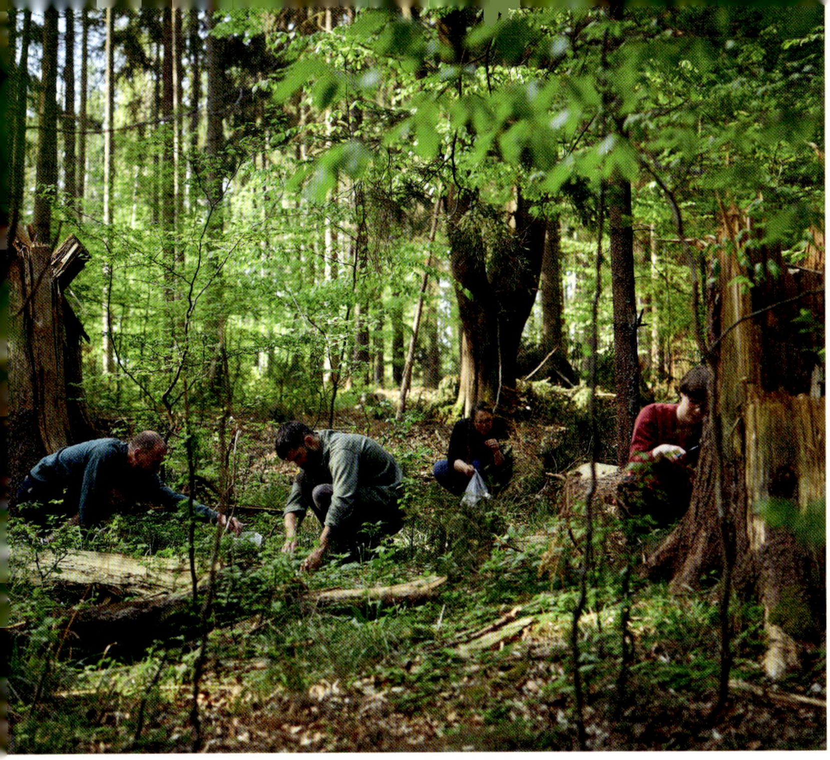

Petr doesn't work by following rigid recipes—he cooks based on intuition, imagination, and seasonality. Drawing on Japanese, or Nordic influences, he always adapts ideas and techniques to local Czech ingredients. Mixing fruits for flavor and texture, he highlights fresh herbs and often seasons with juices from fermented fruit. His sensitive perception and open mind also show in how he preserves the harvest: pickling green strawberries, elderberry capers, or even pinecones.

"The foundation is quality ingredients, but there also needs to be enthusiasm in the kitchen," he says. "Being a chef isn't just about cooking. You need to be curious and look around. If you're serious, you should know what you're cooking with, who the producers are, where and how the ingredients are grown, how animals are raised and slaughtered. And you have to know what kind of statement you want to make with the food on the plate."

Chef Petr Židek proves that being a chef isn't just about cooking—it also requires the courage to do things differently.

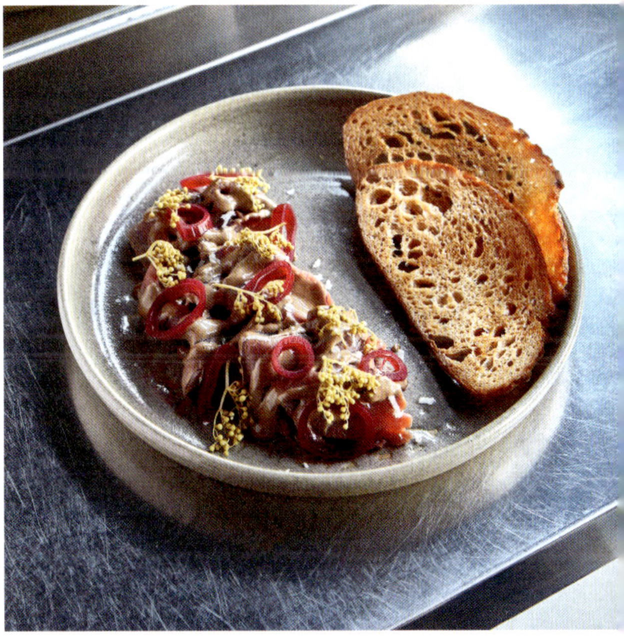

As a young boy, Petr loved being in the kitchen, watching his mother and aunt cook and bake. Over time, he decided that he wanted to be a professional cook. His family, however, wasn't exactly thrilled when he told them he wanted to study to become a chef. Still, Petr didn't give up, and he has found his way into professional gastronomy.

His trial by fire came a few years later at La Finestra. It was a hot summer's day, everyone was out swimming, and it seemed unlikely the restaurant would be busy. But the opposite happened. Suddenly, Petr was left alone at his station, with orders piling up in no particular order and the kitchen in chaos. In his own words: "hell." However, instead of discouraging him, the experience fired his passion for cooking. From then on, compared with taking his first steps into the world of gastronomy, everything else moved quickly.

He first gained experience at the well-known restaurant Výčep in Vinohrady, and also cooked over open flames with friends in the ZE MĚ project, created menus and weekend brunches at Café Hrnek, and grew creatively at KRO Kitchen. He also spent time in London on internships before returning to Prague to become head chef at Alma.

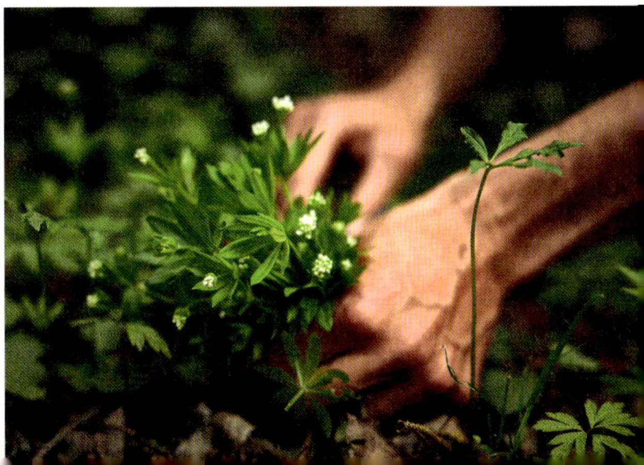

Candied Pinecones

For 3 small canning jars (8 ounces / 250 ml each)

Ingredients

7 ounces (200 g) baby (green) pinecones
1½ cups (300 g) granulated sugar
3⅓ cups (800 ml) water

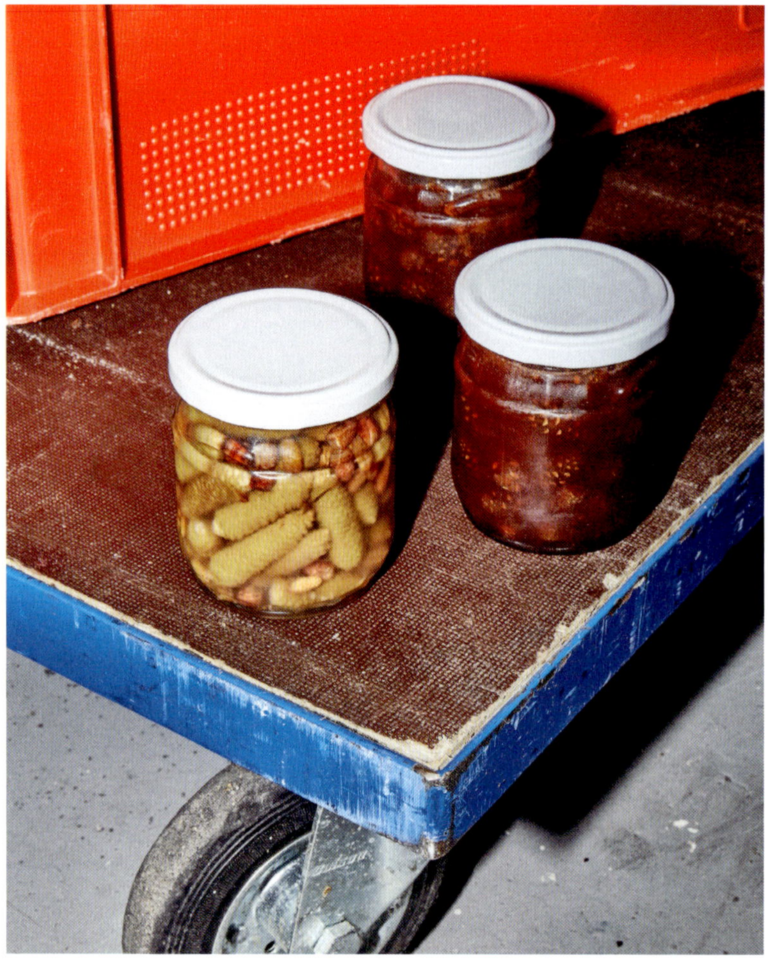

Clean the pinecones by removing any pine needles or debris and wash well under cold running water.

Put the pinecones, sugar, and water into a pot and bring to a boil over medium heat. Reduce the heat to low and simmer gently for about 3 hours, until the pinecones are almost falling apart. Candying removes the bitter taste from the pinecones and caramelizes the syrup until it is thick and dark.

Divide the warm pinecones into the small sterilized canning jars and cover with the syrup, then close tightly and process in a water bath. Let cool. Use the candied pinecones immediately or store the jars in a cool, dark place.

Tip Candied pinecones go well with vegetable salads and cheese. In winter, they can also be added to hot beverages, including mulled wine and punch. They're hidden gems that elevate desserts, such as ice cream and apple pie.

Pickled Elderflower Bud Capers

For 1 canning jar (16 ounces / 500 ml)

Ingredients

10 ½ ounces (300 g) elderflower buds (about 60 heads)

Scant 1 cup (200 ml) apple cider vinegar

Scant ½ cup (100 ml) water

2 ½ teaspoons (10 g) granulated sugar

1 ½ teaspoons (10 g) salt

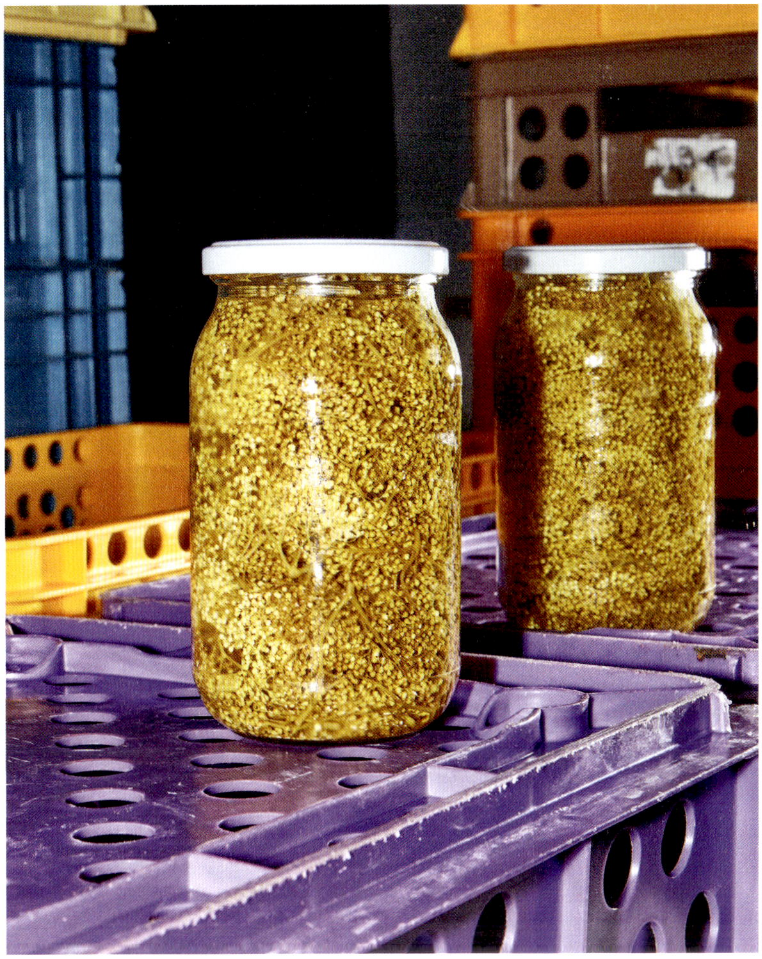

Wash the elderflower buds well under cold running water. Put the buds into a sterilized canning jar (you can leave the stems attached).

To make the pickling liquid, mix the vinegar, water, sugar, and salt in a saucepan and bring to a boil for 3 minutes. Pour the hot liquid over the buds, covering them completely in the liquid. Close the jar tightly and process in a water bath. After cooling, store the jar of elderberry capers in a cool, dark place. Pickle for a minimum of 2 weeks before using.

Tip Elderflower bud capers pair well with steak tartar, grilled fish, and pan-fried schnitzel. They also make a delicious accompaniment for a trout ceviche and can be enjoyed with hollandaise sauce.

Sweet Pickled Green Strawberries

For 2 canning jars (8 ounces / 250 ml each)

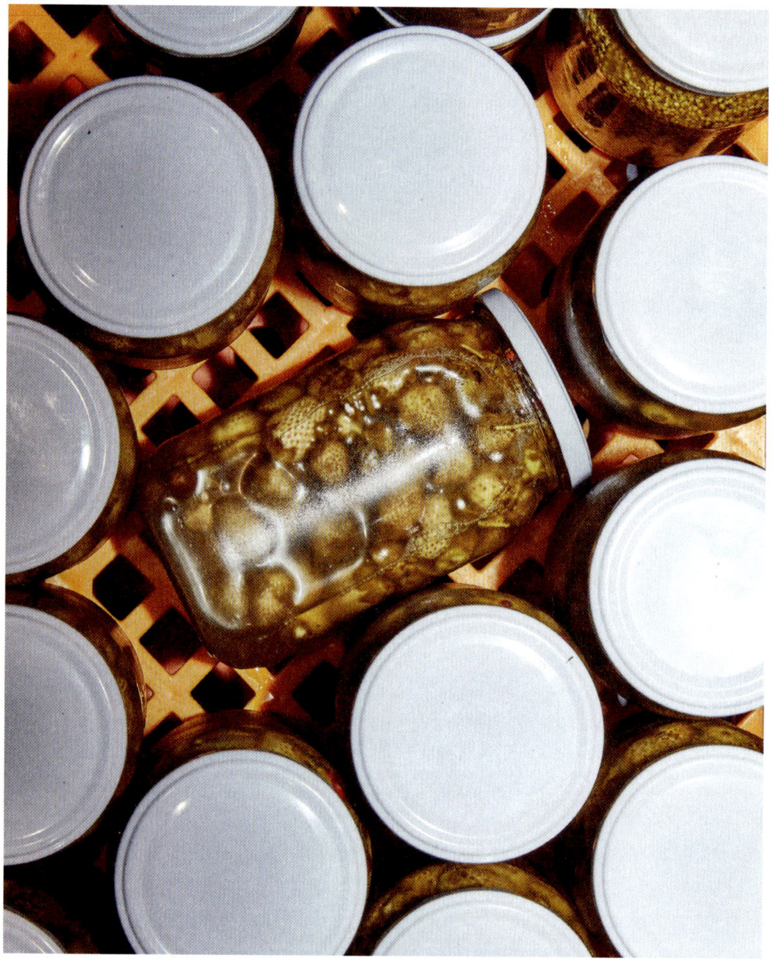

Ingredients

2 cups (300 g) green (unripe) strawberries

2 strips of rind from 1 organic lemon

10 pink peppercorns

⅔ cup (150 ml) Elderflower Syrup (see p. 47)

Wash the strawberries under cold running water and remove the leaves (you can leave the stems attached). Arrange the strawberries in layers inside the sterilized canning jars, then add the lemon rind and pink peppercorns. Pour the elderflower syrup over the contents of the jars, then close the jars tightly and process in a water bath. Pickle the strawberries for at least 2 weeks before use.

Tip These pickled strawberries go well with tomato and lovage salad, game tartar, and grilled fish. They can also be combined with classic pancakes or traditional Czech *lívance* (yeast pancakes).

Unripe Strawberries in Vinegar

For 2 canning jars (8 ounces / 250 ml each)

Ingredients

1⅔ cups (250 g) green (unripe) strawberries

Scant 1 cup (200 ml) water

Scant ½ cup (100 ml) vinegar (see tip)

¼ cup (50 g) granulated sugar

1 teaspoon (7 g) salt

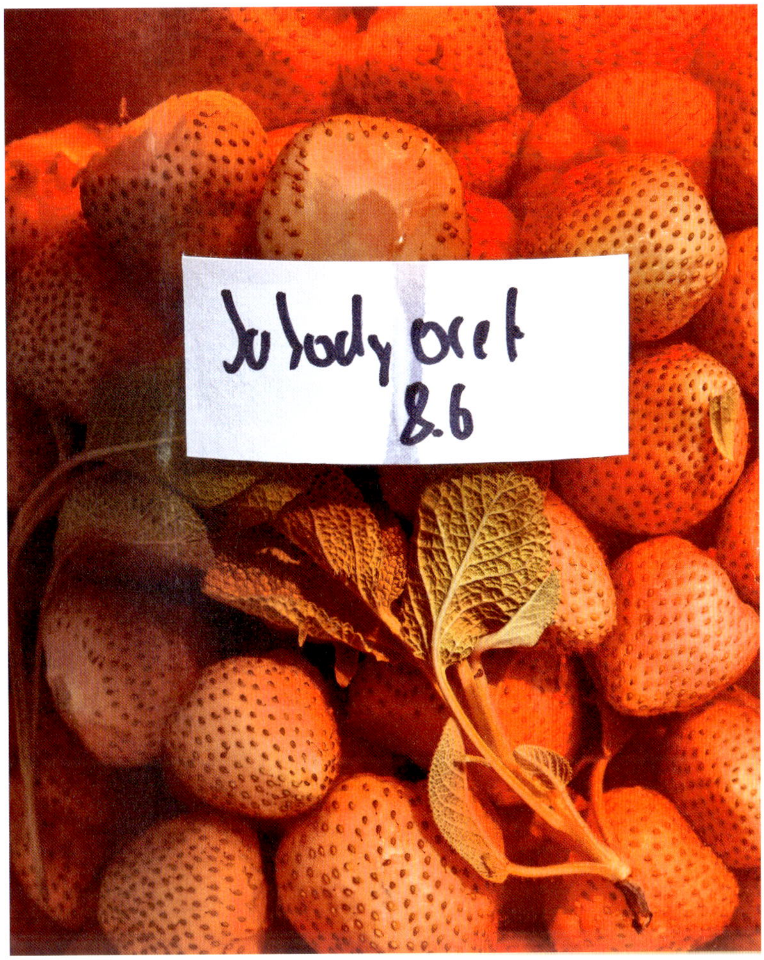

Wash the strawberries under cold running water and remove the leaves and stems. Arrange the strawberries in layers inside the sterilized canning jars.

To make the sweet-and-sour pickling liquid, mix the water, vinegar, sugar, and salt in a saucepan, put it over medium heat, and stir continuously until the sugar dissolves. Remove the pan from the heat.

Pour the slightly cooled, yet still hot liquid over the strawberries. Close the jars tightly and briefly process in a water bath. Store in a cool, dark place. Pickle the strawberries for at least 1 week before use.

Tips These pickled strawberries are the perfect accompaniment for steak tartar.

For a fresh note, add a sprig of mint or lemon balm to each jar.

Apple cider vinegar or wine vinegar works well, but it's up to you which one you use.

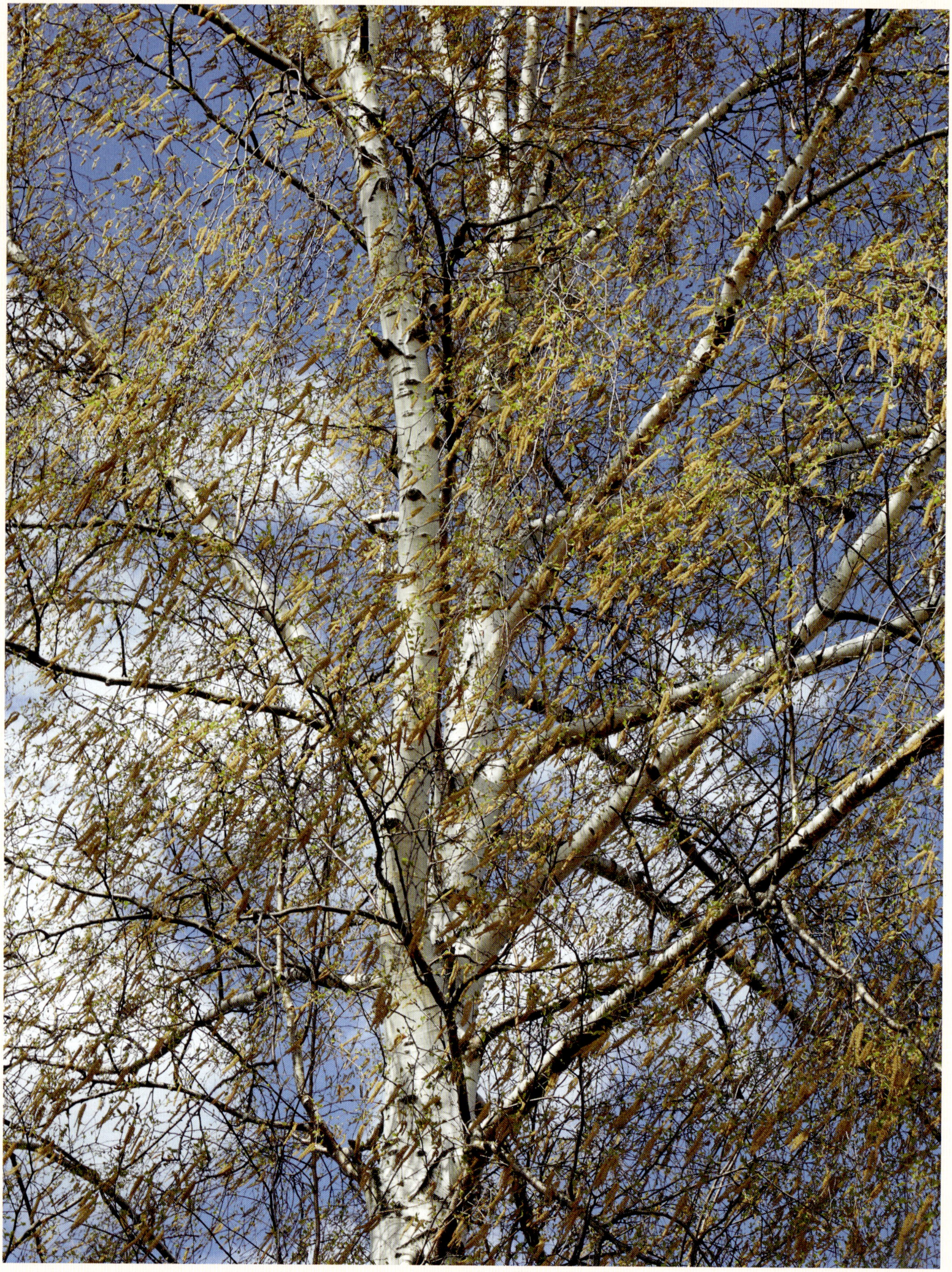

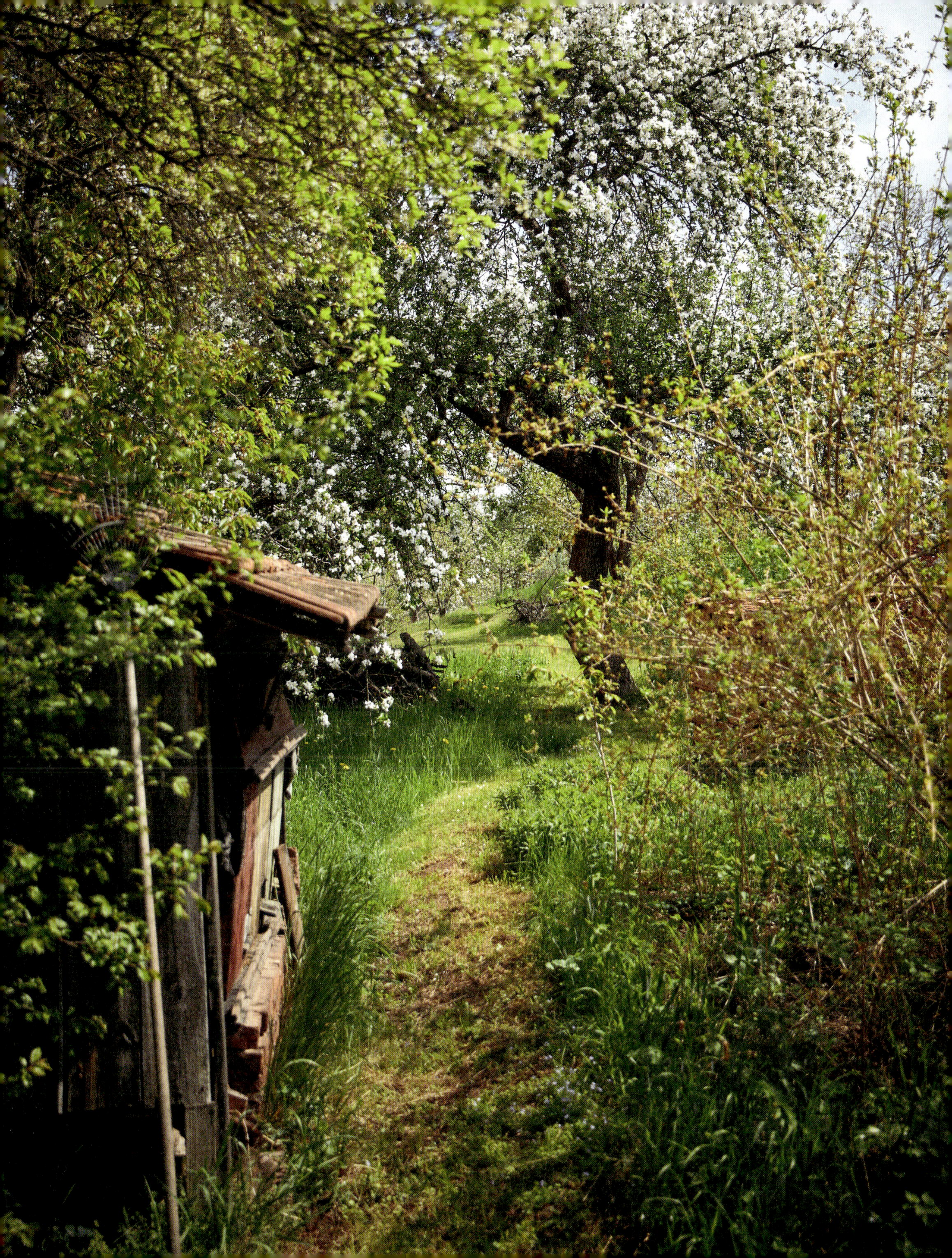

Rhubarb Compote with Honey and Vanilla

For 4 canning jars (8 ounces / 250 ml each)

Ingredients

2 ¼ pounds (1 kg) rhubarb

1 vanilla bean (pod)

1 cup (200 g) granulated sugar

3 ½ cups (700 ml) water

Juice of 1 lemon

¼ cup (80 g) honey

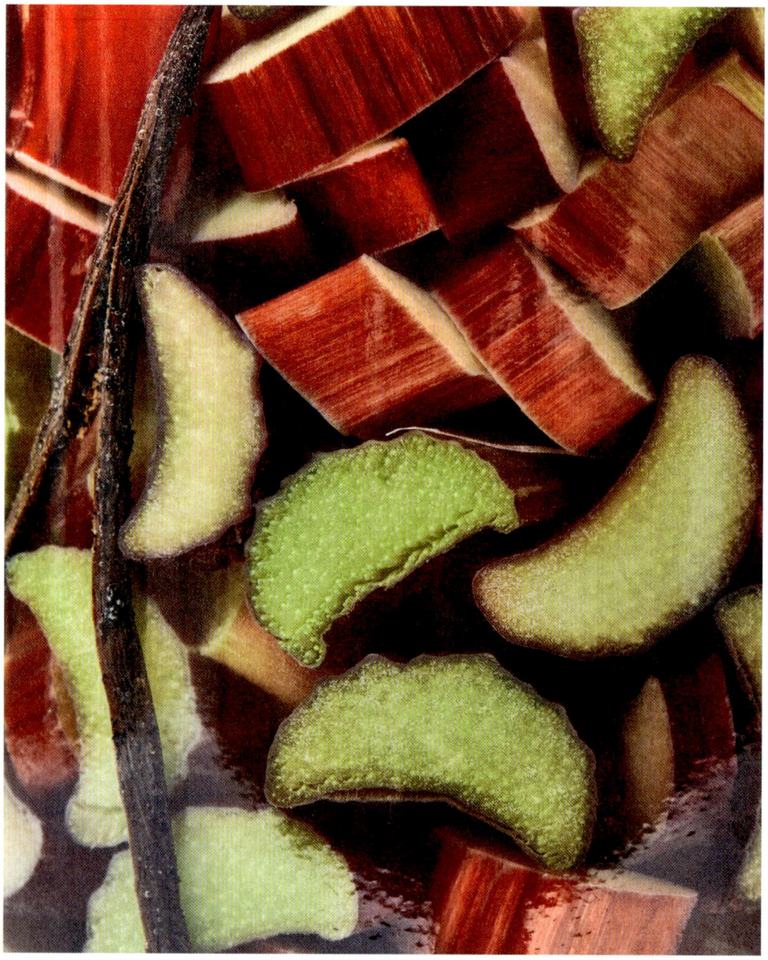

Wash the rhubarb stalks and trim off the leaves and woody ends. There is no need to peel the stalks. However, if they are very fibrous, they may need destringing. Cut the stalks into small pieces and put them into the sterilized canning jars. Cut the vanilla bean into small pieces and put one into each jar.

To make the syrup, mix the sugar, water, and lemon juice in a saucepan. Bring to a boil, stirring continuously to dissolve the sugar, then remove from the heat—don't let the syrup boil any further. Stir in the honey until completely dissolved.

Pour the hot syrup over the rhubarb. Close the lids tightly and process the jars in a water bath—due to its oxalic acid content, the rhubarb must undergo sufficient heat treatment; cook for 30 to 40 minutes at 185 °F (85 °C). Remove the jars, turn them upside down, and let cool. Store in a cool and dark place. Let the rhubarb compote mature for at least 2 weeks before use. This will give the rhubarb time to absorb the flavor and aroma of the vanilla.

Rhubarb Jam

For 4 canning jars (8 ounces / 250 ml each)

Ingredients

2 ¼ pounds (1 kg) rhubarb

3 ½ cups (700 g) cane sugar

Juice of 1 lemon

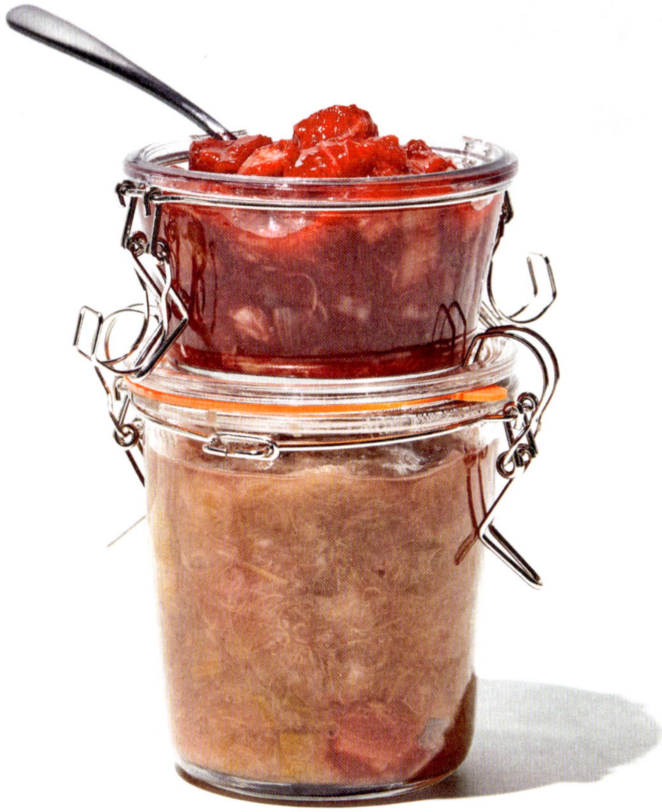

Wash the rhubarb stalks and trim off the leaves and woody ends. There is no need to peel the stalks. However, if they are very fibrous, they may need destringing. Cut the stalks into small pieces, put them into a ceramic or glass mixing bowl, and mix with the sugar. Cover the bowl and let the mixture infuse in a cool place for 12 hours (preferably overnight).

Pour the juice released by the rhubarb into a pot. Put it over low heat, bring to a boil, and simmer for a few minutes until the juice thickens. Add the rhubarb pieces. Continue to cook for 15 to 20 minutes, until they break down and the jam thickens to the desired consistency. Stir regularly, because the rhubarb will quickly stick to the bottom of the pan. Finally, stir in the lemon juice.

Transfer the finished jam to the sterilized canning jars, close the lids tightly, and place upside down. Let cool. Use the jam immediately or store the jars in a cool, dark place.

Tips You can replace half of the rhubarb with chopped ripe strawberries, adding them both to the pan to cook. If you like larger pieces of fruit in your jam, add a few strawberry pieces later, so that they don't boil away completely.

Rhubarb jam can also be flavored with freshly grated ginger, cloves, ground cinnamon, or the seeds scraped out of a vanilla bean (pod). Simply add the spices to the pan with the rhubarb and cook as directed.

This jam will be a little runnier because rhubarb has a lower pectin content. The color of the jam depends on the type of rhubarb used: rhubarb can have both red and green stalks.

The typical tart rhubarb flavor of this jam goes well with sweet desserts, such as a Fluffy Rhubarb Sponge Cake (see p. 60)

Fluffy Rhubarb Sponge Cake

Makes 1 cake (7 inches/18 cm in diameter)

Ingredients

For the cake batter

6 tablespoons (80 g) unsalted butter, plus extra for greasing

1⅔ cups (200 g) cake flour or all-purpose (plain) flour, plus some for the work surface

2 teaspoons baking powder

1 pinch of salt

1 vanilla bean (pod)

2 eggs

scant 1 cup (180 g) granulated sugar

⅓ cup (80 ml) milk

For the filling

1¾ cups (400 g) cream cheese

5 tablespoons powdered (icing) sugar, plus some for dusting

About ¾ cup (180–200 ml) whipping cream (33 percent fat)

A few drops of lemon juice

Generous 1 cup (250 g) Rhubarb Jam (see p. 59)

Grease the bottom and sides of a springform (7-inch/18-cm)-diameter cake pan with butter and line with parchment (baking) paper. Preheat the oven to 325 °F top/bottom heat (160 °C/Gas Mark 3).

Melt the butter in a saucepan and let cool a little. Sift the flour into a bowl, then add the baking powder, salt, and the seeds scraped from the vanilla bean. Mix everything together.

Crack the eggs into the bowl of a stand mixer and add the granulated sugar. Using a wire whip (whisk), beat the eggs and sugar on the highest speed for 5 to 10 minutes, until thick and pale. Gently fold the flour mixture, butter, and milk into the egg mixture, in small portions, ideally using a spatula by hand. Pour the batter into the cake pan and bake for about 45 to 50 minutes (every oven bakes differently). Don't open the oven door during this time or the cake may collapse.

In the meantime, to make the filling, mix the cream cheese with the sifted powdered (icing) sugar until smooth. Whip the cream with a little lemon juice to stiff peaks and gently fold it into the sweet cream cheese. Refrigerate the filling for at least 1 hour to firm up, making it easier to use later.

As soon as the cake starts to smell fragrant, starts to come away from the sides of the cake pan, and its surface becomes firmer, cracks slightly, and turns golden, insert a toothpick or wooden skewer into the center of the cake; if it comes out clean, the cake is done. Take the cake out of the oven and let cool on a wire rack for 20 minutes. Unlock and carefully remove the outer ring. If the cake top is slightly domed, place it on a plate with the domed side down; the surface will even out nicely. Let cool completely.

Cut the cake in half horizontally. Spread half of the filling over the bottom half, cover with rhubarb jam, then top with the second half of the cake. Cover the cake with the remaining filling and spread the top with rhubarb jam. Dust with powdered (icing) sugar before serving.

Tips For a large cake, simply double the quantities given. The batter can then be divided between 2 smaller springform pans and the cake assembled with 4 layers. If a single large springform pan is used, only cut through the cake once.

All the cake ingredients should be at room temperature before use. Take the eggs and milk out of the refrigerator at least 2 hours before making the cake. However, the cream cheese for the filling should be chilled. The filling should also be chilled to make it easier to whip. If you like, you can make both cake and filling the day before. In that case, cover the cake in plastic wrap (clingfilm). Cover the filling with a lid or plate and refrigerate.

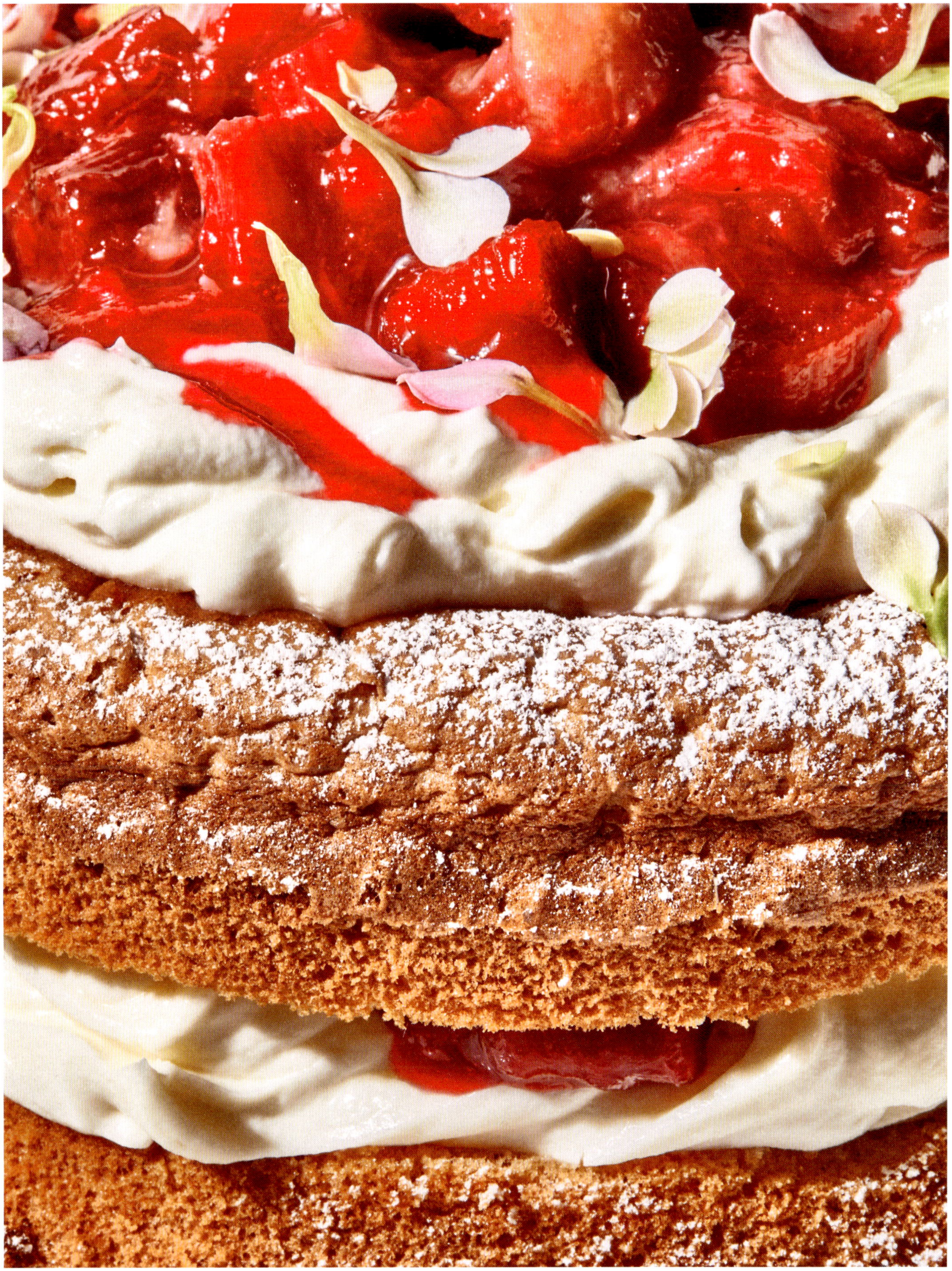

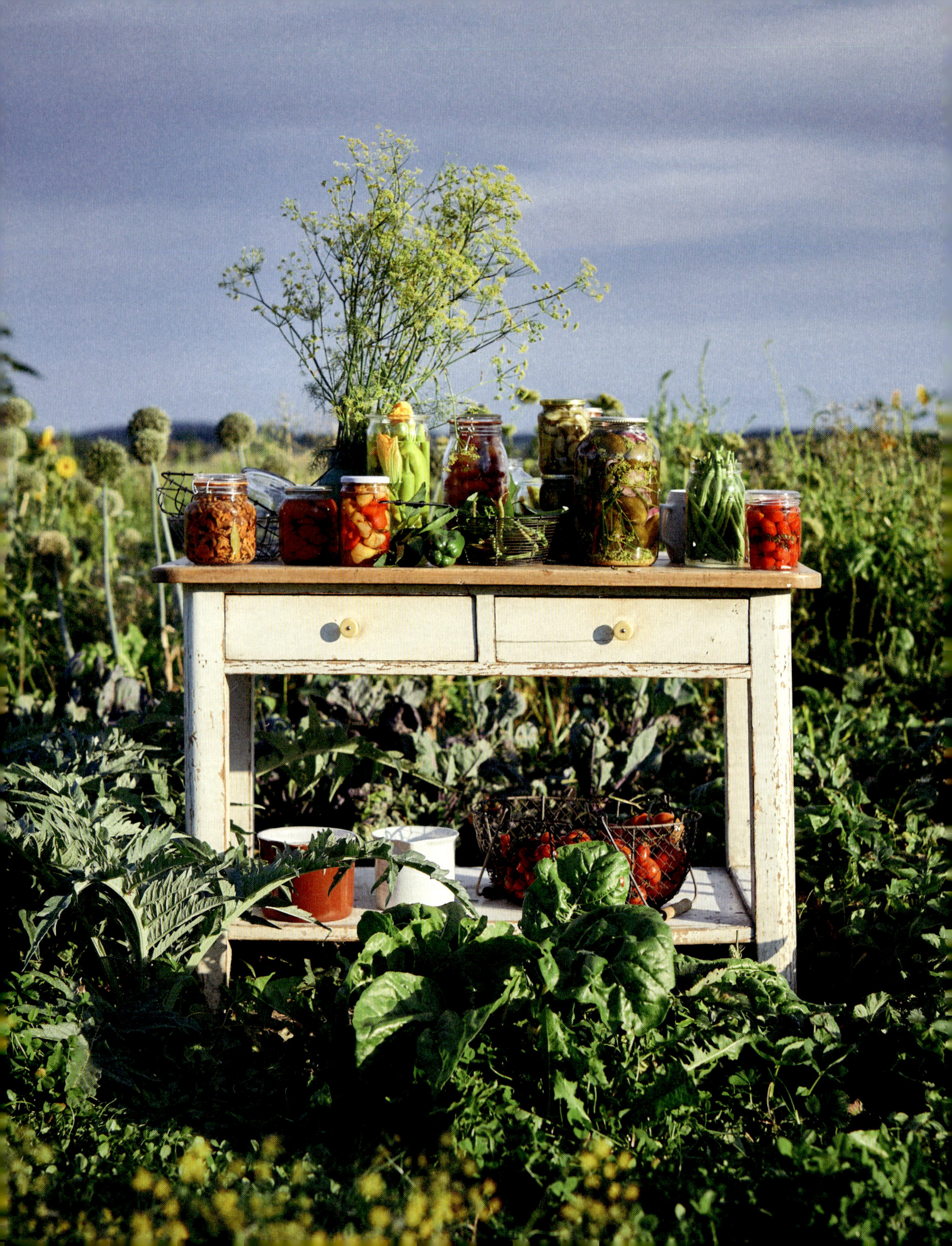

SUMMER

Kdo se v létě nezapotí, v zimě se nenasytí.

He who doesn't toil in the summer
shall hunger in the winter.

The Long Road to the Perfect Strawberry Jam

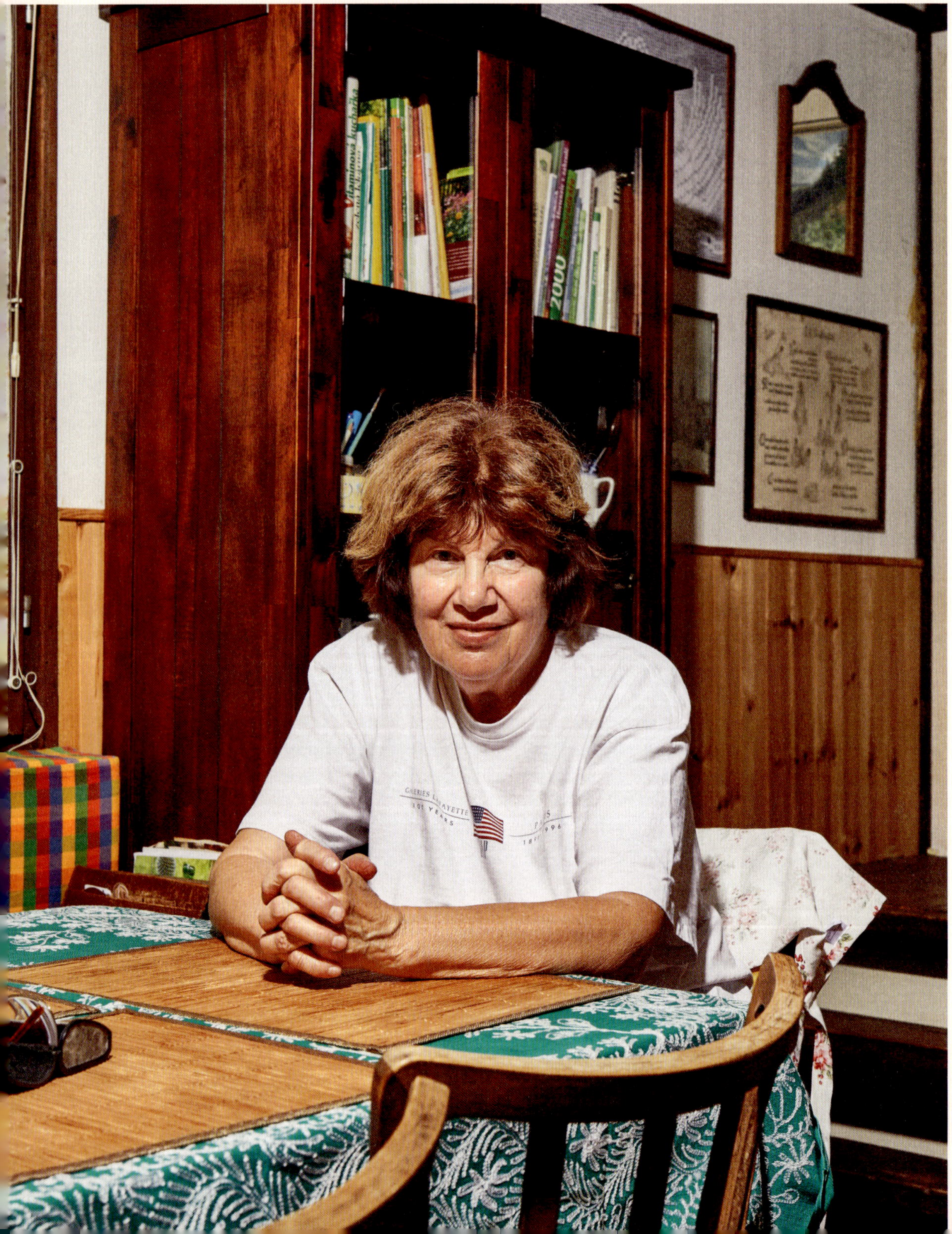

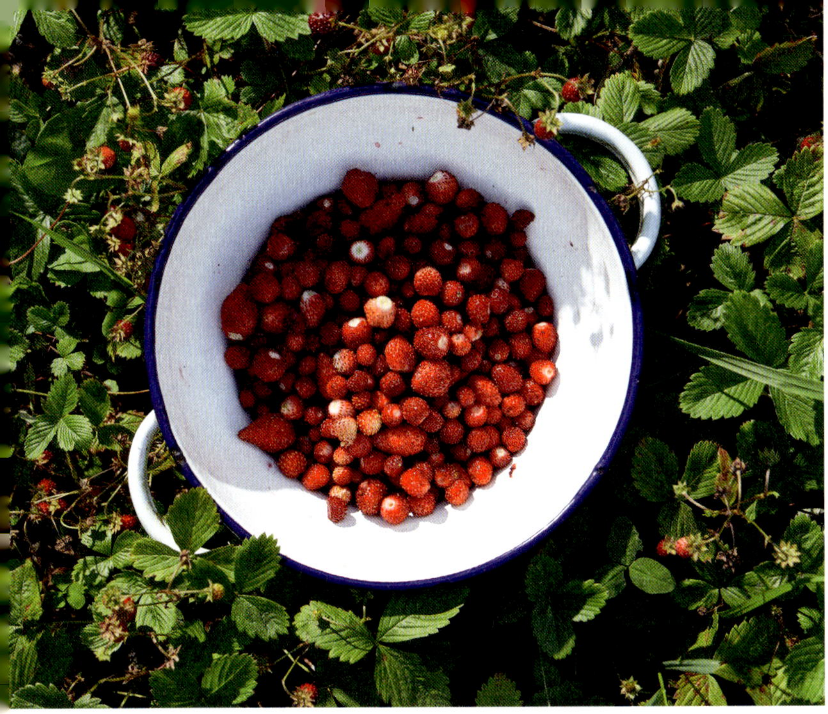

A wood-fired stove, no artificial additives, and only hand-picked wild strawberries. Welcome to Marie Hannová's cottage, where making jam follows clearly defined rules!

When Marie Hannová permanently moved from Syria to the Czech Republic after the Velvet Revolution in 1989, she decided to return to her roots in the Klatovy region. Back in the First Republic, her grandparents had built a wooden cabin (called *chata* in Czech) in a valley with a stream running through it, and the whole family has been coming here ever since. For Marie, it was a second home from childhood. Her mother passed on not only a love of nature but also a whole set of traditional cottage habits. Still, the difference in character and generation soon showed.

In the 1990s, Marie set up her own cottage a little farther from the old one and closer to the forest, and she did everything her own way—including following her own rules for cooking jams and marmalades.

As a child, she used to head into the woods to pick raspberries and wild strawberries. A former doctor, Marie has kept her curiosity for science and innovation, and so she decided to bring a piece of the forest to her garden beds. They've been expanding every year—much to her children's dismay—especially the particular patch devoted entirely to wild strawberries. What started out as tossing a few wild berries into regular strawberry jam soon turned into a full-on wild version. Well, half-wild, anyway. Years of testing and tasting have taught Marie that pure wild strawberry jam isn't truly sweet enough; the perfect flavor comes from a 50:50 mix of wild forest and regular garden strawberries.

Although it feels like time has stopped at Marie's cottage, with the wood squeaking underfoot and crackling in the oven, her way of growing and preserving fruit is far more sustainable and careful than in the untamed 1990s. To thicken her preserves, Marie no longer uses commercial gelling agents but citrus pectin. She cooks everything the traditional way on a tiled oven, letting the fruit mixture drip slowly through a special three-tier pot that separates the seeds from the juice.

Her daughter Daniela Hannová (see p. 250) still remembers how, as a child, she and her grandmother used to grind currants by hand in an old metal mill. Three generations, three very different relationships with making preserves. The cautious grandmother didn't trust anything new; the adventurous Marie loved trying out fresh ideas; and the youngest, Daniela, had to grow into her love of the cottage and canning. But she got there in the end.

It's June 25, 2022, and we're taking photographs at Marie's cottage. "The big revolution in making strawberry jam came to me in 2016, when natural citrus pectin hit the market," says a handwritten note surrounded by little hearts in her thick recipe book. Outside, pine trees from the nearby forest cast dappled shadows over the strawberry patch, a brook babbles lazily and blithely in the distance, the scent of Arabic coffee with cardamom drifts in from the kitchen, and the hot strawberry jam (see p. 67) that Marie and her daughter have just finished making together is gently bubbling on the stove (hob), filling the room with its sweet, summery aroma.

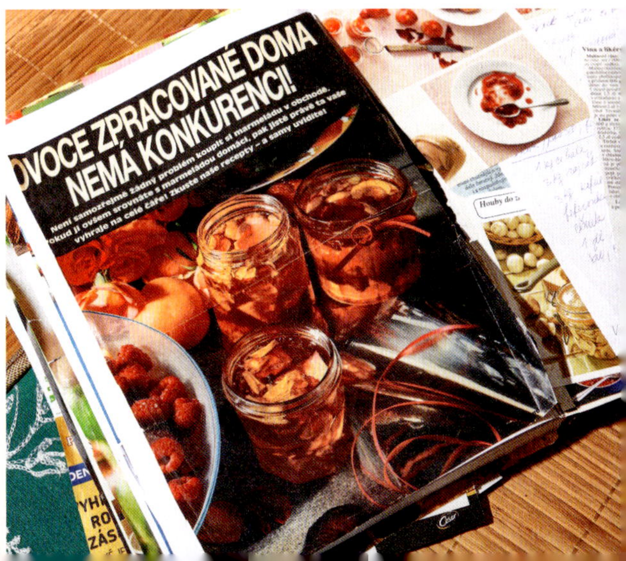

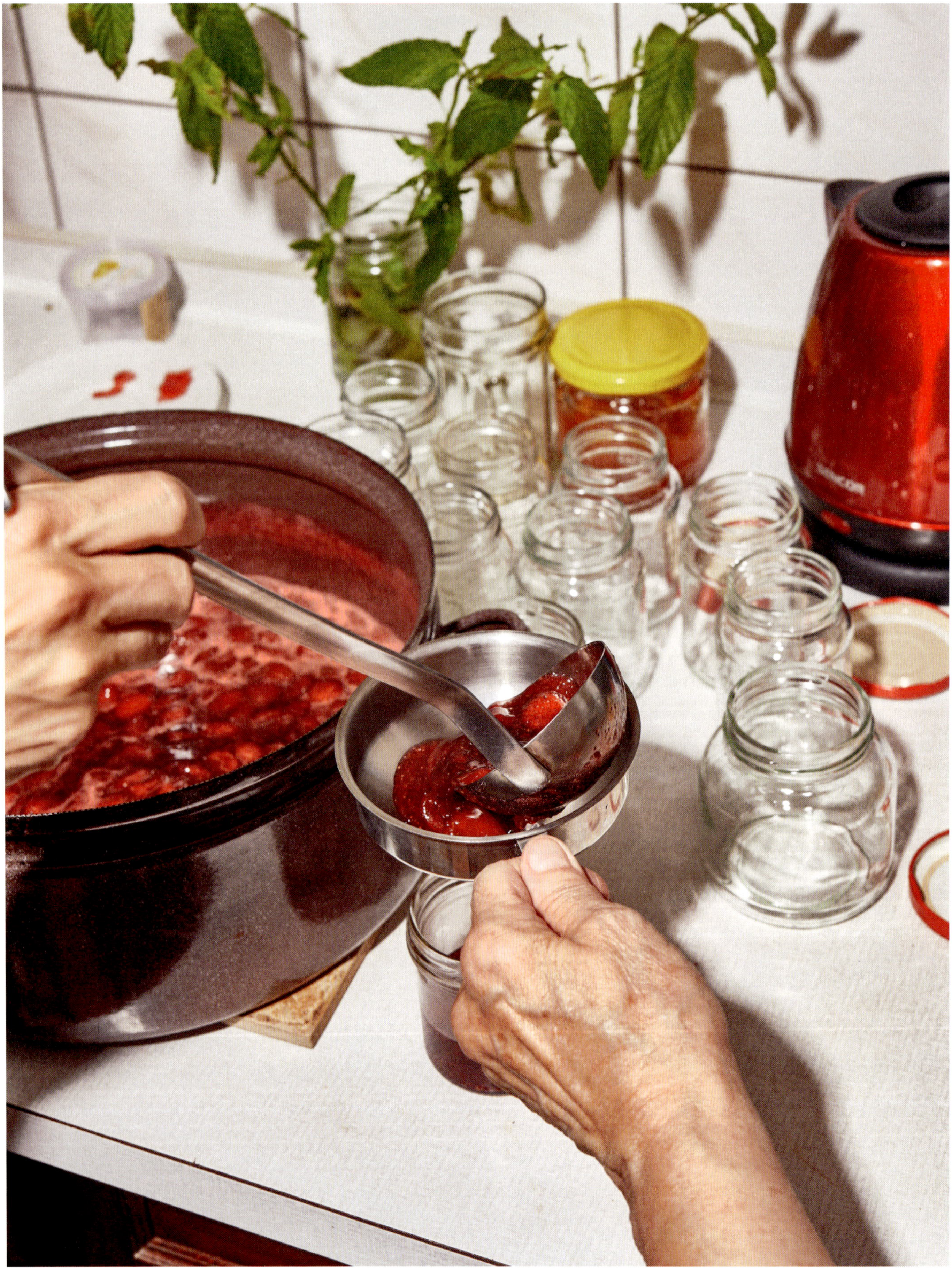

Wild Strawberry Jam

For 4 canning jars
(4 ounces / 125 ml each)

Ingredients

2 ¼ pounds (1 kg) wild strawberries (about 6 ½ cups)

4 teaspoons to 2 tablespoons plus 2 teaspoons (20–40 ml) water

2–4 teaspoons citrus pectin

3 cups (600 g) granulated sugar

Juice of ½ lemon

Wash the strawberries and put them into a wide saucepan. Add a little water and bring to a boil. Reduce the heat and let simmer for about 5 minutes.

Mix the pectin with about 1 tablespoon of the sugar and add to the strawberries in the pan. Simmer for another 5 minutes, then sprinkle over the remaining sugar and cook until the mixture thickens. Stir regularly to keep the strawberries from sticking to the bottom of the pan.

Remove the pan from the heat and stir in the lemon juice (the jam must not be allowed to boil). Transfer the hot jam to the sterilized canning jars, close the lids tightly, and place upside down for 5 minutes. Turn them over again and let cool. Use the jam immediately or store the jars in a cool, dark place.

Tip You can substitute half of the wild strawberries with regular garden strawberries. Cut larger fruit into small pieces before cooking. This makes the jam sweeter and gives it a more intense strawberry flavor.

Koblihy

Makes about 10 doughnuts

Ingredients

⅔ cup (150 ml) milk

1 small (⅔-ounce/19 g) cake fresh yeast

3 ½ tablespoons (40 g) granulated sugar

1 ⅔ cups (200 g) pastry flour, plus extra for dusting

1 ¼ cups (150 g) all-purpose (plain) flour

¼ teaspoon vanilla seeds

1 pinch of salt

4 tablespoons (60 g) unsalted butter

2 eggs

2 tablespoons rum

About ½ cup (150 g) Wild Strawberry Jam (see p. 67)

Canola (rapeseed) oil, for deep-frying

Powdered (icing) sugar, for dusting

Activate the fresh yeast: In a saucepan, lightly warm the milk—do not let it boil. Crumble the fresh yeast into the milk, then add 1 teaspoon of the sugar and 1 teaspoon of the pastry flour. Stir well and cover with a clean cloth. Rest at room temperature for 5 to 15 minutes.

Sift both types of flour into a bowl. Add the remaining sugar, vanilla seeds, and salt and mix well. Add the milk mixture with activated yeast, butter, eggs, and rum to the flour mixture. Using a wooden spoon or in a stand mixer, mix everything together to form a dough. Knead for at least 10 minutes, until the dough is smooth and supple and easily comes away from the sides of the bowl. Cover the bowl with a clean cloth and let the dough rise in a warm place for about 1 hour, until doubled in volume.

Dust the work surface with a little flour. Cut the dough into 10 pieces of about 3 ounces (80 g), shape them into balls, and place spaced well apart on the floured work surface. Cover with a clean cloth and proof for 20 to 30 minutes.

Fill a deep saucepan to a depth of at least 2 inches (5 cm) with oil and place over medium heat. To check the temperature of the oil, add a small piece of dough. If the dough rises to the surface immediately and plenty of bubbles form around it, the oil has reached the right temperature. Fry the doughnuts in the oil in batches. As they will puff up a little more in the hot oil, use a slotted spoon to position the doughnuts in the oil and keep them from touching. Do this carefully, because there is a risk of splashing. Fry the doughnuts for 2 to 3 minutes on one side, until golden, then flip over and fry the other side for the same time, making sure they are cooked through.

Using a slotted spoon, lift out the cooked doughnuts, drain on absorbent paper towels, and let cool completely. Put the jam into a pastry (piping) bag fitted with a small plain tip (nozzle). Using a knife, pierce a hole in the doughnuts and pipe full of jam. Dust with powdered (icing) sugar and enjoy.

Tips Only have instant yeast at home? Go ahead and use it—just remember that you cannot substitute fresh yeast 1:1 with instant yeast. Instant yeast is 1.5 times stronger, so always use 1.5 times less! You also don't need to activate instant yeast in advance; simply sprinkle it over the flour and work it into the dough.

Koblihy can also be filled with Spiced Blackberry Jam (see p. 97) or Apricot and Thyme Jam (see p. 119).

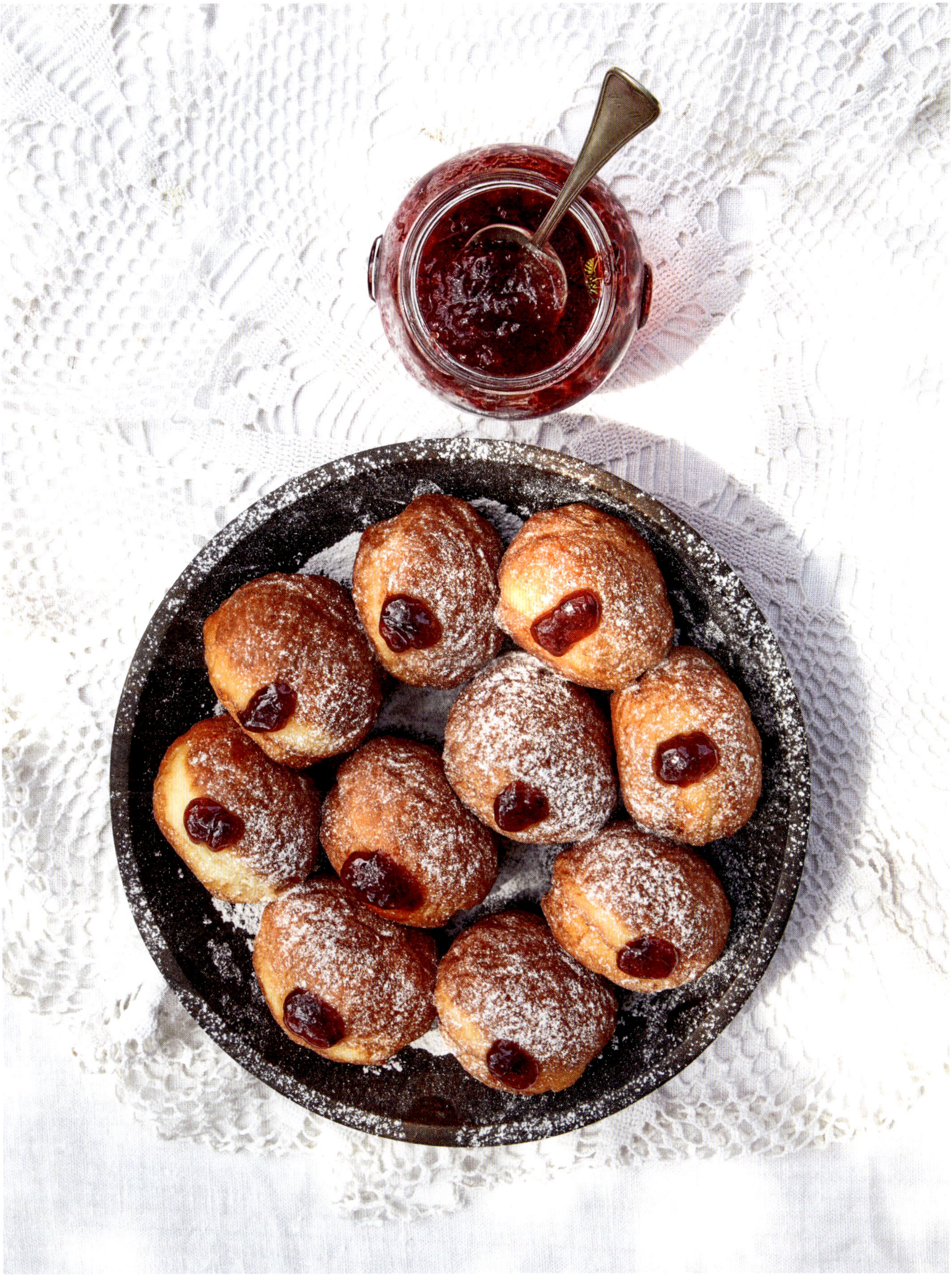

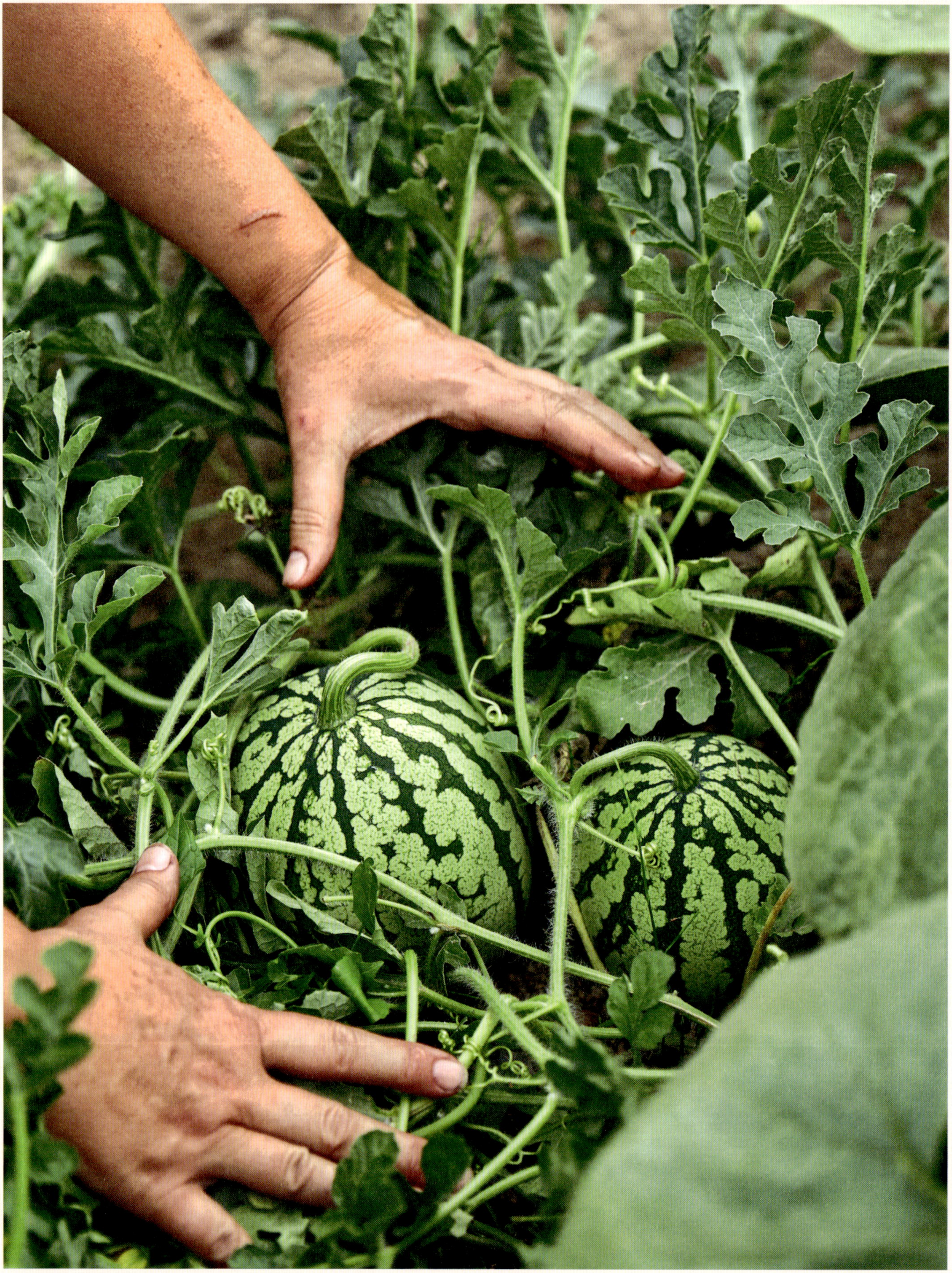

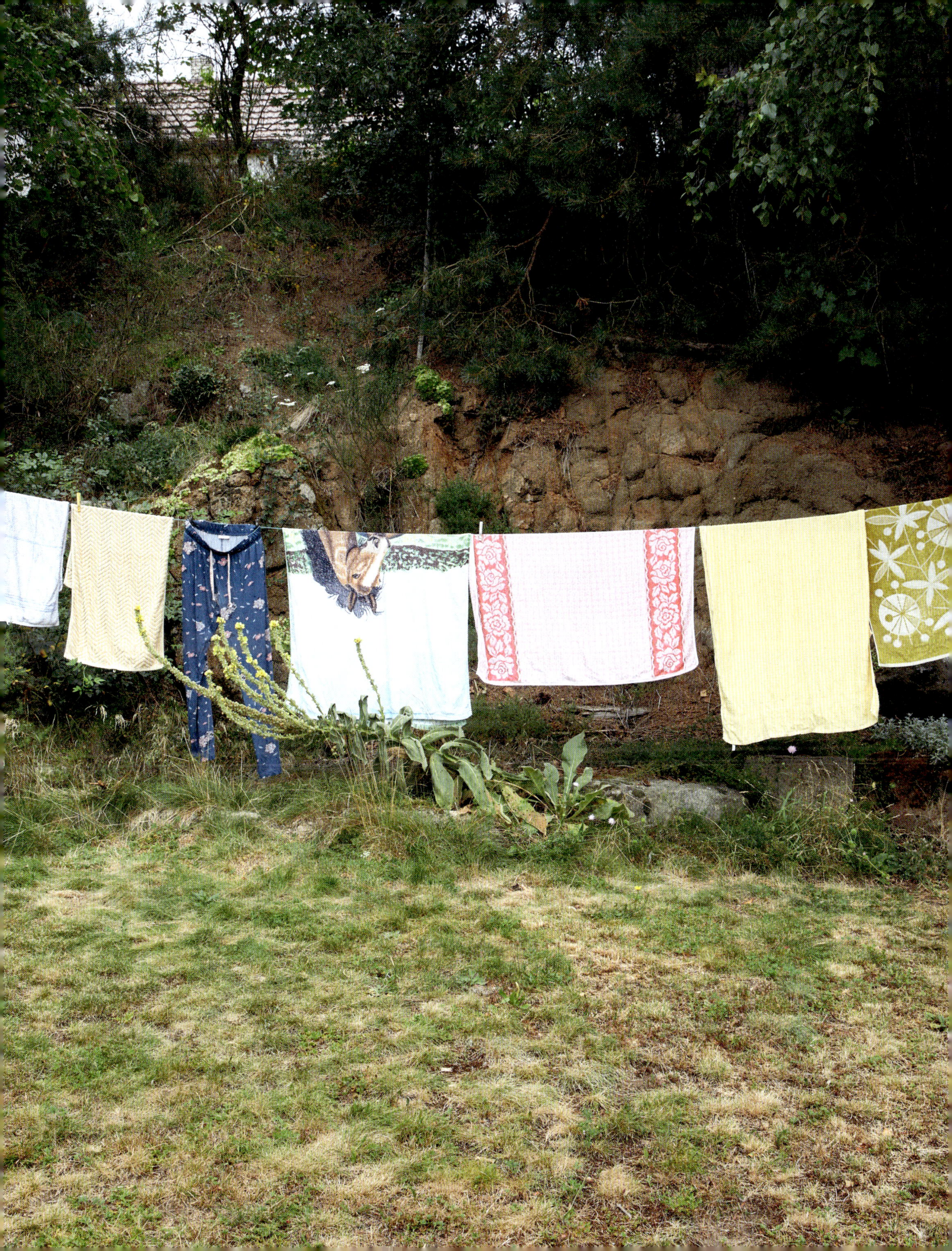

Lovage Salt

For 1 canning jar (8 ounces/200 ml)

Ingredients

1½ ounces (40–50 g) fresh lovage (about 2 cups)

⅔ cup (150 g) kosher (coarse) sea salt

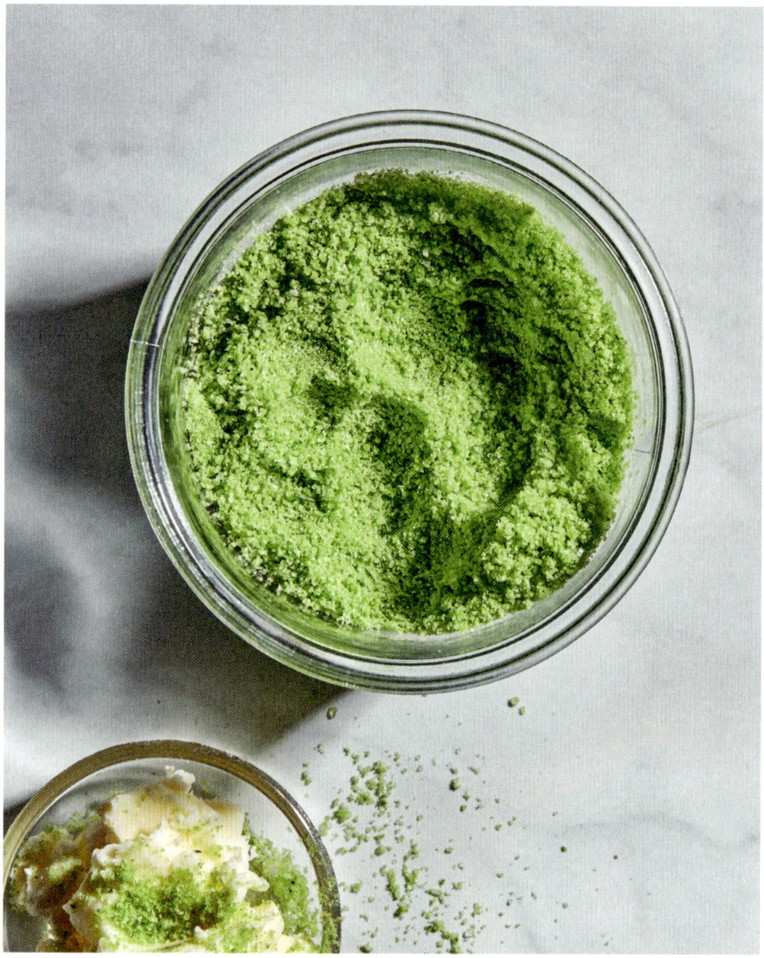

Wash the lovage, shake dry, and pluck the leaves from the stems. (Only the leaves will be used for this herb salt, but you can reserve the stems for another use, such as a vegetable or meat broth/stock.)

Place the lovage leaves and salt in a blender and pulse to grind. If the lovage sticks to the sides of the blender jar, push them down and pulse again.

Transfer the lovage salt to the canning jar and seal. Use the salt immediately or store in the refrigerator or freezer (this herb salt will quickly lose its green color at room temperature).

Tips The intensely aromatic lovage shines on a slice of sourdough bread spread with butter, in boiled potatoes, or in subtly flavored creamy root vegetable soups.

Lovage salt is a fantastic seasoning, but keep in mind that it is still salt, so it's not advisable to consume it in large quantities.

Other herb salts can be made in the same way using parsley, sage thyme, rosemary, oregano, or lavender, or you can try a combination of these herbs.

Pickled Dill

For 2 canning jars (8 ounces / 250 ml each)

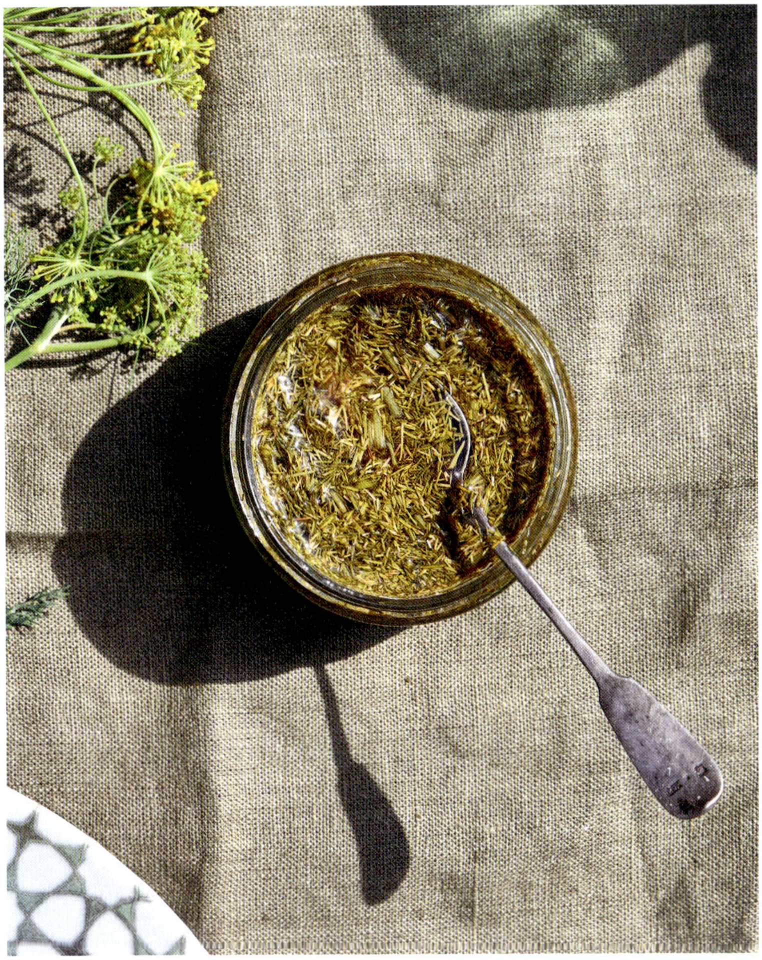

Ingredients

1 cup (250 ml) water

½ cup (125 ml) distilled white vinegar

1 tablespoon granulated sugar

½ teaspoon salt

1 large bunch of fresh dill

To make the pickling liquid, mix the water, vinegar, sugar, and salt in a saucepan and bring to a boil. Stir until the sugar and salt dissolve completely. Remove the pickling liquid from the heat and let cool slightly.

Wash, shake dry, and chop the dill, then put it into the sterilized canning jars and pour over the liquid while still warm. Close the jars tightly, process in a water bath, and let cool. Use the pickled dill immediately or store the jars in a cool, dark place.

Tip Use the pickled dill to make, for example, a traditional Czech main dish called *koprová omáčka* (a creamy sauce, most often served with bread dumplings or potatoes and beef or boiled eggs) or a *kulajda* (a sweet-and-sour soup made from potatoes, mushrooms, and whipping cream, typical of the region of South Bohemia). It also makes a good accompaniment for fish and can be used in salad dressings and dips.

Parsley Oil

For 1 bottle (12 ounces / 300 ml)

Ingredients

1 large bunch of parsley

1 cup (250 ml) canola (rapeseed) oil

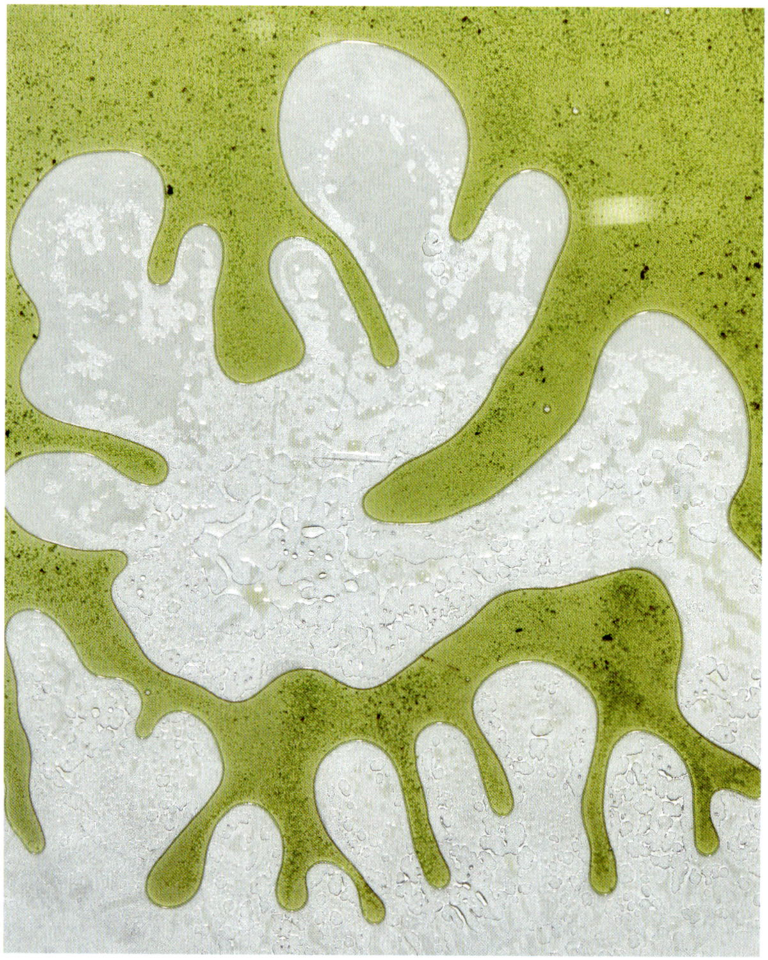

Bring water to a boil in a saucepan. Prepare a bowl with cold water and ice cubes.

Wash the parsley and shake dry. Do not pluck the leaves, because the whole parsley, with the stems, are used to make this oil. When the water comes to a simmer, briefly blanch the whole parsley, then immediately put it into the ice water to shock the herb so that it keeps its rich green color. Pat dry thoroughly.

Pour the oil into the blender jar, add the parsley, and blend until smooth. Filter the green oil through cheesecloth (muslin) or a fine-mesh strainer or sieve into a sterilized glass bottle. Use the oil immediately or store in a cool, dark place.

Tips There are plenty of uses for this parsley oil, such as in salad dressings and risotto. You can also drizzle it over a homemade Cream of Jerusalem Artichoke Soup (see p. 218). However, it is not suitable for cooking.

Homemade herb oils are a great way to use up large quantities of different herbs, instead of letting your leftover herbs wilt and spoil. The exception is basil, given that it will turn black quickly and become unsightly.

When making flavored oils, choose a base oil with as neutral a taste as possible, such as canola (rapeseed) or sunflower oil. Note: Olive oil and flaxseed oil have an intense flavor of their own, so they will mask other flavors. Whichever oil you choose, it should always be a high-quality one. Lower quality oils have an off-flavor that will linger on your palate.

Green Walnut Liqueur

For 1 bottle (64 ounces / 2 l)

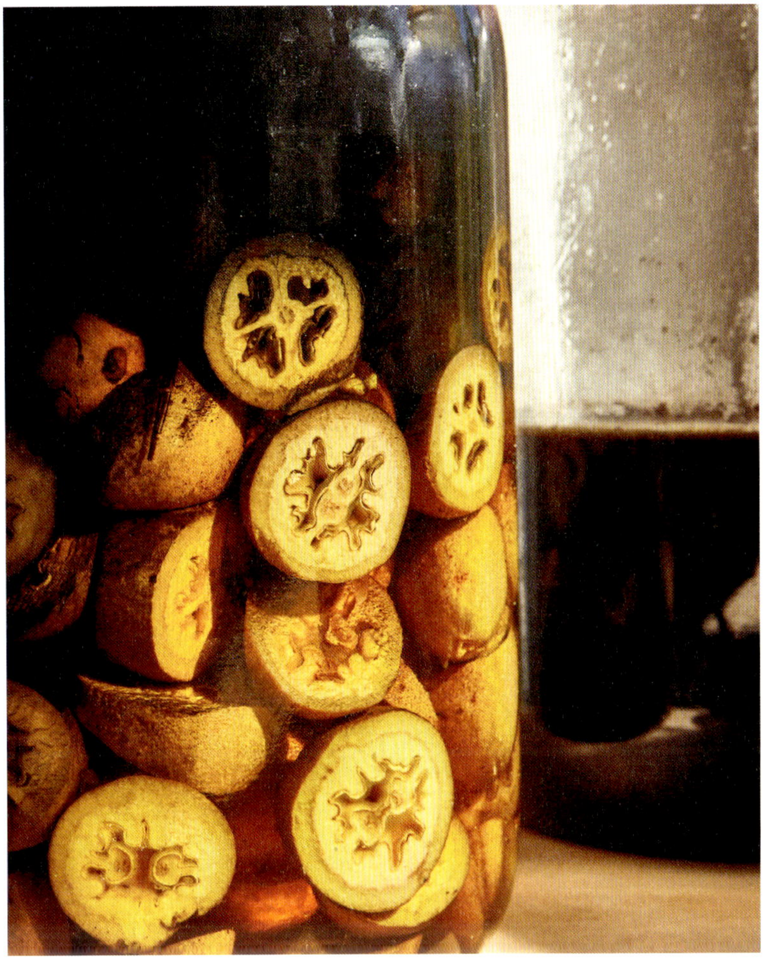

Ingredients

30 green walnuts

1 organic lemon

1 stick of cinnamon

4 cloves

3 juniper berries

1 nutmeg

4 ¼ cups (1 l) slivovitz (plum brandy) or vodka

¾ cup (250 g) honey or 1 ¼ cups (250 g) granulated sugar

2 cups (500 ml) water

Rinse the green walnuts, pat dry, and cut them into pieces. Using a vegetable peeler, zest the lemon.

Put the walnut pieces into a large sterilized canning jar and add the lemon zest, cinnamon, cloves, and juniper berries. Grate a little fresh nutmeg over the top. Add the liquor (spirit) to cover everything. Cover the jar with a lid or plastic wrap (clingfilm) secured with a rubber band, place in a sunny position, and let infuse for 5 to 6 weeks, until the liquid turns a nice brown color.

Make a syrup by mixing the honey and water in a saucepan and bringing to a boil. Filter the liquid from the jar through a fine-mesh strainer or sieve into a container. Discard the nuts and spices. Mix the syrup with the filtered liquid. Transfer the mixture to a sterilized glass bottle and close tightly. The liqueur should be allowed to mature in a cool, dark place for some time before drinking, at least until Christmas. Only then will its special aroma be completely developed.

Tips You should pick green walnuts around June 24 (St. John's Day). They will not have yet developed a hard shell and their husks will still be soft. To test their suitability, simply prick the nut with a needle or pin. If you come across something hard, the nuts will already be too ripe.

You can zest an orange instead of a lemon to make this liqueur. If you prefer a less sweet liqueur, you can also omit the syrup.

This walnut liqueur aids digestion, making it an ideal digestif.

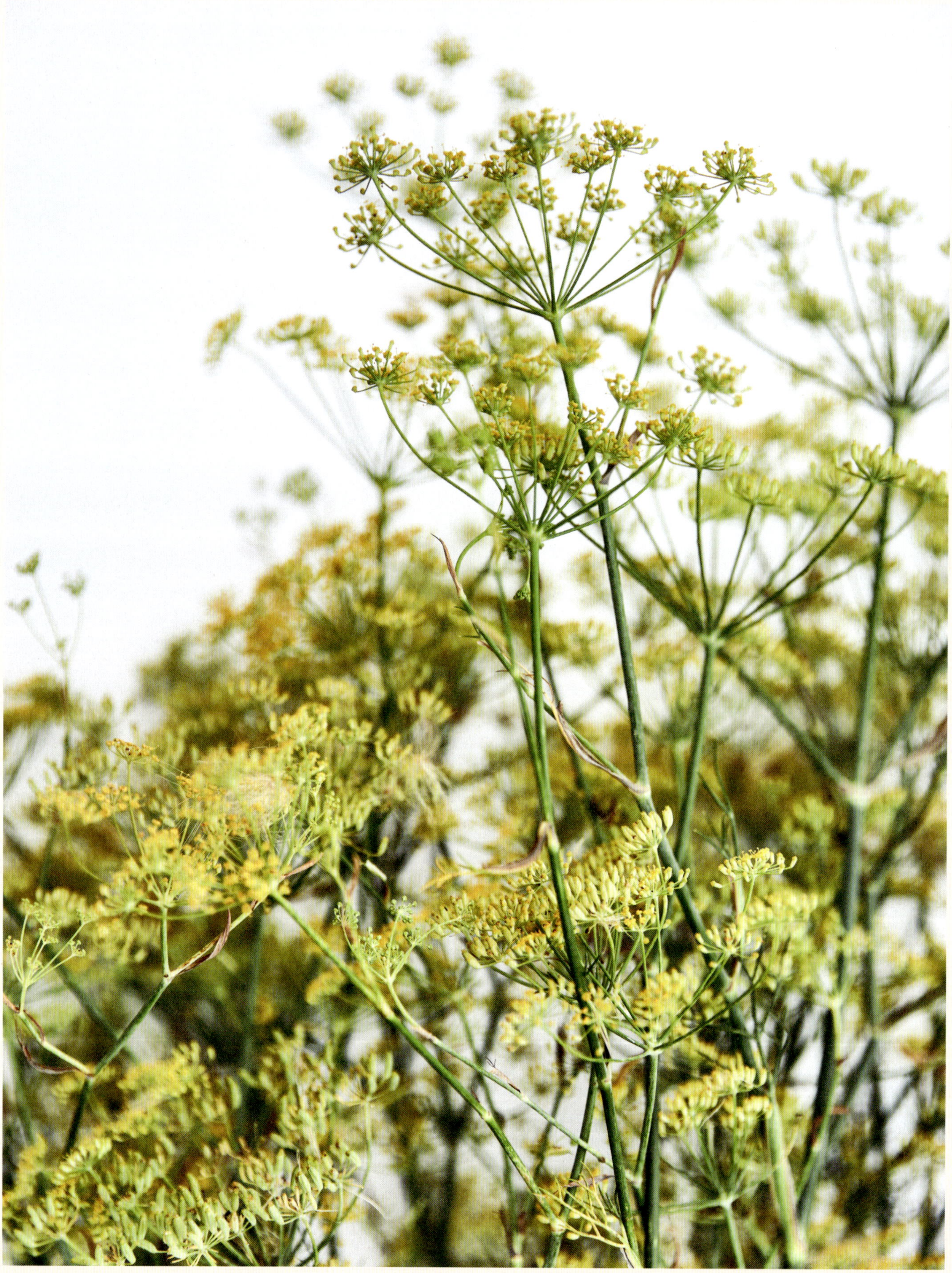

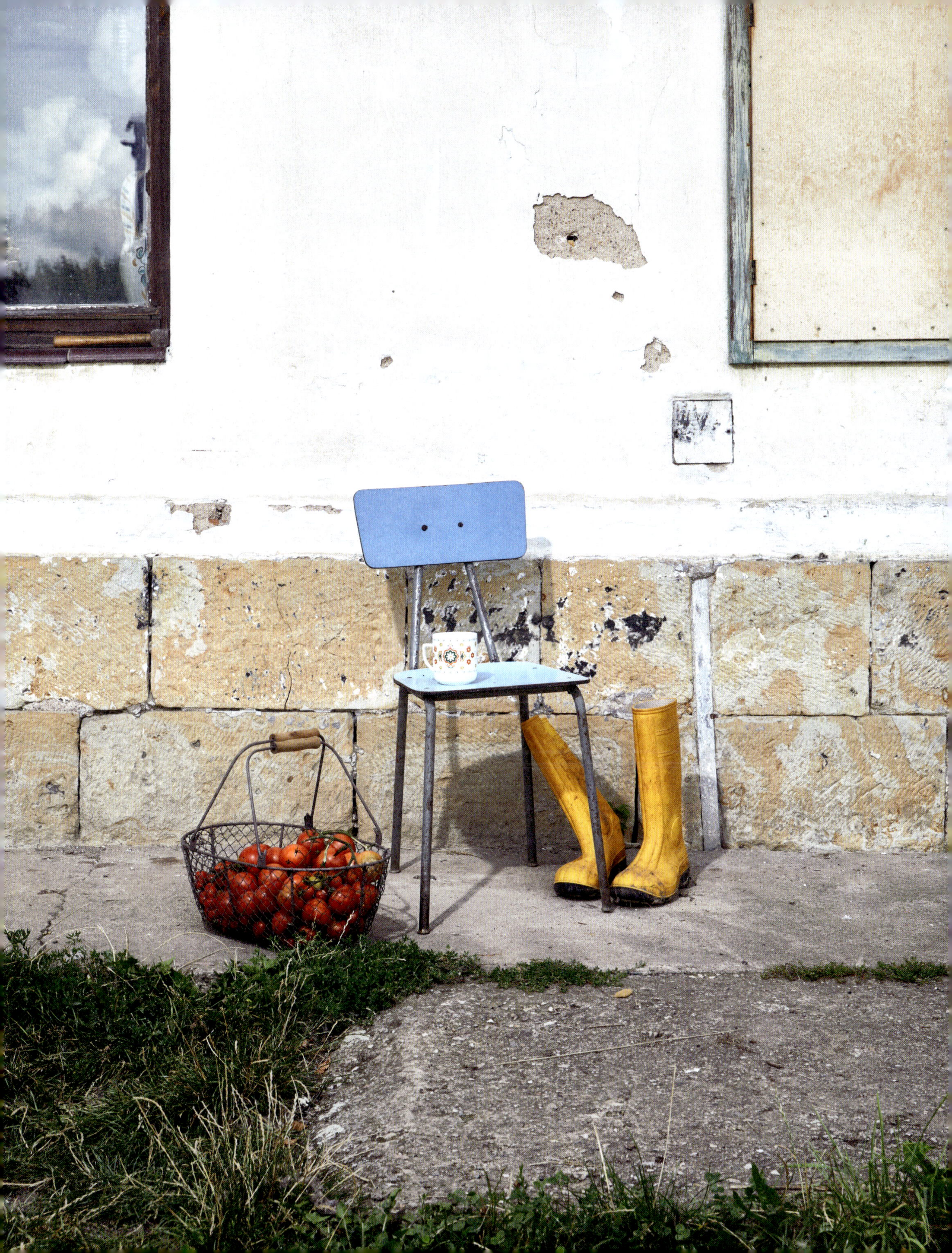

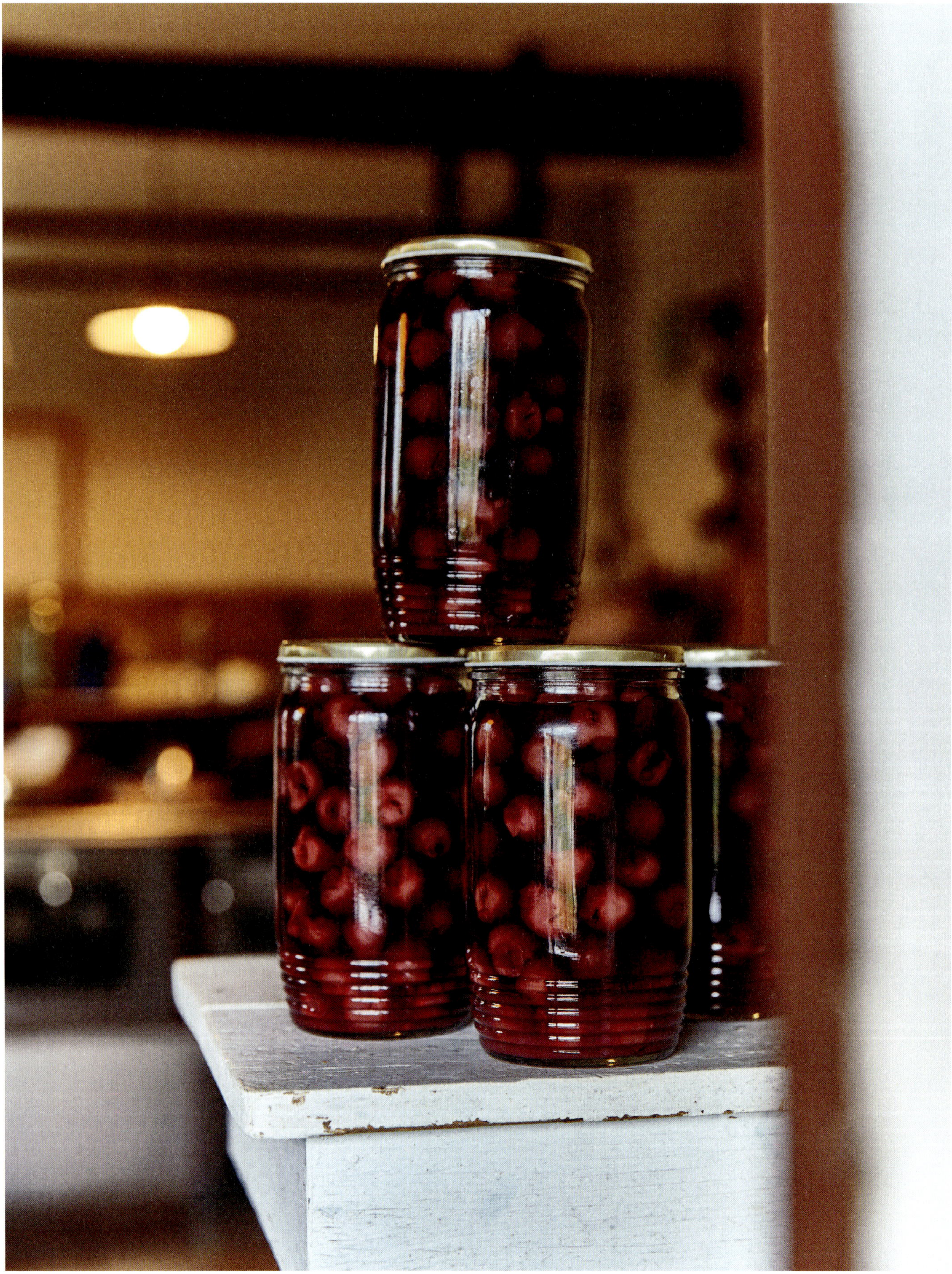

Cherry Compote

For 4 canning jars (16 ounces / 500 ml each)

Ingredients

2 ¼ pounds (1 kg) ripe sweet cherries (about 7 ¼ cups)

4 ¼ cups (1 l) water

1 ½ to 1 ¾ cups (300–350 g) granulated sugar

Sort the cherries and discard any bruised or damaged ones. Remove the stems from the cherries, then wash well under running water and let drain. You can also pit the cherries if you prefer. The best way to do this is by using a cherry pitter. However, the cherries will keep their shape better if left unpitted.

Mix the water and sugar in a saucepan (adjust the amount of sugar to the sweetness of the cherries) and bring to a boil, then let simmer, stirring occasionally, until the sugar dissolves completely. Remove the syrup from the heat and let cool slightly.

Fill sterilized canning jars with the cherries, leaving a gap of about ¾ inch (2 cm) below the rim. Carefully tap the open jars on the work surface to compact the fruit, so that as much as possible will fit into each jar. Pour the hot syrup over the cherries, close the jars tightly, and process in a water bath. Let the jars rest for at least 2 weeks so the cherries can soften and absorb the sweetness.

Tips You can also preserve sweet or sour cherries in rum. For this, you will need to arrange the cherries in layers inside the jars, sprinkling each layer with sugar. Adjust amount of sugar according to the sweetness of the fruit. Fill the jars with high-quality rum to completely cover the cherries. Seal the jars tightly and let the fruit mature in a cool, dark place for about 2 months. The cherries will be infused with the sweetness and aroma of the rum.

You can use these cherries to make *bublanina,* the traditional Czech Fruitcake (see p. 80), among others.

Bublanina—Czech Fruit Cake

For 1 deep rectangular cake pan (12 by 8 inches / 30 × 20 cm)

Ingredients

1½ cups (400 g) Cherry Compote (see p. 79)

1½ teacups all-purpose, pastry or cake flour
1½ teacups of wheat semolina, plus extra for dusting

1 teacup granulated sugar

2½ teaspoons (12 g) baking powder

½ teaspoon ground cinnamon

1 vanilla bean (pod)

1 pinch of salt

1 teacup milk

1 teacup canola (rapeseed) oil, plus extra for greasing

2 eggs

Powdered (icing) sugar, for dusting

Place the cherry compote in a strainer or sieve and let drain. Preheat the oven to 350 °F top/bottom heat (180 °C/Gas Mark 4).

Grease the cake pan with oil and dust with flour.

To make the cake batter, sift the flour into a large bowl and mix with the sugar, baking powder, cinnamon, seeds scraped from the vanilla bean, and salt. Add the milk, oil, and eggs and beat with a whisk until smooth.

Pour two-thirds of the batter into the pan and spread most of the cherries on top, spacing them apart a little. Spread the remaining batter on top and cover with the remaining cherries. This will ensure that the fruit is evenly distributed throughout the cake and will not all sink to the bottom.

Bake for 45 to 60 minutes, until golden. To check whether the cake is cooked through, insert a toothpick or skewer all the way through to the bottom of the cake and then pull it out. No batter should be stuck to it—only a few dry crumbs if anything.

Take the cake out of the oven and let cool. Dust the cake with powdered (icing) sugar, cut into slices, and serve.

Tips Ideally, the teacup measures should be a little on the smaller side, equivalent to about ⅔ cup (150 ml).

When making this cake in summer, you can create variations using other fresh fruit. Or out of season, use any fruit compote or frozen fruit. However, don't defrost frozen fruit beforehand, otherwise it will become too soft and release too much juice.

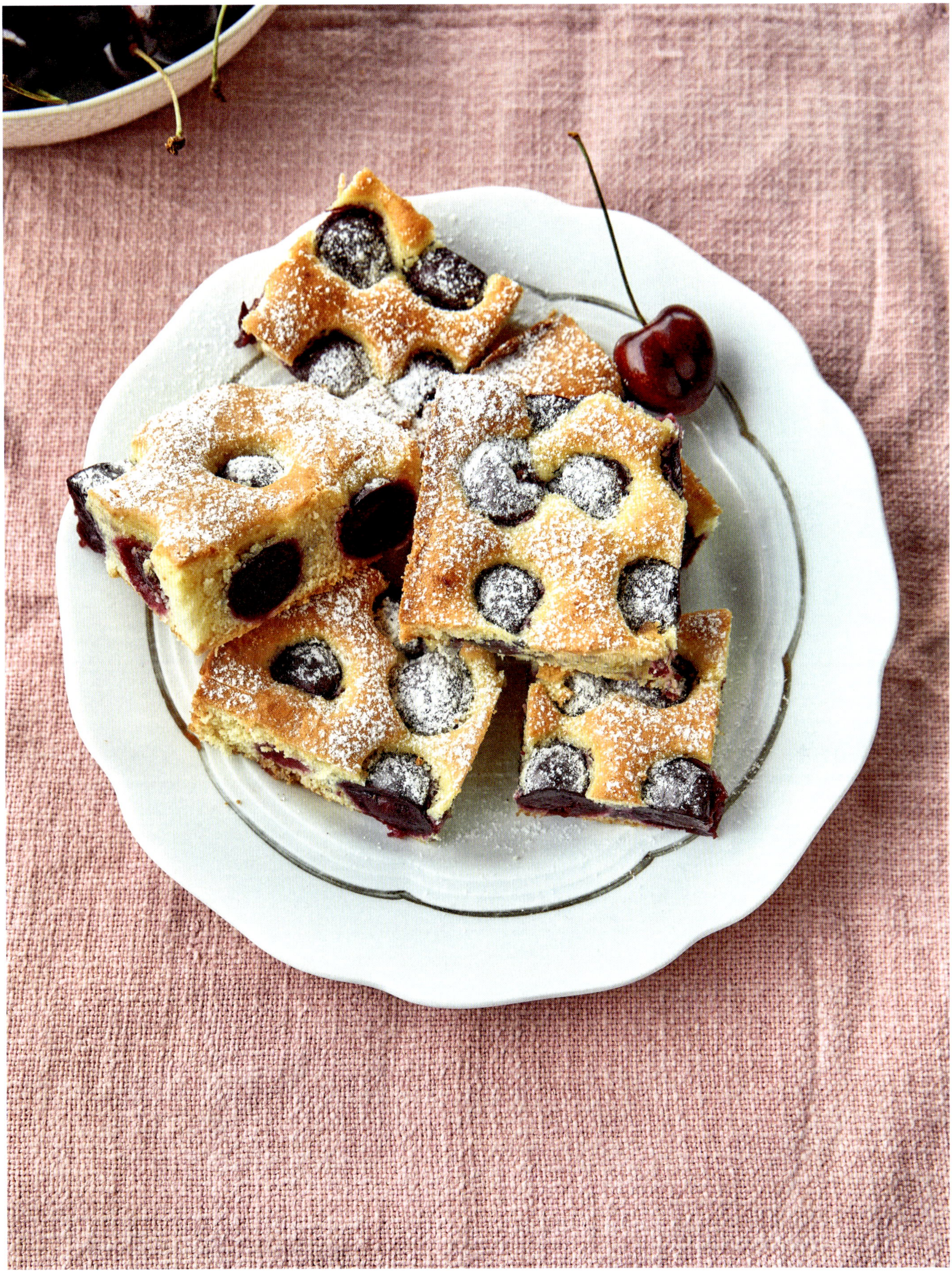

Lemon Balm–Mint Syrup

For 2 bottles (32 ounces/1 l each)

Ingredients

6 ⅓ cups (1.5 l) water

7 ½ cups (1.5 kg) cane sugar

2 bunches of fresh lemon balm

2 bunch of fresh mint

3 organic lemons

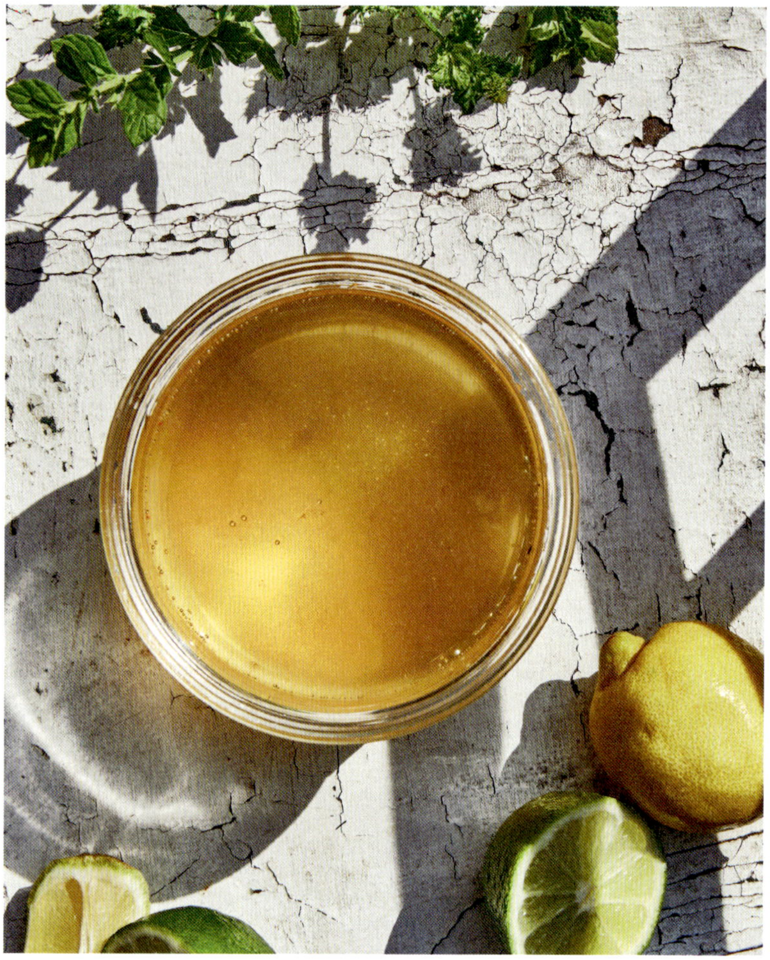

Mix the water and sugar in a pot and bring to a boil, stirring occasionally, until the sugar dissolves.

In the meantime, wash the herbs under cold running water, shake dry, and coarsely chop along with their stems. Wash the lemons in hot water and cut into slices.

As soon as the syrup comes to a simmer, reduce the heat. Add the herbs and stir, covering them completely in the syrup. Let boil for 2 to 3 minutes, remove from the heat, stir in the lemon slices, and cover the pot. Let infuse in a cool place for 20 to 48 hours.

Strain the syrup through cheesecloth (muslin) into a clean pot, then squeeze out as much liquid as possible out of the herbs and lemon slices and discard. Place the pot over medium heat. As soon as the first bubbles form at the bottom of the pot, pour the hot syrup into sterilized and preheated glass bottles. Close the bottles tightly, let cool, and refrigerate. For a refreshing summer drink, dilute the herbal syrup with tap water, sparkling mineral water, or club soda (soda water).

Tips You can vary the flavor of your syrup by substituting some of the lemons with limes or adding a few slices of ginger.

The syrup will keep longer if you add 1 tablespoon vodka or other pure high-proof liquor (spirit) to each bottle. This will stop bacteria from forming.

Cherry Vinegar

For 2 bottles (32 ounces / 1 l each)

Ingredients

4 ¼ cups (1 l) water

Generous ⅓ cup (80 g) granulated sugar

2 ¼ pounds (1 kg) sweet cherries (about 7 ¼ cups)

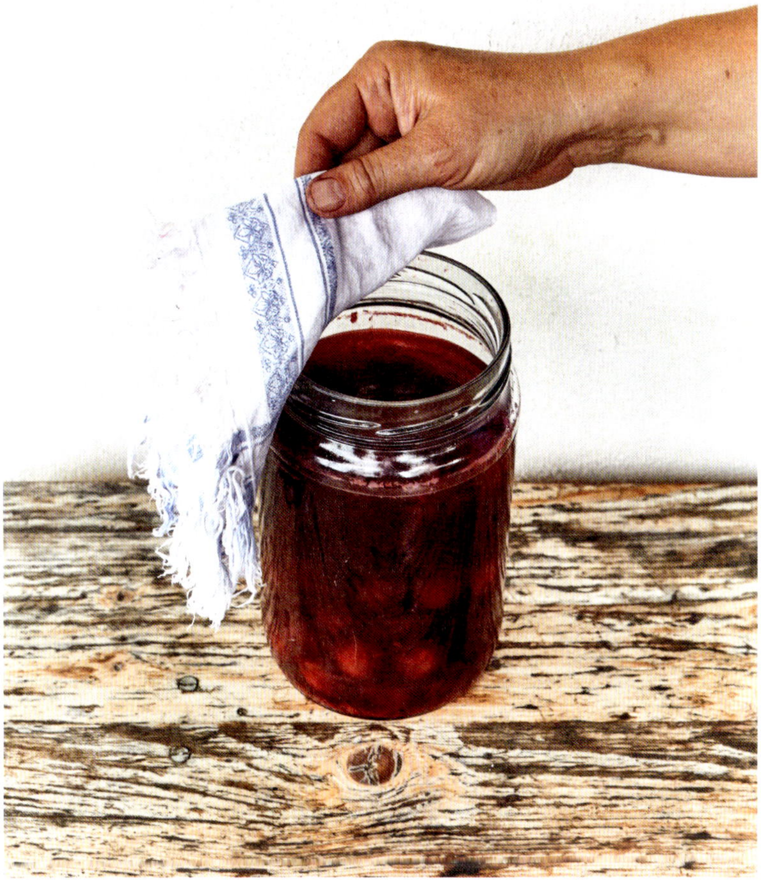

In a saucepan, mix the water with the sugar and bring to a boil, stirring well until the sugar dissolves. Let cool.

Wash the cherries, keeping stems and pits intact. Place them in a large sterilized jar (3-quart / 3-l) until it is half full, then pour in the syrup. Leave enough headspace between the fruit and the rim for foam to form during fermentation.

Cover the jar with a clean cloth and secure with a rubber band. Let ferment at room temperature away from direct sunlight for 2 to 3 weeks, stirring several times a day with a wooden or plastic spoon. A thick, gelatinous film, known as a vinegar mother, should gradually form on the surface of the mixture. Although it looks a little unappetizing, it shows that the fermentation process is proceeding normally. If the entire surface is covered by the vinegar mother, press it down slightly so that air can reach the bottom.

Line a funnel with cheesecloth (muslin) and filter the vinegar into sterilized bottles. Cover the opening of each bottle with a clean cloth. Rest the bottled vinegar at room temperature for at least a few days and up to a month without stirring. In the meantime, taste the vinegar regularly. It is ready as soon as it develops a pleasantly sour taste. Now close the bottles tightly. Use the cherry vinegar immediately or store in the refrigerator.

Tips You can use the fermented cherries. Pitted, they make a delicious component for vegetable salads, such as a Summer Salad with Fermented Cherries (see p. 84).

You can save the vinegar mother and use it for the next batch of vinegar, which you can make, for example, by using apple peels. The vinegar mother will help to boost and speed up the entire fermentation process.

Summer Salad with Fermented Cherries

Serves 2 to 4

Ingredients

4 handfuls of lettuce leaves

1 handful of Swiss chard

1 handful of fermented cherries (from Cherry Vinegar, see p. 83)

6 tablespoons olive oil

2 tablespoons Cherry Vinegar (see p. 83)

½ teaspoons honey

½ teaspoon Kremser mustard or other whole-grain mustard

Salt and freshly ground black pepper

7 ounces (200 g) sheep milk cheese

2 tablespoons sliced almonds

Wash the lettuce and chard well under cold running water and drain. Tear the leaves into smaller pieces, if necessary. Place the lettuce and chard in a salad bowl and add the fermented cherries.

To make the dressing, add the olive oil, vinegar, honey, and mustard to a small bowl and season with a little salt and pepper. Whisk the dressing to a slightly creamy emulsion. Adjust the seasoning, if necessary.

Pour the dressing over the salad and toss well. Coarsely crumble the cheese over the salad and finish by sprinkling with sliced almonds. Serve immediately, because the salad will be at its best when served freshly made.

Tips This summer salad is great when simply accompanied with whole-wheat (wholemeal) bread, but it also makes a fantastic side dish for grilled meat.

Toasting the almonds in a dry skillet or frying pan gives them a more intense flavor. Alternatively, use chopped walnuts or pecan nuts.

You can also embellish this summer salad with edible summer flowers, such as pumpkin and zucchini (courgette) blossoms, cornflowers, and calendula, as well as oregano and lavender flowers.

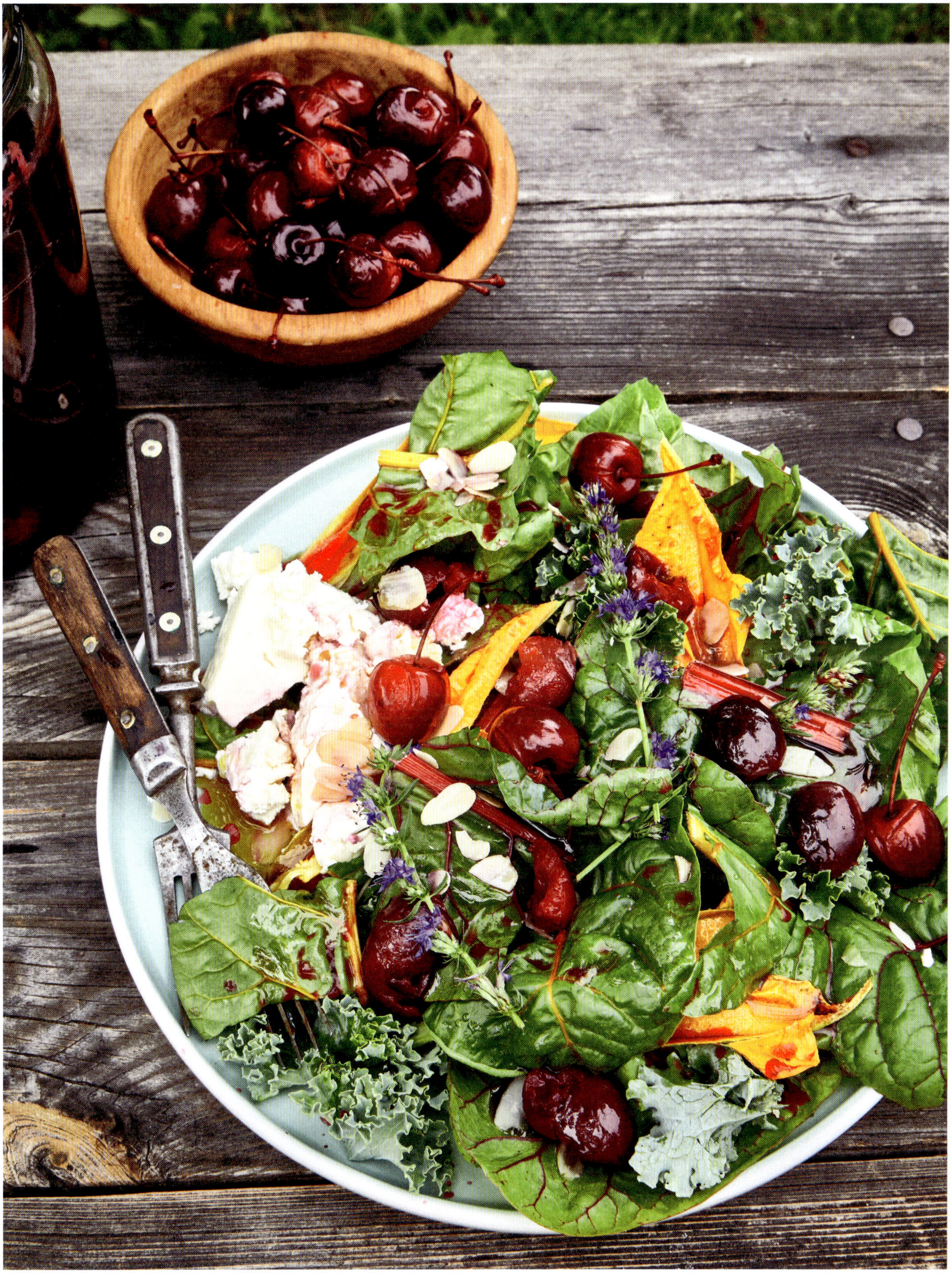

Where Nature Does All the Work

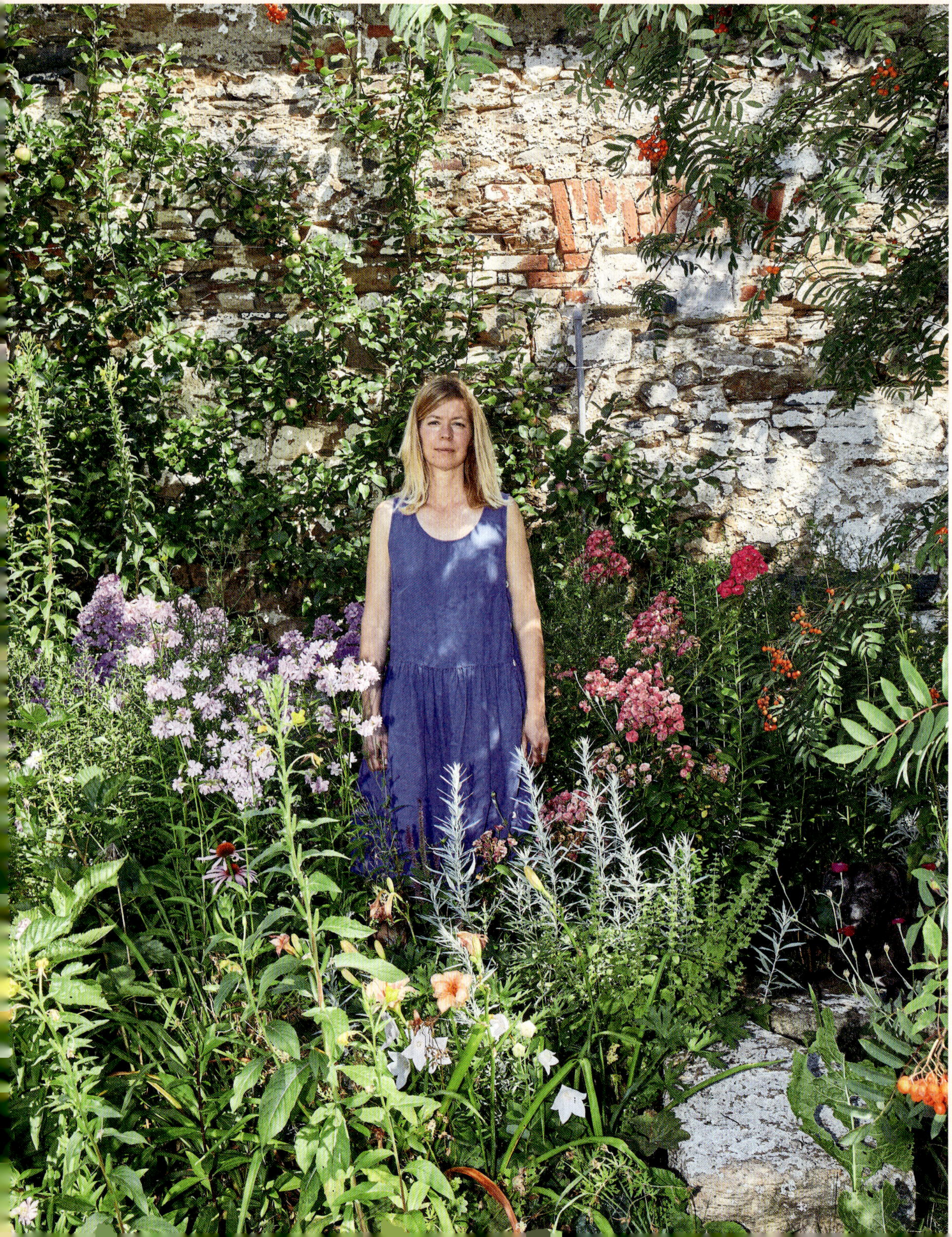

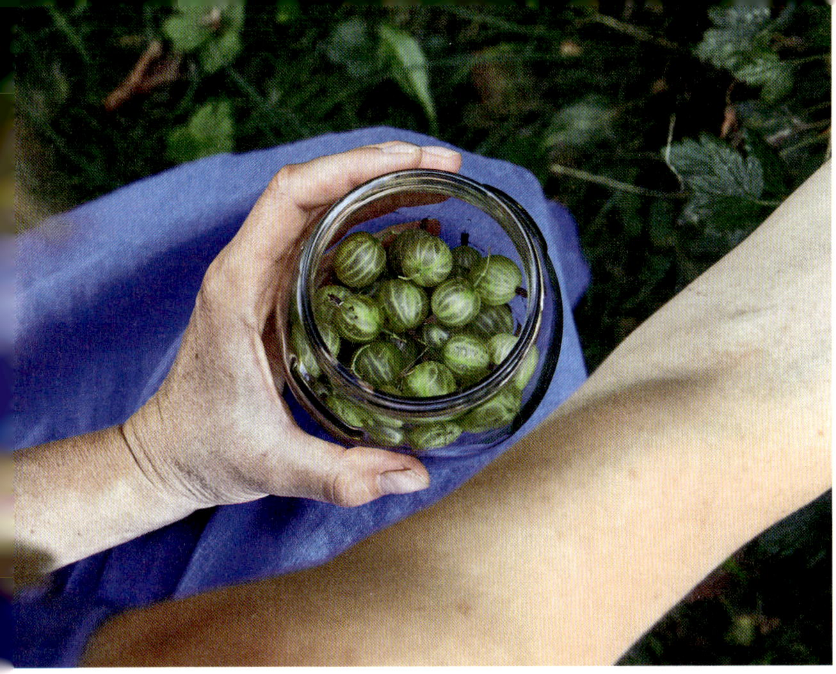

Utopia in today's industrialized world? Discover heritage apple ciders and playful drinking vinegars that brought Eva Laurinová acclaim at home and overseas.

A few years ago, Eva and Ivo Laurin bought a homestead with a medieval fortress in Sudkův Důl, left Prague behind, and started fermenting natural Utopia ciders from old apple varieties. "We wanted to eat clean, so we moved to the Vysočina region," Eva says. "We planted trees, shrubs and flower beds, and we keep bees, sheep, geese, ducks, chickens, and fish, all in a preindustrial way. The idea is to have nourishing, healthy food and beverages for the family and the many friends who visit."

Eva and Ivo also started their own apple orchard. They use no sprays or rodenticides, fertilize the trees with well-rotted horse manure from a neighbor, and add compost made from apple pomace. The voles? The local foxes take care of those. It'll be years before their trees grow tall and strong, so for now they harvest apples for their cider from magnificent old orchards, with a deep sense of gratitude to the people who planted them 80 years ago.

When it comes to making cider, the Laurins stick to pure natural processes. Their ciders ferment spontaneously with local wild yeasts cultures in oak barrels, with no filtration, clarification, pasteurization, added carbonation, or unnecessary additives. After a few years in the craft, they now joke that they don't really *make* cider at all—it's the yeast and bacteria that do the work.

Eva's enthusiasm and determination eventually led her to create fine apple drinking vinegars, infused with all kinds of ingredients: black elder, smoked plum, thyme, Douglas fir, quince, and other fruit, flowers, and leaves. Most of these are gathered from the Vysočina valley, are grown in the Laurin family's own garden, or are bought from local organic farmers. Mixed with water, tonic, or a splash of gin, the result is a refreshing drink for any season. Eva's vinegars also add a surprising twist of flavor to both sweet and savory dishes. "At the beginning, we gave vinegar away to friends in the restaurant world in exchange for feedback," Eva says. "Now we've got dozens of barrels in our vinegar house."

And so it was that, although made in an almost utopian way in an age of industrialized food, their ciders and vinegars quickly found their way into Czech homes, bistros, cafés, and the kitchens of gourmet restaurants. They have even found their way abroad.

Alongside making cider and vinegar and running the farm, Eva has a handful of quirky and deeply satisfying hobbies. One of them is to seal in fresh fruits (see p. 89). You read that right: not jams or compotes, but raw preserved fruit. "I've been making it regularly for about six years now," she says. "You just seal fresh fruit in a jar, no sugar, no preservatives. I read about it ages ago and thought it was a strange idea. Then I found an article by a chemist, and that persuaded me that this kind of fruit isn't just harmless—it's actually really good for you and, most importantly, tastes amazing!"

Eva explains that raw preserved fruit isn't meant as a way to preserve an excess harvest from the garden but instead as a special treat during the months when local fruit is scarce. Around 20 jars per season is plenty. "I love grapes and wild cherries the most, and I'm also fond of fresh currants with gooseberries. Some fruit, such as blackberries or raspberries, release too much juice for my taste." She mostly uses her fruit in salads or as toppings for ice cream sundaes. Give it a stab—you might just get hooked!

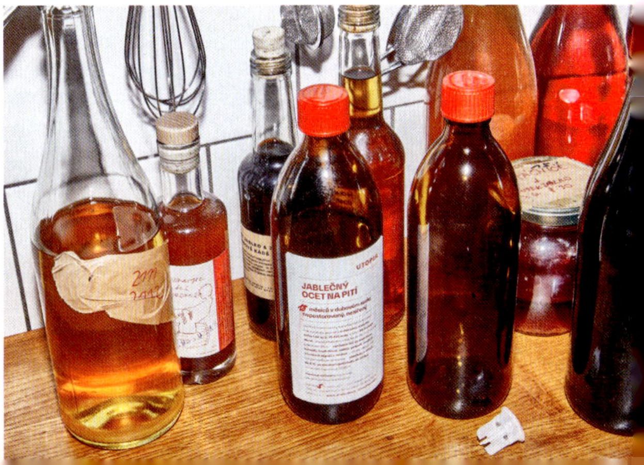

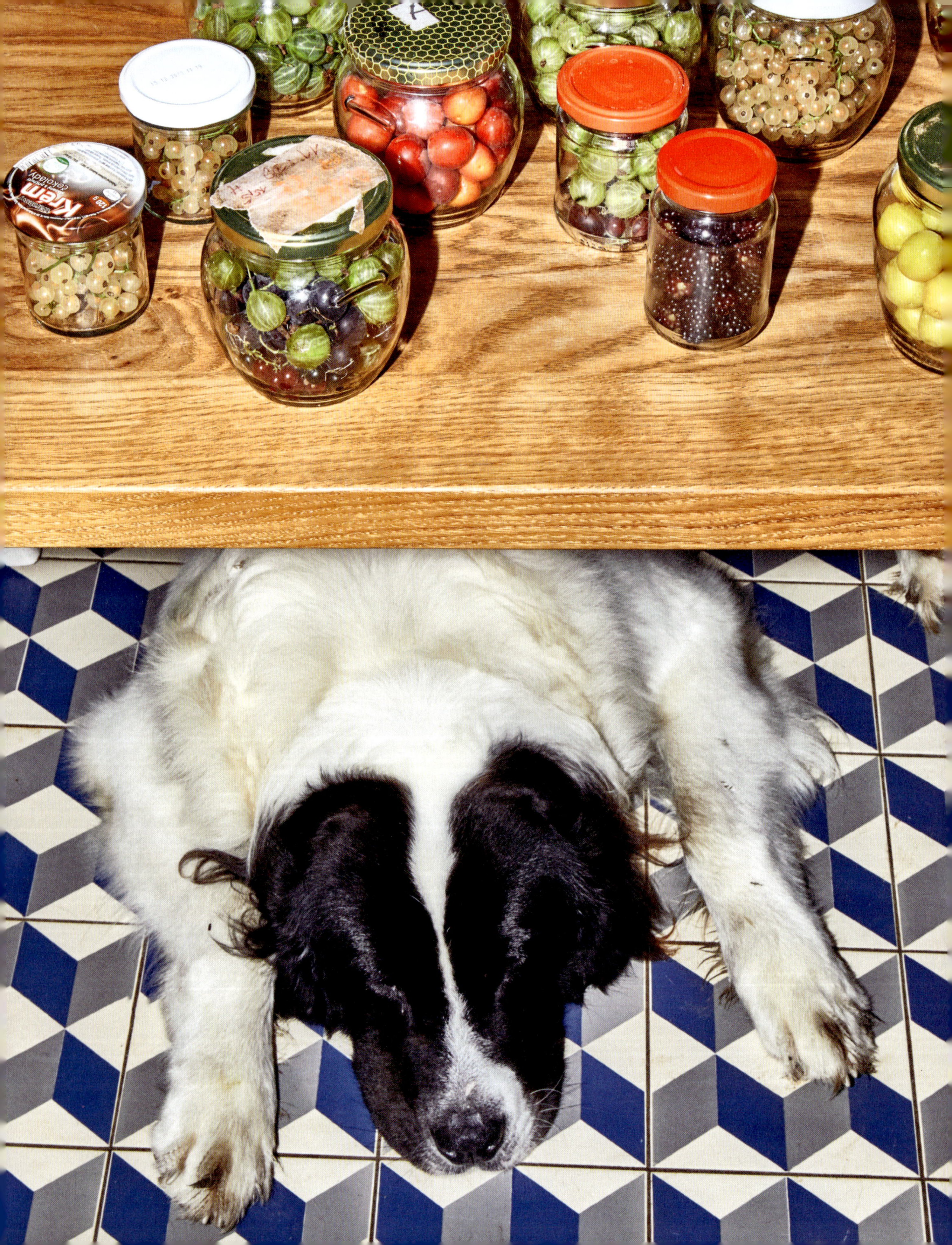
Krem

The Ancient Method of Sealing In

There is an easy way to prolong the life of a fruit well beyond its season while retaining all of its vitamins and beneficial nutrients. You can seal it in a passive controlled atmosphere in a canning jar.

For our ancestors, "sealing in" was a common method of preserving the fruit that they picked in the wild or later learned to grow themselves. Because many different types of fruits are now available in supermarkets practically throughout the year, people have generally forgotten this ancient preservation method. However, jars of fruit can still be found in the pantries of experimenters, locavores, and history buffs.

How it works

Put firm, undamaged fruit, ideally with stems still attached, into sterilized canning jars and create an airtight seal. The best way to do this is to go fruit picking with a basket of sterilized canning jars and put the freshly picked fruit directly into the jars. If possible, the fruit should be sealed in the jars within 15 minutes of picking. This creates a protective atmosphere around the fruit, because carbon dioxide is released through their skin, depleting any oxygen and preventing them from spoiling.

Store the jars in a cool, dark place. Although the fruit will turn somewhat pale, it will retain its flavor and aroma, as well as much of its structure. After some time, it will ferment slightly and its natural acidity will become more pronounced. The fruit will release liquid as it ferments.

Which fruit is suitable for this?

This method works best with small fruit, such as fresh currants, gooseberries, blueberries, and mirabelle plums. Grapes and sweet cherries are also very popular. Raspberries and blackberries work just as well, although some juice may leak out. Delicate fruit with a thin skin can become very soft or mushy. If you want, you can also try lesser-known fruit, such as juneberry, barberries, chokeberries, and sloes. Freshly picked flower buds, spruce tips, and lavender spikes also stay superfresh when sealed in this way.

Because the fruit must not be washed before being sealed in the jar, it shouldn't be picked near busy roads and industrial areas. Never use chemically treated fruit!

Uses

Fruit stored in a controlled atmosphere can replace fresh fruit. It tastes great on its own, with yogurt and granola, and in cakes and salads. It also works well in desserts, marinades, and with grilled meat. It is best to consume this fruit within the same year, so a new batch should be prepared each season. However, fruit preserved through sealing in will keep for up to 2 years when stored in a cellar.

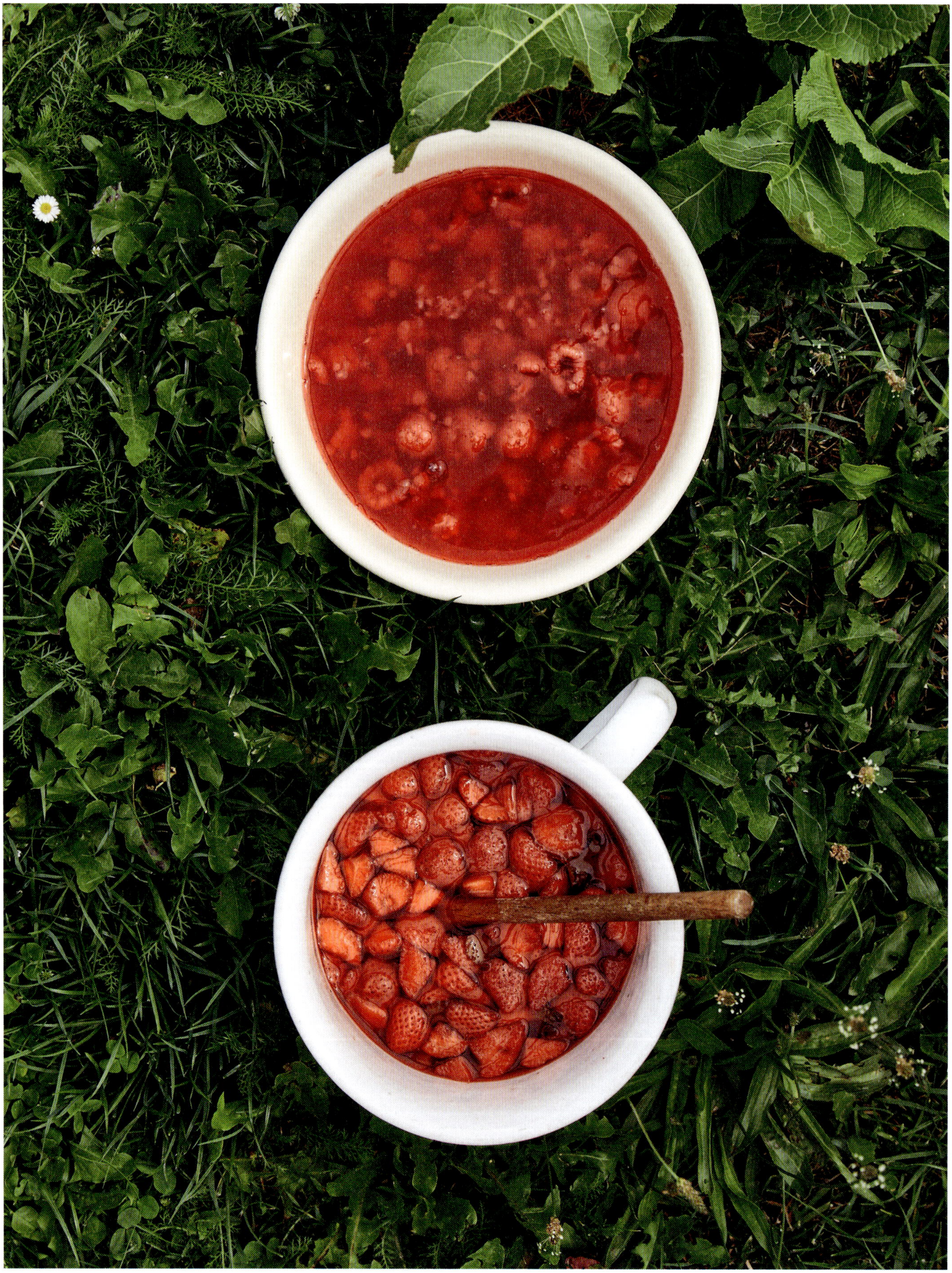

Raspberry Vinegar

For 1 bottle (25 ounces / 750 ml)

Ingredients

4 cups (500 g) raspberries

2 cups (500 ml) apple cider vinegar

½ to ¾ cup (100 – 150 g) granulated sugar

Sort the raspberries, wash carefully in a strainer or sieve under cold running water, then drain. Put the berries into a large, sterilized canning jar with a wide opening, crush with a potato masher, and pour in the vinegar. Seal the jar and store in a cool, dark place for about 1 week.

Filter the liquid through cheesecloth (muslin) or a fine-mesh strainer or sieve into a saucepan and add the sugar. Put over low heat and gradually warm the vinegar while stirring continuously. As soon as the sugar has completely dissolved, remove the vinegar from the heat and transfer it to a sterilized bottle. Close tightly and let cool.

Strawberry Vinegar

For 1 bottle (25 ounces / 750 ml)

Ingredients

2 cups (500 ml) white wine vinegar

1¾ cups (250 g) strawberries

In a saucepan, bring the white wine vinegar to a boil in a pan and let cool until lukewarm. Carefully wash and trim the strawberries. Quarter or halve any larger fruit. Put the strawberries into a large, sterilized canning jar with a wide opening and crush them a little with a potato masher. Pour in the lukewarm vinegar.

Cover the jar with a cloth and secure with a rubber band, or loosely cover with a lid. Let the vinegar mixture mature in a light place at room temperature for about 2 weeks. Stir the mixture with a wooden spoon every other day.

When ready, filter the vinegar through a strainer or sieve into a sterilized bottle and close tightly.

Tips Only use very ripe fruit and a high-quality vinegar for these recipes. You can also flavor the vinegar with a cinnamon stick, a few cloves, or cardamom pods.

Fruit vinegars can be used immediately after filtering. They are ideal, for example, to enhance vegetable salads and light desserts. They can be diluted with sparkling mineral water or club soda (soda water) to make a delicious and refreshing drink.

Raspberry Compote

For 6 canning jars (8 ounces / 250 ml each)

Ingredients

4 ¼ cups (1 l) water

2 ½ to 3 cups (500–600 g) granulated sugar

Juice of ½ lemon

2 ¼ pounds (1 kg) raspberries (about 8 cups)

To make the syrup, put the water into a saucepan and add the sugar. Adjust the amount of sugar according to the sweetness of the fruit. Place the pan over medium heat and let simmer, stirring, until the sugar dissolves. Stir in the lemon juice, remove from the heat, and let cool.

Sort the raspberries, wash carefully under cold running water, then drain. Fill sterilized canning jars with the raspberries, leaving a gap of about 1 ¼ inches (3 cm) below the rim. Pour over the syrup, covering the fruit completely. Cover the jars tightly and process in a water bath, then let cool and store in a cool, dark place. Let the raspberry compote rest for at least 2 weeks before use.

Tip You can elevate your raspberry compote by adding 2 to 3 tablespoons of red wine vinegar. To enhance the flavor, add a vanilla bean (pod), star anise, cinnamon stick, or cloves to the jars.

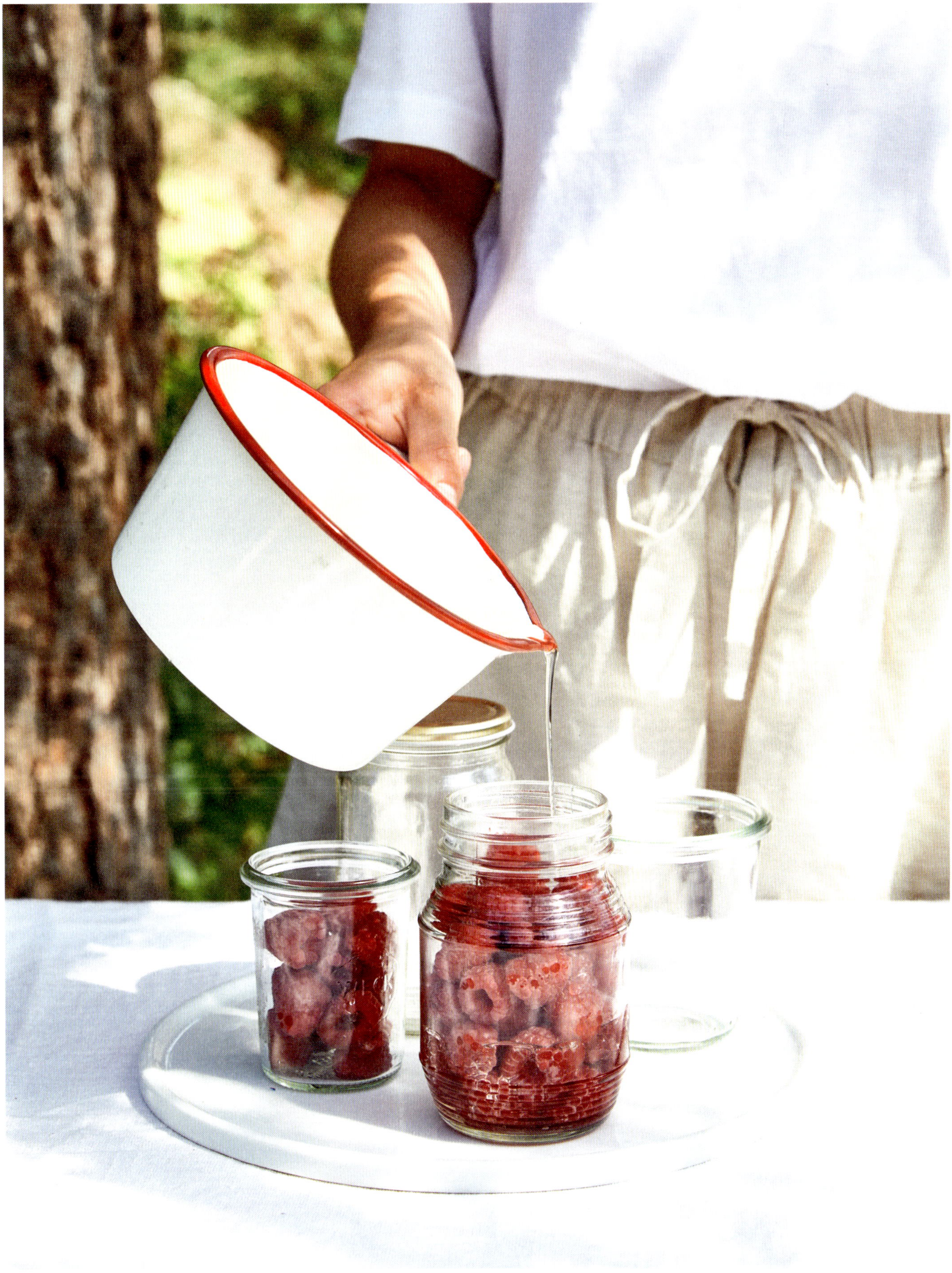

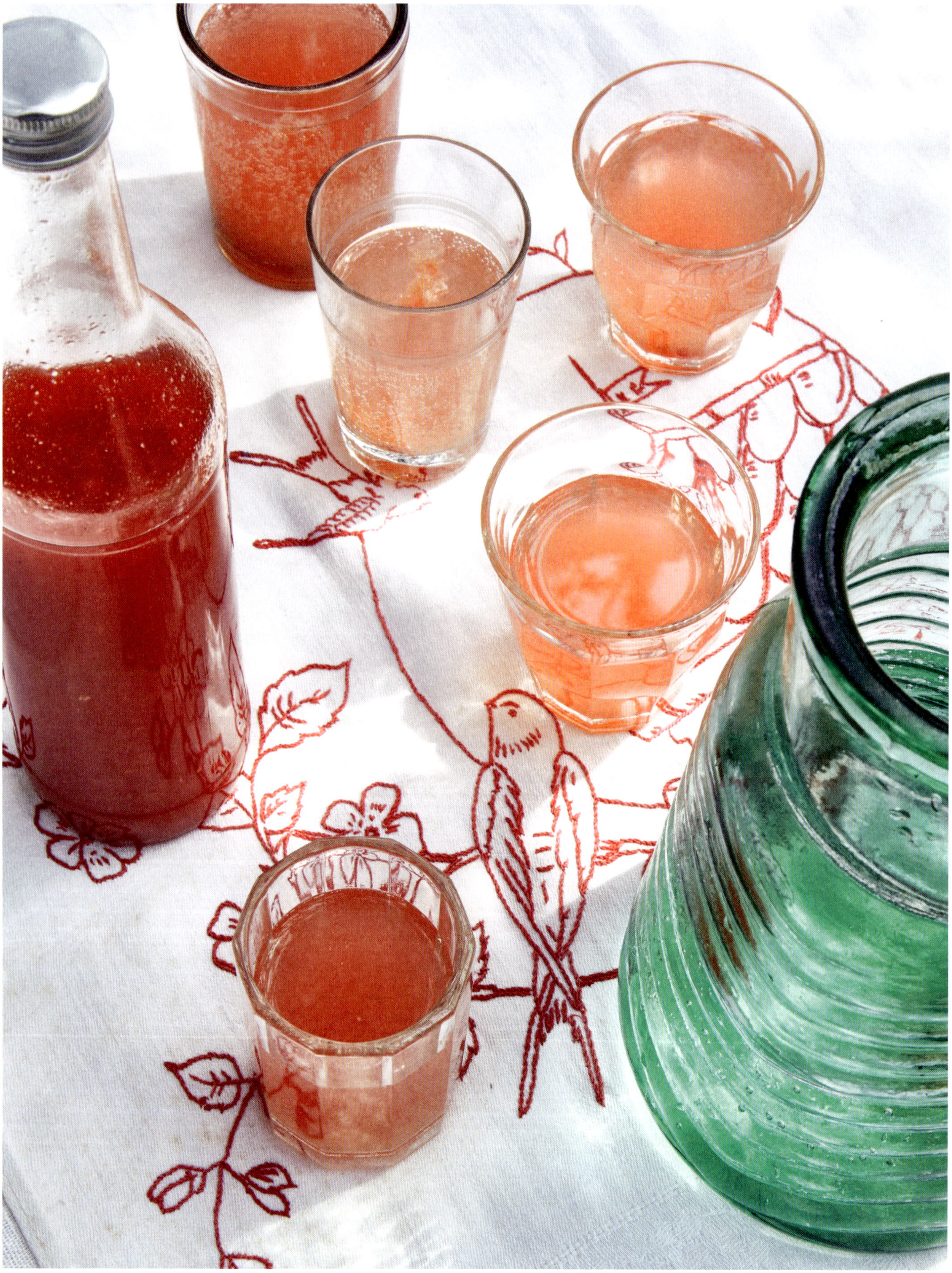

Raspberry Soda Syrup

For 2 bottles (25 ounces / 750 ml each)

Ingredients

3 cups (750 ml) water

3 ¼ pounds (1.5 kg) raspberries (about 12 cups)

3 ½ tablespoons (40 g) citric acid

5 to 7 ½ cups (1–1.5 kg) granulated sugar

Bring the water to a boil in a saucepan, then let cool completely. Sort the raspberries, discarding any bruised, damaged, or rotten fruit. Carefully wash the berries under cold running water and place them in a large glass, ceramic, or porcelain bowl.

Lightly crush the berries, then add the citric acid and water. Stir everything together, cover with a lid or a clean cloth, and let infuse in a cool, dark place for 20 to 24 hours.

Filter the resulting liquid through cheesecloth (muslin). Add the sugar (adjust the amount depending on the sweetness of the fruit) and mix well until the sugar dissolves. The result should be a thick, sweet syrup. Pour into sterilized bottles, create an airtight seal, and store in the refrigerator. Use the syrup immediately, diluted with sparkling mineral water or club soda (soda water).

Tips You can pick wild raspberries to make this syrup. Although they are not as large and perfectly formed as cultivated raspberries, they have a much more intense aroma and a fuller flavor.

Don't discard the raspberries left in the cheesecloth; you can use them along with fresh berries to make Raspberry Vinegar (see p. 91).

You can also replace the raspberries in this recipe to make blackberry, strawberry, black currant, or gooseberry syrup.

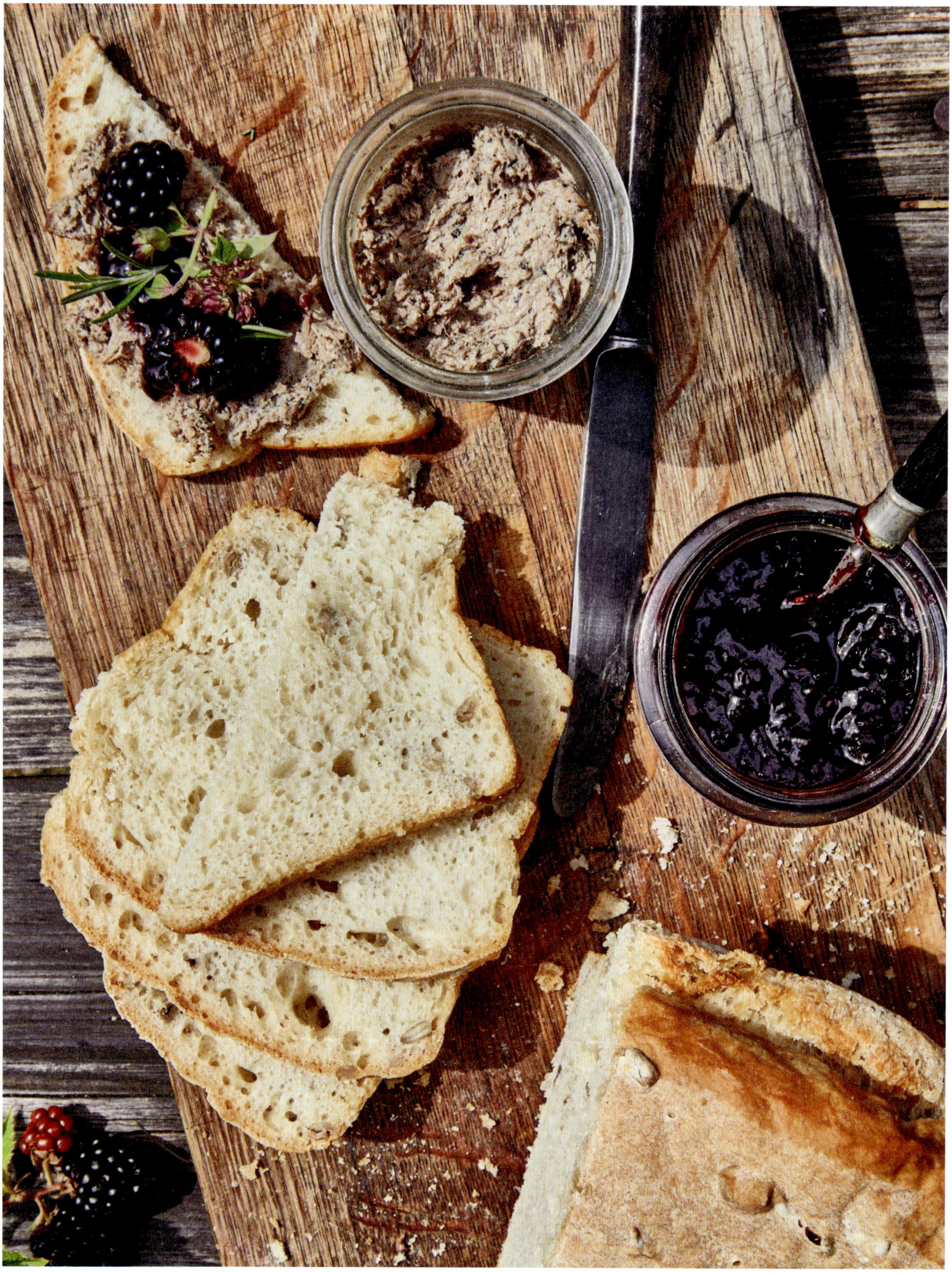

Spiced Blackberry Jam

For 4 canning jars (8 ounces / 250 ml each)

Ingredients

2 ¼ pounds (1 kg) blackberries (about 7 cups)

5 cups (1 kg) granulated sugar

1 heaping teaspoon (6 g) citrus pectin

1 teaspoon ground cinnamon

½ teaspoon ground cloves

½ teaspoon ground allspice (mixed spice)

Sort the blackberries, remove any stems, and wash under cold running water, then drain and set aside. Mix a few tablespoons of sugar with the pectin in a small bowl.

Transfer the blackberries to a pot and bring to a boil. You can lightly crush the berries with a potato masher, but ripe berries usually cook quickly. Add the spices and let simmer, stirring continuously, for 3 minutes. Stir in the sugar and pectin mixture and lower the heat. Add the remaining sugar and cook for another 5 to 10 minutes, until the mixture thickens, stirring occasionally. Be careful not to burn the jam.

Transfer the hot jam to small, sterilized canning jars and close tightly. Place the jars upside down and let cool. Store in the refrigerator and consume within 2 weeks. If you want to store the blackberry jam for longer, process the jars in a water bath after filling.

Tips If you prefer your jam less sweet, simply reduce the amount of sugar to 4 cups (800 g).

Blackberry jam makes a great topping for pancakes and crepes and is a good accompaniment for plain (natural) yogurt and chicken terrine.

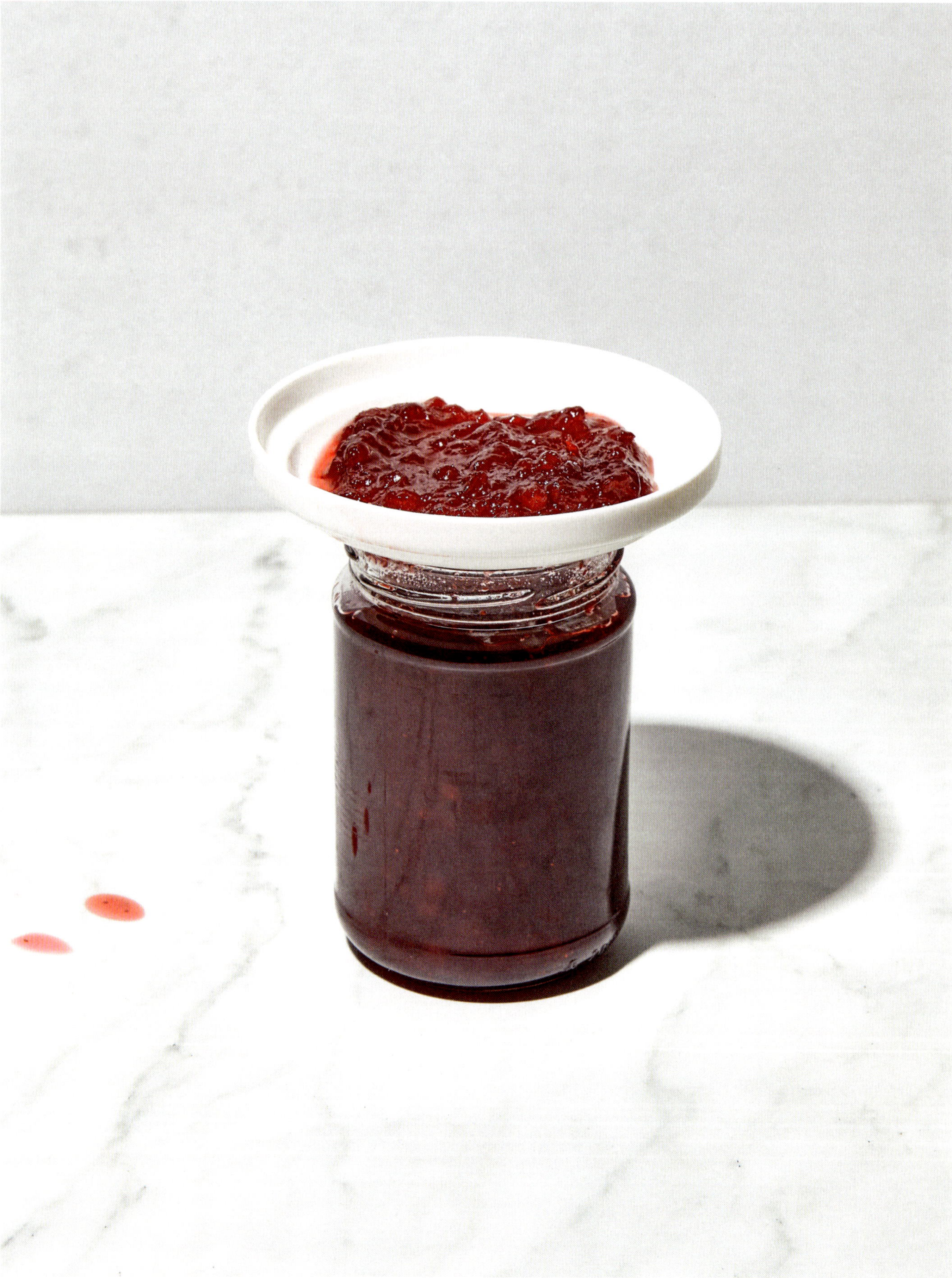

Red Currant Jam

For 6 canning jars (8 ounces / 200 ml each)

Ingredients

2 ¼ pounds (1 kg) red currants (about 7 cups)

3 ¾ cups (750 g) granulated sugar

2 teaspoons ground cinnamon

6 cloves

Juice of 1 lemon

3 to 5 tablespoons rum

Strip the currants from their stems. Discard any leaves and rotten fruit. Rinse the berries in a strainer or sieve under cold running water, then drain and place in a wide saucepan. Add the sugar. Mix well, cover the pan, and let infuse overnight in a cool, dark place for the berries to release their juice.

The next day, add the spices and lemon juice. Bring to a boil, then lower the heat and let simmer, stirring occasionally, for about 15 minutes. The berries should be slightly overcooked and most of the juice should evaporate. As soon as the mixture thickens a little, stir in the rum and let simmer for another 5 minutes. Remove from the heat.

Transfer the hot jam to small, sterilized canning jars and close tightly. Place the jars upside down and let cool. If you want to store the jam for longer, process the jars in a water bath after filling. Use the jam immediately or store in a cool, dark place.

Tips The jam will still be a little runny after cooking, but it will firm up as it cools. Fresh currants are naturally very sour and contain a lot of natural pectin. When combined with lemon juice, it has a gelatinizing effect. This means that no additional pectin is required for this recipe.

Red currant jam goes well with crepes, gingerbread cake, *lívance* (traditional Czech yeast pancakes), and Linzer Tart (see p. 100).

Linzer Tart with Red Currant Jam

For 1 baking pan (12 by 16 inches / 30 × 40 cm)

Ingredients

5 cups (600 g) pastry flour or all-purpose (plain) flour, plus extra for dusting

1⅔ cups (200 g) powdered (icing) sugar, plus extra for dusting

½ teaspoon Bourbon vanilla bean powder

2½ teaspoons (12 g) baking powder

1 pinch salt

Finely grated zest of 1 organic lemon

1 cup plus 2 tablespoons (250 g) unsalted butter, plus extra for greasing

2 eggs

About 1 cup (300 g) Red Currant Jam (see p. 99)

1 handful of slivered (flaked) almonds

Sift the flour and sugar into a large mixing bowl, then add the vanilla, baking powder, salt, and lemon zest and mix together. Grate the butter or cut it into small cubes and add to the flour mixture. Add the eggs, then using your hands, work the mixture into a smooth dough without excessive kneading, otherwise it will become too firm after baking. Shape the dough into a ball, cover with plastic wrap (clingfilm), and refrigerate for at least 1 hour.

Preheat the oven to 350 °F top/bottom heat (180 °C/Gas Mark 4). Grease a baking pan with a little butter.

Roll out three-quarters of the dough into a rectangle on a floured work surface. Roll the dough onto the rolling pin and unroll it into the greased baking pan. Raise the edges of the dough by pinching it with your fingers. Prick the dough several times with a fork. Stir the red currant jam until smooth and spread a thick layer of jam evenly over the dough. Roll out the remaining dough into a rectangle and cut into strips about ¾ inch (2 cm) wide. Arrange the dough strips into a lattice over the jam. Use the remaining strips of dough to form a border along the sides of the tray. Sprinkle the slivered almonds over the top, lightly embedding them into the dough.

Bake for 40 to 50 minutes, until golden. After 35 minutes, test to see if the pastry is cooked by by inserting a toothpick or bamboo skewer into the edge. If it comes out clean, the pastry is done. Let rest in the turned-off oven for another 5 minutes.

Remove the baked tart from the oven and let it cool completely before serving. While you can enjoy it as soon as it has cooled, it tastes even better the next day. Store it in a cool, slightly humid place so the flavors can develop. Before serving, dust it with powdered (icing) sugar.

Tips For a round 11-inch (28 cm)-diameter cake pan, halve the specified quantities of ingredients.

If you want the finished tart to be glossy, brush the dough with beaten egg yolk before baking.

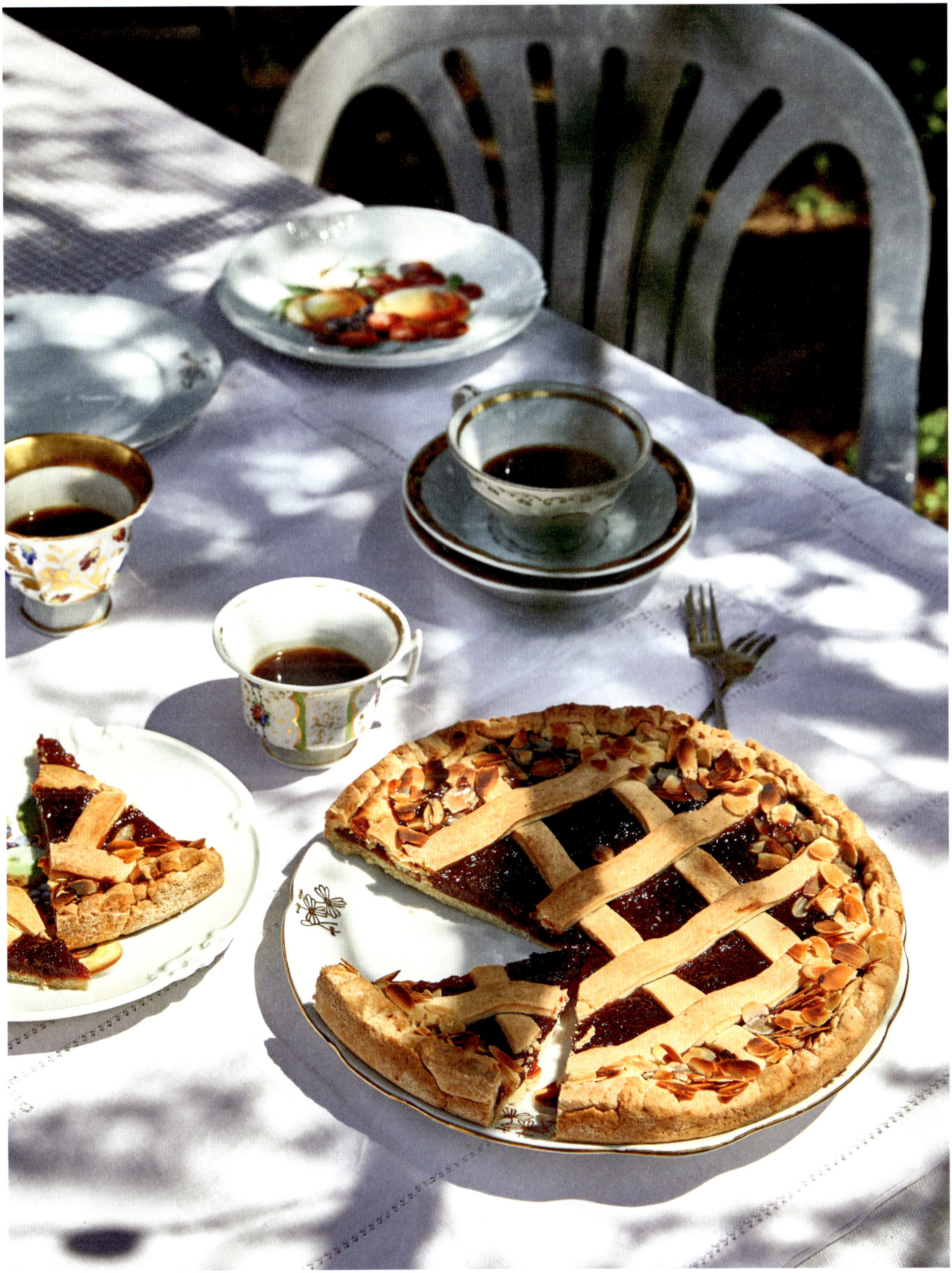

Svíčková—Mock Tenderloin Steak with Cream Sauce

Serves 4

Ingredients

2 large carrots

½ celery root (celeriac)

2 parsley roots

2 onions

2 tablespoons lard

1½ pounds (700 g) mock tenderloin (chuck tender steak or shoulder tender steak)

1 to 2 sprigs fresh oregano

1 to 2 sprigs fresh thyme

2 bay leaves

3 juniper berries

3 to 4 allspice berries

Salt and freshly ground black pepper

3 cups (700 ml) beef broth (stock) or water

2 tablespoons (25 g) unsalted butter

1 cup (250 g) whipping cream

Bread dumplings, to accompany

Lingonberry-style Red Currants (see p. 105), to accompany

1 lemon, sliced

Preheat the oven to 340 °F top/bottom heat (170 °C/Gas Mark 3). Peel the carrots, celery root, parsley roots, and onions. Cut everything into small dice and put into a roasting pan. Melt the lard in a large pan and sear the meat well on all sides until golden brown. Place the meat on top of the vegetables in the roasting pan.

Stir in the herbs and spices, season with salt and pepper, and pour in the broth or water. Cover with a lid or aluminum foil and braise in the oven for about 2 hours 30 minutes, until the meat is tender. Check occasionally that there is still enough liquid in the roasting pan. Add a little more broth, if necessary. About 15 minutes before the end of the cooking time, remove the lid and let the meat brown a little.

Remove the meat, herbs, and spices from the roasting pan. Transfer the vegetables to a saucepan, add a little butter, and puree everything with an immersion stick blender until you get a smooth, creamy sauce. If the sauce turns out too thick, you can dilute it with a splash of hot broth or water. Stir in a few tablespoons of room-temperature cream, bring the sauce to a boil, and let simmer for 5 minutes. If necessary, adjust the seasoning with salt, pepper, and lemon juice.

Cut the meat into slices and divide among plates with bread dumplings and the sauce. For additional flavor, top with lingonberry-style red currants. Whip the remaining cream to stiff peaks, then garnish the dish with a tablespoon of whipped cream and lemon slices.

Tip This recipe can also be made using beef round or shank (shin). Wrap the roasted meat in aluminum foil or place in the still-warm oven after turning it off to keep warm until serving. Rest the meat for at least 5 minutes before slicing. This closes the pores on the surface and keeps it nice and juicy.

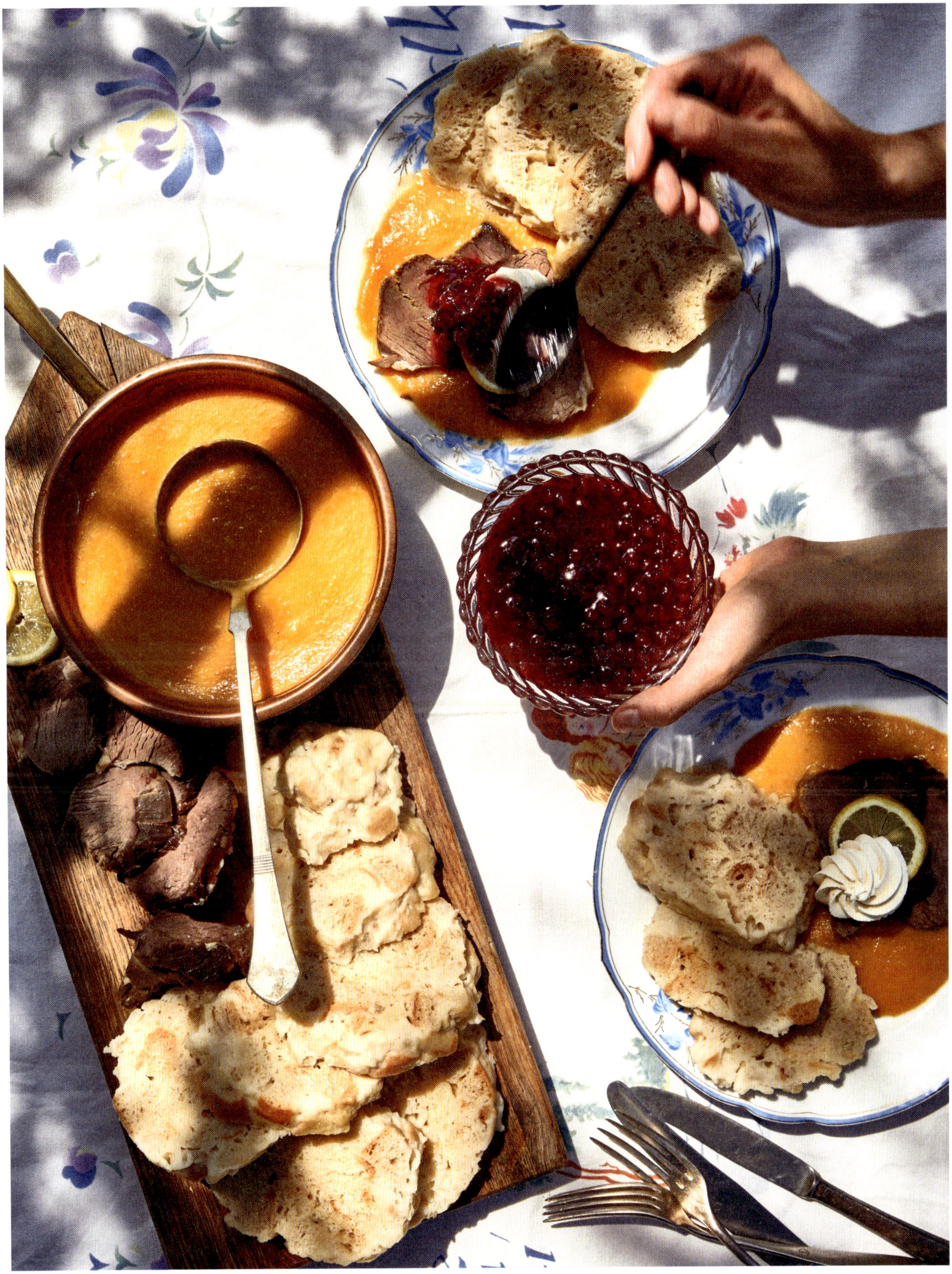

Sugared Wild Blueberries

For 2 canning jars (16 ounces / 500 ml each)

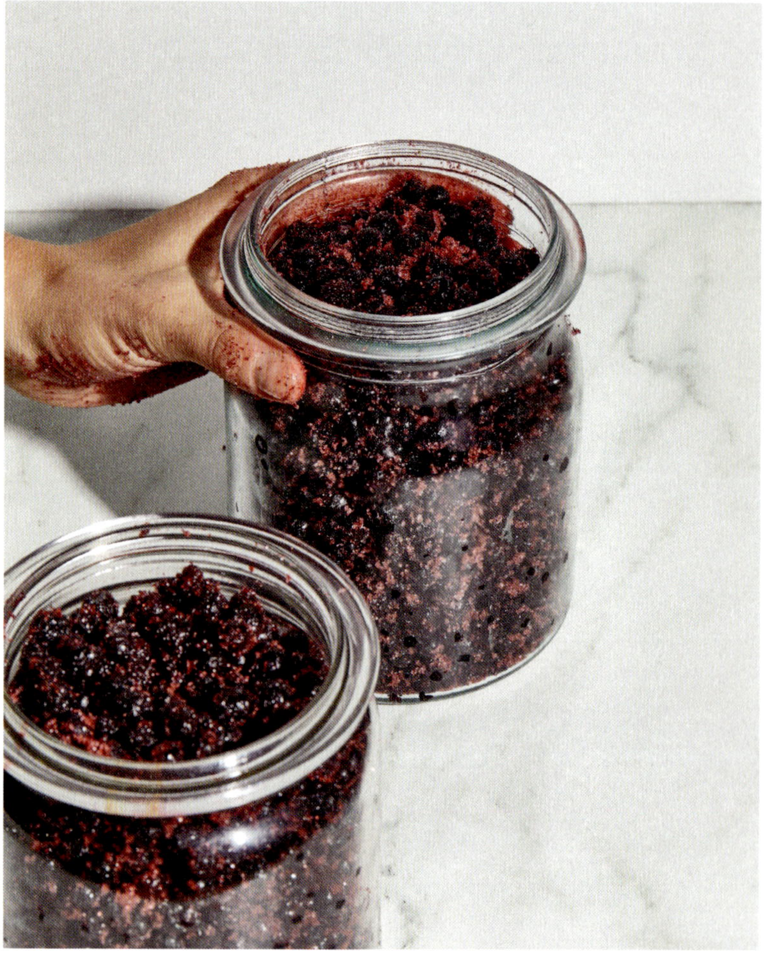

Ingredients

2 ¼ pounds (1 kg) wild blueberries (about 7 cups)

1 cup (200 g) granulated sugar

This recipe works best with freshly picked blueberries. Sort the berries and discard any leaves. Carefully wash the berries in a strainer or sieve under cold running water and drain. Transfer to a large bowl and mix with the sugar.

Spoon the blueberries into sterilized canning jars as quickly as possible (otherwise they will turn mushy). Close the jars tightly and process in a water bath. Let cool, then store in a cool, dark place.

Tips In winter, these wild blueberries are good to use as an ingredient for different cakes and *kolaches* (see p. 106), sweet *Germknödel* (yeast dumplings), and *lívance* (traditional Czech yeast pancakes). They also go well with *lejoky* (Bohemian-style Pancakes, see p. 254).

Other berries and small fruit can also be preserved in the same way, including fresh raspberries, blackberries, currants, wild strawberries, lingonberries, and cranberries.

Lingonberry-style Red Currants

For 5 canning jars (8 ounces / 250 ml each)

Ingredients

1 cup (250 ml) distilled white vinegar

1¼ cups (270 – 290 ml) water

2¼ pounds (1 kg) red currants (7 cups)

3½ cups (700 g) granulated sugar

5 cloves

1 small cinnamon stick

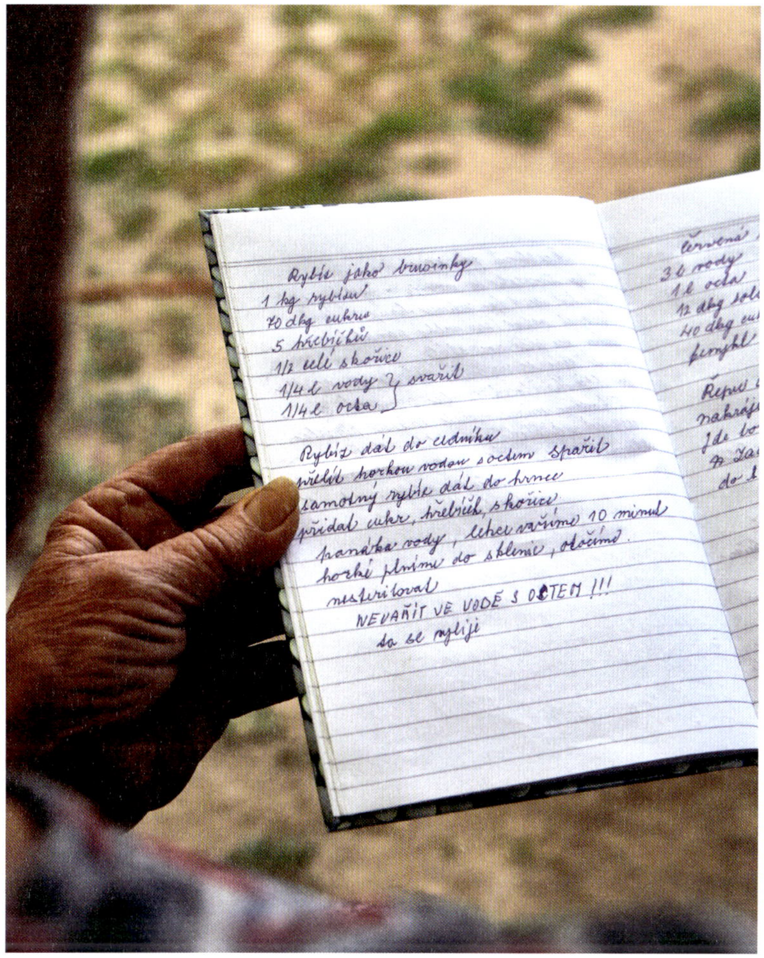

Mix the vinegar with 1 cup (250 ml) of the water in a saucepan, bring to a boil, and let simmer for 5 minutes.

Strip the currants from their stems, sort, and rinse in a stainless steel strainer or sieve. Place the strainer in the sink and pour the hot vinegar mixture over the currants.

Transfer the berries to a pot, add the sugar and spices, and pour in the remaining 2 to 3 tablespoons (20 – 40 ml) of the of water. Bring everything to a boil, then reduce the heat and let simmer for 10 minutes.

Transfer the hot currants to sterilized canning jars, close the lids tightly, and place upside down. Let cool, then store in a cool, dark place.

Tip Lingonberry-style red currants make a good accompaniment for *svíčková* (see p. 102), grilled meat, and cheese. This mock lingonberry jam can also be used to enliven salad dressings.

Blueberry Kolaches

Makes about 20 kolaches

Ingredients

7 tablespoons (100 g) unsalted butter, plus 1½ tablespoons (20 g) for brushing

About 1 cup (200–250 ml) milk

1 small (⅔ ounce/19 g) cake fresh yeast

4 cups (500 g) pastry flour or all-purpose (plain) flour

Scant ½ cup (90 g) granulated sugar

¼ teaspoon Bourbon vanilla bean powder

1 pinch of salt

2 egg yolks, plus 1 beaten egg for brushing

About 3½ cups (500 g) Sugared Wild Blueberries (see p. 104)

2 to 3 tablespoons rum

Powdered (icing) sugar, for dusting

Melt the 7 tablespoons (100 g) of butter in a saucepan and let cool. Heat a scant 1 cup (200 ml) of the milk in a second saucepan until lukewarm—do not let it overheat. To activate the yeast, crumble the yeast into the lukewarm milk and stir in 1 tablespoon of the flour and 1 tablespoon of the sugar. Cover the pan with a clean cloth and let rise at room temperature for about 10 minutes.

Sift the remaining flour into a bowl. Add the remaining sugar, vanilla bean powder, and salt and mix everything together. Add the activated yeast, melted butter, and 2 egg yolks. Using a wooden spoon or in a stand mixer, mix everything together to form a dough. If the dough is too dry, add the remaining milk. Knead for at least 10 minutes, until the dough is smooth and easily comes away from the sides of the bowl. Cover the bowl with a cloth and let rise in a warm place for 1 hour, until doubled in size.

In the meantime, line 2 baking sheets with parchment (baking) paper. Put the blueberries into a strainer or sieve to drain. Next, divide the risen dough into 20 equal pieces (about 2 ounces/60 g each). Using the palms of your hands, shape them into compact balls. Arrange the dough balls spaced well apart on the prepared baking sheets. Using the bottom of a glass, flatten the center of each dough ball to make a well. Brush the edges and sides of the kolaches with the beaten egg and fill the wells with the blueberries. Let proof for 15 to 20 minutes. Preheat the oven to 350 °F top/bottom heat (180 °C/Gas Mark). Bake the kolaches for about 15 minutes, until golden.

In the meantime, melt the remaining butter in a saucepan and stir in the rum. Brush the edges of the hot kolaches with the rum and butter mixture. Let the kolaches cool, then dust with powdered (icing) sugar immediately before serving.

Tips Only have instant yeast at home? Go ahead and use it—just remember that you cannot substitute fresh yeast 1:1 with instant yeast. Dried yeast is 1.5 times stronger, so always use 1.5 times less! You also don't need to activate instant yeast in advance; simply sprinkle it over the flour and work it into the dough.

You can add 1 tablespoon quark or cream cheese to each well before filling them with blueberries, which will also keep the kolaches soft and fluffy until the next day.

Another variation is to sprinkle the kolaches with a crumb topping before baking. To make the topping, mix about 3½ tablespoons (50 g) melted and then cooled butter with ⅓ cup (70 g) granulated sugar and ⅔ cup (80 g) wheat semolina.

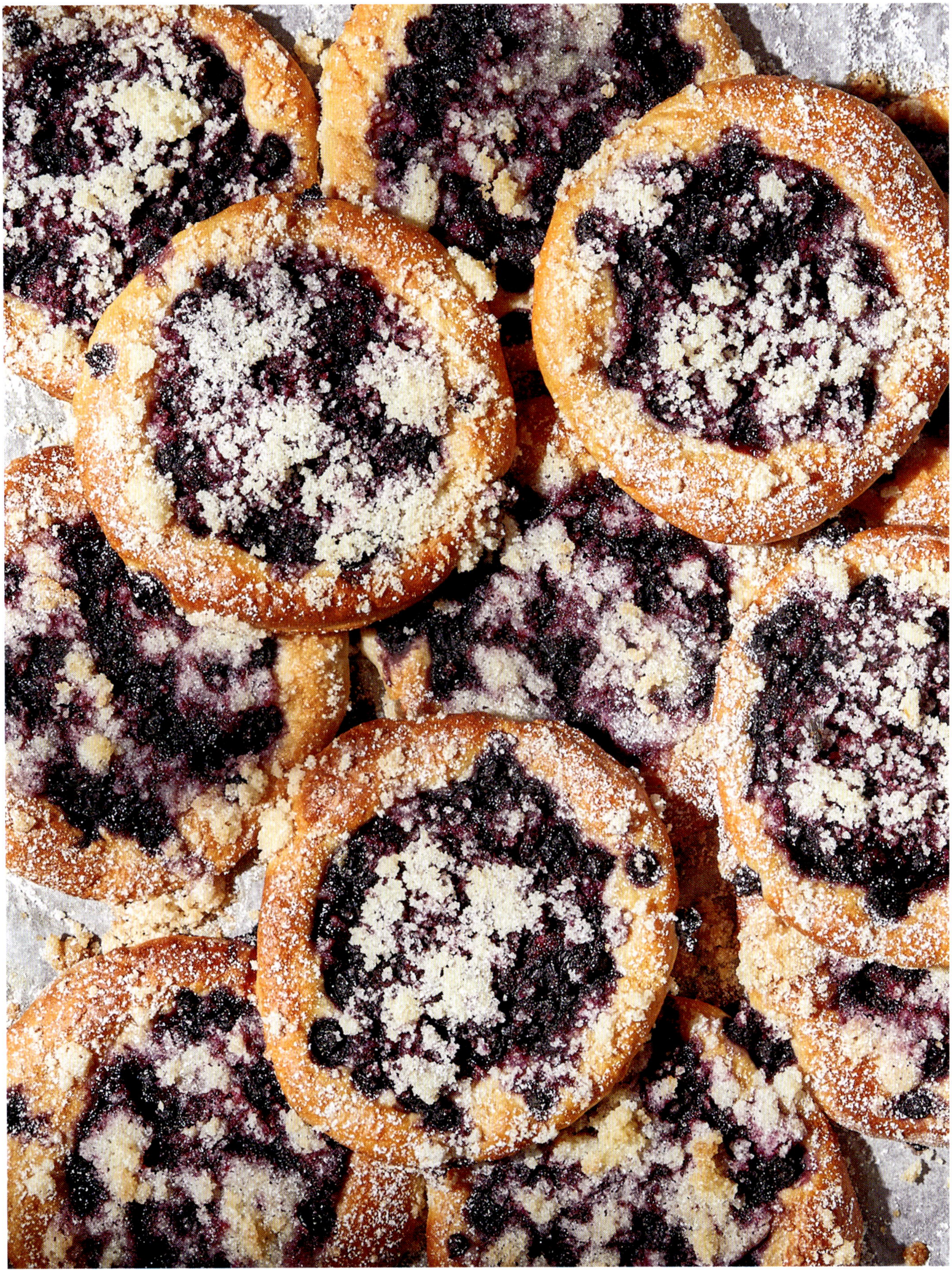

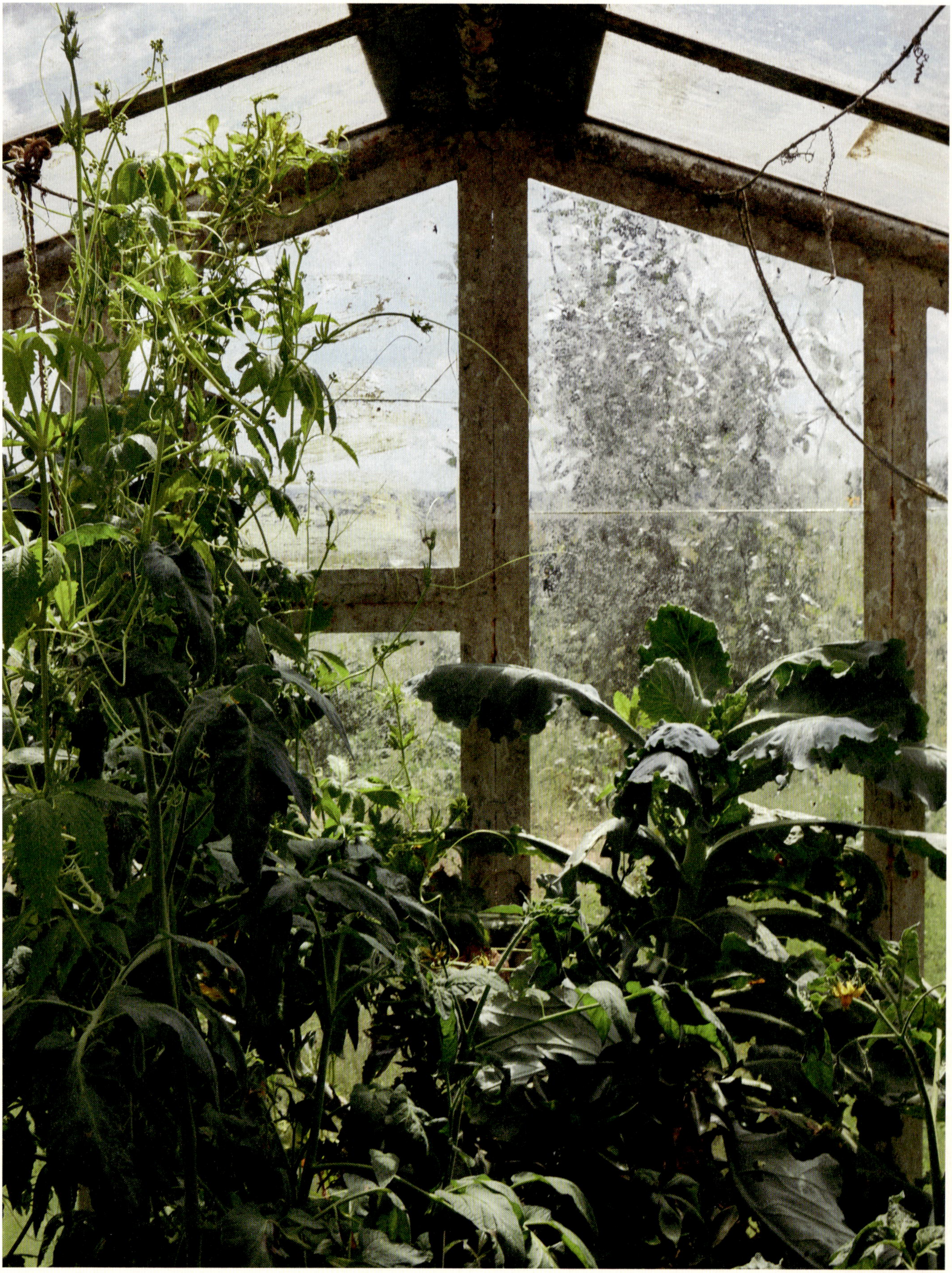

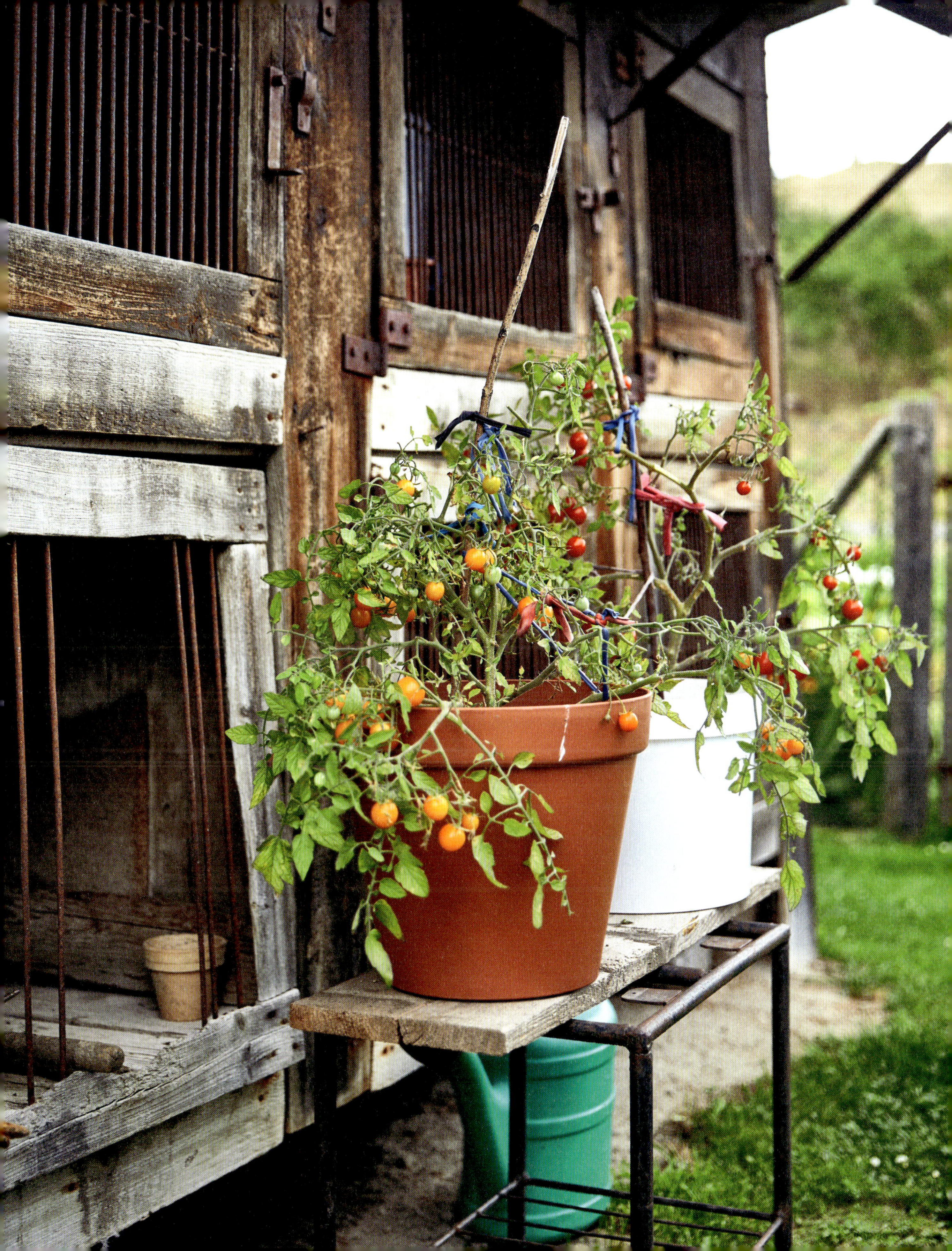

A Jar for Every Neighbor

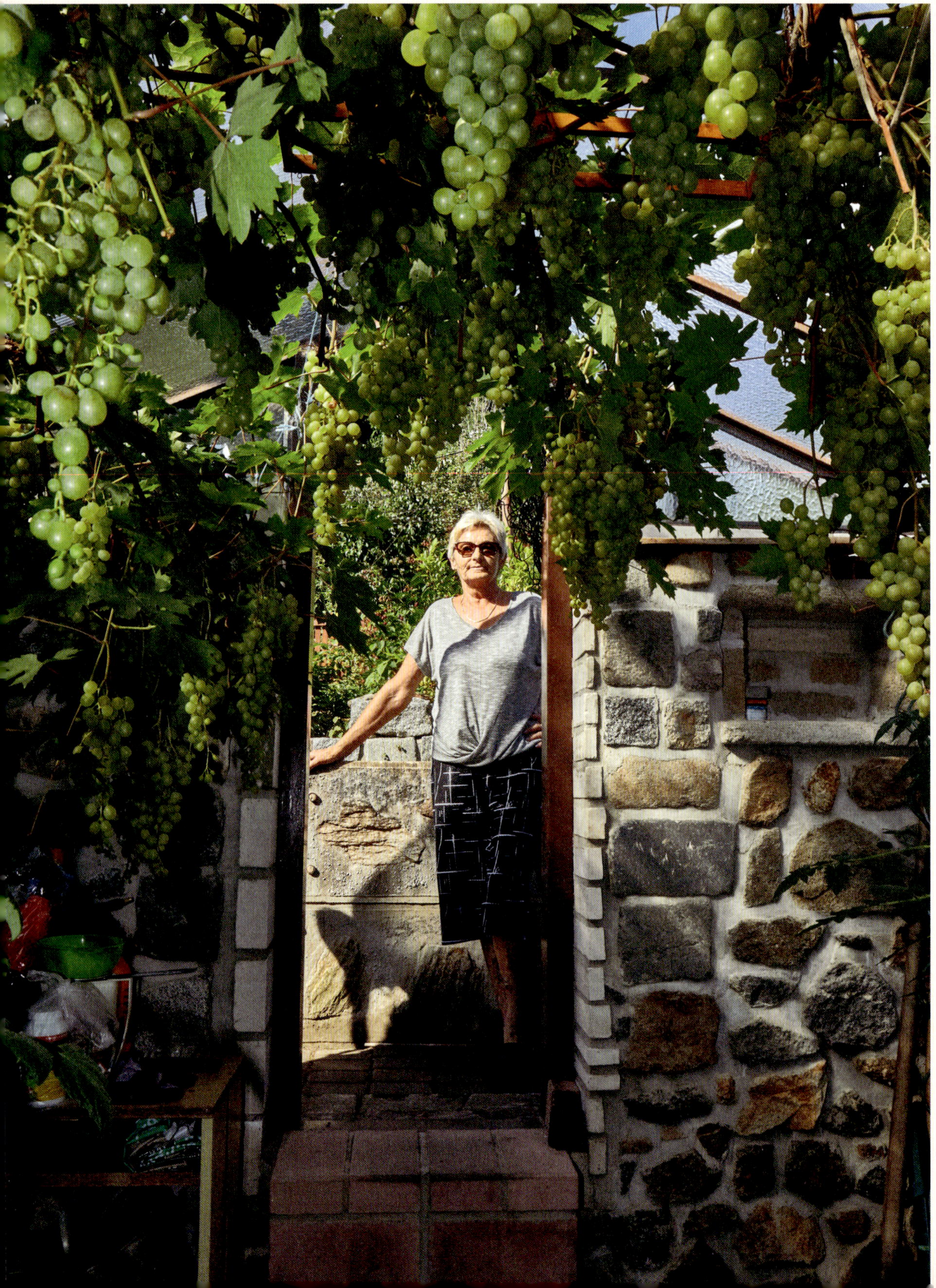

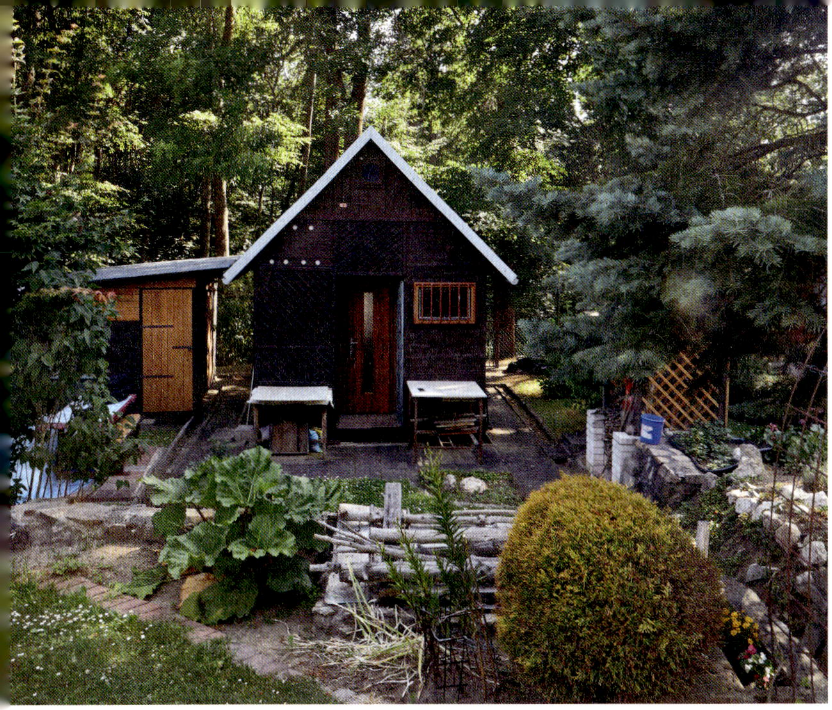

Věra Kutišová preserves unusual exotic vegetable, pickles her signature salad mix, and secretly spreads joy throughout her apartment building.

At first glance, Věra Kutišová is a really cool lady. She once worked as a bartender, and even now, in retirement, she's always smiling, radiating warmth and loving every chance to talk with people. As soon as the weather turns mild and the forest greens up after winter, she escapes to her tiny cottage tucked away in the woods, just a stone's throw from the historic center of Tábor in South Bohemia.

Věra insists she "doesn't fuss too much over the beds," yet her little plot overflows with fruit and vegetables. Dominating the garden is a greenhouse made from large glass canning jars. Peek inside and you'll see the whole inner frame draped with grapevines, heavy with sweet, fragrant grapes.

"My pride and joy are my pickles. Everyone comes for them—they say they've never had better," she grins. Along with her famous pickles, Věra also makes traditional jams and marmalades, and she preserves the unusual vegetable *ačokča* or *achocha* (see p. 113), also known as caigua (and often called the slipper gourd or stuffing cucumber), as well as a homemade root vegetable mix (see p. 113) for traditional Czech Christmas potato salad. "I can't stand those big, hard chunks of vegetables you get in a store-bought salad. I tried grating them and blending them, but that just turned into mush. So I've been making my own salad mix for years. I do it in two ways: I dice some of the root vegetables finely and cut others into larger cubes. Which vegetables end up in the salad on Christmas Eve depends on how many of us are at the table. If I'm making just a small amount, say for three people, I go for the finely chopped vegetables; when all seven of us are gathering, the salad works better with coarser root vegetables that hold up well." By adding colorful carrots, celeriac, parsley root, and even peas, this traditional Eastern European winter comfort food transforms into a festive mosaic that makes everyone at the table smile even before the first bite.

Věra may claim she's slowed down, but she's still unstoppable. "I don't preserve as much as I used to," she admits, walking back and forth to the pantry to bring out jar after jar of preserves, each accompanied by its own vivid story, "but I still love sharing what I make." Most of her jars of fruit and vegetables go to family and friends, although she always keeps a few on the side. Back home in her typical Czech apartment building called *panelák*, she sometimes leaves a few jars by the pipes in the shared hallway. Before long, they're gone! It's her quiet way of brightening her neighbors' day—one jar at a time.

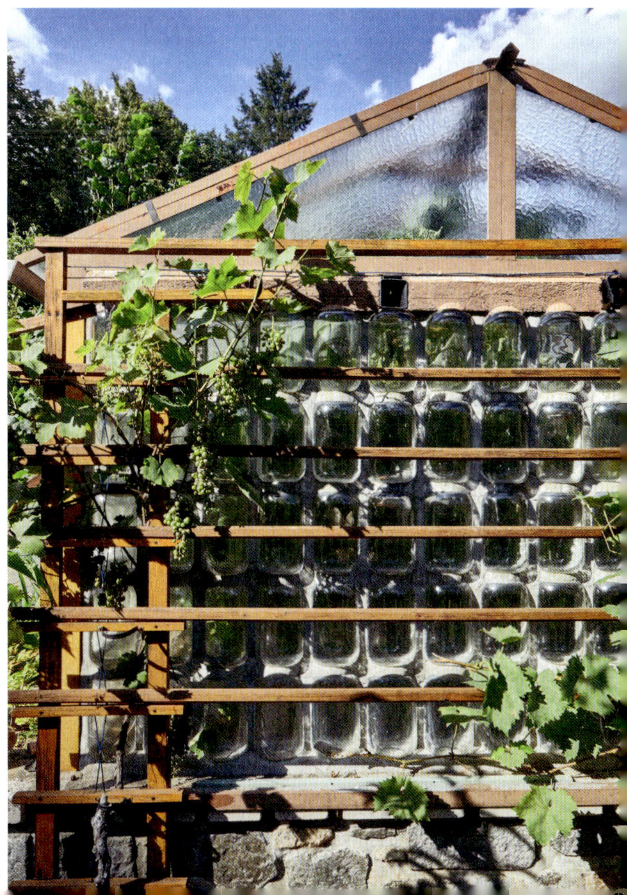

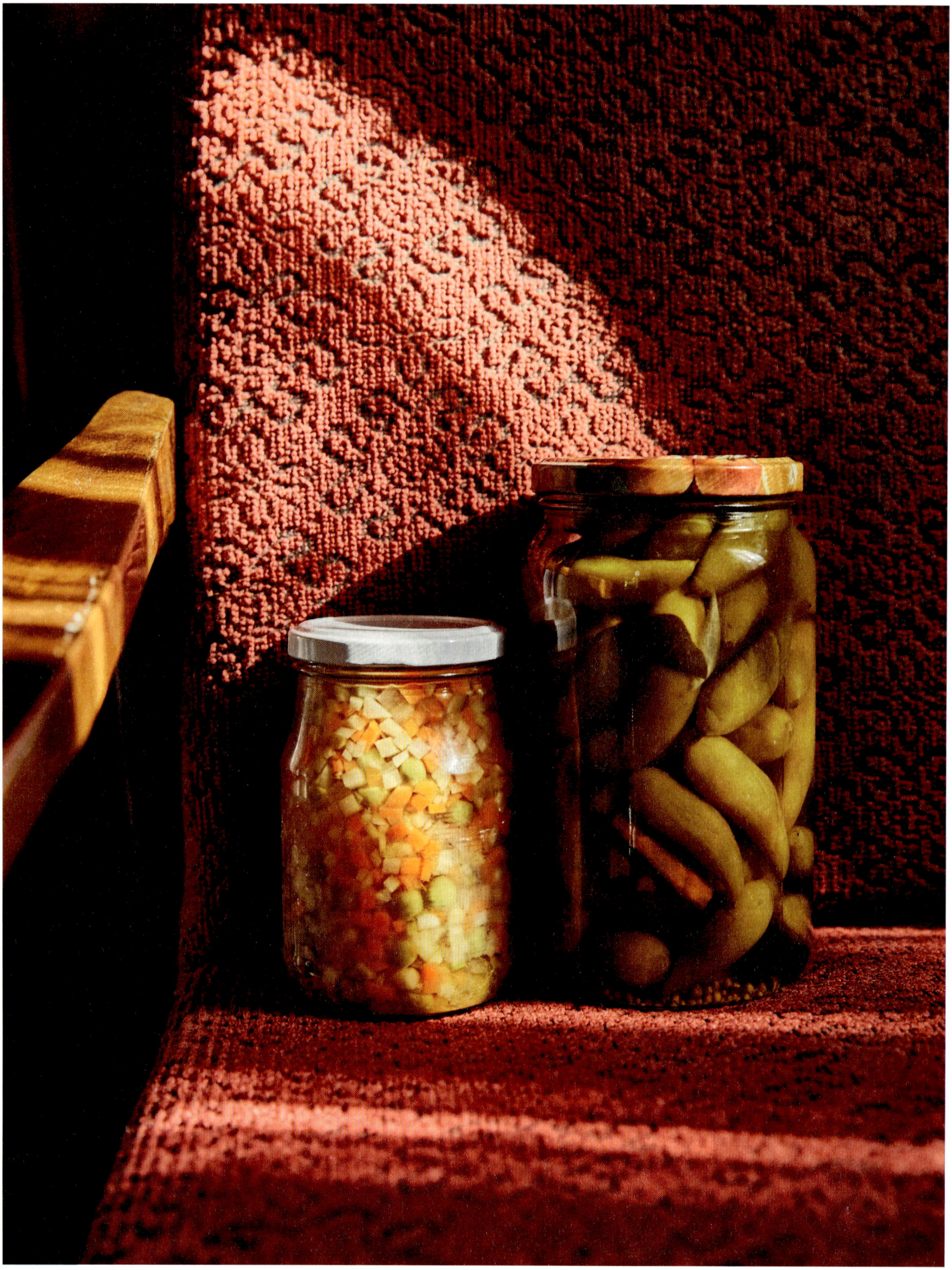

Root Vegetables

For 8 canning jars (8 ounces / 250 ml each)

Ingredients

3 cups (750 ml) water

1 cup (250 ml) distilled white vinegar

⅓ cup (70 g) granulated sugar

1½ tablespoons (30 g) salt

4½ pounds (2 kg) mixed root vegetables (such as carrots, celery root / celeriac, and parsley root)

1 pound (500 g) pickling cucumbers

1¼ cups (200 g) freshly shelled peas

To make the pickling liquid, mix the water and vinegar in a saucepan and add the sugar and salt. Bring to a boil over medium heat, stirring occasionally, until the sugar and salt dissolve. Boil the liquid for about 3 minutes, then remove from the heat.

Clean the root vegetables, peeling them, if necessary. Wash the cucumbers. Cut the root vegetables and cucumbers into small dice. Mix them with the peas and divide everything among the sterilized canning jars. Pour the hot liquid over the vegetables, close the jars tightly, and process in a water bath. Let cool, then store in a cool, dark place.

Tips If you prefer your pickled root vegetables somewhat softer, first cut the vegetables into small dice and blanch them in a little water for 3 minutes. Strain the blanched vegetables, collect the cooking liquid, and use it as the base for the pickling liquid. Transfer the diced vegetables to the canning jars and pour the hot liquid over them.

If freshly shelled peas aren't an option, frozen peas are a good alternative; simply defrost, blanch in hot water, and put immediately into ice water to shock them.

Before pouring the pickling liquid over the vegetables in the jars, taste it—if it seems too bland or not sweet enough, stir in additional sugar.

Pickled Achocha

For 5 canning jars (25 ounces / 750 ml each)

Ingredients

6⅓ cups (1.5 l) water

2 cups (500 ml) distilled white vinegar

Scant ¾ cup (140 g) granulated sugar

3½ tablespoons (60 g) salt

3 bay leaves

6 cloves

10 allspice berries

10 peppercorns

1 onion

1 carrot

About 4½ pounds (2 kg) achocha (also known as caigua, slipper gourds, or stuffing cucumbers)

To make the pickling liquid, mix the water and vinegar in a saucepan. Add the sugar, bay leaves, salt, and spices. Peel the onion and carrot. Cut the onion into eighths, slice the carrot, and add both to the liquid. Bring to a boil over medium heat, stirring occasionally, until the sugar and salt dissolve completely. Let simmer for a few minutes, then remove from the heat. You can either strain the liquid or leave the spices and vegetables in it.

Wash the achocha and arrange them in layers in the sterilized canning jars. Pour over the hot liquid, close the jars, process in a water bath, and let cool. Store in a cool, dark place.

Tips Only the very young achocha fruit (up to 2 inches / 5 cm long) are suitable for pickling, because they will not have yet developed their typical hard, black seeds.

If you prefer a sweeter pickle, simply stir more sugar into the hot liquid before adding it to the jars.

To give your pickled achocha a kick, slice up a piece of horseradish and add it to the pickling liquid with the onion and carrot. For extra flavor, add a garlic clove or small chili pepper.

You can use pickled achocha in a variety of ways, as you would traditional pickles.

Traditional Pickled Cucumbers

For 8–10 canning jars (16 ounces / 500 ml each)

Ingredients

6 ½ pounds (3 kg) pickling cucumbers

3 large carrots

2 onions

8 ½ cups (2 l) water

2 cups (500 ml) distilled white vinegar

1 ⅔ cups (325 g) granulated sugar

¼ cup (75 g) salt

10 peppercorns

10 allspice berries

1 teaspoon mustard seeds

2 bay leaves

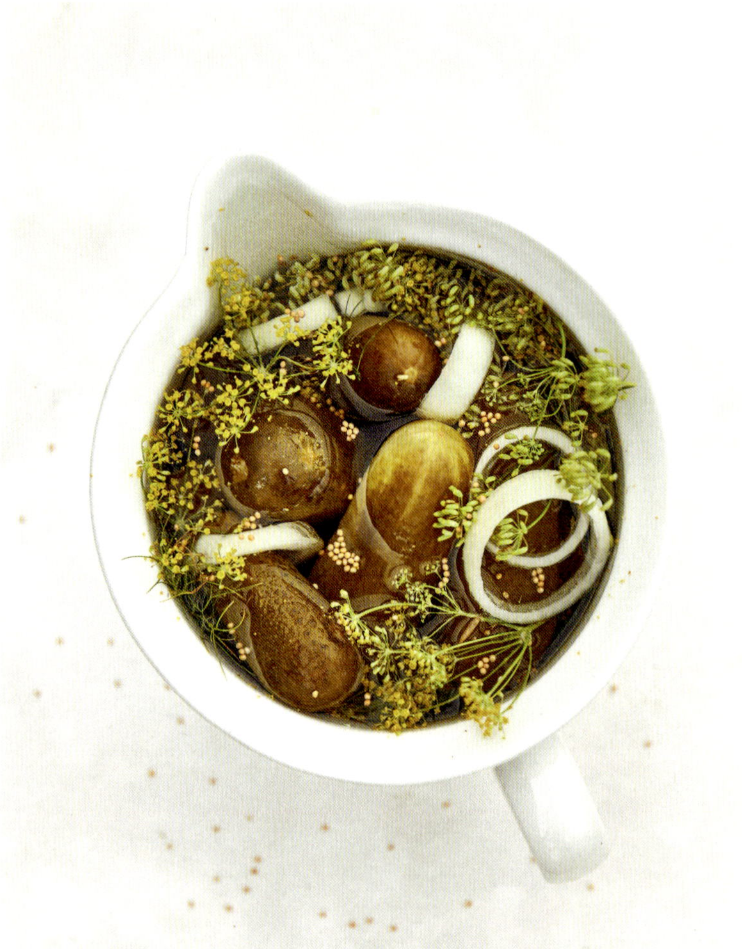

Thoroughly wash the cucumbers, ideally using a vegetable brush under running water in the sink. Spread out the cucumbers on a cloth and pat dry. Peel and slice the carrots and onions into rounds.

To make the pickling liquid, mix the water and vinegar in a saucepan and add the sugar, salt, spices and bay leaves. Bring to a boil over medium heat, stirring occasionally, until the sugar and salt dissolve completely. Let cook for about 5 minutes, then remove from the heat.

Arrange the cucumbers in layers inside sterilized canning jars, leaving as little space as possible between them. Insert the carrot and onion slices between the cucumbers. Finally, pour over the hot liquid until everything is completely covered. Close the jars tightly and process in a water bath. Place the jars upside down, let cool, and store in a cool, dark place. Pickle the cucumbers for at least 2 weeks before use.

Tip For a special hint of flavor, lay a fresh grape (vine) leaf on the bottom of the canning jars before filling. You can also add dill stems and dill flowers or feathery fennel fronds to the jars. Black currant leaves, oak leaves, and horseradish leaves will also add a delicious flavor.

Fermented Cucumbers

For 1 large canning jar (64 ounces / 3–4 l)

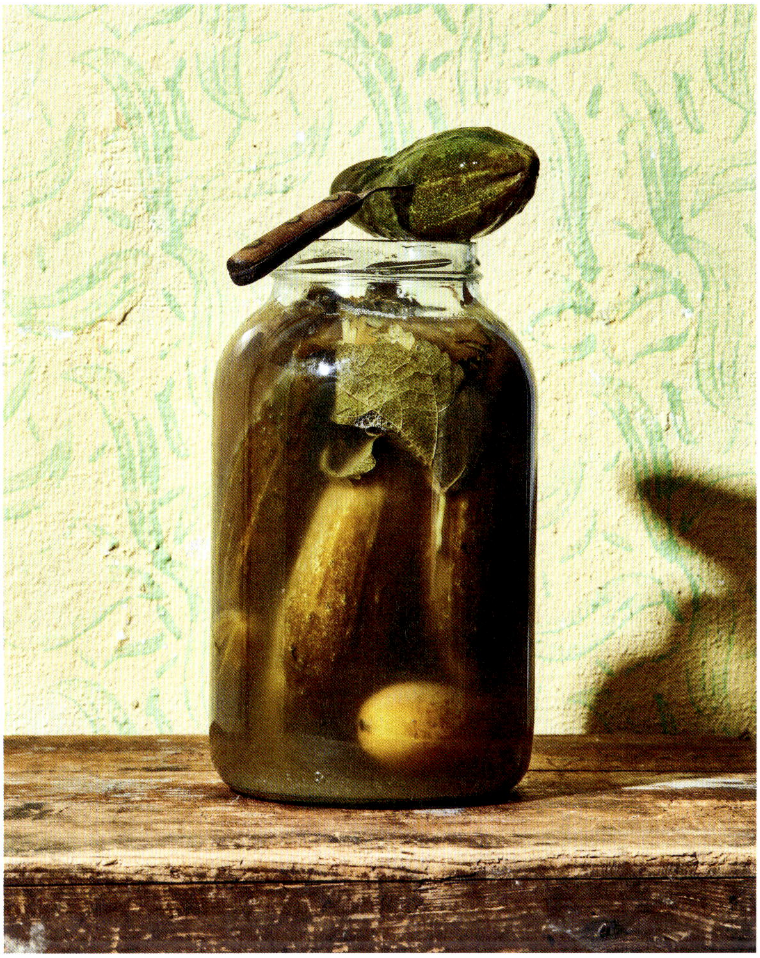

Ingredients

4 ¼ cups (1 l) water

2 tablespoons (40 g) salt

4 ½ pounds (2 kg) large pickling cucumbers

1 (2-inch / 5-cm) piece horseradish root

3 cloves garlic

4 grape (vine) leaves, black currant leaves, or sour cherry leaves

To make the brine, bring the water to a boil in a saucepan and immediately remove it from the heat. Add the salt and stir until completely dissolved. Let cool to lukewarm. Wash the cucumbers thoroughly and pat dry. Prick the larger cucumbers with a fork. Peel and slice the horseradish and garlic. Wash the leaves and lightly crush them to release their aroma.

Arrange the cucumbers in compact layers with the horseradish, garlic, and leaves in a large sterilized canning jar. Pour the lukewarm brine over the cucumbers, leaving a space of at least 2 inches (5 cm) between the liquid and the rim of the jar, because foam may form during the fermentation process. The cucumbers must be completely covered with the brine and not come into contact with air. If necessary, use a sterilized fermentation weight to keep the cucumbers in place.

Place the lid on the jar without tightening it, or cover the opening with a clean cloth and secure it with a rubber band. Stand the jar in a shallow bowl to collect any overflowing liquid during the fermentation process. Let the cucumbers ferment in a warm place for at least 5 days. They are now ready to use, but they will be at their best after 10 to 14 days.

Close the jar tightly and store in a cool, dark place to stop the fermentation process. The best place for this is in the refrigerator or in a cellar. Ideally, eat the fermented cucumber by the end of the winter.

Tips Use overgrown pickling cucumbers for fermenting, but avoid over-fermenting to prevent softness.

Enhance with fresh dill, bay leaves, peppercorns, or allspice.

Skim off any harmless white Kahm yeast with a spoon. If mold appears, discard the entire contents.

Spiced Pickled Cucumber Salad

For 2 canning jars (16 ounces / 450 ml each)

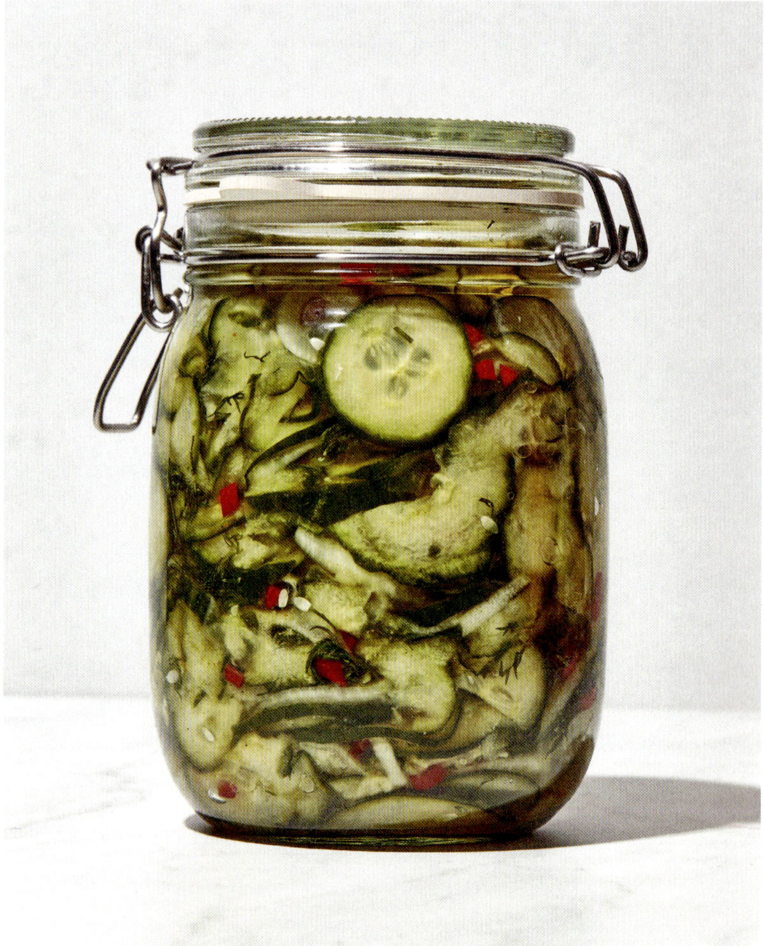

Ingredients

2 to 3 salad cucumbers
1 large onion
1½ teaspoons salt
1¼ cups (300 ml) distilled white vinegar
1 cup (200 g) granulated sugar
½ teaspoon curry powder (see tips)
¼ teaspoon freshly ground pepper
2 sprigs fresh dill
1 (¾-inch/2-cm) piece fresh chili pepper

Wash the cucumbers and pat dry. Peel the onion. Using a knife or mandoline, thinly slice the cucumbers and onion, then put them into a bowl, sprinkle with the salt, mix together, and let stand for at least 1 hour.

To make the pickling liquid, mix the vinegar, sugar, curry powder, and pepper in a saucepan and bring to a boil. Let simmer for a few minutes until the sugar dissolves, then let cool until lukewarm.

Wash the dill, pat dry, and mince (very finely chop). Cut the chili into thin rings. Drain the liquid released by the cucumber and onion slices, lightly squeeze the vegetables, and mix them with the dill and chili. Divide the vegetables among the sterilized canning jars. Leave a space of about ¾ inch (2 cm) between the filling and the rim of the jar. Pour over the lukewarm liquid until the vegetables are completely covered. Close the jars tightly and process in a water bath. Let cool and store in a cool, dark place. Pickle the cucumbers for at least 2 weeks before use.

Tips This recipe can also be used for both slicing and pickling cucumbers that are overly large.

Most European curry powders are based on their Indian counterparts. As a rule, however, they are mild and have very little kick. They usually contain turmeric, coriander seeds, cumin, fenugreek, pepper, ginger, cloves, cardamom, mace, and a pinch of chili powder.

You can use these pickles for any dishes where you would normally use Traditional Pickled Cucumbers (see p. 114). They are a good accompaniment for meatballs, schnitzel, or pan-fried meat, among others.

Zucchini Kraut

For 3 or 4 canning jars (16 ounces / 650 ml each)

Ingredients

4 ½ pounds (2 kg) zucchini (courgettes)

2 tablespoons (25 g) granulated sugar

1 ½ tablespoons (25 g) salt

¼ cup plus 1 teaspoon (65 ml) distilled white vinegar

1 ½ teaspoons crushed caraway seeds

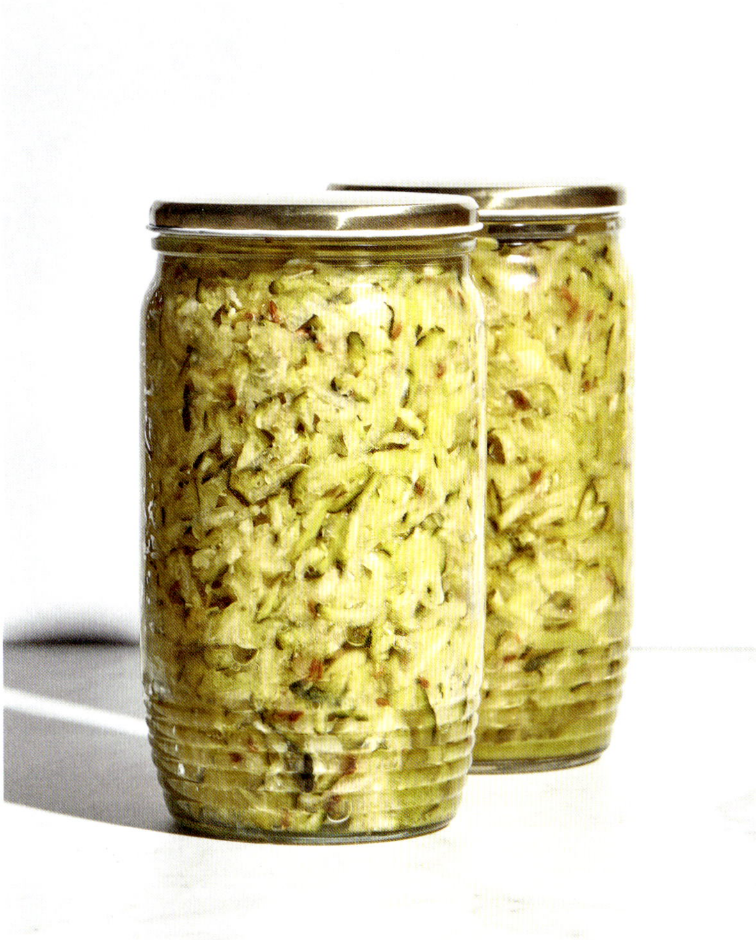

Wash the zucchini and pat dry (leave them unpeeled). Cut the zucchini in half lengthwise, seed, and shred (coarsely grate into a ceramic or glass mixing bowl). Mix the sugar and salt with the vinegar and pour the mixture over the zucchini. Sprinkle with the caraway seeds, mix well, and let stand for 15 to 30 minutes. Adjust the seasoning, adding more sugar or vinegar as required.

Transfer the zucchini to sterilized canning jars, leaving a space of about ¾ inch (2 cm) between the zucchini and the rim of the jar and making sure everything is completely covered in the liquid. Cover the jars tightly, process in a water bath, and store in a cool, dark place. Let mature for about 2 weeks before use.

Tips You can use this zucchini kraut like you would conventional sauerkraut. Drain the liquid. Melt butter or lard in a skillet or frying pan, sauté finely chopped onions, and then add the zucchini kraut and briefly sauté. You can also thicken the mixture with a little flour. Adjust the seasoning with salt, pepper, sugar, vinegar, or caraway seeds, if necessary.

This recipe is perfect for using up oversize ripe zucchini (marrows).

Peach Compote with Rosemary

For 5 to 7 canning jars (16 ounces / 700 ml each)

Ingredients

8 ½ cups (2 l) water

3 cups (600 g) granulated sugar

¼ cup to ⅓ cup (50–100 ml) honey

4 ½ pounds (2 kg) peaches

4 to 8 sprigs of fresh rosemary

Juice of 2 lemons

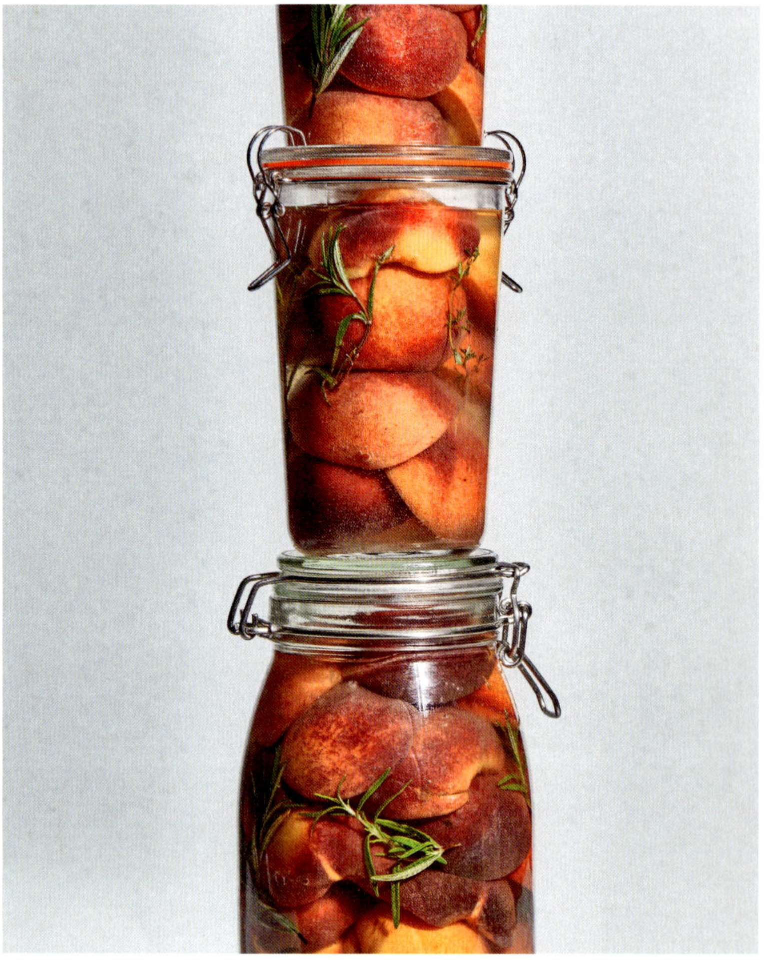

To make the syrup, mix the water and sugar in a pot and bring to a boil. Reduce the heat and let simmer for 5 minutes, stirring regularly, until the sugar dissolves. Remove from the heat and stir the honey into the syrup. Adjust the amount of honey according to the sweetness of the fruit.

Wash the peaches and pat dry, then halve and pit them. Arrange the peach halves, cut side down, in sterilized canning jars. Wash the rosemary and pat dry. Place 1 or 2 sprigs of rosemary in each jar and sprinkle with 1 tablespoon of the lemon juice. Pour the hot syrup over the peaches until completely covered. Close the jars tightly and process in a water bath. Let cool, then store in a cool, dark place.

Tips To make this compote, you should use peaches that are very ripe but still firm. Soft peaches are better for making jam, otherwise they would fall apart in the hot syrup.

You can also add a star anise or cardamom pod to the peaches.

Apricot and Thyme Jam

For 4 canning jars (8 ounces / 200 ml each)

Ingredients

2 ¼ pounds (1 kg) apricots

2 to 2 ½ cups (400–500 g) granulated sugar

Juice of 1 lemon

A few sprigs fresh thyme

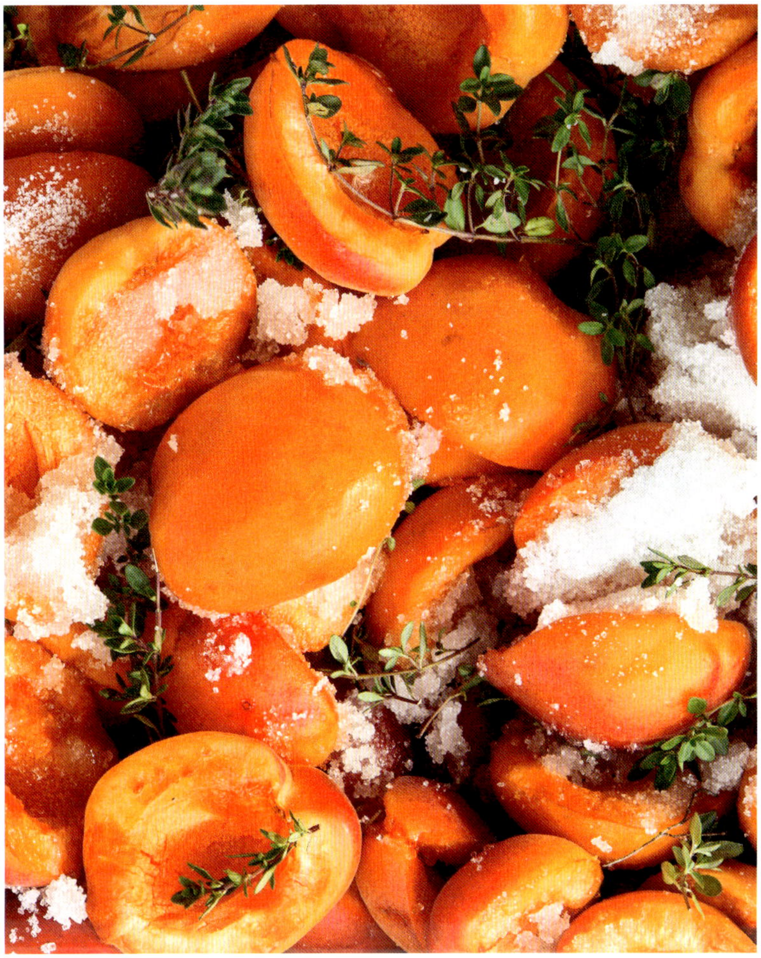

Wash the apricots and pat dry, then pit and cut into quarters. Place the apricot pieces in a ceramic or glass bowl, sprinkle with the sugar and lemon juice, and mix everything together. Let infuse in a cool place for 4 to 6 hours, preferably overnight.

Strain the resulting juice through a strainer or sieve into a pot. Bring to a boil, then lower the heat and reduce the juice by about half until a thick syrup. Wash the thyme. Add about two-thirds of the apricots and thyme sprigs to the syrup and let boil for 5 minutes. When the apricots turn soft and begin to fall apart, add the remaining apricots. (This retains pieces of fruit in the preserves.) Cook until the preserves thicken.

Transfer the hot preserves to small, sterilized canning jars. Close the jars tightly, place upside down, and let cool. Use the preserves immediately or store in the refrigerator and consume within 2 weeks. If you want to store the preserves for longer, process the jars in a water bath after filling.

Tips Adjust the amount of sugar according to the sweetness of the apricots. If you use apricots that aren't completely ripe, the preserves will be slightly tart. However, it will thicken better because sour fruit has a higher pectin content.

If you prefer a jam with smaller pieces of fruit, let the apricots soften a little in the pan, puree with an immersion stick blender, and only then add the thyme. This will make the jam a little runnier, so it will need to be cooked longer to thicken.

If you don't like the idea of thyme leaves in your preserves, put them into a spice bag, so that you can simply remove them when the preserves are ready.

Blending Trends with Traditions

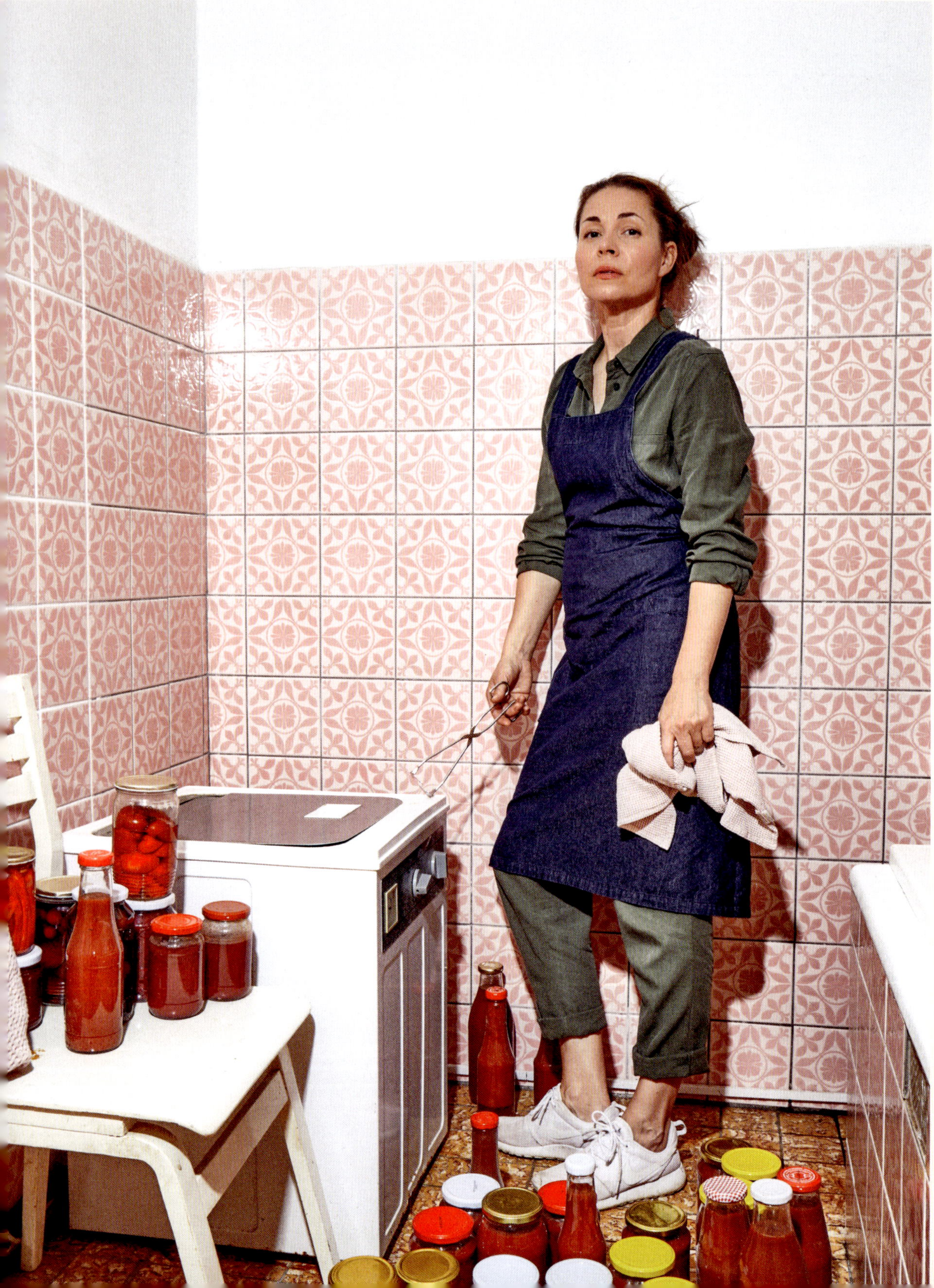

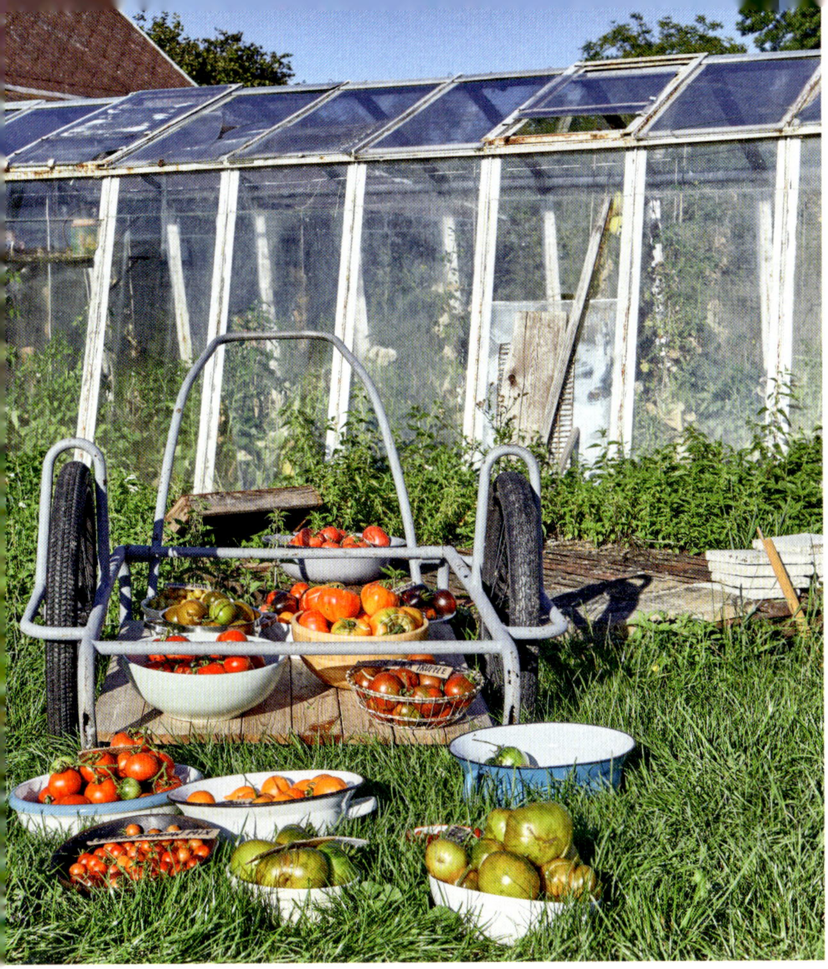

With rare tomato varieties, homemade ketchups, and vibrant garden life, Kateřina Winterová brings the legacy of our ancestors to life with a modern twist.

When you meet Kateřina Winterová, you instantly understand what it means to be a Renaissance woman. With the cult band *Ecstasy of Saint Theresa*, she made a name for herself both abroad and at home. She's been a Prague National Theatre regular for more than twenty years, has starred in movies, has written books about cooking, baking, and gardening, and has supported countless charities. And for more than a decade, TV audiences have known her as the radiant face of *Herbář* (*Herbarium*).

Through that show, Kateřina picked up the torch once carried by the Czech gastronomic revivalists—those who spread awareness about good food, mindful eating, organic farming, and living in harmony with nature. She has helped awaken a national curiosity about what we put on our plates, what we cook, and where those ingredients actually come from. She made it cool, even sexy, to grow your own vegetables and get your hands dirty in the garden, proving it's as meaningful now as it ever was.

One of my first memories of Kateřina goes back to a photo shoot for her book *Herbář ze zahrady přímo na talíř* (*From the Garden Straight to the Plate*). "That's a book I grew entirely in my own garden!" she said with a laugh. She greeted me at her farmhouse with no makeup, in rain boots (wellies), and glowing with good energy. Within minutes she'd made breakfast for the team, fed the cats, dashed out to the field for a handful of ripe tomatoes and herbs, then disappeared into the pantry for a jar of pickles. While the photographer clicked away, she told stories about the last pumpkin harvest, shared culinary discoveries from her travels across Europe, and quoted odd little gems from antique cookbooks she'd tracked down in antiquarian bookstores. That day, it was clear: the recipes, the stories, the tips she shares with her readers and TV audience aren't just for show—this is how she lives.

Kateřina keeps up with the latest in gastronomy, yet her kitchen, garden, and fields are rooted in time-honored traditions. She draws on the wisdom of generations, bringing age-old methods into the modern kitchen and adapting them with care for today's cooks. And returning to her roots, she spends every season canning, preserving "sweet things" from the past—alongside the favorites her family devours year after year.

Her real specialty, however, is ketchup, made from tomatoes she's raised, from seed. Her garden beds are a kind of open-air laboratory where she plants rare and heirloom varieties, many long forgotten. In summer, she watches the plants sway, the fruit ripen in unexpected colors and shapes—and, of course, she tastes them all. "Ketchup is a welcome rescue in the sea of tomatoes," she smiles.

She shows me her favorite: a spiced one with fruit (see p. 125). "The first recipe for tomato ketchup didn't appear until around 1812," she explains. "Before that, people thought tomatoes were poisonous. The original Chinese version was made from fermented oysters, soybeans, and meat—the liquid left from fermentation was called *ketchup*. My own recipe is inspired by Victorian versions that used fruit and spices. Sugar was already available back then, but very expensive, so people often used fruit for sweetness. When you bake the tomatoes with the other ingredients, they caramelize wonderfully, the excess liquid cooks off, and then you just blend and preserve."

Her advice as she turns back toward her garden: "Discover and grow native varieties. The more types of tomatoes you harvest the more types of ketchup you can make!"

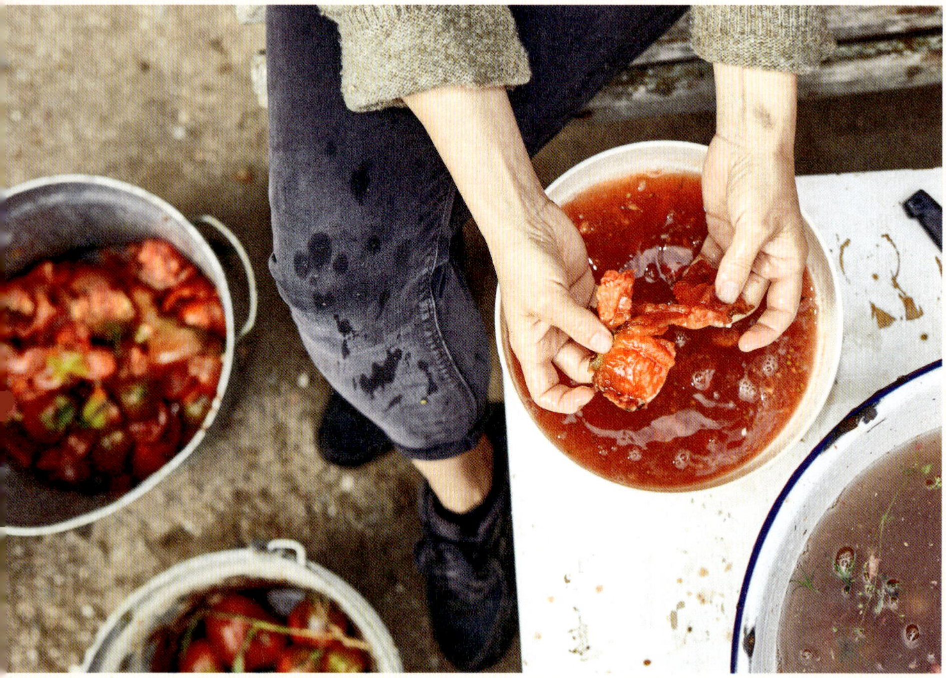

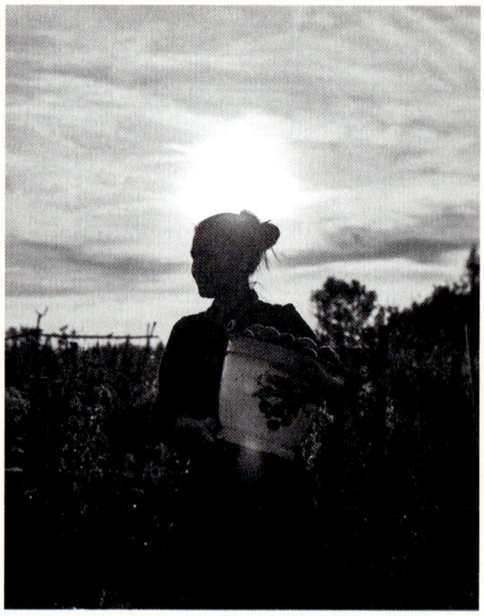

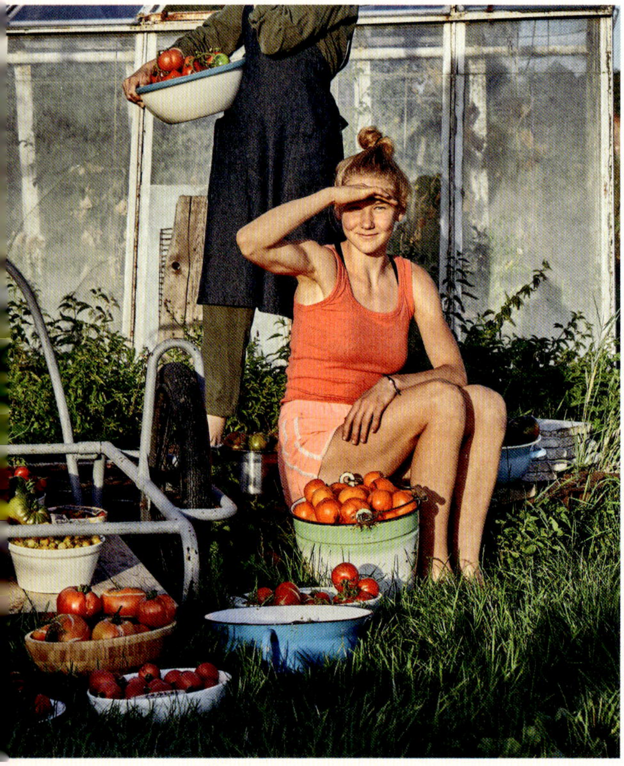

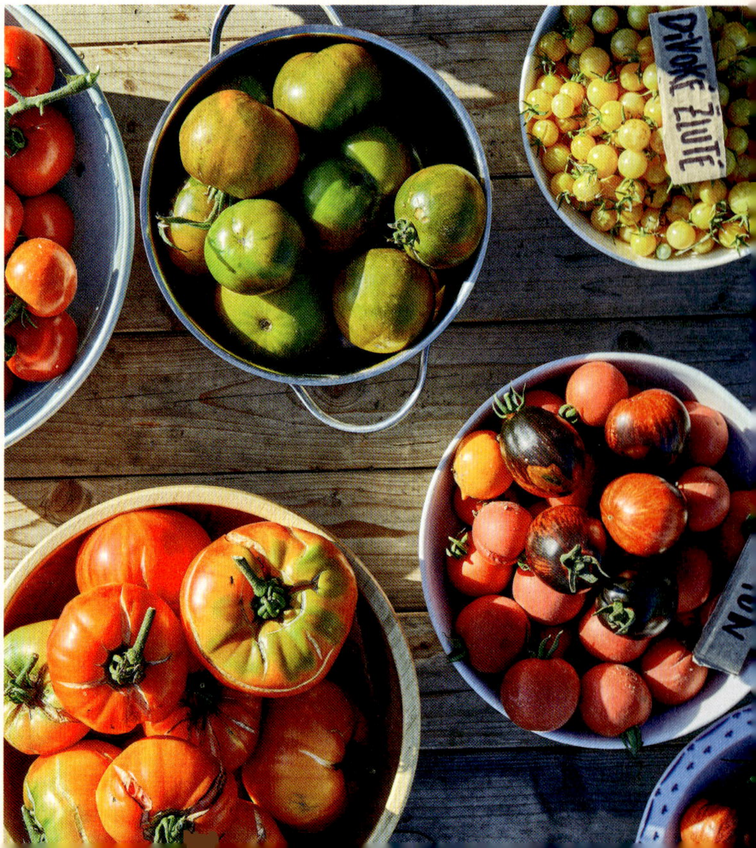
DIVOKÉ ŽLUTÉ

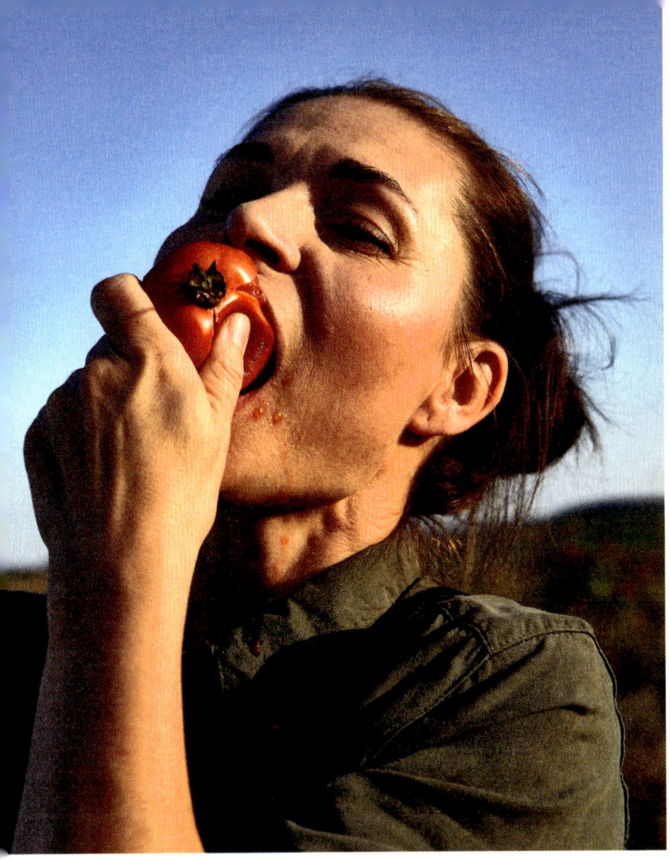

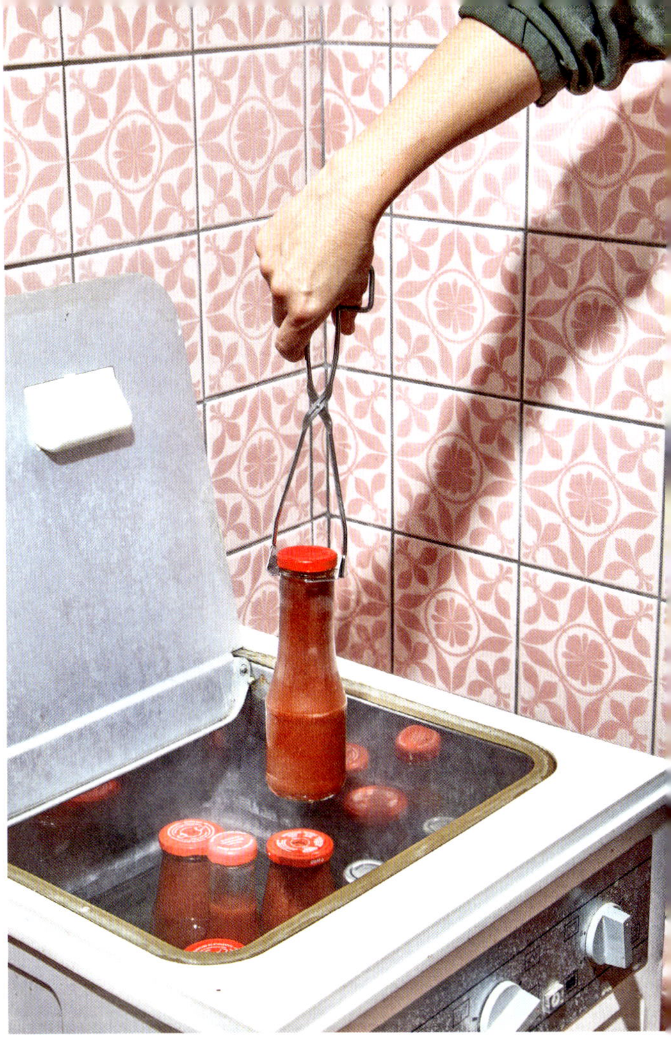

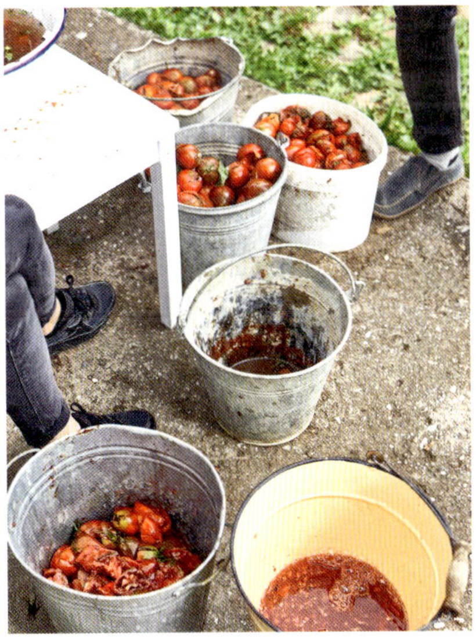

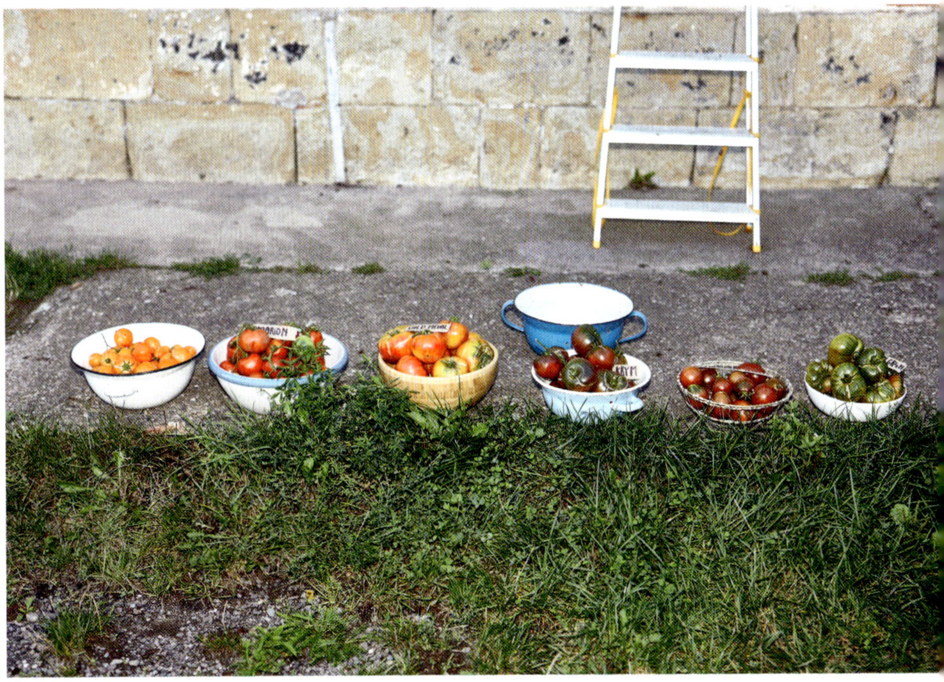

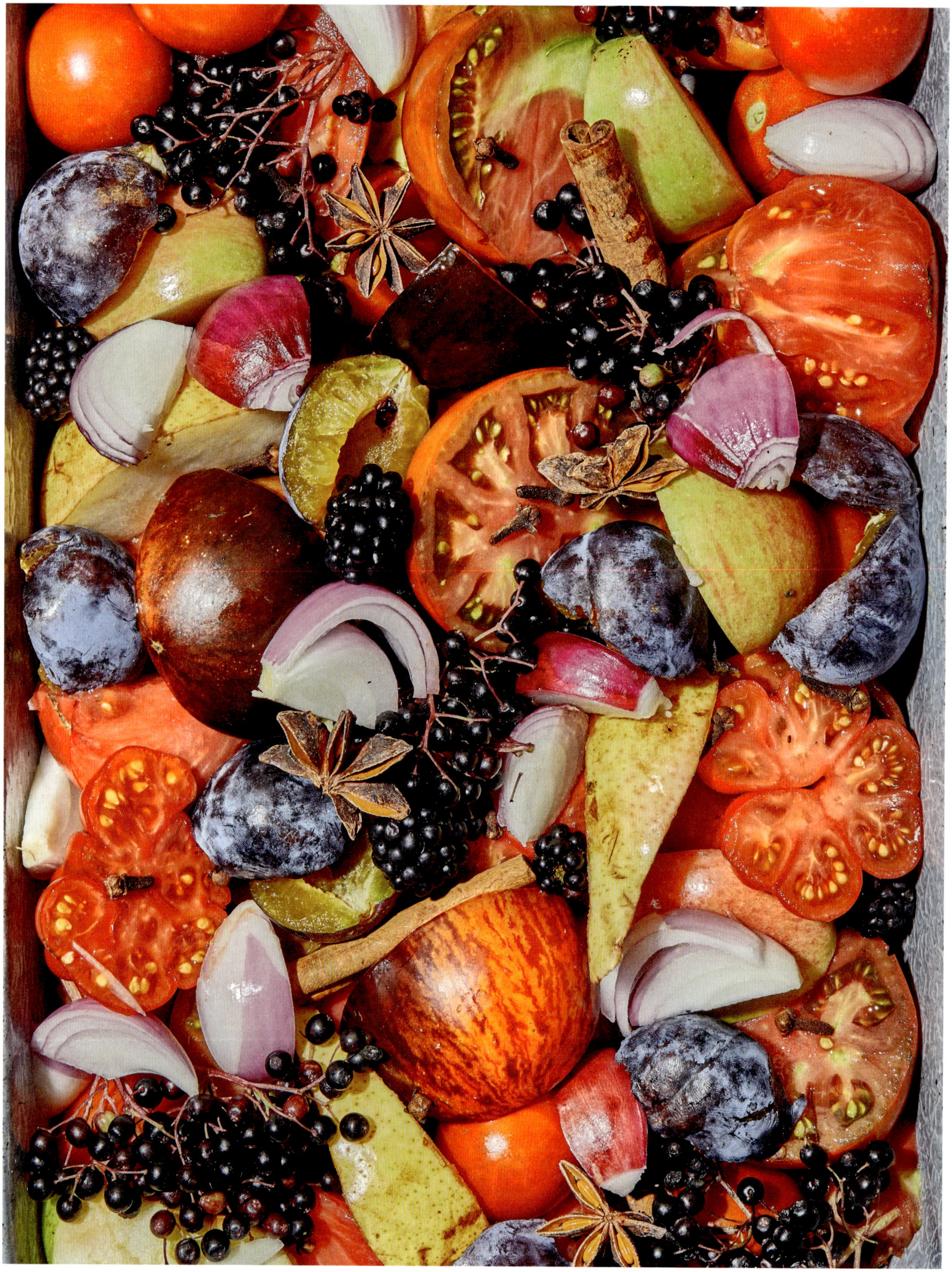

Spiced Fruit Ketchup

For 8 canning jars (8 ounces / 250 ml each)

Ingredients

8 ¾ pounds (4 kg) tomatoes
2 apples
3 pears
10 ½ ounces (300 g) plums
6 large onions
1 handful of blackberries
2 elderberry blossoms
¾ cup (150 g) granulated sugar
2 tablespoons sweet paprika
4 cinnamon sticks
½ teaspoon freshly grated nutmeg
1 pinch chili powder
4 star anise
1 teaspoon allspice berries
1 teaspoon cloves
4 teaspoons salt
1 cup (250 ml) apple cider vinegar

Preheat the oven to 350 °F top / bottom heat (180 °C / Gas Mark 4).

Wash the tomatoes and fruit, then pat dry. Cut the tomatoes into chunks. Core the apples and pears, pit the plums, and cut them into chunks. Peel and coarsely chop the onions. Put them all into a roasting pan along with the blackberries and eldberry sprigs.

Sprinkle the contents of the pan with the sugar, add the spices and salt, and pour over the vinegar. Cook in the preheated oven for 30 to 45 minutes (depending on the size and ripeness of the tomatoes and fruit) until soft.

Take the pan out of the oven and discard the cinnamon sticks, star anise, allspice berries, and cloves. Puree the vegetable and fruit mixture with an immersion stick blender until smooth, and adjust the seasoning as needed. Transfer the hot ketchup to sterilized canning jars and close the lids tightly, then place upside down and let cool. Use the ketchup immediately or store in a cool, dark place.

Tip If your fruit isn't sweet enough, simply add more sugar. If you prefer a tangier ketchup, add more vinegar.

Tomato Ketchup

For 4 canning jars (8 ounces / 250 ml each)

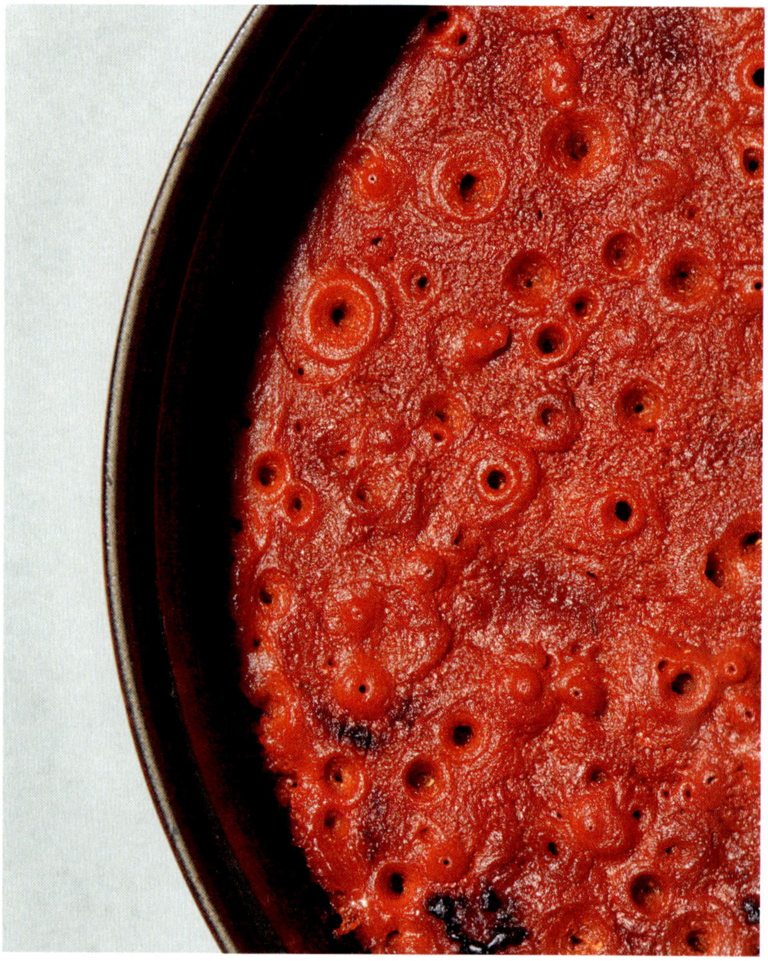

Ingredients

4 ½ pounds (2 kg) tomatoes
3 onions
2 apples
⅓ cup (80 ml) distilled white vinegar
3 ½ tablespoons (50 ml) water
3 bay leaves
4 cloves
1 tablespoon sweet paprika
½ teaspoon ground allspice (mixed spice)
½ teaspoon ground cinnamon
¼ teaspoon freshly ground pepper
1 tablespoon salt
⅓ to ½ cup (80–100 g) cane sugar

Wash the tomatoes, pat dry, and cut them into small pieces. Peel and mince (very finely chop) the onions. Peel, core, and coarsely grate the apples. Place the tomatoes, onions, and apples in a skillet or frying pan. Add the vinegar and water, then the bay leaves, spices, and salt. Mix it all together.

Put the pan over medium heat and cook the mixture, uncovered, for about 1 hour. Stir regularly to keep the mixture from burning. Remove the bay leaves and cloves. Transfer the mixture to a blender, puree until very smooth, then filter through a strainer or sieve back into the pan. Place the pan over low heat, stir in most of the sugar, and let the ketchup simmer for 15 minutes. Adjust the seasoning and sweeten with the remaining sugar, if necessary. Continue to cook for about 30 minutes, until the ketchup thickens (depending on how juicy the tomatoes are and the size of the pan), stirring occasionally.

Transfer the hot ketchup to sterilized canning jars, close the lids tightly, and place upside down. Let cool, then store in a cool, dark place.

Tips Using a cast iron skillet is recommended when making this ketchup, because the heat will be evenly distributed and the material retains heat well.

This recipe is suited to very ripe, and even overripe, tomatoes, because they provide more flavor. However, discard any rotten tomatoes.

You can experiment with this recipe as you please with different ingredients or spices. For example, you can omit the apple or onion, or you can add tomato paste (puree) or mustard for a more intense flavor. However, vinegar, sugar, and salt are essentials, because they act as natural preservatives. You can also season your ketchup with a little ground ginger, chili powder, or freshly grated nutmeg.

Semi-dried Cherry Tomatoes

For 3 canning jars (8 ounces / 250 ml each)

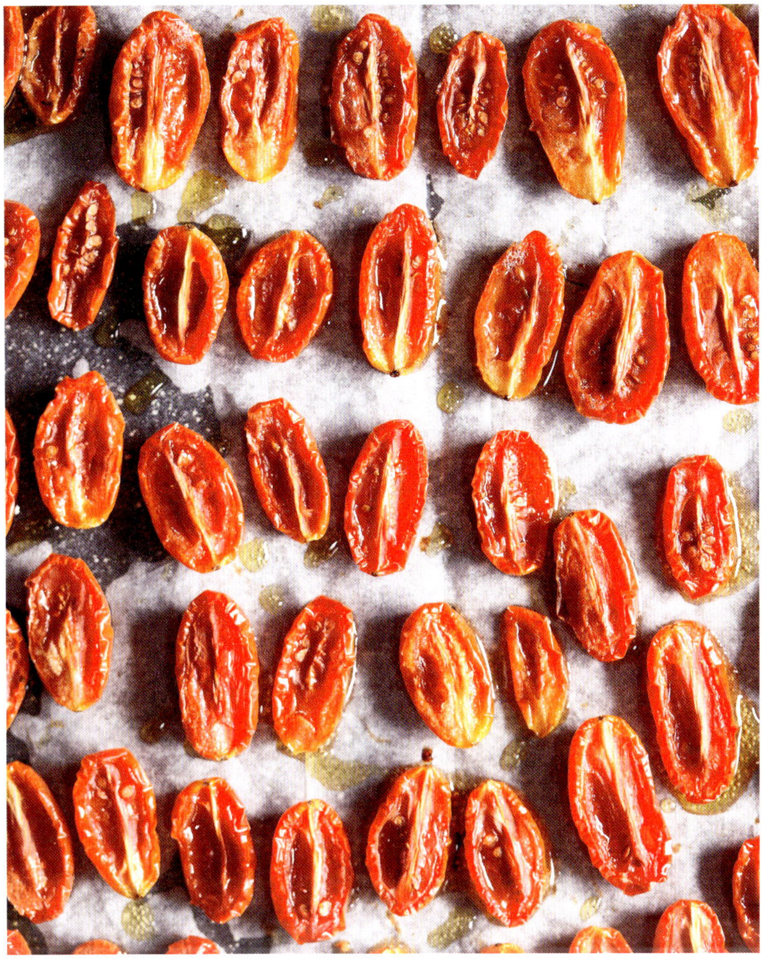

Ingredients

2 ¼ pounds (1 kg) cherry tomatoes (about 7 cups)

3 cups (750 ml) olive oil

2 pinches of salt

3 cloves garlic

3 sprigs of fresh thyme

3 sprigs of fresh oregano

Preheat a convection (fan-assisted) oven to 195 °F (90 °C) and line a baking sheet with parchment (baking) paper.

Wash the tomatoes thoroughly, pat dry, and halve. Place them, cut side facing up, on the baking sheet, drizzle with a little olive oil, and season with the salt.

Partly dry the tomatoes in the oven for 2 to 3 hours (depending on their variety and size). Check the tomatoes regularly. Prop the oven door open with a wooden spoon or open the oven door regularly to vent steam.

Take the tomatoes out of the oven and let cool. Warm the oil in a saucepan. Peel and slice the garlic. Wash the herbs and shake dry. Transfer the semi-dried tomatoes to small sterilized canning jars. Insert the garlic slices and small sprigs of the herbs between the tomatoes. Pour the warm oil over the tomatoes until they are completely covered. Finally, close the jars tightly and let cool. Store the semi-dried cherry tomatoes in a cool, dark place.

Tips You should use ripe but still firm tomatoes for this recipe. Tomatoes containing a great deal of water are unsuitable. If you don't have fresh herbs, dried ones will work just as well.

You can speed up the drying process by preheating the convection (fan-assisted) oven to 250 °F (120 °C). Check the tomatoes more often to keep them from burning.

Semi-dried cherry tomatoes are delicious on their own or on toast with cheese and basil. They are also great in salads, pasta and couscous dishes, and vegetable casseroles.

Bold Flavors, Fearless in the Kitchen

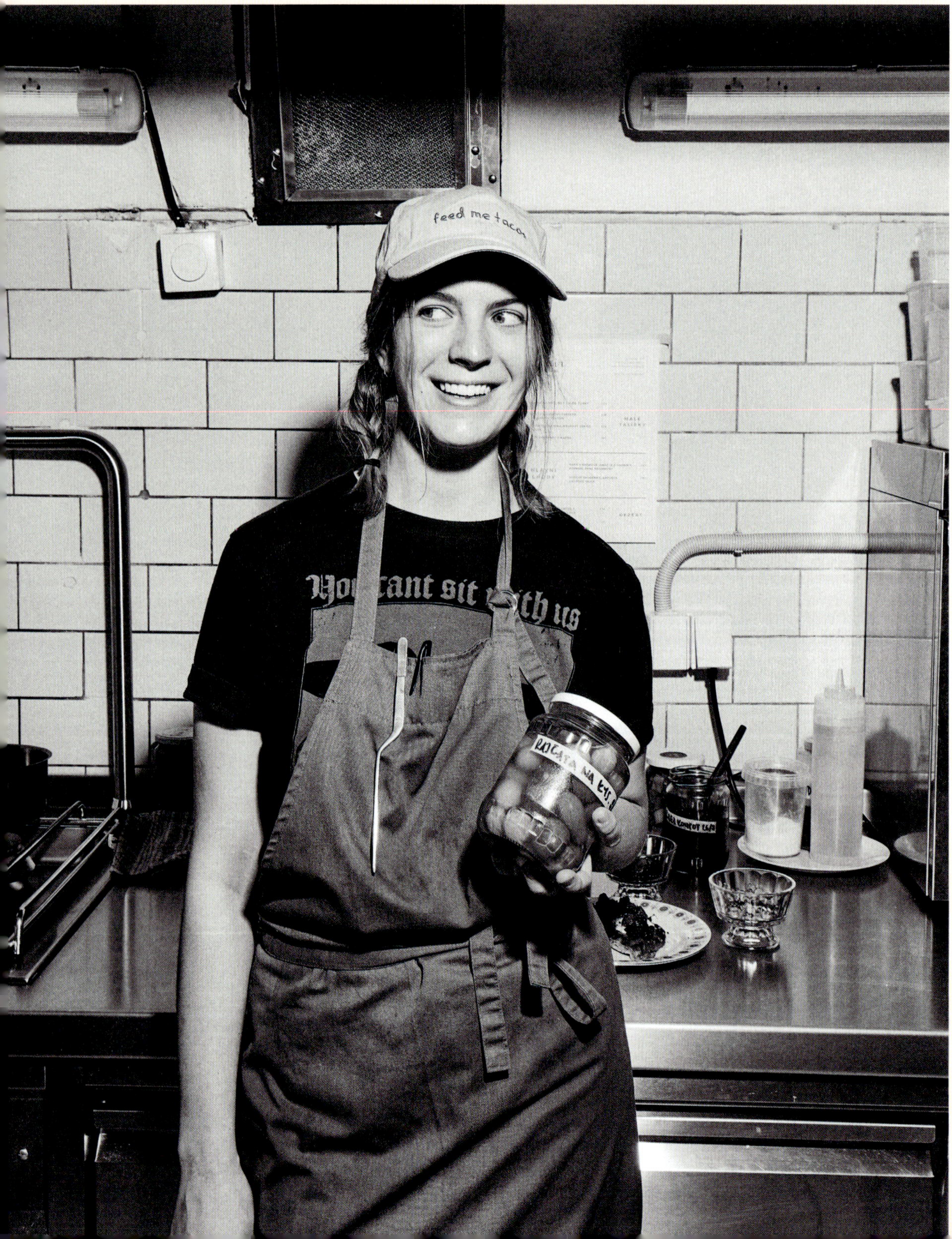

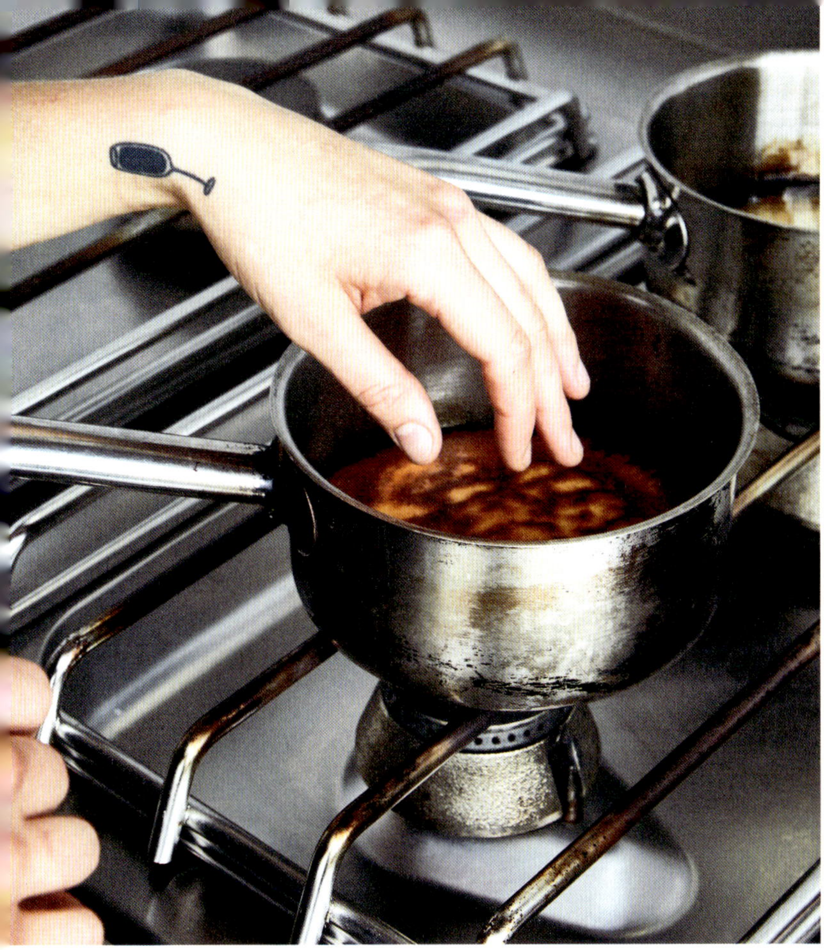

Though never formally trained in cooking, Anna Vejvodová helped restore the fame of Czech carp and creates daring preserves that push the boundaries.

She never went to culinary school, but when Prague's celebrated restaurant Eska put out a call for new kitchen talent, Anna Vejvodová raised her hand. She started out at the breakfast station—not with formal training but just instinct and curiosity—and within months she'd worked her way up to cook.

Then came the COVID-19 pandemic, and with it, a call from Jan Čulík of Thir in Tábor. He asked if she'd join him in reimagining his popular South Bohemian restaurant. Anna packed her bags, moved south, and together they set out on a mission few would have dared: to restore the reputation of Czech carp.

And that's exactly what they did. The press soon spoke of a "carp renaissance" while diners traveled from all over the country to taste her inventive fish dishes paired with natural wines.

"Carp is a wonderful fish, it's got excellent, high-quality flesh," Anna says. "But it's been unfairly maligned. It hasn't tasted muddy or bland for years. You just have to know how to handle it," she laughs. "Yes, it's trickier to fillet and full of bones, but with a little patience you get the hang of it. And you have to break free from the traditional deep-fried breaded version. Be bold! Have you ever tried smoked carp? Pair it with green tomato *čalamáda*, a sweet-and-sour Czech pickle—it's fantastic." She's right. It really is.

Anna may no longer be cooking carp in Tábor since she's flown as far as Montreal, Canada, to sharpen her skills, but her South Bohemian chapter still inspires. Why not give carp another chance? Or at least try her *čalamáda* recipe (see p. 132), which is a perfect way to use up those garden tomatoes that never ripened. And if that's not your thing, there's always the Elderberry Compote (see p. 131)—another one of her unassuming masterpieces.

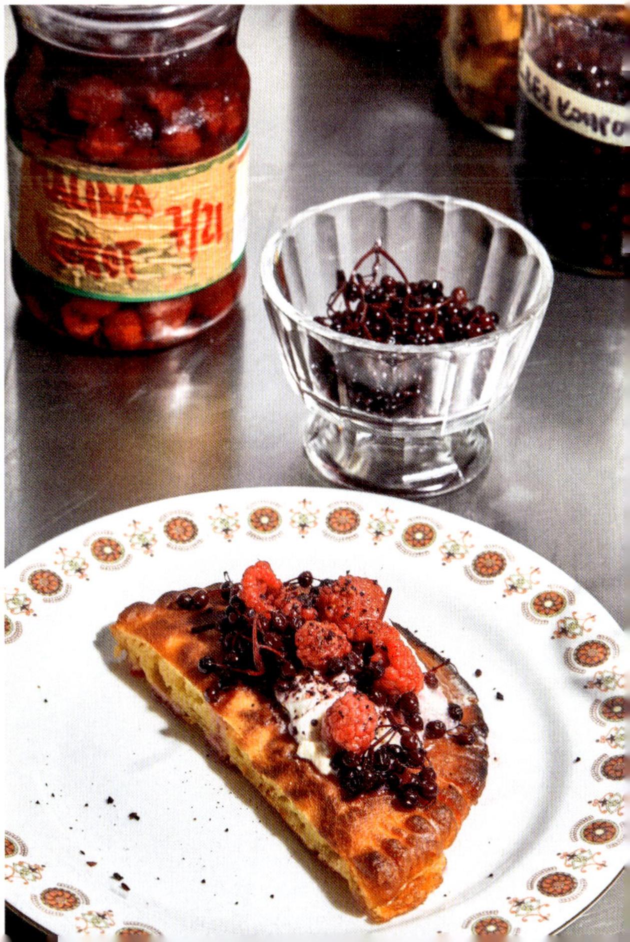

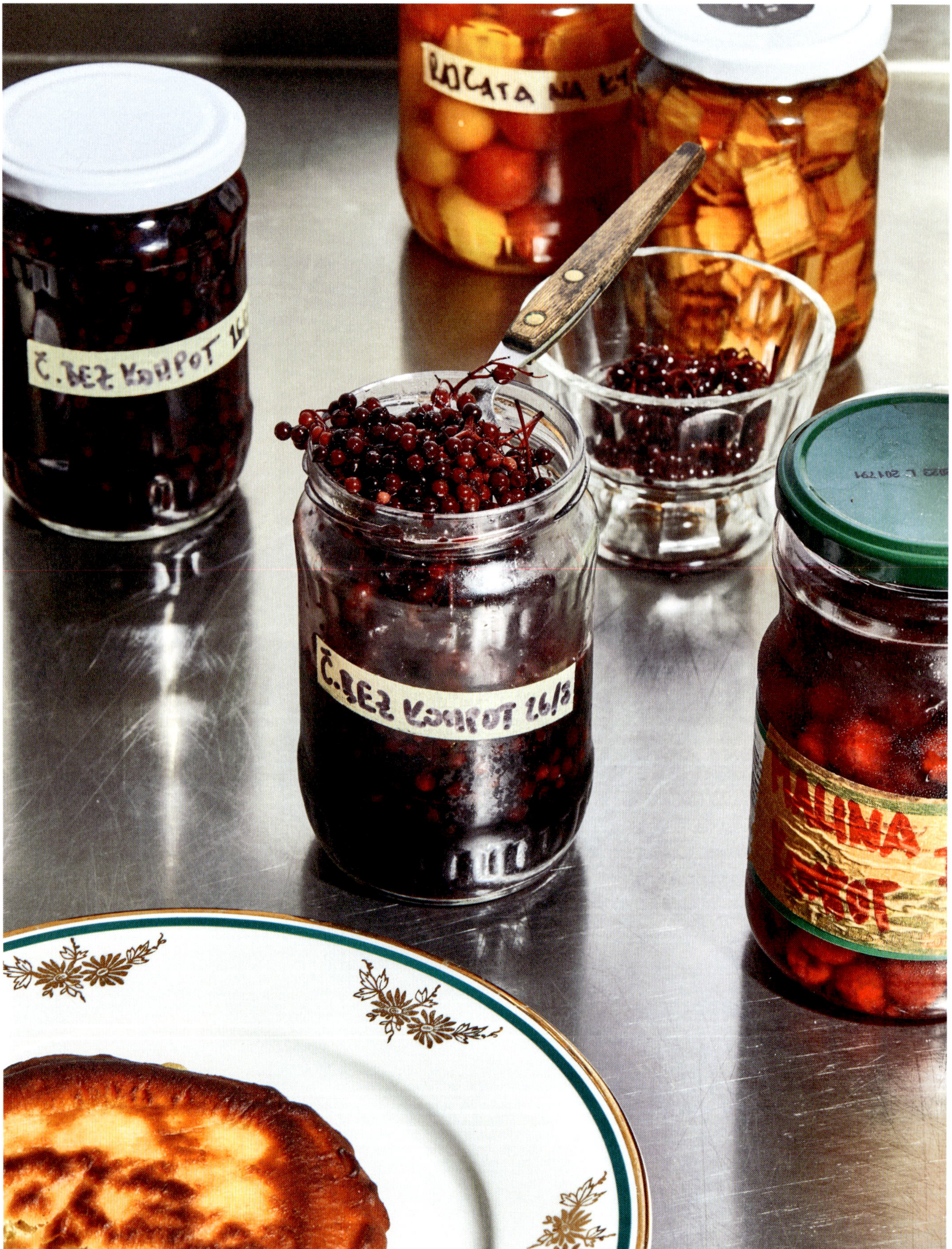
Č.BEZ KOMPOT 26/8

Elderberry Compote

For 5 or 6 canning jars (16 ounces / 350 ml each)

Ingredients

3 ¼ pounds (1.5 kg) ripe elderberries

2 cups (500 ml) water

¾ cup (150 g) granulated sugar

Juice of 1 lemon

Rinse the elderberries under cold running water and drain on a clean cloth.

To make the syrup, put the water and sugar into a saucepan and bring to a boil, stirring regularly, until the sugar dissolves completely. Let cool. Filter the lemon juice through a fine-mesh strainer or sieve into the cooled syrup and mix well.

Transfer the elderberries to sterilized canning jars, leaving a space of about ½ inch (1 cm) between the berries and the rim of the jar. Pour the syrup over the elderberries. Wipe the jars with a clean cloth, close the jars tightly, and process in a water bath. Let the compote cool, then store in a cool, dark place.

Tips You can leave the stems on the elderberries. If you prefer not to have any stems in your compote, strip the berries off them with a fork. Be careful not to crush them.

Raw elderberries are slightly poisonous in large quantities and can cause diarrhea. They must therefore be heated through before they can be eaten. The best way to do this is to process them in a water bath as a compote—definitely don't skip the water bath canning step!

Green Tomato Čalamáda

For 4 canning jars (8 ounces / 250 ml each)

Ingredients

4 ½ pounds (2 kg) unripe green tomatoes

2 ¼ pounds (1 kg) onions

1 cup (250 ml) water

Scant ½ cup (135 g) salt,
plus 1 pinch for the pickling liquid

2 cups (500 ml) apple cider vinegar

Scant ½ cup (100 g) whole-grain mustard

1 cup (200 g) cane sugar

10 peppercorns

10 allspice berries

3 bay leaves

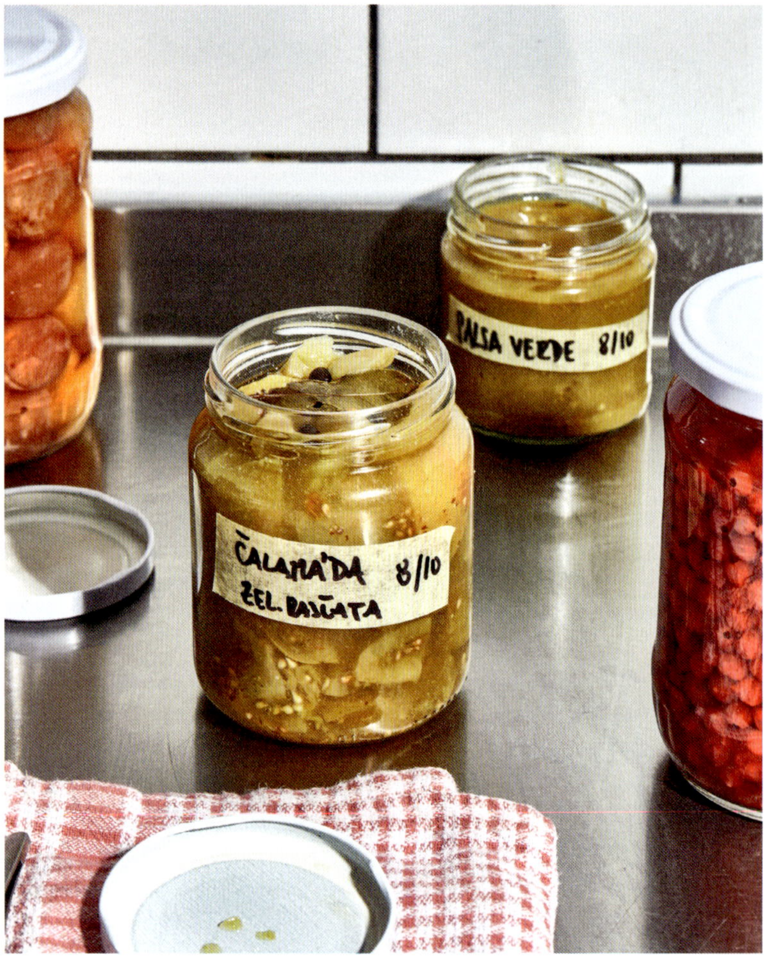

Wash the tomatoes, pat dry, and cut them into small pieces. Peel and cut the onions into thin wedges. Mix the tomatoes with the onions in a pot.

Make a brine by mixing the water with the salt and stirring until the salt dissolves. Pour the liquid over the tomato and onion mixture and cover the pot with a lid. Let stand overnight in a cool place.

The next day, bring the tomato and onion mixture to a boil for 2 minutes, then drain in a strainer or sieve and collect the liquid. Set aside the tomatoes and onions in a container.

To make the pickling liquid, mix the vinegar with the liquid collected from the tomato and onion mixture. Add the mustard, sugar, spices, and bay leaves, and season with a little salt, if necessary (carefully, because the tomatoes already contain salt from the previous day). Bring the pickling liquid to a boil, stirring continuously, then remove from the heat and let cool.

Pour the pickling liquid over the tomatoes and onions, mix well, and transfer to sterilized canning jars. Close the jars tightly, process in a water bath, then let cool.

Tips Green tomato relish is a good accompaniment for smoked or grilled dishes, and it is great on toast and in wraps.

This recipe is a wonderful way to use up any tomatoes in your garden that won't ripen properly in late summer.

Follow all of the recipe steps; to ensure the green tomatoes are safe to eat, they must be boiled, pickled in a sufficient amount of vinegar, and processed in a hot water bath.

Chili Oil

For 1 large canning jar (25 ounces / 750 ml)

Ingredients

7 ounces (200 g) chili peppers

1 sprig of fresh thyme

1 sprig of fresh rosemary

1½ tablespoons (25 g) salt

Scant ½ cup (100 ml) white wine vinegar

2 cups (500 ml) olive oil

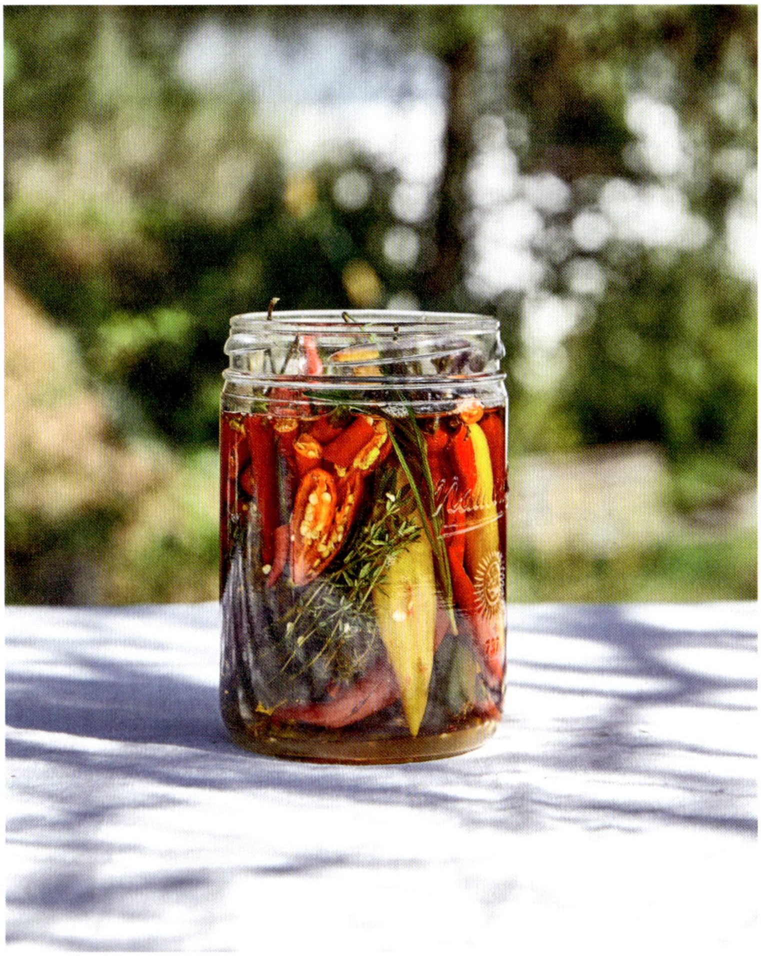

Wash the chili peppers and herbs and pat dry. Cut the chilies into rings or long strips. For less intense heat, remove the seeds. Place the chilies in a glass or ceramic bowl. Sprinkle with the salt, mix well, and let stand for at least 2 hours. Drain the chilies and return them to the bowl. Add the vinegar and let infuse for at least 30 minutes. Drain off the liquid.

Arrange the chilies and herb sprigs in a sterilized canning jar with a wide opening. Pour over the oil until the chilies are completely covered, then close the jar tightly. Let the chilies infuse in the oil in a cool, dark place for about 1 month before use.

Tips Choose the type and amount of chili peppers according to your taste and tolerance for heat. You can also use dried chili.

You should wear disposable gloves when preparing chilies, because contact with large amounts of them can lead to allergic reactions and skin irritation. More important, make sure you do not touch your eyes or face with your hands!

This chili oil goes well with pasta dishes, many Asian dishes, and Turkish poached eggs. You can also use it in different dips and barbecue marinades, and on pizza.

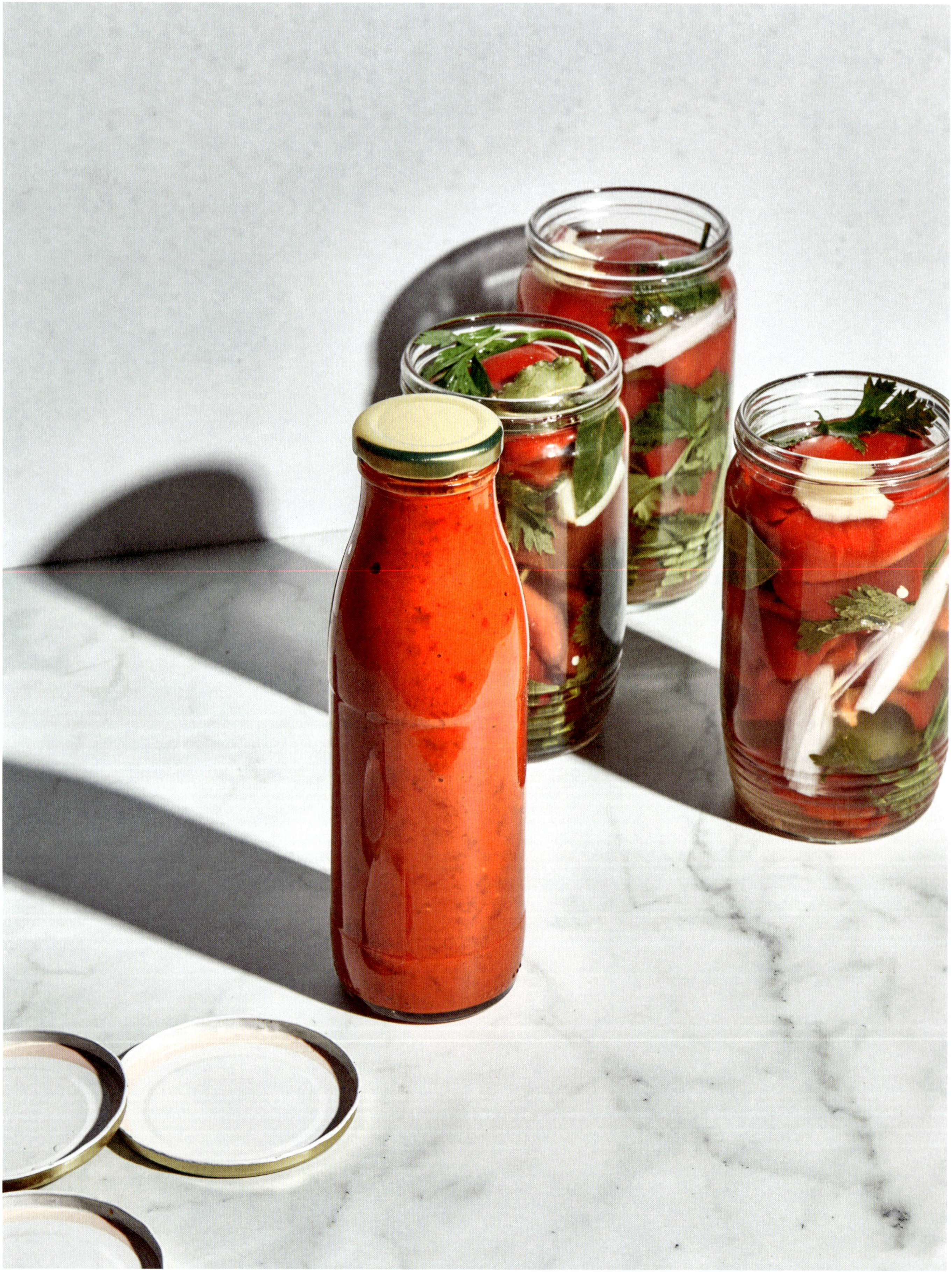

Fermented Bell Pepper Sauce

For 3 canning bottles (25 ounces / 750 ml each)

Ingredients

4 ¼ cups (1 l) water

1 tablespoon (20 g) salt

6 red or orange bell peppers

1 onion

3 to 5 cloves garlic

3 sprigs of fresh parsley or lovage

3 to 6 bay leaves (optional)

To make the brine, put the water into a saucepan, bring to a boil, and let cool completely. Add the salt and stir until completely dissolved. Halve the bell peppers lengthwise, remove the white ribs and seeds, and wash. Cut the halves into chunks. Peel the onion and garlic. Cut the onion into wedges and halve the garlic cloves.

Place the bell pepper pieces in sterilized canning jars. Add 1 parsley sprig, a few onion and garlic pieces, and 1 bay leaf, if desired, to each jar. Leave a space of at least 1 ¼ inches (3 cm) between the contents of the jar and the rim. Pour the brine over the vegetables. The bell pepper pieces should be completely covered to prevent contact with the air. If necessary, use a sterilized fermentation weight to keep them in place. Leave some space between the brine and the rim of the jar to allow room for the formation of foam on the surface of the liquid.

Close the jars with their lids but without tightening. Place them on a tray or baking sheet and let ferment at room temperature (preferably at 65 to 70 °F / 18–21 °C) in a dark place for 5 to 7 days. The exact fermentation time will vary depending on the temperature of the room (a warmer temperature speeds up the fermentation process). Check and taste the contents of the jars regularly (always use an impeccably clean fork). The bell peppers will be ready when no more bubbles form or the foam dissipates. They should now have a pleasantly sour and mildly spicy taste.

Drain the contents of the jars through a strainer or sieve and collect the liquid. Discard any bay leaves. Puree the vegetables and herbs until thick and creamy. Dilute the sauce with the collected liquid, if necessary. Fill sterilized bottles with the bell pepper sauce and use immediately or store in the refrigerator.

Tips You can modify this recipe to suit your taste, for example, by using different types of bell peppers, replacing some of the peppers with tomatoes, or adding other herbs and spices.

You can also use this recipe to make your own hot sauce. Just replace the bell peppers with chili peppers.

This sauce has a flavor that is reminiscent of the red pepper condiment known as *ajvar,* which means you can use it in a similar way: as a sauce for grilled meat and kebabs, burgers or sandwiches, as a dip for different vegetable side dishes, as an accompaniment for bulgur and couscous, or spread on toast.

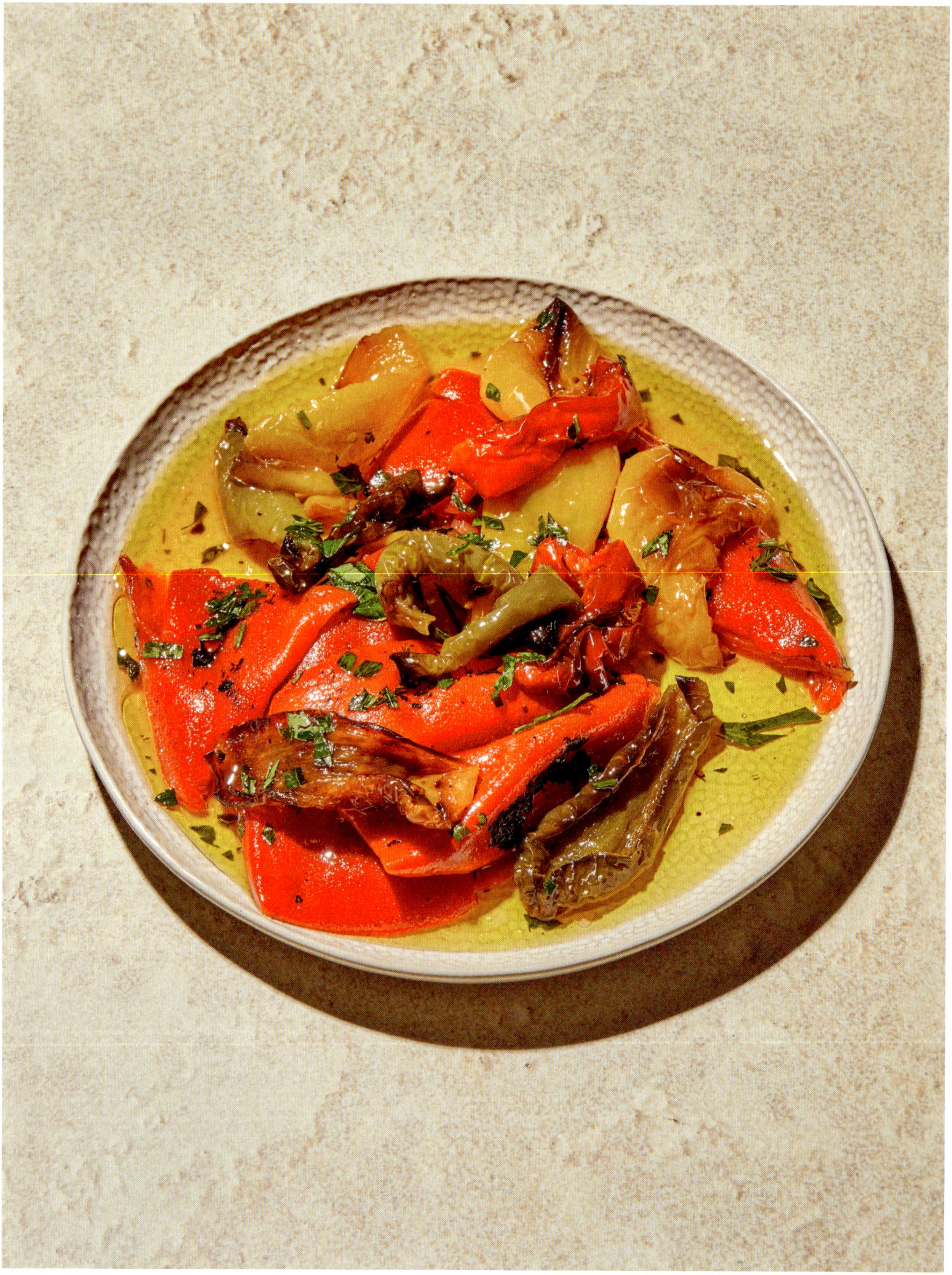

Roasted Peppers in Oil

For 2 canning jars (8 ounces / 250 ml each)

Ingredients

2 ¼ pounds (1 kg) bell peppers

1 ¼ cups (300 ml) olive oil

½ teaspoon salt

4 tablespoon white wine vinegar

4 cloves garlic

2 sprigs of fresh thyme

2 sprigs of fresh rosemary

1 teaspoon peppercorns

Preheat the oven to 425 °F top / bottom heat (220 °C / Gas Mark 7) and then switch to the broiler (grill) setting. Line a baking sheet with parchment (baking) paper. Halve the bell peppers lengthwise, remove the white ribs and seeds, and wash. Arrange the bell pepper halves on the baking sheet and drizzle with a little oil. Roast the bell peppers in the oven for about 20 minutes, until large black blisters form on their surface.

Transfer the roasted peppers to a bowl along with the juices released. Cover with a plate and let stand for 15 minutes—this will steam the peppers, making them easier to peel. Peel the bell pepper halves and discard the charred skin. It doesn't matter if not all the skin comes off. Cut the bell pepper halves into smaller pieces or strips and return them to the bowl.

Gently heat the remaining oil in a pan; it should not exceed a temperature of 175 °F (80 °C). Season the bell peppers with salt and mix with 3 tablespoons of the vinegar. Pour the remaining vinegar into two small sterilized canning jars. Peel and thinly slice the garlic. Wash the herbs and shake dry. Add ½ teaspoon of the peppercorns, 2 sliced garlic cloves, 1 thyme sprig, and 1 rosemary sprig to each jar. Arrange the bell pepper pieces in layers inside the jars. Leave a space of about 1 ¼ inches (3 cm) between the bell peppers and the rim of the jar. Gently tap the open jars on the work surface to remove any air pockets. Finally, pour the oil over the bell peppers until completely covered and close the jars tightly. Marinate the bell peppers in the oil for at least 2 weeks before use.

Tips Fleshy bell peppers are the most suitable for this recipe. For added kick, add some crushed red pepper (chili) flakes to the jars.

These preserved bell peppers make an excellent accompaniment for broiled (grilled) meat. They also taste wonderful in sandwiches and spreads. Combined with oven-roasted tomatoes and ricotta cheese, they can quickly be turned into a delicious pasta sauce.

Just Like Your Beloved Grandmother

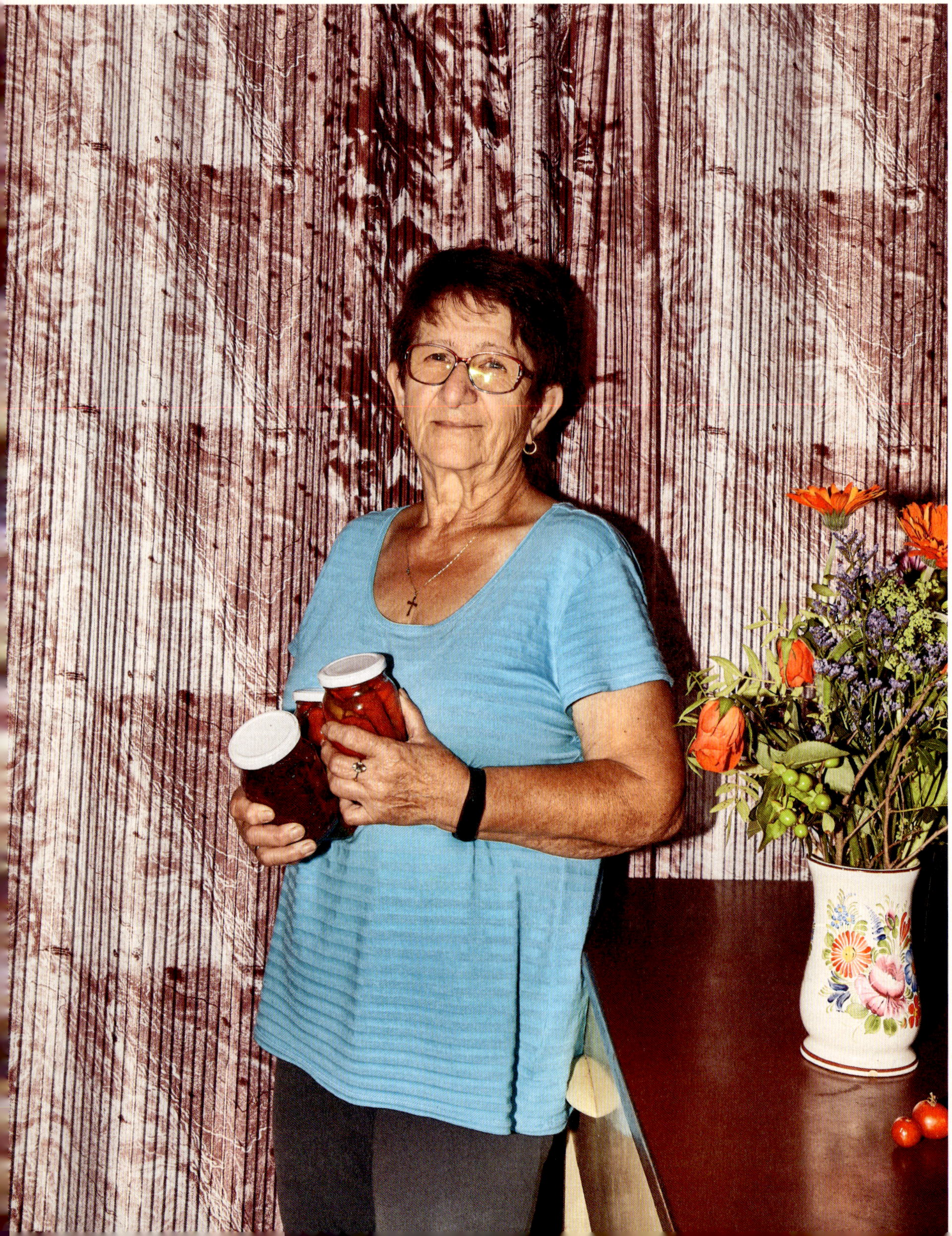

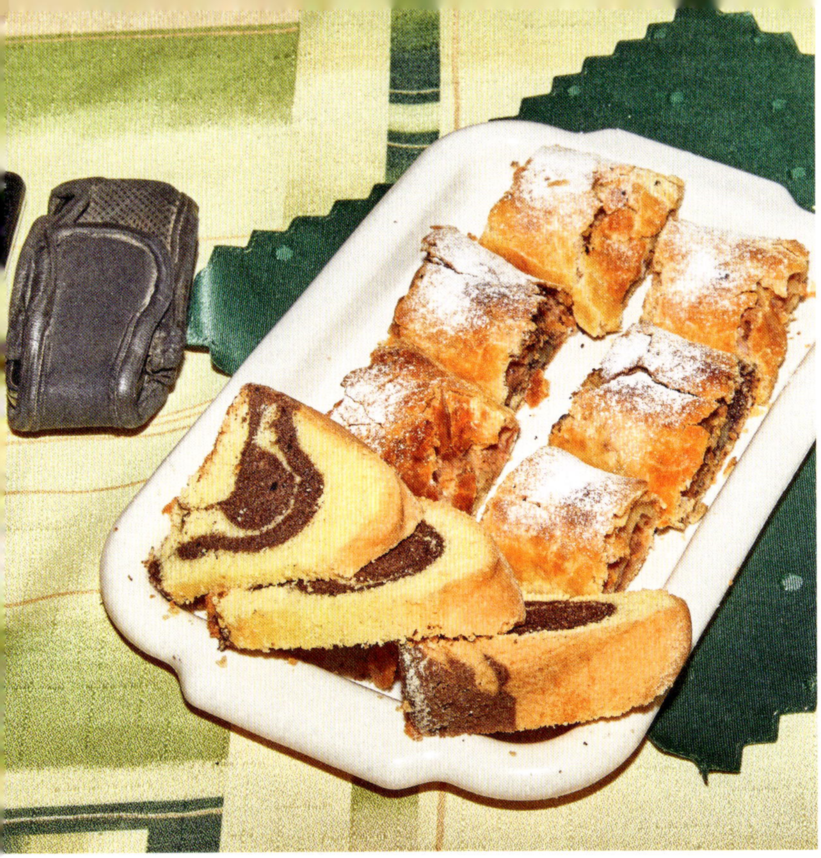

Lunch, afters, and, of course, some treats to take home! That's Miluše Švecová in a nutshell—pressing a few jars of her preserves into your hands before you go.

"Pull in your stomach, Grandpa!" calls out Miluše Švecová, with a laugh, as we snap her husband's photograph for the book. The two of them live in a house surrounded by a garden and vast fields, located in a little village not far from Planá nad Lužnicí. The moment you step through their front door, you're hit with an unmistakable feeling that says *you're at Grandma and Grandpa's*.

What do you picture when you hear that phrase? Chances are it looks a lot like the Švecs' place. A tall, proud walnut tree towers in the yard. Chickens cluck from the coop, sheep bleat somewhere in the background, birds chirp in the trees, and every now and then an annoying fly lands right on you. In the midst of it all are a few plastic chairs and table covered with an oilcloth waits under a cheerful sun umbrella, casting just the right amount of shade. Around the edges, lush hydrangeas bloom like they're showing off, and bright annuals add splashes of color. Behind the house, hidden from view, there's a greenhouse and a vegetable plot.

"They said they liked goat horn peppers back home, so I bought some seeds, and ever since, we've been growing these in our greenhouse," Miluše explains. "It's like Russian roulette; every now and then one burns like crazy. You never know which one you'll get!" She's talking about her pepper preserve (see p. 141), which is very popular with her family.

Within minutes, mugs of *turek* (Czech-style freshly brewed coffee with grounds settling at the bottom called „Turkish coffee"), a tray of *chlebíčky* (Czech open sandwiches), and plates of delicious homemade *bábovka* and strudel (see p. 188 and 162) land on the table. "Mmm, you can eat these. They're good," she says, evaluating a jar of goat horn peppers that she's just opened.

While the photographer Marek and I admire the organized freezer inventory—there's a color-coded chart on the door so you can tell at a glance what's in each bag—we learn that Miluše's other specialty is beet (beetroot) salad (see p. 141). The secret to its unbeatable flavor? A touch of horseradish.

"I always say I've got plenty of food, I don't need a thing," Denisa, Miluše's granddaughter laughs. "And every time, I leave with something from the garden—a jar of jam, some veggies, whatever's ripe that week. I already have a jar of beet salad in my trunk today." Sound familiar? Classic Grandma!

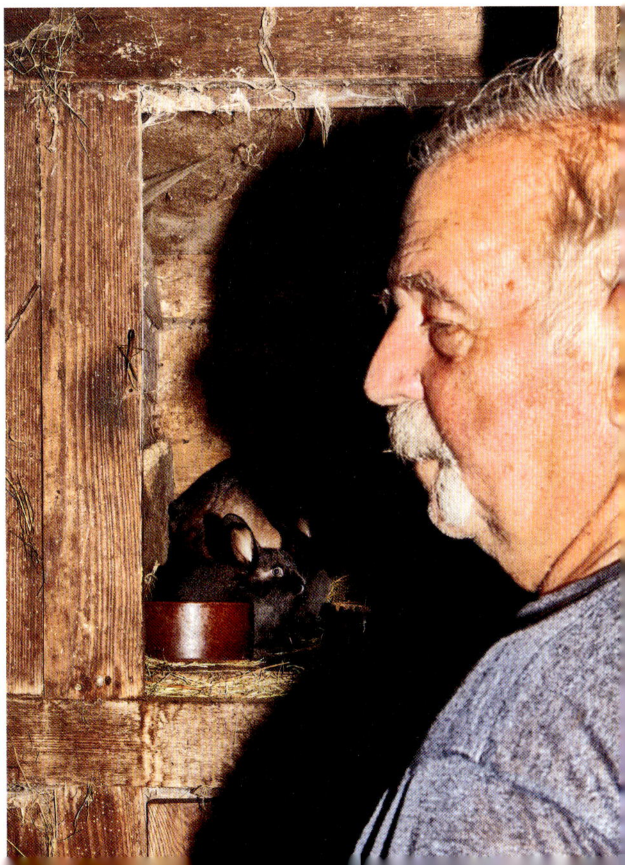

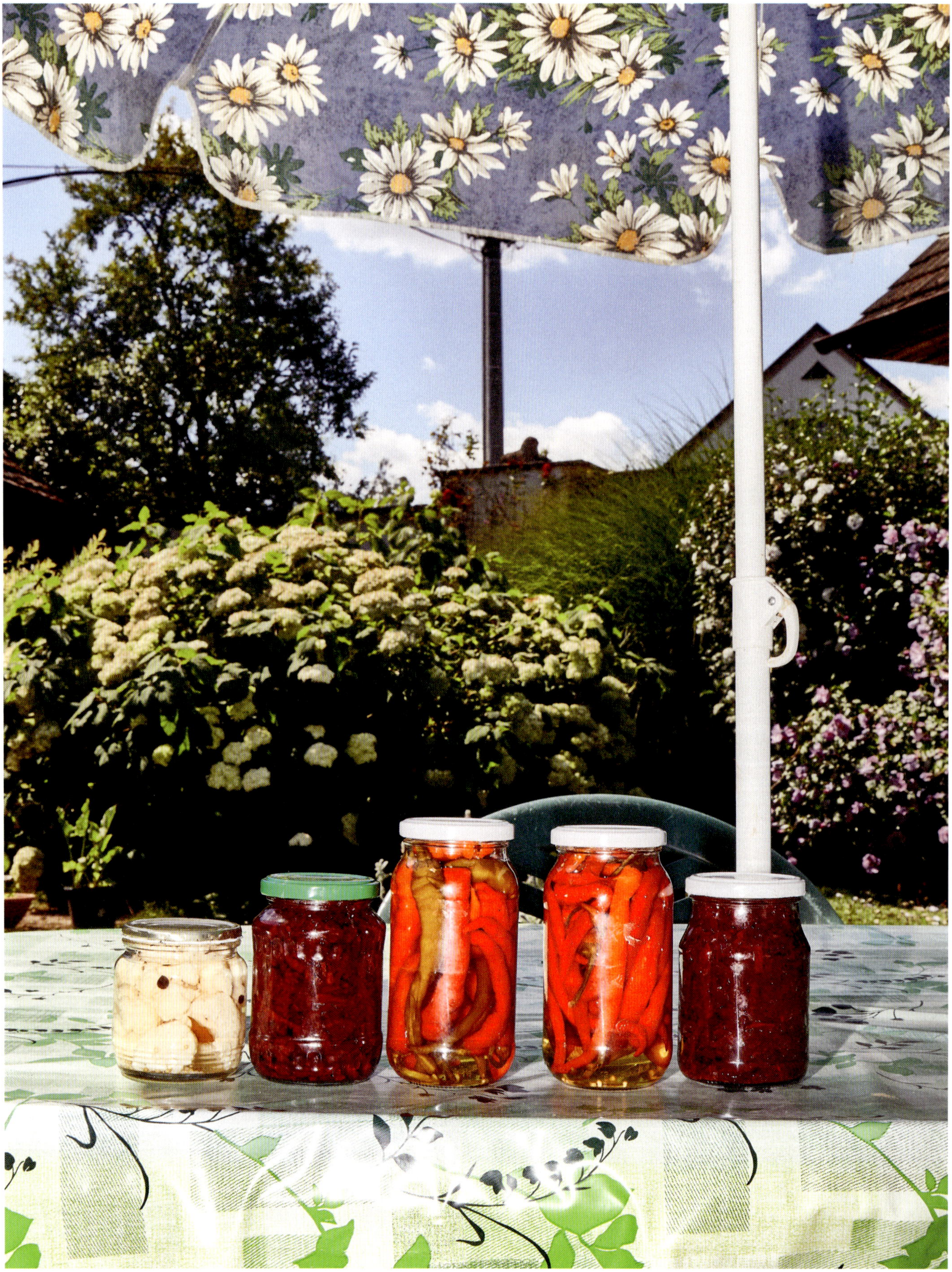

Pickled Goat Horn Peppers

For 6 to 8 canning jars (16 ounces / 700 ml each)

Ingredients

3 quarts (3 l) water

4 ¼ cups (1 l) distilled white vinegar

1 ⅓ cups (280 g) granulated sugar

Scant ½ cup (120 g) salt

About 6 ½ pounds (3 kg) goat horn peppers

Vegetable oil

To make the pickling liquid, mix the water and vinegar in a pot, add the sugar and salt, and bring to a boil over medium heat. Stir occasionally until the sugar and salt dissolve completely. Let the liquid boil briefly and then remove from the heat.

Wash the peppers, pat dry, and arrange in layers in the sterilized canning jars. Drizzle ½ teaspoon of oil over each pepper layer (this will help to release the flavors in the vegetable). Pour the warm liquid over the peppers until completely covered. Close the jars tightly, process in a water bath, and let cool. Store the jars in a cool, dark place.

Tip These pickled goat horn peppers are excellent served with sausages, hams, or cheese and go well with broiled (grilled) meat.

Pickled Beets with Horseradish

For 8 to 10 canning jars (16 ounces / 700 ml each)

Ingredients

3 quarts (3 l) water

4 ¼ cups (1 l) distilled white vinegar

1 ⅓ cups (280 g) granulated sugar

Scant ½ cup (120 g) salt

6 ½ pounds (3 kg) beets (beetroot)

1 teaspoon caraway seeds

1 teaspoon fennel seeds

1 teaspoon anise seeds (aniseed)

1 small piece of horseradish root

To make the pickling liquid, mix the water and vinegar in a pot, add the sugar and salt, and bring to a boil over medium heat. Stir occasionally until the sugar and salt dissolve. Let boil for about 3 minutes, then remove the pot from the heat.

Wash and peel the beets, then coarsely grate them over a large bowl. Add the spices and mix well. Peel and thinly slice the horseradish root.

Place 2 slices of horseradish in each sterilized canning jar. Loosely fill the jars with the grated beets. Pour the warm liquid over the beets until completely covered. Close the jars tightly and process in a water bath. Let cool and then store in a cool, dark place.

Tips For a twist, add finely shredded cabbage to the beets in a 2 : 1 ratio (2 parts beets to 1 part cabbage).

Cold pickled beets make a great accompaniment to many dishes.

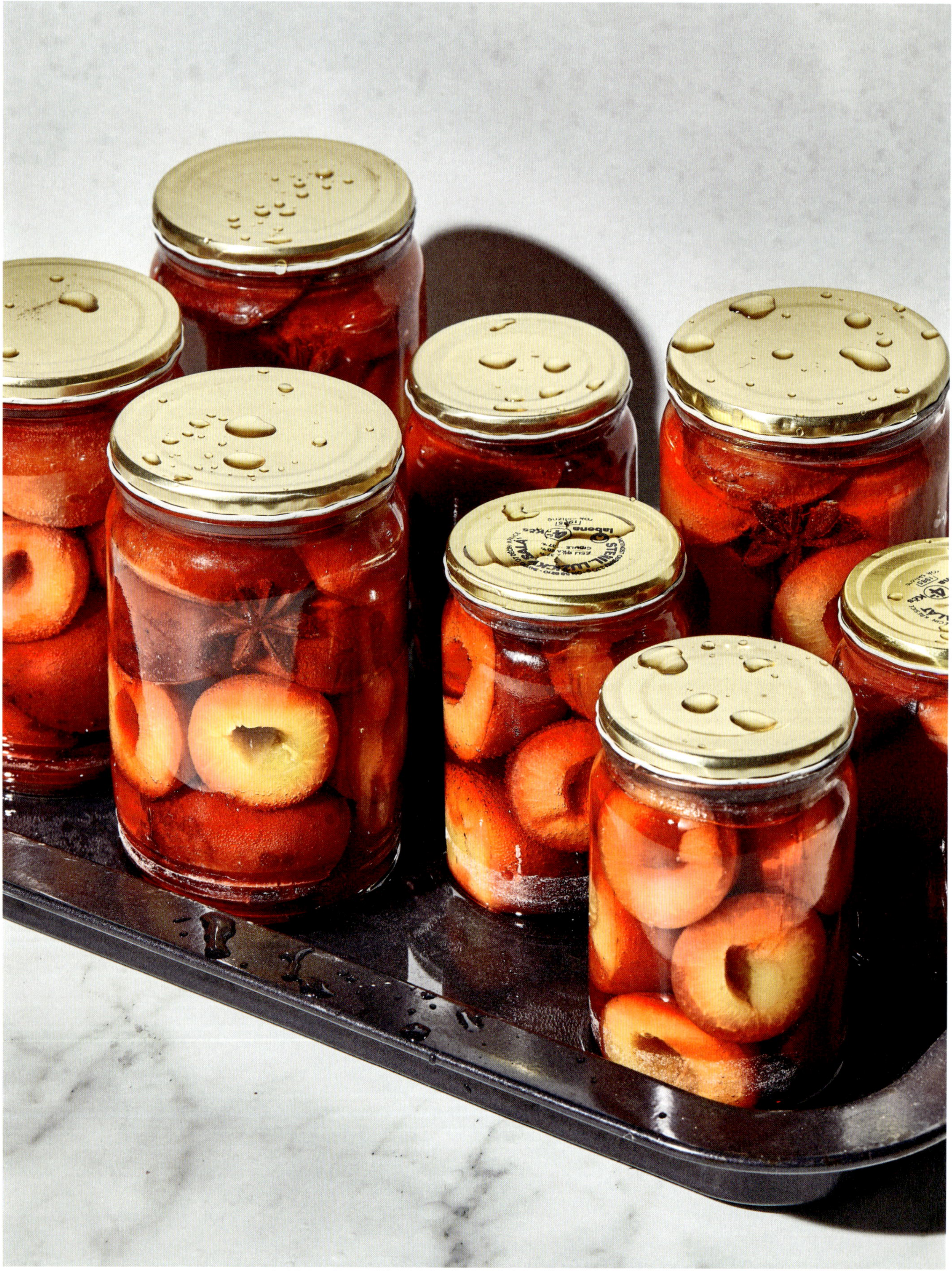

Plum Compote with Star Anise

For 4 canning jars (16 ounces / 500 ml each)

Ingredients

4 ¼ cups (1 l) water

1 ½ to 2 cups (300 – 400 g) granulated sugar

4 ½ pounds (2 kg) plums

4 star anise

Put the water into a saucepan and add the sugar (adjust the amount depending on the sweetness of the plums). Stir and bring to a boil. Reduce the heat and let the syrup simmer, stirring occasionally, for about 5 minutes, until the sugar dissolves completely.

In the meantime, wash the plums, pat dry, halve, and pit. Arrange the plum halves, ideally cut side down, in sterilized canning jars. Add 1 star anise to each jar.

Pour the hot syrup over the plums until completely covered. Close the jars tightly, process in a water bath, and let cool. Store in a cool, dark place.

Tips Firm fruit is more suitable for this recipe, because softer plums will fall apart. Soft plums can be used to make *povidla* (see p. 144).

To give your compote extra flavor, add 1 cinnamon stick or 2 to 3 cloves to each jar.

Old cookbooks advise: "He that desires a compote of yellow hue shall first scald and peel the plums."

Povidla—Oven-baked Plum Butter

For 4 canning jars (8 ounces/200 ml each)

Ingredients

2 ¼ pounds (1 kg) plums

1 cup (200 g) cane sugar

2 tablespoons plus 2 teaspoons (40 ml) distilled white vinegar

Rum

Wash, stem, halve, and pit the plums. Puree the fruit with an immersion stick blender until smooth (alternatively, coarsely blend to leave chunks). Transfer the puree to a deep roasting pan to control splattering as it cooks. Add the sugar and vinegar and mix well. Cover the roasting pan with a clean cloth and let stand overnight in a cool place.

The next day, preheat the oven to 450 °F top/bottom heat (230 °C/Gas Mark 8). Bake the plum puree, uncovered and without stirring, for 30 minutes. Reduce the oven temperature to 325 °F (160 °C/Gas Mark 3) and continue to bake for about 5 hours, until the puree caramelizes and thickens. Halfway through baking, you can stir the puree to see how it is thickening. Check occasionally to make sure it doesn't burn.

Stir the thicken, hot *povidla* well and fill the sterilized canning jars. Drizzle the surface with a little rum to prevent bacteria from forming and allow for the puree to last longer without spoiling. Close the jars tightly, place upside down, and let cool. Store in a cool, dark place.

Tips Very ripe to almost overripe plums are the most suitable ones for this recipe. Their higher sugar content will make the puree sweeter.

After baking, you can enhance the flavor of the *povidla* with ground spices, including cinnamon, star anise, and cloves. Alternatively, add the spices to the *povidla* before its next use in the kitchen.

The *Povidla* will continue to thicken as they cool and rest. If the fruit butter is too firm, loosen it with a little rum or hot water.

You can use this plum butter to fill *buchty* rolls (see p. 158), sweet *Germknödel* (yeast dumplings), and different cakes and *kolaches* (see p. 106). It is also delicious with *lívance* (traditional Czech yeast pancakes) and as a filling for *přesňáky* (thin potato dough pancakes).

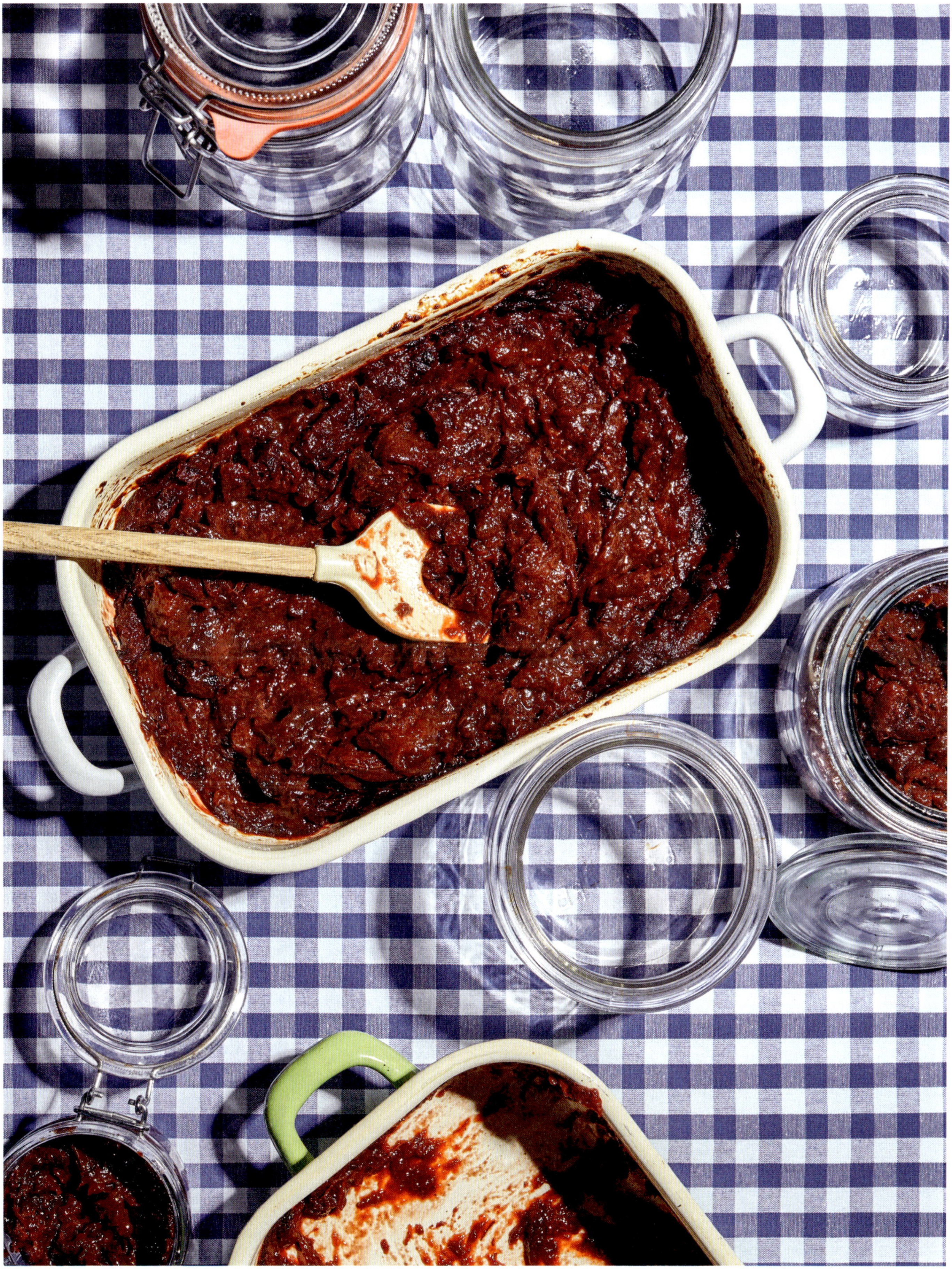

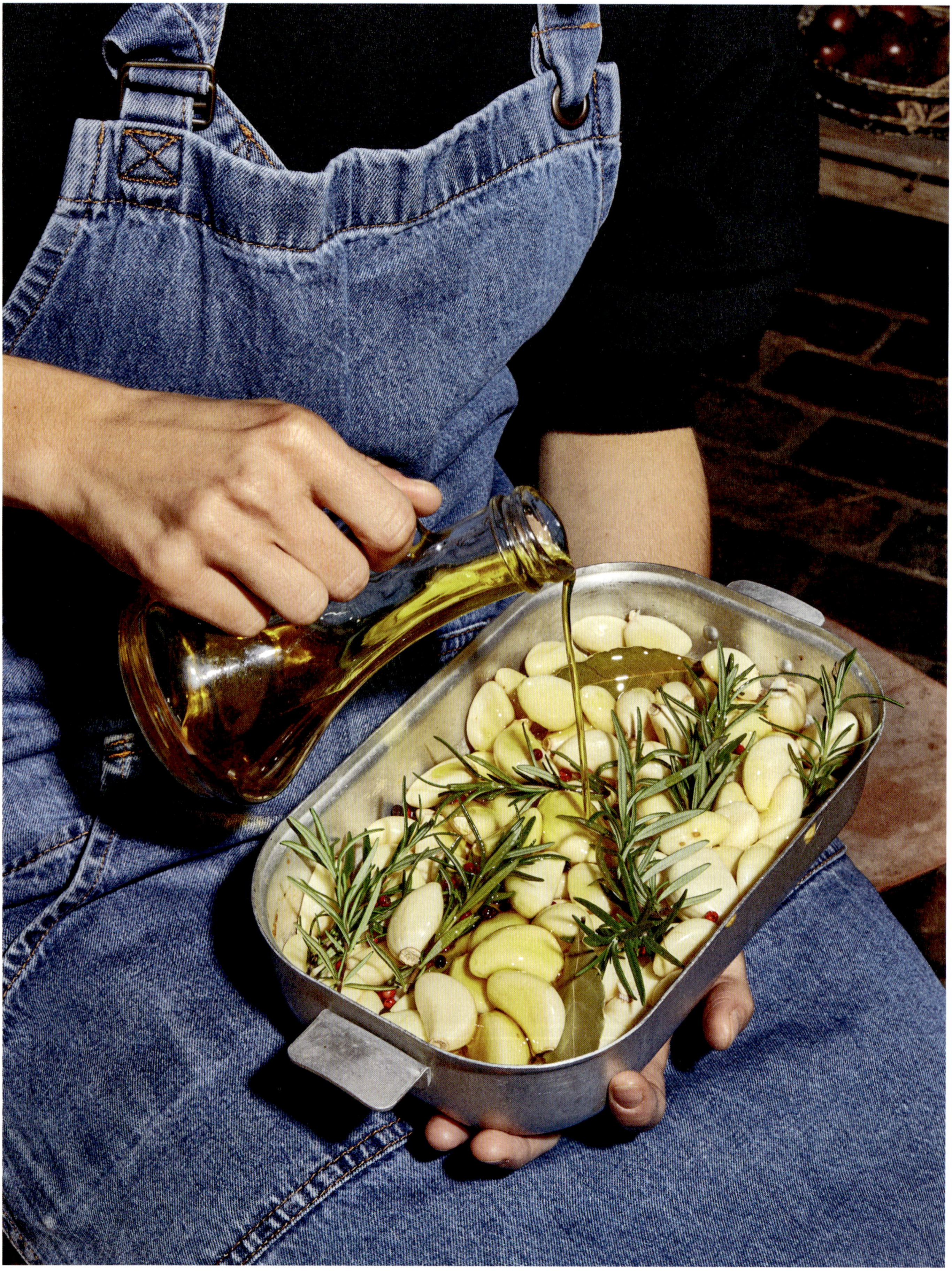

Garlic Confit

For 2 canning jars (4 ounces / 125 ml each)

Ingredients

1 cup (250 ml) olive oil

2 to 3 whole garlic heads

2 sprigs of fresh rosemary

3 bay leaves

1 teaspoon pink peppercorns

Gently heat the olive oil in an ovenproof saucepan over medium heat. Preheat the oven to 175 to 195 °F top/bottom heat (80–90 °C).

Divide the garlic heads into their individual cloves and peel. Carefully add the garlic cloves to the warm oil. Wash the rosemary sprigs, shake dry, and add to the pan along with the bay leaves and peppercorns. Heat the oil to 175 °F (80 °C)—the oil should not boil so that the garlic, herbs, and spices do not burn.

Put the pot into the preheated oven. Confit the garlic for about 1 hour, until soft, making sure that it doesn't burn. Reduce the oven temperature slightly, if necessary.

Transfer the garlic, oil, rosemary, and spices to small sterilized canning jars. The garlic should be completely covered in oil. Close the jars tightly, then store in a cool, dark place.

Tips In addition to herbs and spices, you can also add 1 chili pepper sliced into rings to the oil.

You can use the leftover oil from the garlic confit and the oil from the jars in the same way as garlic oil bought in a grocery store. This oil has a pleasantly mild taste and a lovely aroma.

Garlic softens and caramelizes when cooked in the oven, as well as loses its typical pungency and becomes easier to digest. It can be used to make garlic mayonnaise (aioli) and spreads, and to enhance mashed potatoes. You can mix it with fresh herbs and whole-grain mustard to make a wonderful marinade for broiled (grilled) meat. The garlic also goes well with pasta dishes and freshly baked rolls.

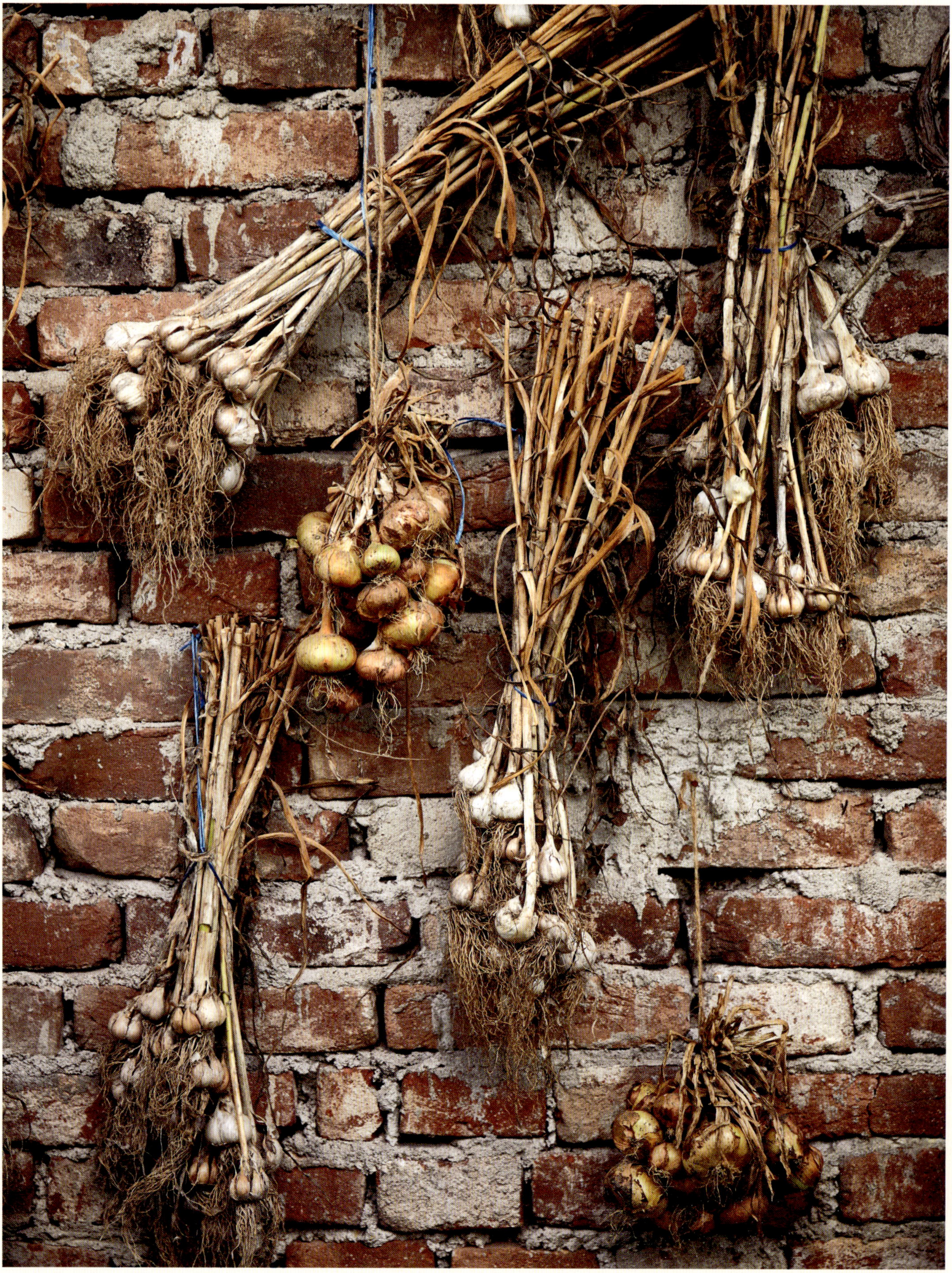

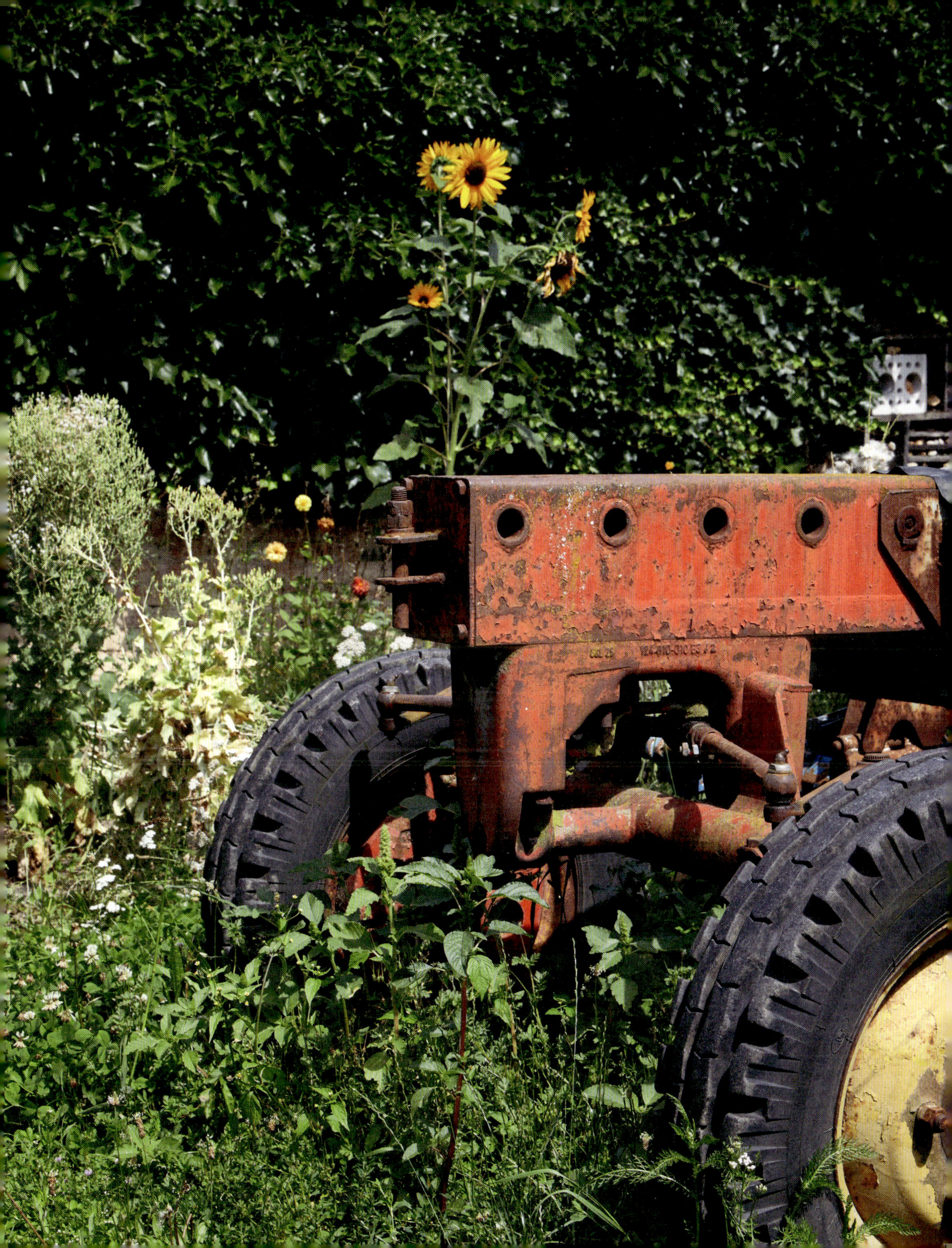

Man with “Golden Czech Hands”

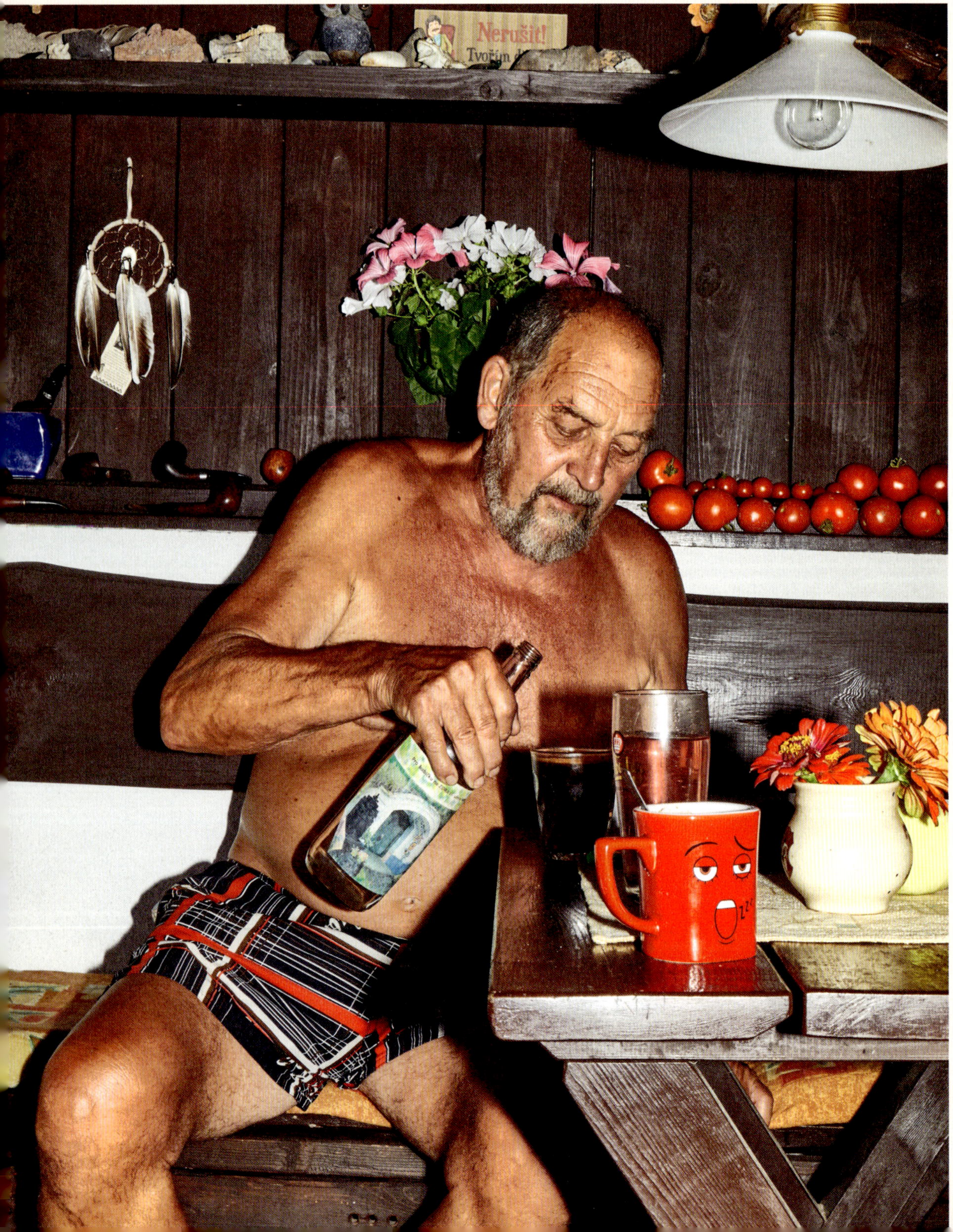

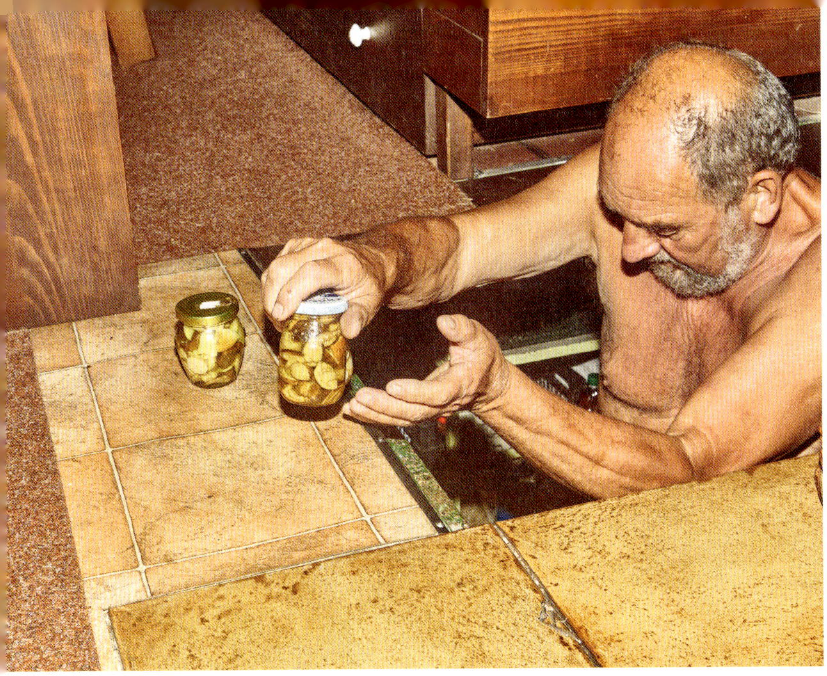

With a pipe in his mouth and jars of forest mushrooms on the shelf, Miloš Potocký lives the art of Czech cottage life. Retired in name, busier than ever!

"Welcome to our cottage village!" calls out the friendly Miloš Potocký as we step out of the car. "Do come in! What'll it be, coffee? A shot? My wife's not home, but she baked you an apple strudel."

Miloš is a cheerful soul. He spent his life working for an insurance company and was once even named National Insurance Worker of the Year. Now retired, he finally has time for his grandchildren and great-grandchildren, tends the garden with his wife, hosts regular get-togethers with his friends, and smokes meat in his own backyard smokehouse. He's the very picture of a man with "golden Czech hands", as we say in the Czech Republic—the kind of man who can make or fix just about anything. He loves working with wood and, because he's a man of action, you instantly notice the garden furniture, swing, shed, and little *kadibudka* (outhouse) he built himself. Every item is perfected down to the last detail!

In the heat of summer, Miloš paddles down the Sázava, Berounka, Ohře, and Lužnice rivers, or takes a dip in the slow-moving stream that winds through the cottage area. He's also an avid mushroom hunter and loves to preserve his finds. We sit on the veranda while the radio plays Marie Rottrová's song "Love, You Smell Like Rain." As we leaf through a mushroom atlas, Miloš points out the species he collects and pickles, explaining where they grow and how to find them. He tells us about the last time he came across a cauliflower mushroom.

"Pickled Wild Mushrooms make a great sauce, or *kulajda*," he says, puffing on his pipe. "Of course, without dill or any other green nonsense—I don't eat that. We eat plenty of mushrooms; they go great with meat, for instance."

He takes us on a little tour of his vegetable patch, his homemade rowing boat, and his quirky collection of insurance-themed tin signs.

We leave the Potockýs taking with us a bag of apples, tomatoes, and cucumbers—and, most of all, smiles on our faces. As we head to the car, we turn back to see Miloš waving, a puff of smoke drifting from his pipe, calling after us to come back again sometime. Starting the engine, waving back, and watching Miloš fading from view, our minds are already at home in the kitchen, imagining how we'll handle the jars of mushrooms in sweet-and-sour brine (see p. 153), softly clinking on the back seat as we drive.

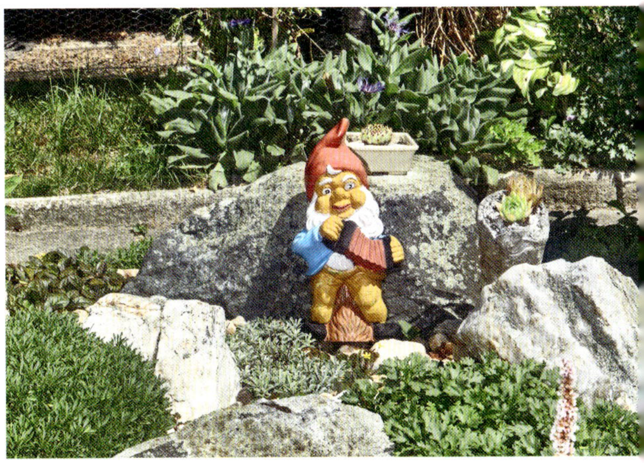

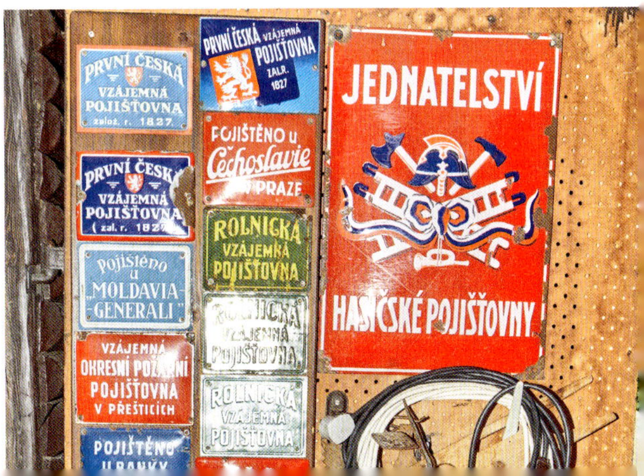

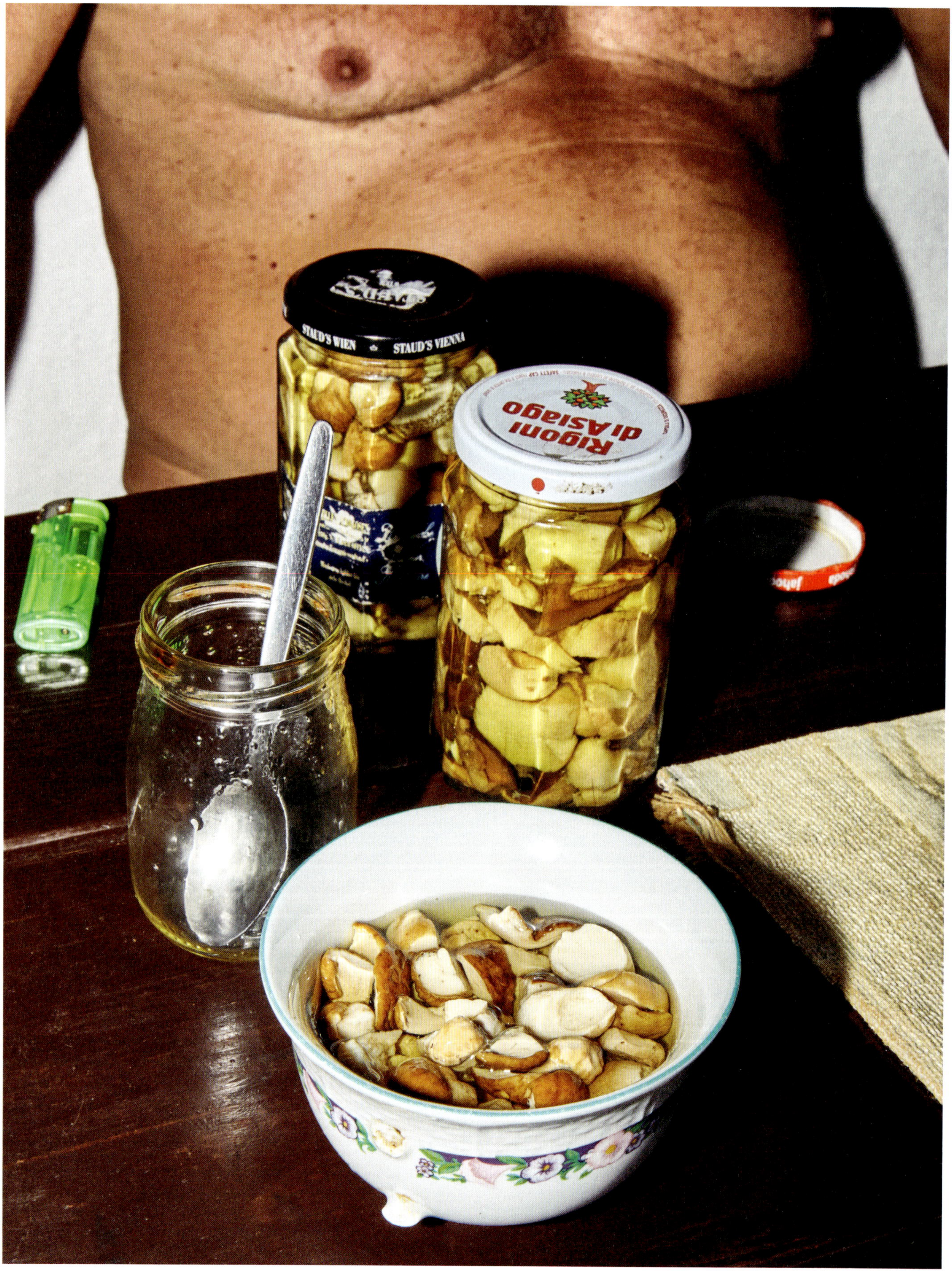
STAUD'S WIEN
STAUD'S VIENNA
Rigoni di Asiago

Pickled Wild Mushrooms

For 12 canning jars (8 ounces / 250 ml each)

Ingredients

Scant 7 ½ cups (1.75 l) water, plus more for parboiling the mushrooms

2 cups (500 ml) distilled white vinegar

⅓ cup (100 g) salt, plus 1 tablespoon salt

1 ½ cups (300 g) granulated sugar

1 tablespoon mustard seeds

1 teaspoon coriander seeds

1 teaspoon peppercorns

½ teaspoon allspice berries

½ teaspoon cloves

½ teaspoon fennel seeds

3 bay leaves

4 ½ to 6 ½ pounds (2–3 kg) mixed wild mushrooms

To make the pickling liquid, mix the water and vinegar in a pot, then add the salt, sugar, spices, and bay leaves. Bring to a boil, stirring regularly until the salt and sugar dissolve. Let the liquid boil briefly and then remove it from the heat.

In another pot, bring water to a boil in a saucepan and stir in 1 tablespoon salt. Keep it at a boil.

Clean the mushrooms with a soft brush, wiping them with a cloth, if necessary, then cut them into larger pieces. Place the mushrooms in the boiling salted water, reduce the heat, and let simmer for 10 minutes. Drain the mushrooms and put them into cold water to shock them, then arrange in layers in sterilized canning jars.

Pour the pickling liquid, including the spices, over the mushrooms until completely covered. Close the jars tightly, process in a water bath, and let cool. Store in a cool, dark place.

Tips The best mushrooms for pickling are the firm varieties, such as porcini (ceps), chanterelles (girolles), and saffron milk caps.

There is a long and strong tradition of preserving mushrooms in the Czech Republic. Writings on mushroom preservation by well-known culinary popularizers date back to the early nineteenth century. Magdalena Dobromila Rettigová (1785–1845), and later Anuše Kejřová (1874–1926), recommended in their manuals that mushrooms be cleaned, peeled, sliced, and paraboiled in heavily salted water with vinegar, and later with citric acid as well. They would then transfer the mushrooms along with the liquid into stone jars, earthenware, or tin containers, allowing them to be preserved. Sometimes the contents were topped with a layer of lard to prevent air from entering. Mařka Kašparová (1856–1934) and Milada Benešová (1900–1970) advised housewives to cover mushrooms in jars with crushed salt—in winter, they could be easily removed, cut in appropriate amounts (as they were very salty), and added to soups.

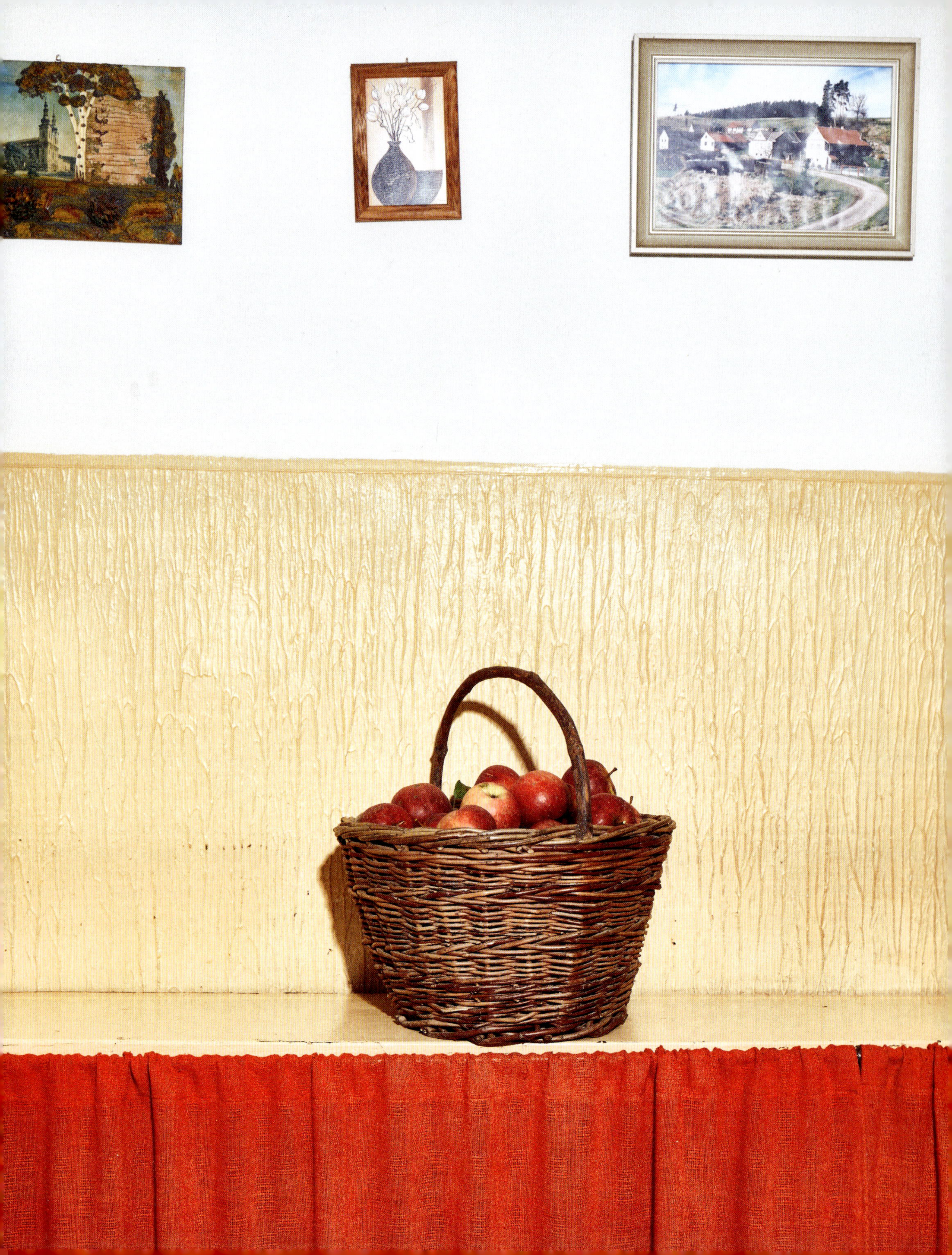

FALL

Září, na léto jde stáří.

September, summer is growing old.

The Secret of Light Apple Butter

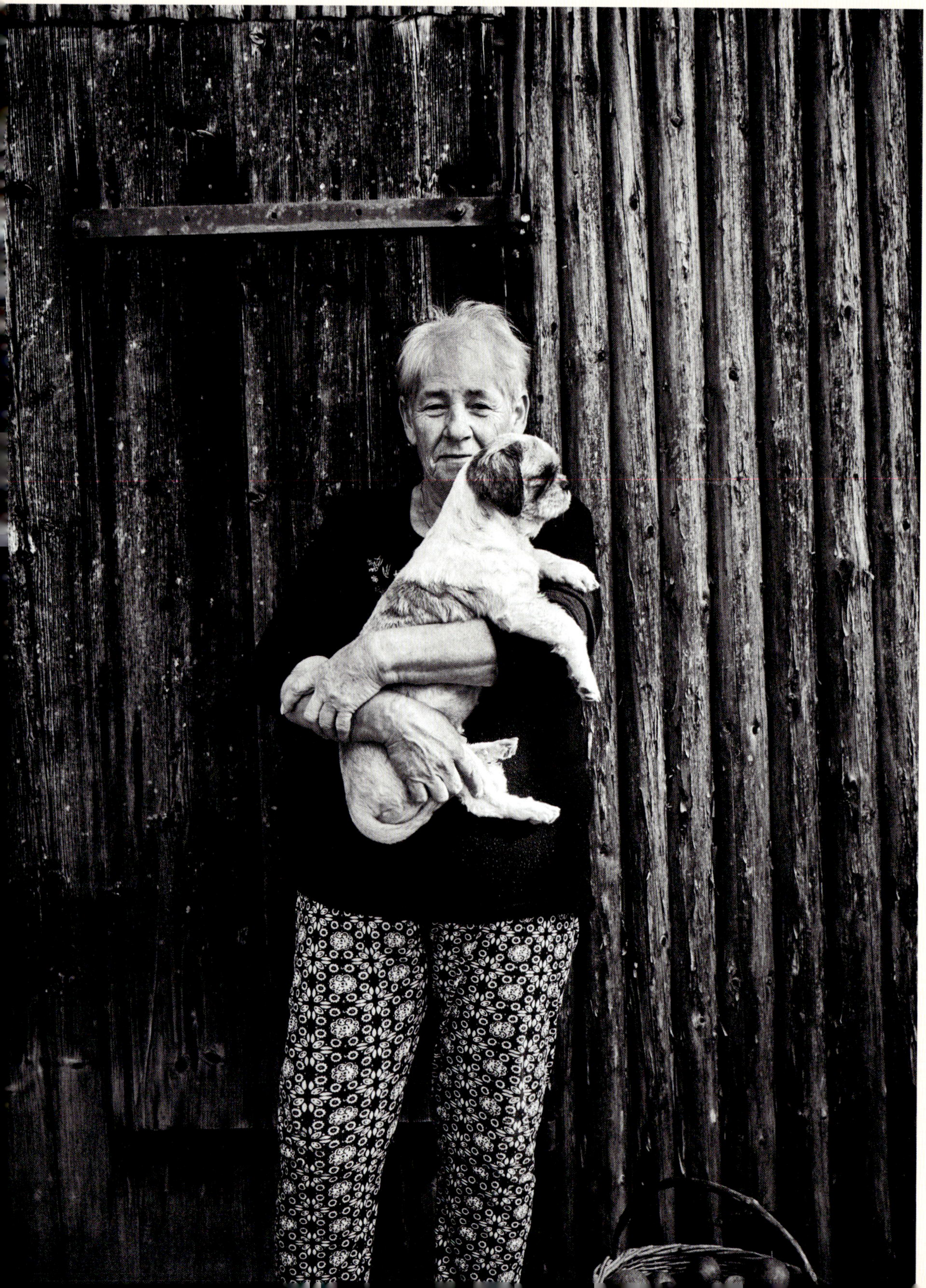

Anna Hlavínová makes famously irresistible apple butter that the whole village would fight over. What's the magic behind its exceptional golden color?

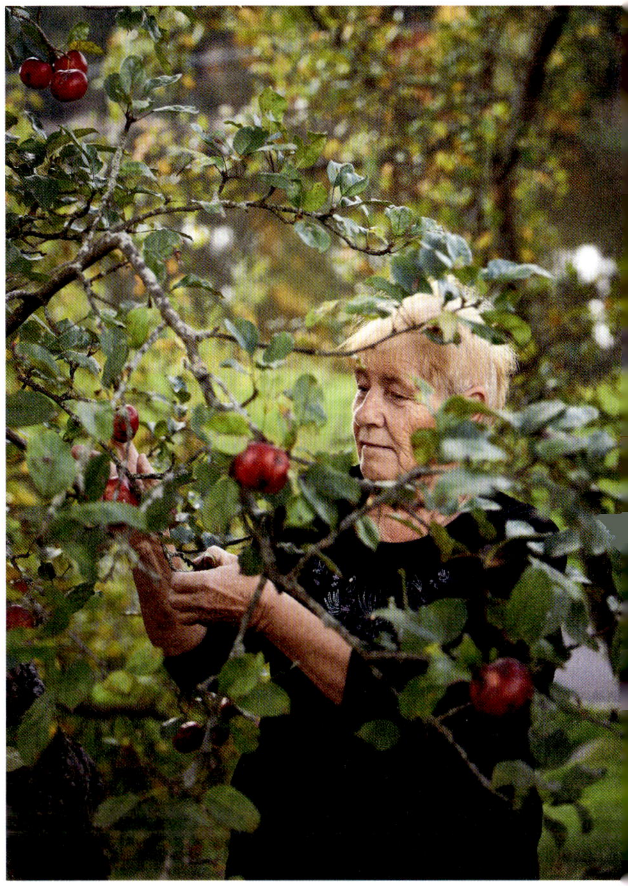

"Apple picking is a ritual I can't imagine late summer and fall without!" says Anna Hlavínová, who has never left the small village in which she lives near Milevsko in South Bohemia.

Anna likes to keep everything in tip-top shape; her house is always spotless, the garden weed-free. Potatoes grow in neat rows, planted with the help of a string. Chickens cluck in the yard. Her family used to keep geese—little Anča (as everyone around still affectionately calls her) would always transfer the freshly hatched goslings to a box she placed on the stove to keep the chicks warm. As soon as they could walk, they would tag along behind her like she was their mother.

Life for Anna revolves around where she lives. She loves fishing, trimming her neighbors' hair, and lending an ear to their troubles. She does express a few sharp words at times, but behind the rough edges is nothing but kindness and affection.

"Anna is a walking pantry!" laughs her neighbor Petra. "When we were kids, we'd roam the village, and if anyone asked where we were going, we'd always say, 'To Anča's greenhouse to eat.' She's a gem, even though she does have some colorful language. She likes to use the word *čůza* (shrew)—unfortunately, that's something I picked up from her ... But people don't buy her tough act. She's a person with her heart on her sleeve.

Behind Anna's house, a small orchard climbs the slope, the trees' branches heavy with apples. She uses these to make preserves—always choosing 'White Transparent' first to make Light Apple Butter (see p. 160). They give her preserves a pale, almost glowing color.

"Anyone can make the dark apple preserves," she says with a grin. "It's the light preserve that's really special—my pride and joy. No one wants to pick apples, but when there are kolaches made with apple butter filling on the table, everyone starts fighting over them!"

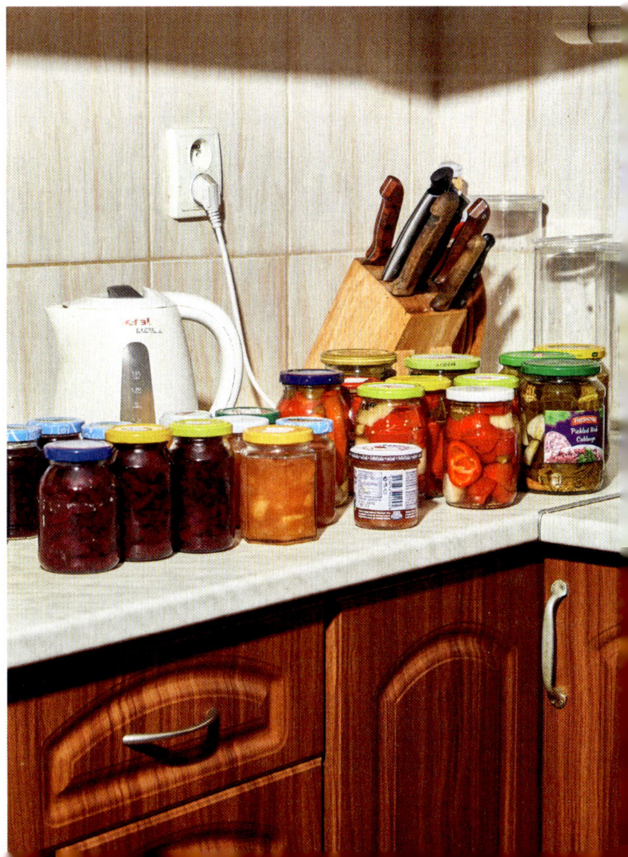

Buchty Rolls

For 1 baking pan (makes 15 to 20 rolls)

Ingredients

1 cup (250 ml) milk

1 small (⅔ ounce/19 g) cake fresh yeast

⅓ cup plus 1 tablespoon (80 g) granulated sugar

½ cup (120 g) unsalted butter, plus extra for greasing

4 cups (500 g) pastry flour or all-purpose (plain) flour, plus extra for dusting

1 pinch of salt

Finely grated zest of ½ organic lemon

1 egg yolk

1 cup (250 g) Plum Butter (see p. 144)

2 tablespoons rum

Powdered (icing) sugar, for dusting

Gently heat the milk until lukewarm—do not let it boil. To activate the yeast, pour half of the milk into a bowl, crumble in the fresh yeast, and add 1 teaspoon of the sugar. Mix well. Cover the bowl with a clean cloth and let the yeast rise for 10 to 15 minutes. In the meantime, melt 4 tablespoons (60 g) of the butter in a saucepan and let cool.

Sift the flour into a bowl and add the remaining sugar, salt, and lemon zest. Add the activated yeast mixture, remaining milk, melted butter, and egg yolk. Using a wooden spoon or stand mixer, mix everything carefully and slowly together to form a dough. Knead for at least 10 minutes, until the dough is smooth and supple and easily comes away from the sides of the bowl. Cover the bowl with a clean cloth. Let the dough rise in a warm place for about 1 hour, until doubled in volume (the warmer the temperature, the faster the dough will rise).

Preheat the oven to 350 °F top/bottom heat (180 °C/Gas Mark 4). Grease a baking pan with a little butter. Melt the remaining butter in a saucepan.

Dust the work surface with a little flour and roll out the dough into a rectangle about ½ inch (1 cm) thick, then cut it into 15 to 20 uniform squares. Place 1 heaping tablespoon of plum butter in the center of each dough square. Bring the corners of each square together over the filling, seal the seams with your fingers, and press together to completely cover the filling. Shape the filled dough pieces into firm balls and place them close together in the greased baking pan with the seams facing downward. Cover with a cloth and let proof for 15 minutes.

Brush the top of the rolls with plenty of melted butter. Bake the rolls for about 30 minutes, until golden. Mix the remaining melted butter with the rum and immediately brush the warm rolls with the mixture. Let the rolls cool, then dust with powdered (icing) sugar and serve.

Tips Only have instant yeast at home? Go ahead and use it—just remember that you cannot substitute fresh yeast 1:1 with instant yeast. Instant yeast is 1.5 times stronger, so always use 1.5 times less! You also don't need to activate instant yeast in advance; simply sprinkle it over the flour and work it into the dough.

In addition to plum butter, these *buchty* rolls can be filled with Light Apple Butter (see p. 160) or Pear Butter (see p. 166).

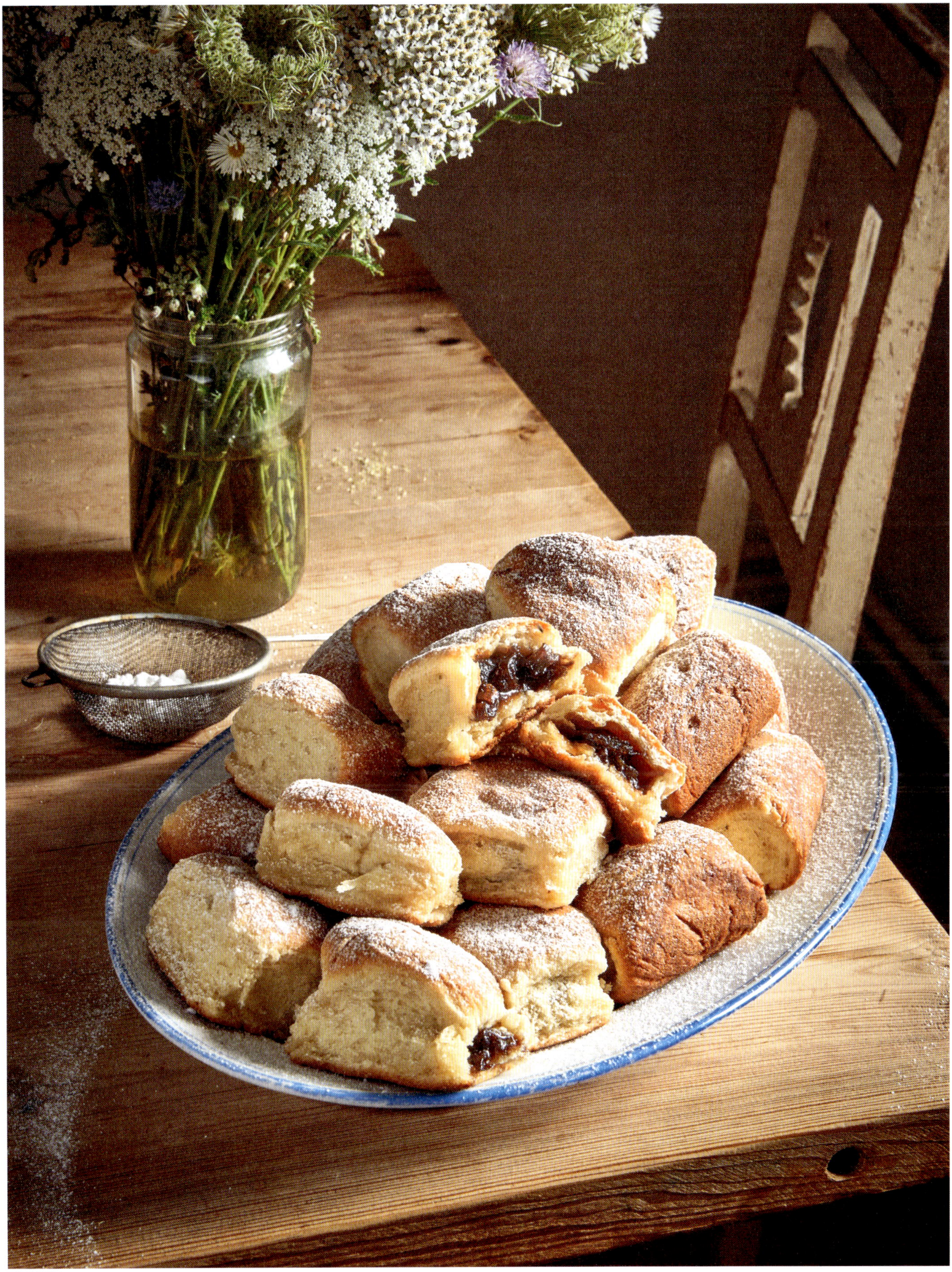

Light Apple Butter

For 4 canning jars (8 ounces / 250 ml each)

Ingredients

2 ¼ pounds (1 kg) White Transparent apples (see tips)
4 cups (800 g) granulated sugar
Juice of ½ lemon

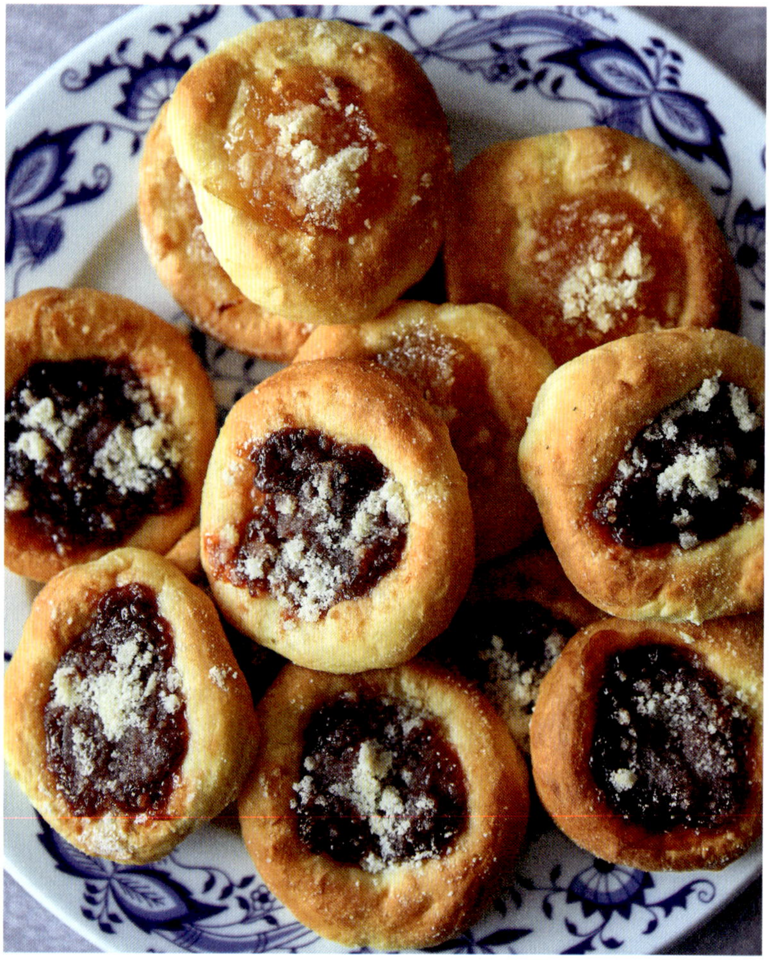

Peel, core, and cut the apples into small pieces. Put the apple pieces into a large saucepan, add the sugar, and mix well. Let stand in a cool place for about 24 hours, stirring occasionally.

Cook the apples over low heat for about 20 minutes, until they fall apart and the mixture thickens. Remove from the heat and stir in the lemon juice. Transfer the hot apple butter to sterilized canning jars, close the lids tightly, and place upside down. Let cool, then store in a cool, dark place.

Tips *White Transparent* is an old apple variety, commonly known in Czech as *letňáky*, which is harvested at the beginning of summer and doesn't keep well in long-term storage. The early-season varieties give this apple butter its beautiful light color, but you can simply use any apples you have at home.

Apple butter makes a delicious filling for *kolaches* (see p. 106) or *buchty* rolls (see p. 158).

Apple Filling for Strudel

For 5 or 6 canning jars (32 ounces / 750 ml each)

Ingredients

8 ¾ pounds (4 kg) apples

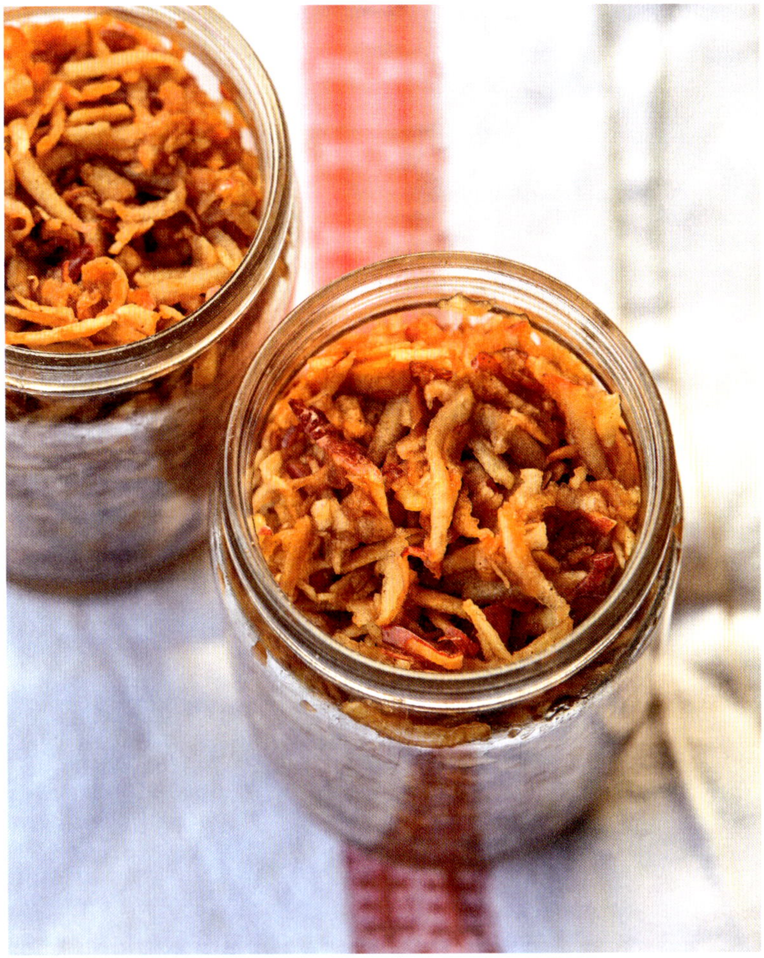

Wash the apples, cut away any bruised or partly rotten areas, and core. Cut the apples into quarters, then either peel or leave unpeeled. Coarsely grate the apple pieces into a bowl or thinly slice them with a mandoline.

Using your clean hands, squeeze out the excess juice. Quickly transfer the apple pieces to sterilized canning jars before they turn brown. Compact them firmly into the jars to prevent the formation of air pockets. Fill the jars to about ¾ inch (2 cm) below the rim. Wipe the rims of the jars with a clean cloth, close the jars tightly, and process in a water bath. Let cool, then store in a cool, dark place.

Tips To prevent the apple from fermenting in the jar, you should always wash your hands thoroughly before starting the process, use very clean bowls during preparation, and sterilize both the canning jars and their lids beforehand. Squeeze as much juice as possible out of the grated apples (you can either drink the juice or freeze it for later). Drizzle the apples with a little lemon juice before sealing the jars.

After canning, the grated apples should be processed in a water bath at 175 °F (80 °C) for about 45 minutes, so the entire contents of the jar heat through properly.

Sweeten the apple filling and add the spices only right before using it; adding sugar in advance could also promote unwanted fermentation in the jar.

The filling works best in a delicate *strudel* (p. 162). By pressing the juice out of the apples, the filling won't run out of the pastries.

Delicate Apple Strudel

Makes 1 strudel

Ingredients

2 cups (240 g) pastry flour or all-purpose (plain) flour, plus extra for dusting

1 pinch of salt

½ cup plus 1 tablespoon (125 g) cold unsalted butter

2 eggs

5 tablespoons cold water

1 tablespoon distilled white vinegar

2 tablespoons bread crumbs

3 cups (400 g) Apple Filling (p. 161)

4 tablespoons granulated sugar

1 teaspoon ground cinnamon

½ teaspoon freshly grated nutmeg

1 handful of walnuts, chopped

1 tablespoon raisins

Powdered (icing) sugar, for dusting

Sift the flour and salt into a bowl. Coarsely grate or dice the cold butter, then add it to the bowl with 1 egg. Add the water and vinegar. Using your hands, quickly work everything into a smooth dough and shape into a ball (knead lightly, otherwise the dough will harden when baked). Cover the dough in plastic wrap (clingfilm) and refrigerate for at least 30 minutes, but preferably for 1 hour.

Beat the remaining egg. Preheat the oven to 400 °F top/bottom heat (200 °C/Gas Mark 6) and line a baking sheet with parchment (baking) paper.

Dust the work surface with flour and roll the dough out thinly into a rectangle. Sprinkle the dough with the bread crumbs, leaving a ¾-inch (2-cm) margin along the edges. Spread the apple filling on top, sprinkle with the granulated sugar, and dust with the cinnamon and nutmeg. Sprinkle the chopped walnuts and raisins over the filling.

Roll up the strudel from a longer edge, then fold the side ends downward and press together well to seal. Carefully place the rolled-up strudel on the baking sheet. Brush with the beaten egg and prick the top several times with a fork to let steam escape while baking. Bake for about 30 minutes, until golden.

Take the strudel out of the oven and let cool, sprinkle with powdered (icing) sugar, cut it into pieces, and serve.

Tips For even more flavor, first soak the raisins in rum, wine, or another high-proof liquor (spirit) of your choice.

For a twist, use pear (see p. 166) or plum butter (see p. 144), quark with raisins, or poppy seeds mixed with plums instead of the apple filling.

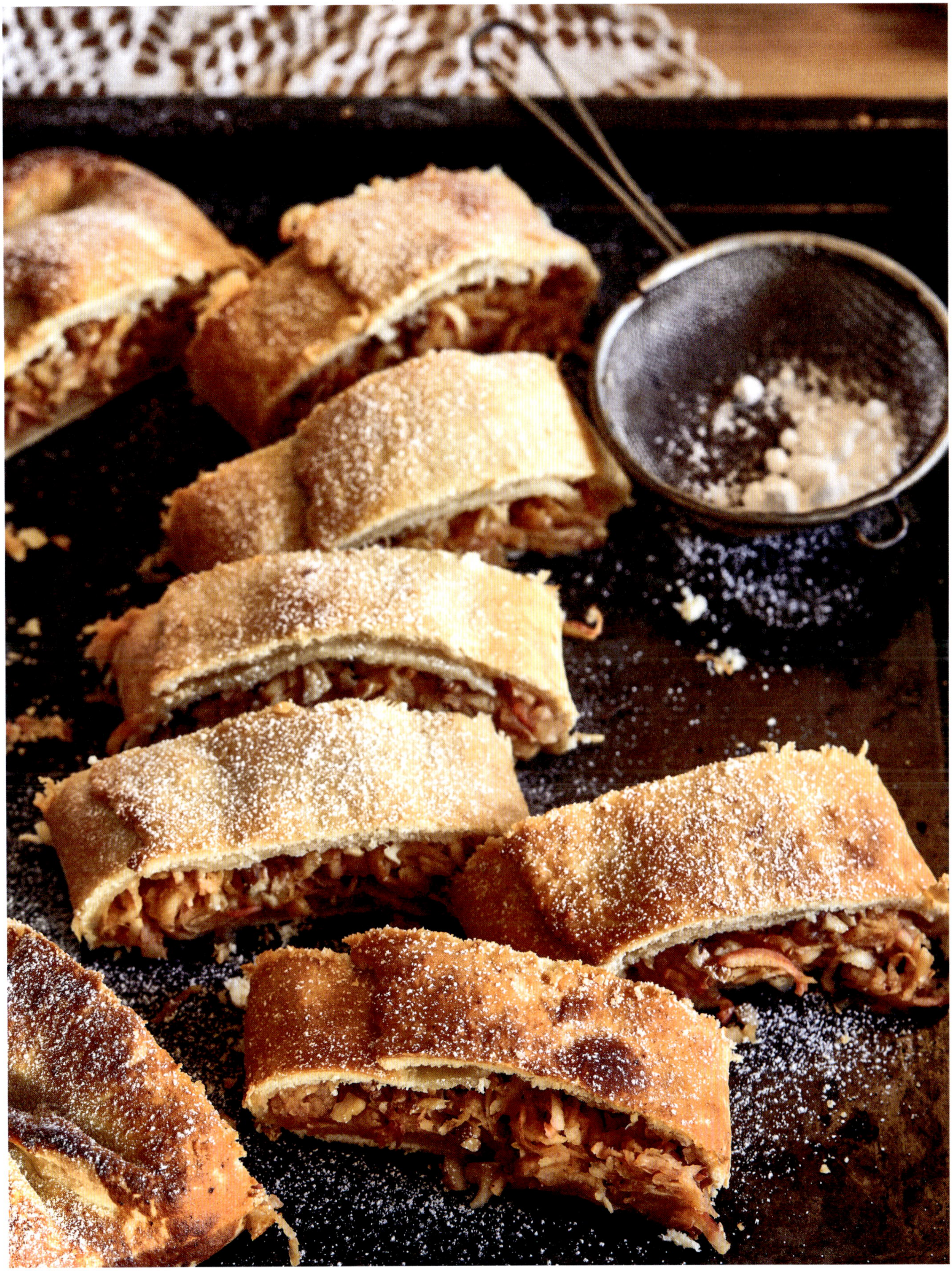

Four Trees, Ninety Bottles of Joy

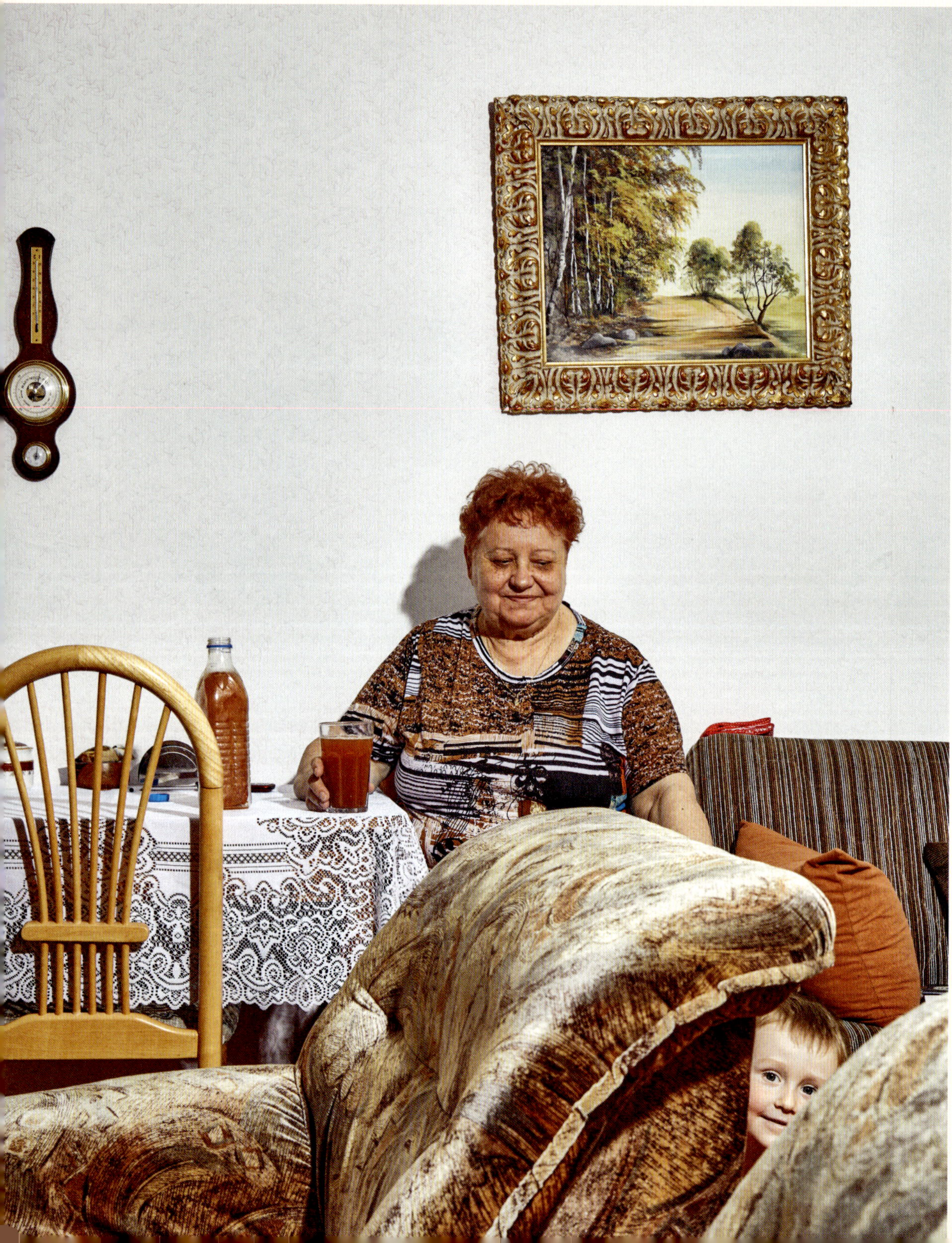

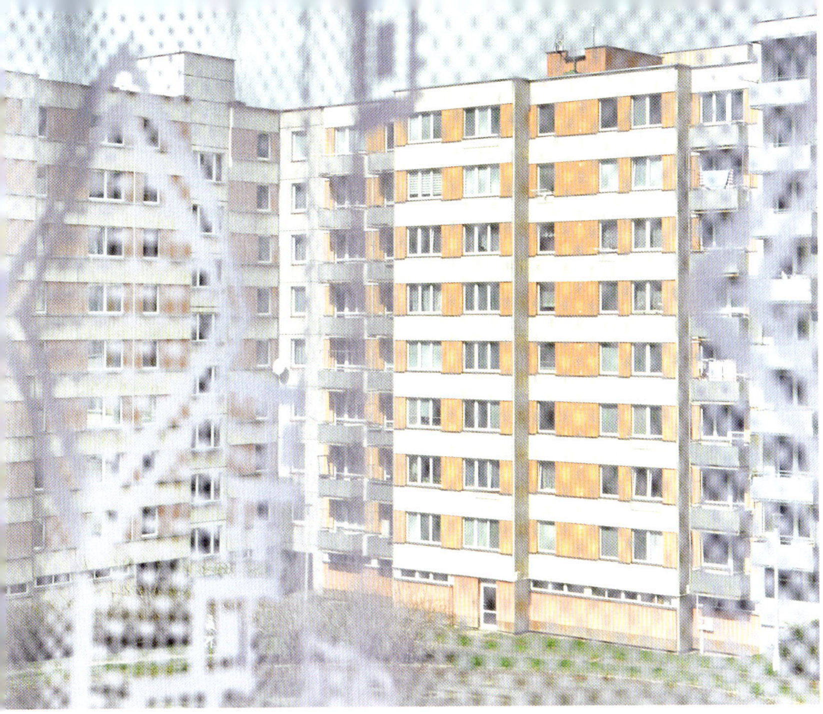

Growing up surrounded by homemade preserves, Marie Camrdová learned the art of turning her own harvest into lasting flavor—bottled and ready to sip.

Marie Camrdová grew up in Mostek, a tiny village near Ratibořské Hory, with a population of fewer than fifty. After elementary school, she headed to Tábor to train as a cook at the Jordán Hotel.

"I never wanted to be a cook," she says with a grin. "I actually wanted to fix farm machinery! I loved anything technical. At driving school, I loved the lessons on car maintenance. Later, when I got a flat tire, I changed it myself without any problem. But the moment I said at home that I wanted to repair machinery, my dad slammed his hand on the table. 'A woman's place is in the kitchen!' he said—and that was that."

So she became a cook. And, to her surprise, she grew to love it. "At work, I always liked making short order dishes, turning out meals quickly, one after another. Cutting, serving, handing out full plates, getting them back licked clean, the speed, the adrenaline—that was fun! And I was always proud when the guests praised the food."

To offset the stress of the kitchen, Marie baked cakes for friends on weekends. She canned fruit and vegetables, too, a habit from her childhood.

She remembers the family farm and its huge garden: "We made wine from almost anything: rose hips, sour cherries, even bread or rice. My mother had this special way of keeping plums. She picked the frosted fruits, stacked them unwashed into a big, dry bottle, flipped it upside down on a plate, and poured a mixture of water and vinegar around the neck and regularly refilled it so that no air or bacteria could get in. She stored the jar this way in the pantry, where the low temperature prevented the plums from fermenting. All winter long the plums tasted like they'd just come off the tree! We also preserved raw eggs in slaked lime. You mixed lime with water, poured it over the eggs, sealed the jar with cellophane, and placed it in the cold. The lime hardened the shells and kept the eggs fresh for ages."

After living in a housing development called *sídliště* with her husband Karel, they bought a plot in a nearby gardening community. They grew strawberries, cucumbers, and cabbage—canning and pickling everything.

"We liked to pickle cabbage with horseradish so there'd be something to nibble on with drinks for New Year's Eve. You're supposed to add just a little horseradish to each kilo (about 2 pounds) of cabbage, but once I messed up and told my husband to grate a kilo of horseradish instead. He couldn't stop crying! We had to throw open every window in the cottage. We both had tears streaming down our faces for ages ... Just don't put that in the book!" Marie laughs.

Time moved on. Now the Camrdas keep only a few apple trees in their garden. Marie no longer cans, but she never misses turning the harvest into cider. Her trick is simple: Freeze it. "Take a bottle out of the freezer in the evening, put it on a plate in the kitchen, and in the morning you've got a fresh drink."

She's still looking for a way to make cider at home without a press. "People say you can grate the apples, but I don't think you can ever squeeze enough juice out by hand. I read about using an old washing-machine wringer—but detergent-flavored juice doesn't sound good to me! So I take the apples to the local cider house. I'd recommend it to anyone. It's hardly any work, it doesn't cost much, and then you can drink cider all winter long. Who would have thought four apple trees could give you 90 bottles of fragrant juice?" Marie finishes with a bright, infectious laugh.

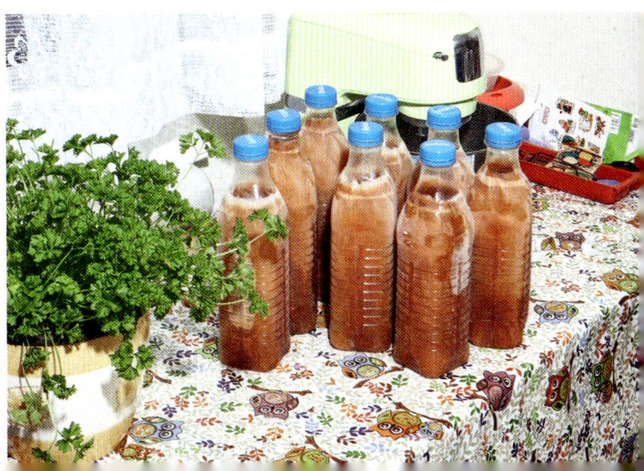

Pear Butter with Rum

For 3 or 4 canning jars (16 ounces / 350 ml each)

Ingredients

4 ½ pounds (2 kg) ripe pears

2 tablespoons distilled white vinegar

2 ½ cups (500 g) granulated sugar

¼ cup (60 ml) rum, plus extra for drizzling

1 teaspoon ground cinnamon

½ teaspoon ground cloves

¼ teaspoon ground star anise

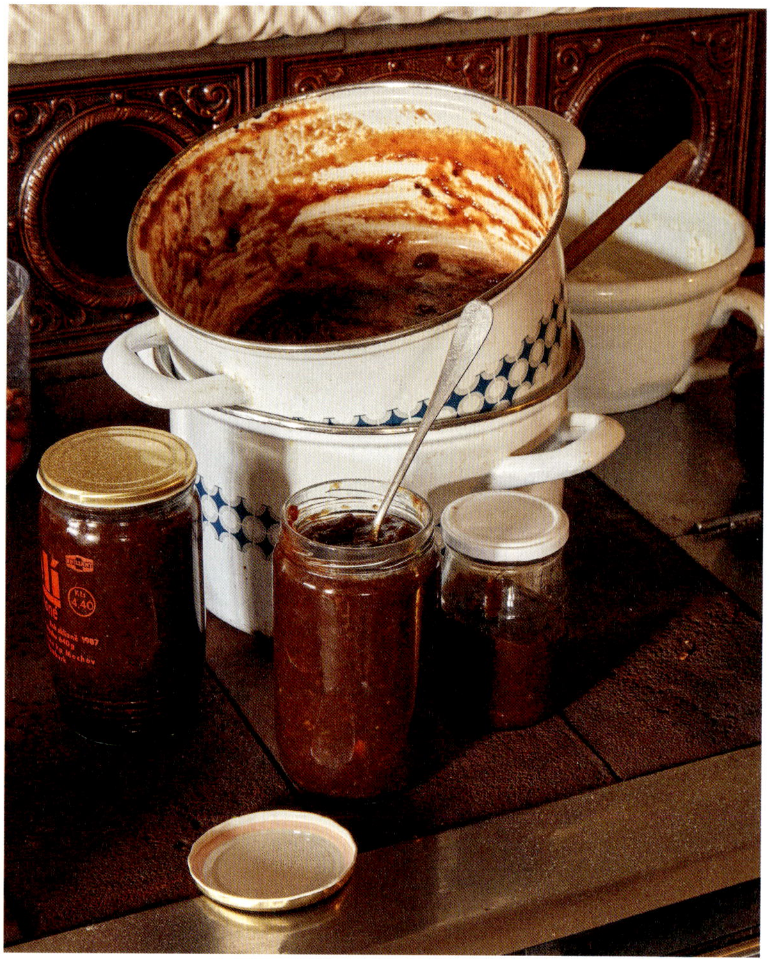

Preheat the oven to 425 °F top/bottom heat (220 °C/Gas Mark 7).

Wash the pears, peeling them if their skin is quite firm, then quarter and core. Cut larger pears into small pieces. Put the pear pieces into a deep roasting pan, drizzle with the vinegar, and mix well. Bake for 20 to 25 minutes without stirring.

Sprinkle the pears evenly with half of the sugar and bake for 15 minutes. Now sprinkle over the remaining sugar and bake again for another 15 minutes, still without stirring.

Add the rum to the pan, then stir in the spices. Using an immersion stick blender, puree the pears until very smooth (optionally, leave a few chunks of fruit). If the pear butter is too runny after blending, put the roasting pan back into the oven and gently cook down for 15 to 20 minutes. The pear butter will thicken even more as it cools.

Transfer the hot pear butter to sterilized canning jars and drizzle over a little rum to prevent it from spoiling quickly. Close the jars tightly, place upside down, and let cool completely. Store in a cool, dark place.

Tips Ripe and even overripe pears are best suited to this recipe. However, if the pears you use are a little firmer and more tart, simply cook them for a little longer.

This pear butter can be used as a filling for *kolaches* (see p. 106) and *buchty* rolls (see p. 158), as well as strudel (see p. 162), jelly rolls (Swiss rolls), and sweet dumplings. It also goes well with *lívance* (traditional Czech yeast pancakes), crepes, and *koblihy* (see p. 68). Use it to sweeten breakfast oatmeal (porridge) or muesli.

Pear Compote with White Wine

For 4 or 5 canning jars (16 ounces/650 ml each)

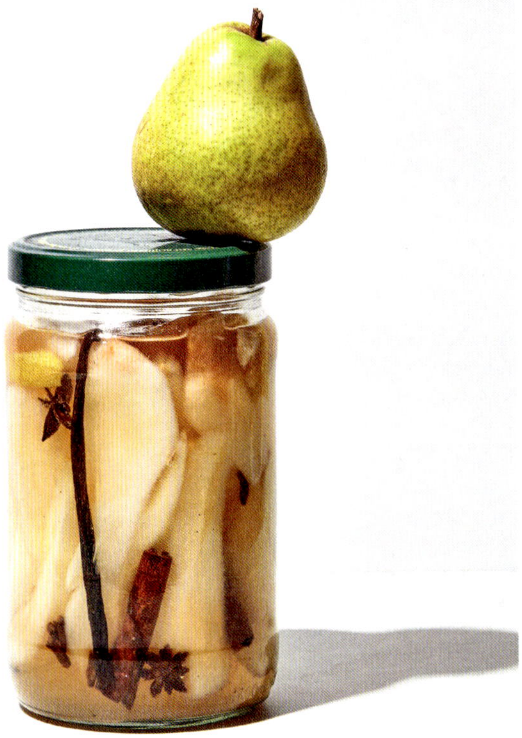

Ingredients

4 ¼ cups (1 l) water
2 cups (500 ml) dry white wine
2 cups (400 g) granulated sugar
6 cloves
4 cinnamon sticks
4 star anise
4 ½ pounds (2 kg) pears
Juice of 1 lemon

To make the syrup, mix together the water, white wine, sugar, and all the spices in a large saucepan. Bring to a boil over medium heat, stirring occasionally, until the sugar dissolves.

Wash, peel, quarter, and core the pears. Add the pear quarters to the syrup. Cook for about 5 minutes (or longer if you want the fruit to be softer). Remove from the heat and stir in the lemon juice.

Transfer the pear quarters to sterilized canning jars and pour over the hot spiced syrup. Close the jars and process in a water bath. Let cool, then store in a cool, dark place.

Tips If you prefer the pears firmer, omit the precooking step. The pears will soften a little in the hot syrup.

Allow the compote to age in the jar for a few weeks before use to let the aroma completely develop. If you want a less intensely flavored compote, simply take the spices out of the syrup before canning.

You can also add a split vanilla bean (pod), leftover from a recipe that used the seeds, for example in baking, by adding it to the syrup for a subtle vanilla flavor.

Pear and Apple Chutney with Shallots and Ginger

For 4 canning jars (8 ounces / 200 ml each)

Ingredients

2 small apples
10 very ripe pears
1 (1½-inch / 4-cm) piece fresh ginger
6 shallots
3½ tablespoons (50 g) unsalted butter
1 teaspoon ground cinnamon
¼ teaspoon ground cloves
¼ teaspoon ground star anise
½ teaspoon ground coriander seeds
¼ teaspoon chili powder
Salt and freshly ground black pepper
2 tablespoons apple cider vinegar

Peel the apples and wash the pears (leave them unpeeled), then core and cut into small dice. Peel and finely grate the ginger. Peel and mince (very finely chop) the shallots.

Heat the butter in a pot and sauté the shallots until golden. Add the grated ginger and cook briefly, stirring continuously, until fragrant. Add the apples, pears, and spices and season with salt and pepper. Bring to a boil until the fruit releases its liquid. Reduce the heat and simmer, uncovered, for 2 to 3 hours, until the fruit falls apart and the mixture thickens, stirring occasionally. When the chutney caramelizes and turns dark, remove from the heat and let cool.

Add the vinegar and adjust the seasoning with salt and pepper. Bring the chutney to a boil again, then lower the heat to a minimum and simmer until the mixture thickens even further. Transfer the hot chutney to small sterilized canning jars. Close the jars tightly, place upside down, and let cool completely. Use the chutney immediately or store in the refrigerator.

Tips Beurre Hardy pears are best suited to this chutney. Their juicy and buttery flesh becomes soft and smooth when cooked down, and their sweetness goes perfectly with the acidity of the vinegar and the spices. You can also use Bosc or Conference pears.

For an even more intense flavor, add the spices directly to the shallot and ginger mixture to release their full aroma.

This pear and apple chutney makes a wonderful accompaniment for cheese. You can also use it as a dip, to spread on burger buns or sandwiches, and as a condiment for steaks and grilled vegetables. It is also excellent with poultry or lamb; you can brush it over meat for roulades.

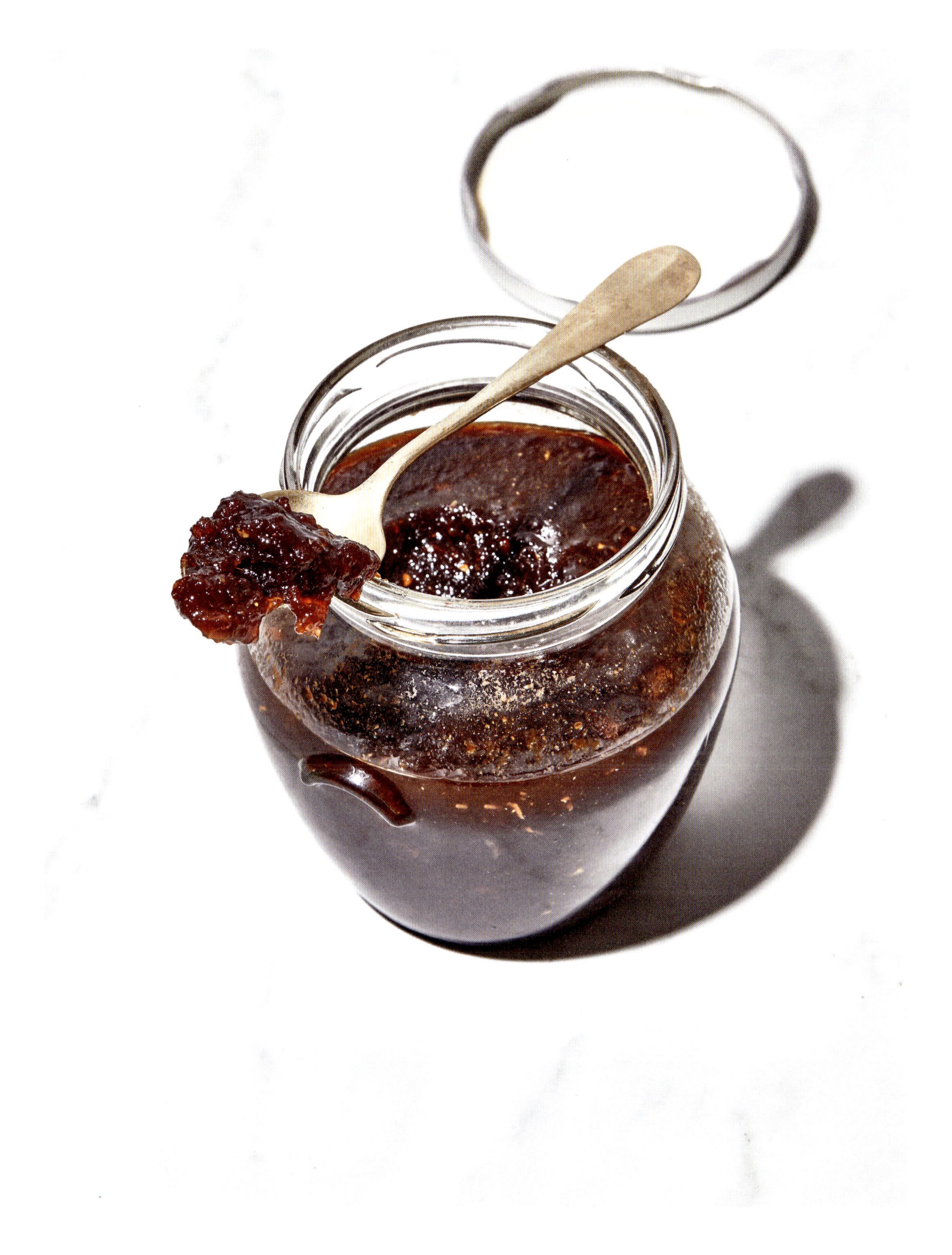

From Root to Stem: Every Part Counts

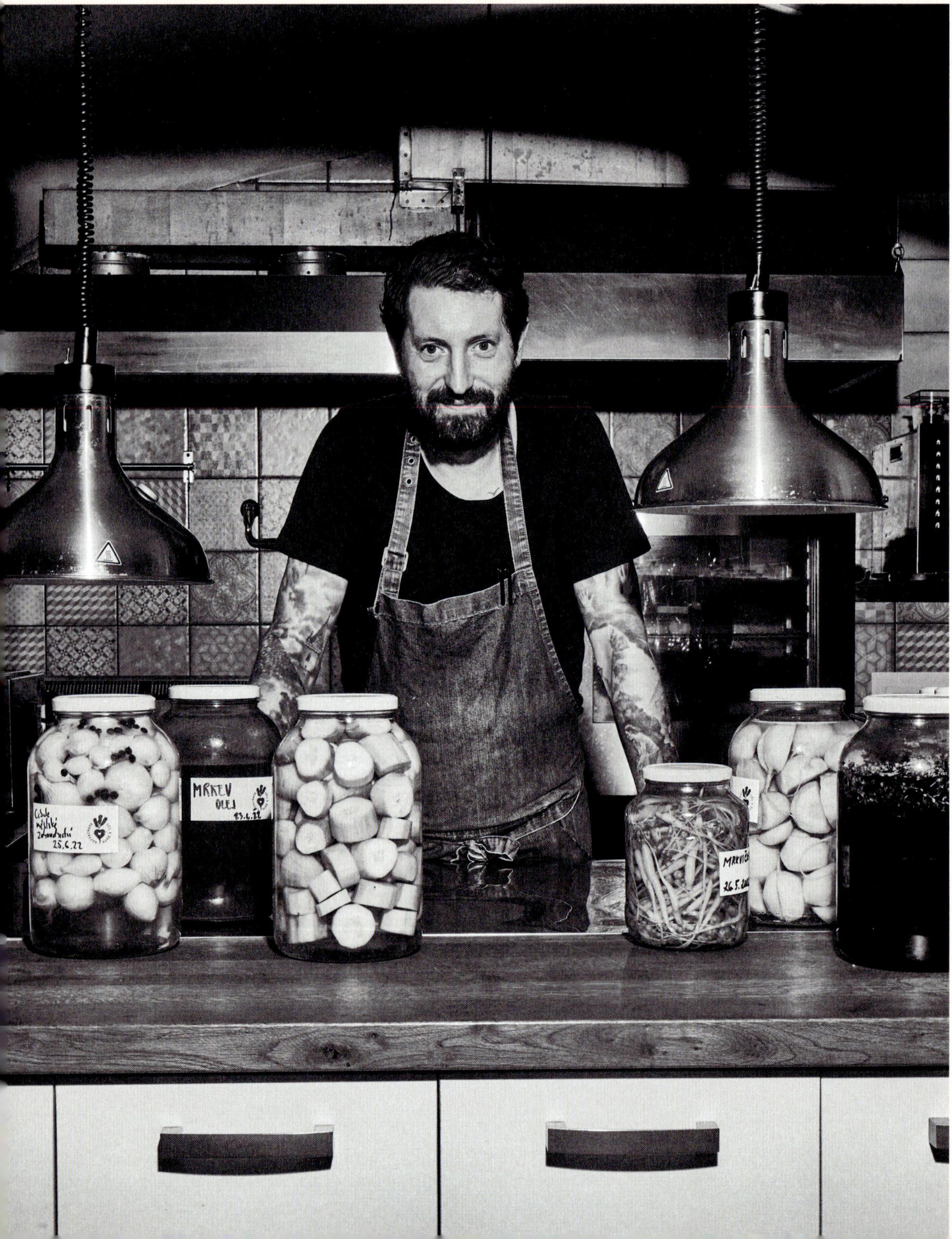

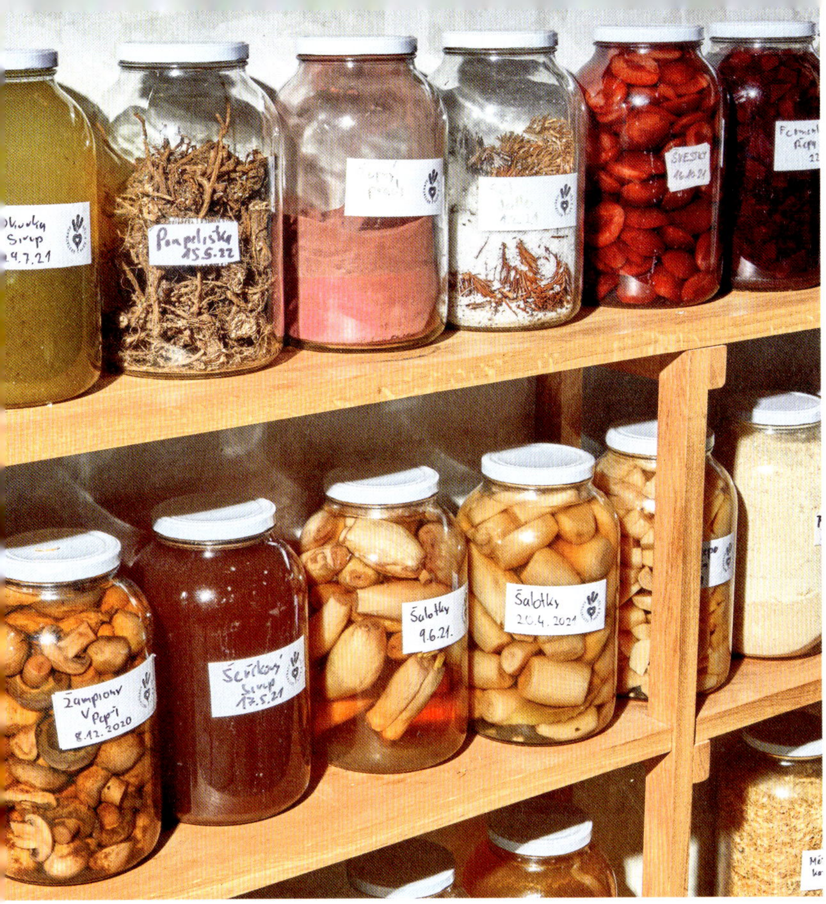

Committed to sustainability and honoring the efforts of local farmers, chef Pavel Drdel makes sure nothing goes to waste in his kitchen.

In a long, dim corridor, barely wide enough to pass, both walls are stacked with shelves of jars and bottles filled with pickled, dried, and fermented fruit and vegetables, all glowing in the half-light. With each step, your mouth starts to water—the closer you get, the more intensely you can smell the enticing aromas drifting in from the open kitchen grow stronger. Welcome to Sůl a Řepa ("Salt and Beet"), the restaurant in Strakonice that has become a must-visit stop in South Bohemia.

The playfully named location has been making waves on the Czech food scene since it opened in 2017. It was cofounded by local chef Pavel Drdel, a local native with many hats. He is a founding member of the association Jíme Jih ("Let's Eat South"), author of the book *Postní kuchařka*, an enthusiastic photographer, ambassador for the charity drive *Postni se* organized by the Diaconia of the Czech Brethren Church, and regular collaborator with the České Budějovice nonprofit charity Active Time.

Pavel trained as a cook, but after school he wanted to try something different. He moved to Milan, Italy, where he worked in a motorcycle factory, building and repairing engines. However, it wasn't long before he was back in the kitchen.

He spent more than seven years cooking in Italy—including internships at Michelin-star restaurants—before moving on to kitchens in Germany and later back in the Czech Republic. When asked where it all began for him, he always returns to childhood summers and weekends with his grandparents. "Grandma would go to the garden and cook lunch from whatever she picked that morning. I was fascinated by the fact that you could pull vegetables from the soil and a few hours later be eating them for lunch."

That same approach followed him to Italy, where he saw chefs in professional kitchens run out to the garden for basil or ripe tomatoes.

His experience abroad eventually motivated Pavel to start thinking about cooking in a different way to what had long been customary in Czech restaurants. For him, cooking starts not in the kitchen but with farmers in the fields. He builds his menus on local ingredients. He blends Czech traditions with modern global techniques and works to a simple philosophy: from root to stem. Out of respect for the hard work of small-scale producers, and with an eye on sustainability, he aims to cook with zero waste. That's why preserving has become central to his craft.

"To me, cooking from scratch with honest farm ingredients means cooking with abundance," he says. "You support local farmers and small producers, strengthen the regional economy, and protect the environment. In the kitchen, you can use everything down to the peel. It's more time-consuming and you have to think harder about the process, but the reward is a clear conscience." His approach has since inspired chefs all over the country.

When you sit down at Sůl a Řepa to enjoy glazed carrots, carrot powder (see p. 174), and carrot-top pesto, all on one plate, take a look around: jars of plum compote, strawberry syrup, beet and parsley root dust, oil infused with charred bark and needles, fir sprigs packed in salt, dried marigolds, and even dandelion roots line the shelves, the bar, and the windowsills. It's sustainability in action—and a reminder that warm-hearted Pavel Drdel really is the preserving king of Czech gastronomy.

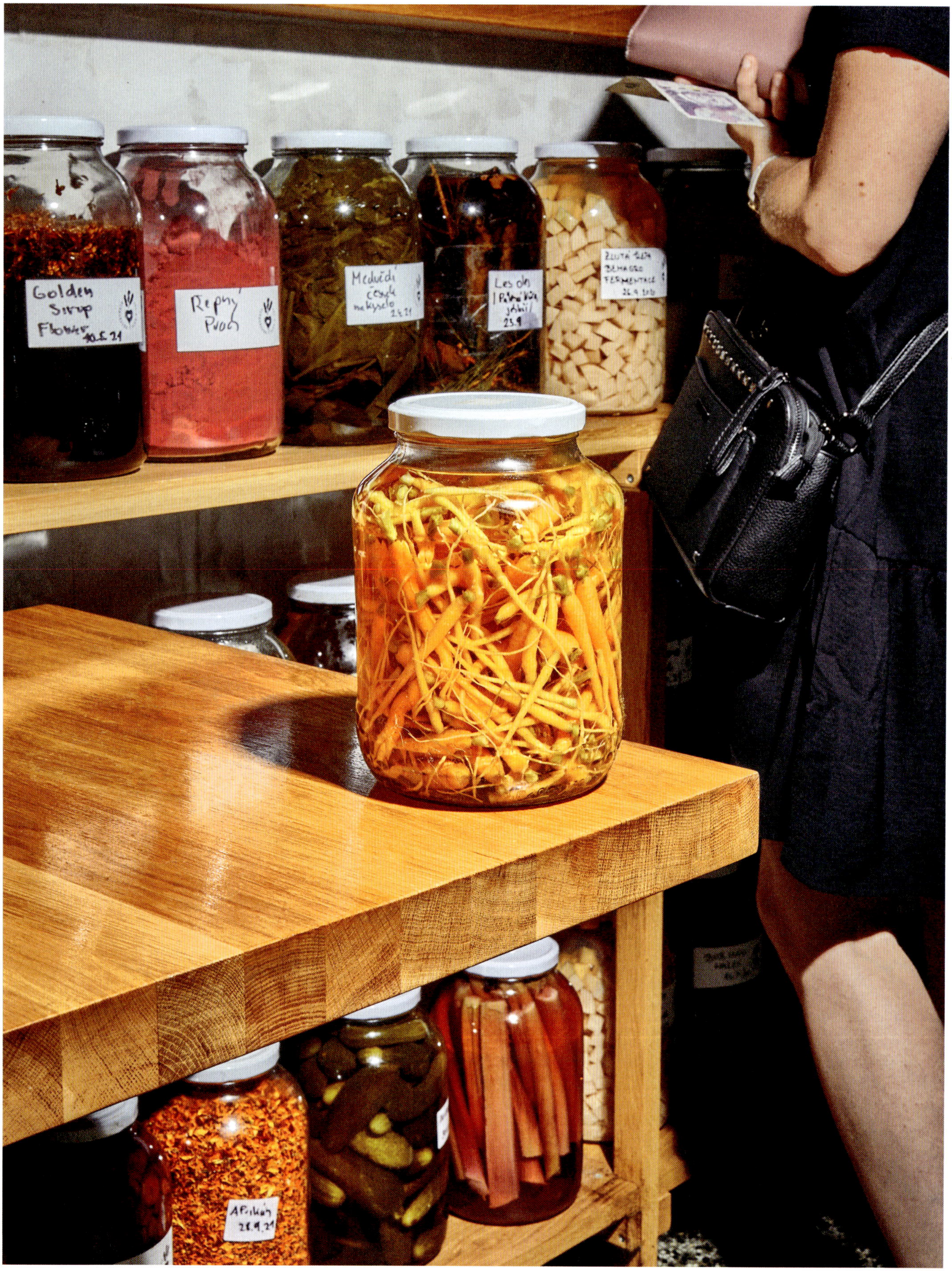
Golden Sirup Flower
FERMENTACE

Fermented Carrots

For 1 canning jar (64 ounces / 1.7 l)

Ingredients

5 ½ cups (1.3 l) water

1 ½ tablespoons (26 g) salt

3 ¼ pounds (1.5 kg) carrots

To make the brine, bring the water to a boil in a pot. Add the salt and stir until completely dissolved. Let cool.

Brush the carrots thoroughly with a vegetable brush, then wash. Peel if necessary. Cut larger carrots into small dice, slices, or sticks.

Arrange the carrots layers in a sterilized canning jar. The vegetables should be layered as tightly as possible in the jar to keep them from floating to the top. Pour over the brine to about ½ inch (1 cm) below the rim of the jar. Place the lid loosely on the jar without closing it tightly. The carrots must be completely covered in the liquid. If necessary, use a sterilized fermentation weight to keep them in place. Because foam can form during the fermentation process, place the preserving jar in a shallow bowl. Let ferment in a dark place at room temperature (62 to 70 °F / 17 – 21 °C). The carrots may spoil at a higher temperature.

Taste the carrots after 14 days. By this time, the bubbles should have stopped forming and the carrots should have a pleasantly sour and spicy taste. Now close the lid tightly and refrigerate to stop the fermentation. The flavor will continue to develop as the carrots mature. These fermented carrots can be stored in a cool place for several weeks up to a few months.

Tips If you want to ferment more or fewer carrots, simply adjust the amount of the brine. As a rule of thumb, use 1 tablespoon (20 g) of salt per 4 ¼ cups (1 l) of water.

Only a clean fork should come into contact with the contents of the jar. Pay attention to cleanliness when preparing and storing fermented vegetables to keep them from spoiling.

This recipe is perfect for using baby carrots leftover from thinning out your carrot patch.

Carrot Powder

Ingredients

Carrot peels and greens (leafy tops)

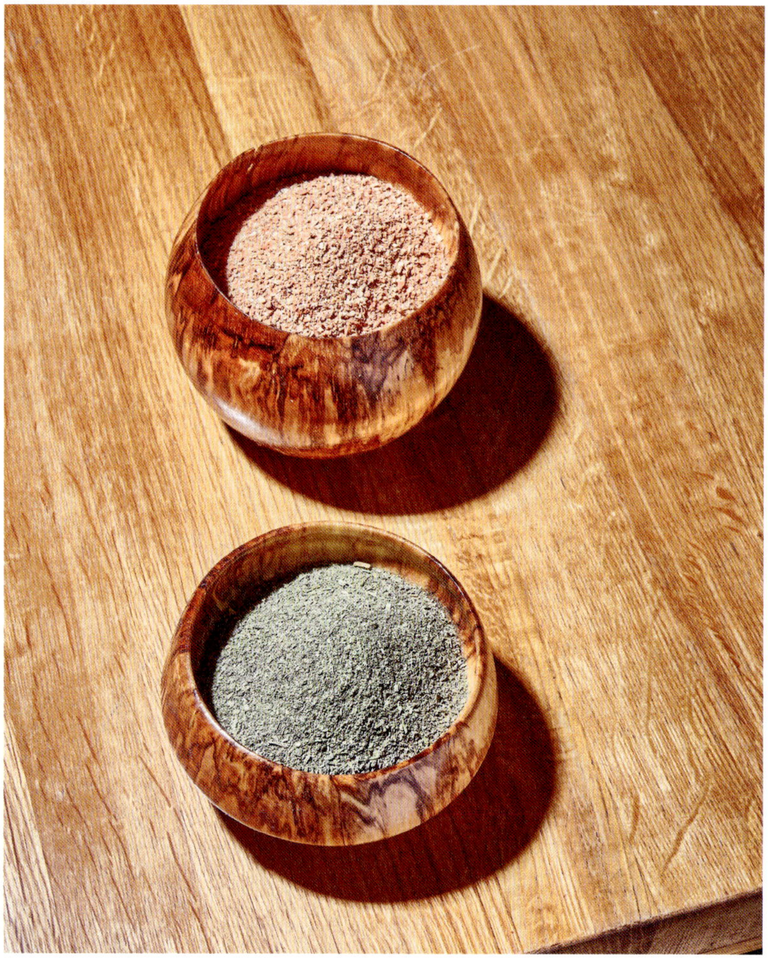

Spread the carrot peels and greens evenly over a baking sheet or large drying rack and let dry out in a warm place for 2 to 3 days. Using a dehydrator will speed up the process.

In a blender, grind the dried peels and greens separately to a fine powder. Transfer each type of powder to a separate jar and close tightly. Carrot powder can be stored for several months and replenished as often as you like.

You can use carrot powder to season sauces, soups, or spreads, among others. You can also use it to garnish different dishes just before serving.

Carrot Leaf Oil

For 1 bottle (16 ounces / 400 ml)

Ingredients

Greens (leafy tops) from 2 bunches of carrots

1¼ cups (300 ml) canola (rapeseed) oil

1 pinch of salt

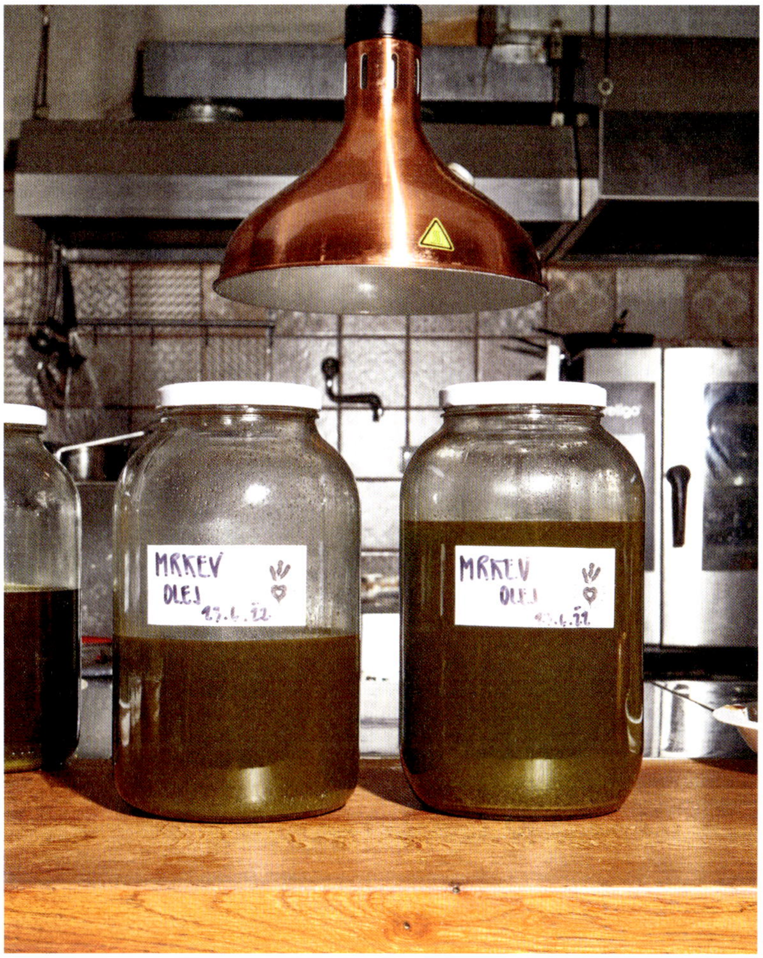

Briefly blanch the carrot greens: Boil them in hot water for 30 to 60 seconds, then drain immediately and place in ice water to shock them. This will allow the greens to retain their beautiful dark green color.

Heat the oil in a saucepan to 140 °F (60 °C)—check the temperature with a probe thermometer. Transfer the heated oil to a blender jar, add the blanched carrot greens, and season with the salt. Puree until smooth, then filter through a clean cheesecloth (muslin). Transfer the oil to a sterilized bottle and store in the refrigerator. Use the carrot leaf oil immediately or store for up to 1 month.

Tips Choose a good-quality, preferably farm-produced oil. Lower quality oils often leave an unpleasant aftertaste in the mouth.

Bring the carrot leaf oil to room temperature before use. If too cold, it can be a little thick or cloudy, although this is purely visual and won't affect its quality.

This way, you can make great use of the left over carrot tops!

Quick Pickled Red Onions

For 2 or 3 canning jars (8 ounces / 150 ml each)

Ingredients

Scant 1 cup (200 ml) apple cider vinegar

⅔ cup (150 ml) water

About ¼ cup (40–60 g) granulated sugar

1 teaspoon salt

3 bay leaves

10 peppercorns

5 allspice berries

3 red onions

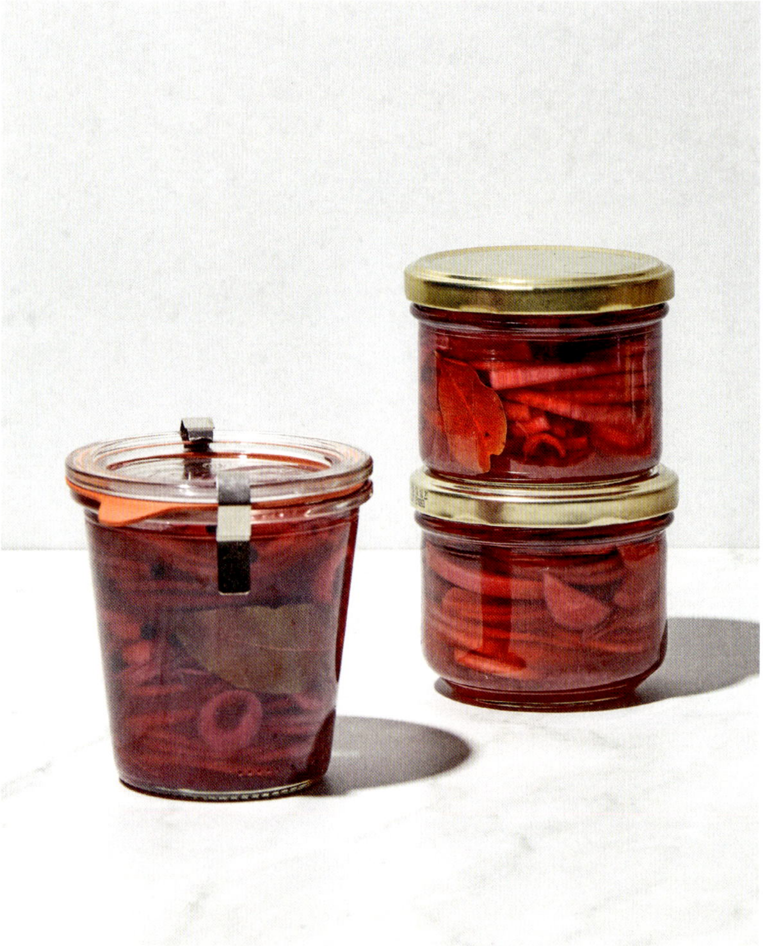

To make the pickling liquid, mix the vinegar and water in a saucepan and add the sugar, salt, bay leaves and spices. Bring to a boil, stirring occasionally, until the sugar and salt dissolve. Let the liquid boil for a few minutes and then remove from the heat.

Peel the onions, halve them, if necessary, and thinly slice. Put the onion slices into sterilized canning jars and pour over the hot liquid until the onions are completely covered. Close the jars, let the onions cool, and store them in the refrigerator. Pickle for at least 3 days before use.

Tip These pickled red onions can be used in salads and as an accompaniment for grilled meat or homemade pork aspic (see p. 248).

Dried Wild Mushroom Oil

For 1 large canning jar (64 ounces / 1.7 l)

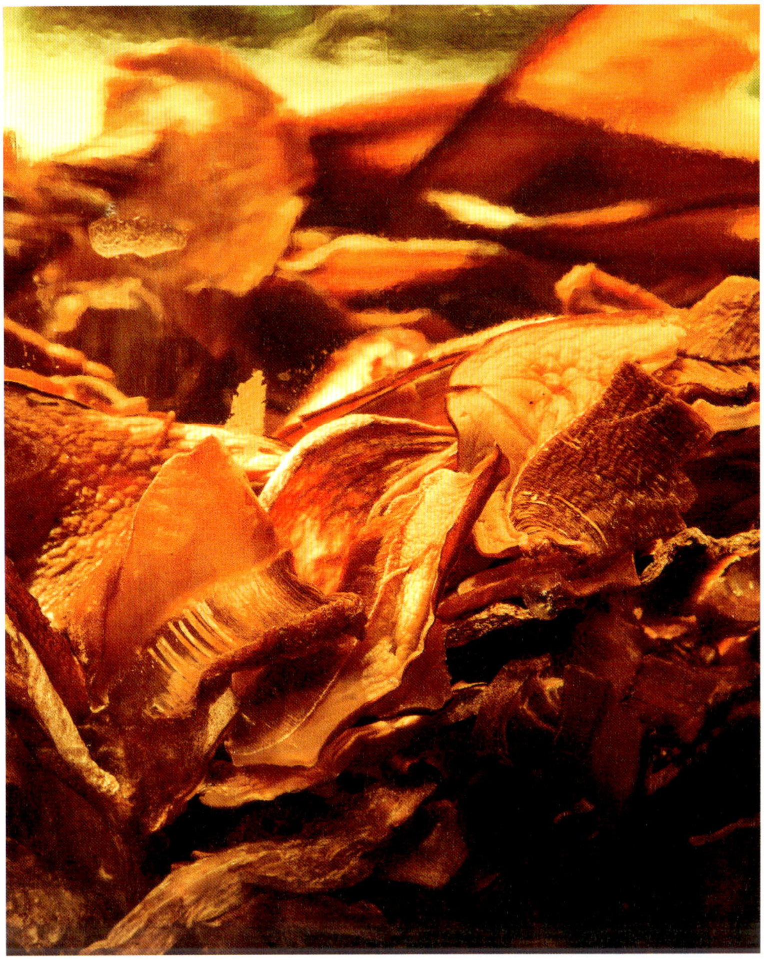

Ingredients

4 cups (150 g) dried mix wild mushrooms

6 ⅓ cups (1.5 l) cold-pressed canola (rapeseed) oil

Preheat the oven to 170 °F top/bottom heat (75 °C).

Spread the dried mushrooms out over a baking sheet and roast for 15 minutes to intensify their aroma and eliminate any microorganisms that could interfere with the oil's long-term aging.

Heat the oil in a saucepan to 150 °F (65 °C)—check the temperature with a probe thermometer. Remove from the heat and set aside.

Transfer the mushrooms to a large sterilized canning jar and pour over the still warm oil. Let the oil cool completely and then close the jar tightly. Store the oil at room temperature in a dark place.

You can use the oil after 6 months, but the flavor becomes more intense with time and is at its best after at least 1 year.

Tip This mushroom oil is packed full of umami. You can use the oil in any mushroom dish in which you want to enhance its flavor, including sauces, cream soups, and risotto. It also adds a special flavor to pizza and an omelet.

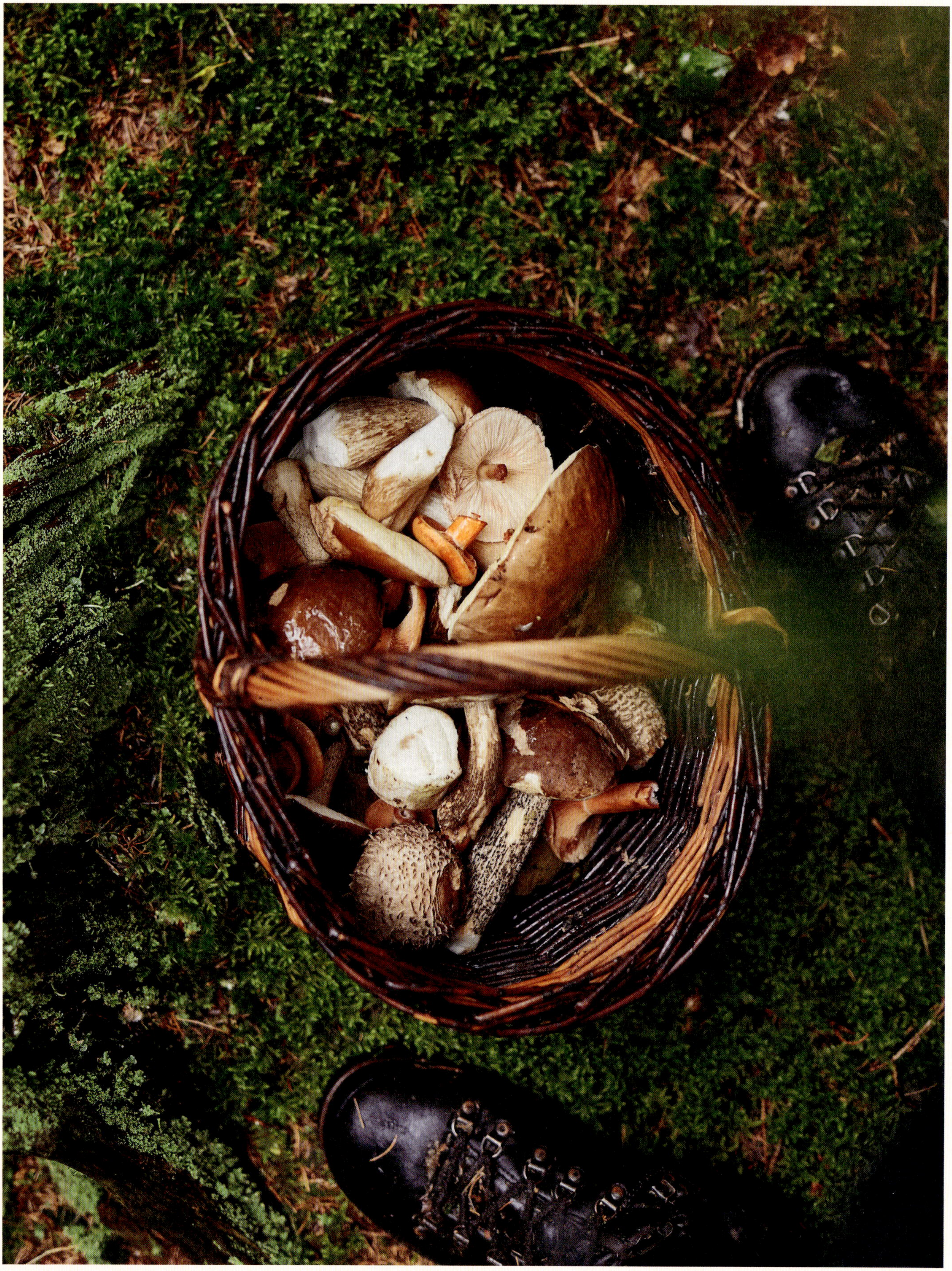

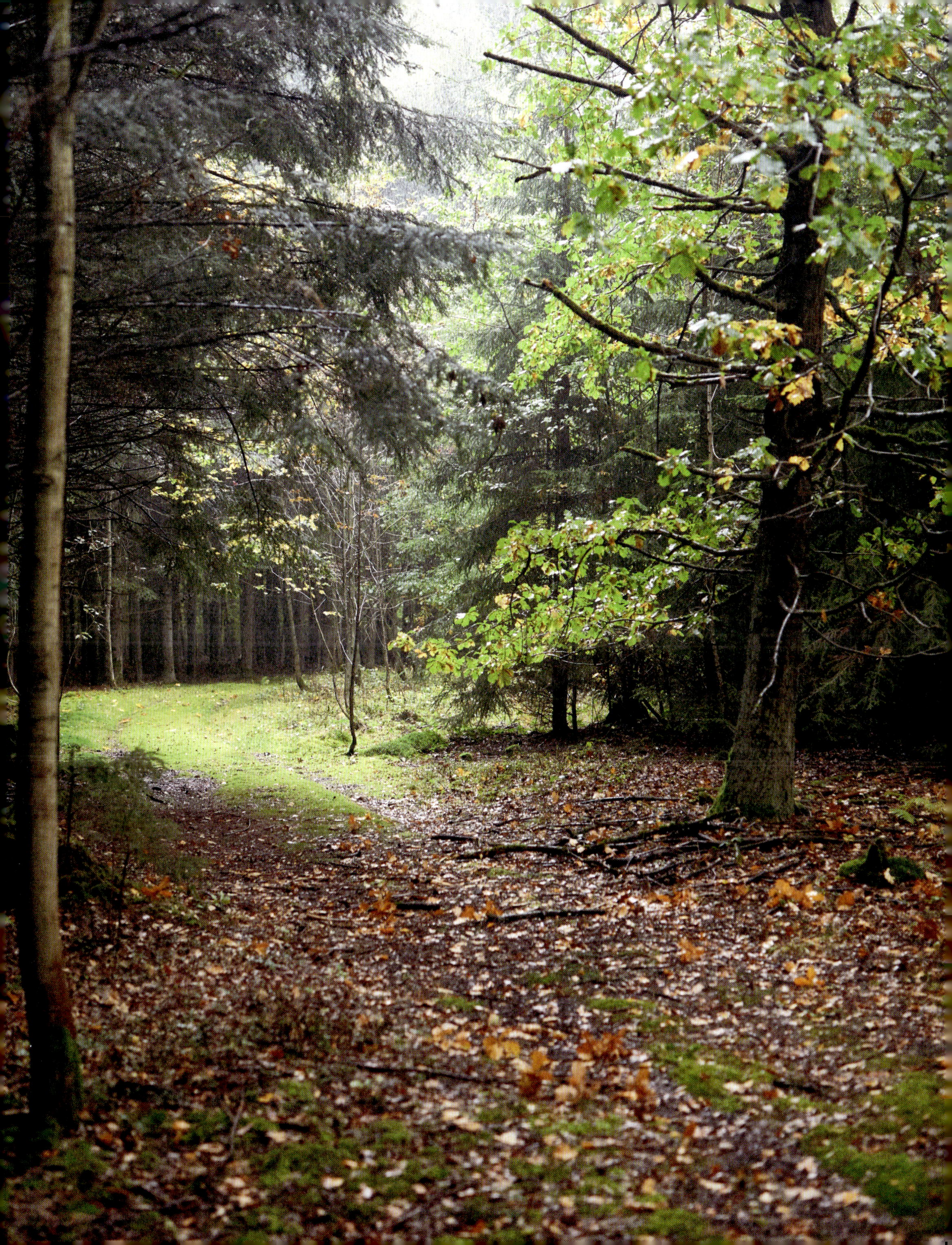

Ukrainian Heritage on the Czech Table

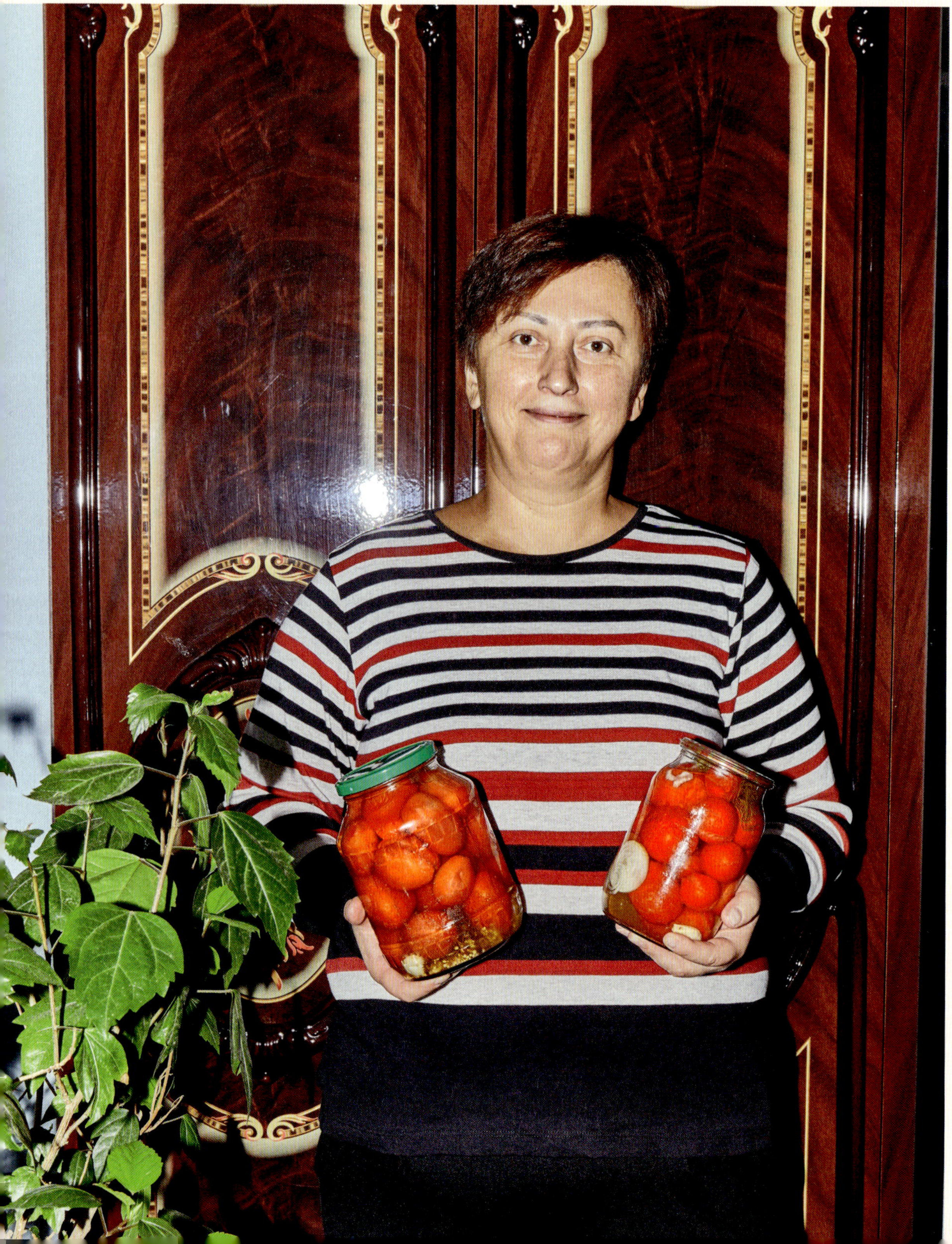

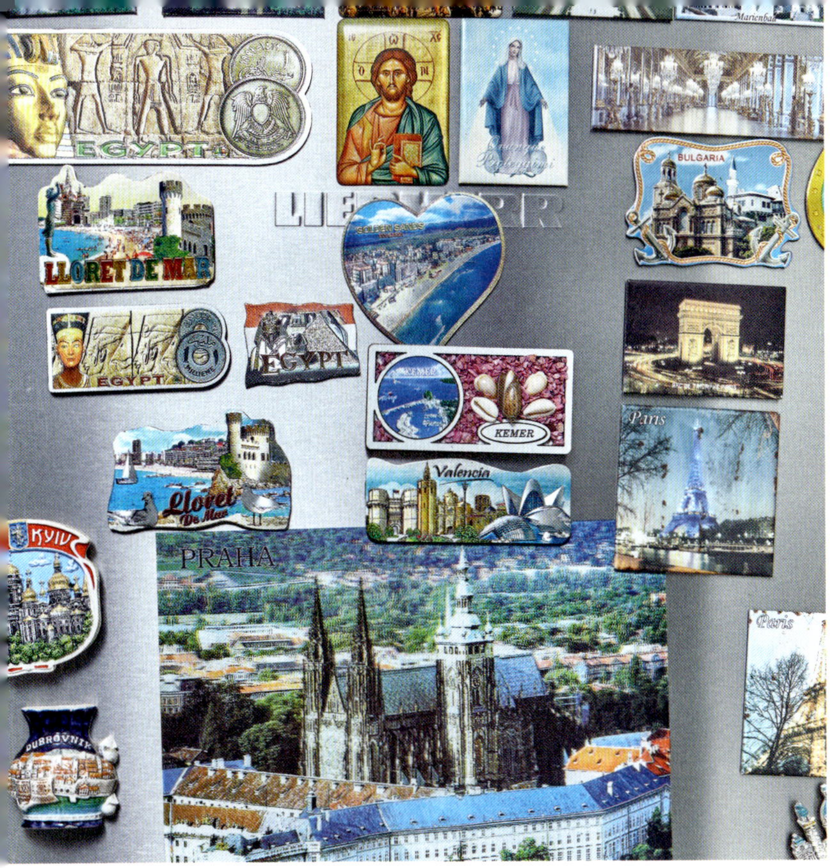

Marija and her family all love the mushroom salad with potatoes boiled in their skins and chopped fresh onions. "It's really delicious with onions. But that's an evening dish—you can't go anywhere after eating it, and it's better not to talk to anyone either!" she laughs. She then pulls out another jar, saying, "This is another delicacy, mushroom pâté, are you familiar with it?" We are now!

Máša, as she is affectionately called, draws her inspiration from both her mother and her Ukrainian roots. We admire the big jars of cabbage. Unlike the sauerkraut that is made shredded in the Czech Republic, whole cabbage heads are often pickled in Ukraine. The large leaves are then used to make stuffed cabbage rolls, which the Ukrainians refer to as *holubky* (see p. 228). Just as eye-catching are the jars of pickled whole tomatoes. In the past, vegetables that spoiled quickly were canned in bulk so there was always something to put on the table during the long, hard winters. In Ukraine, canned tomatoes are served as a side dish or as part of *zakuski*, appetizer-style dishes meant to be eaten with vodka.

Alongside fruit and vegetables, Marija also loves to preserve fish, with her favorite being mackerel slow-cooked in its own juice.

With mushroom salad or pickled cabbage heads, Marija Bartošová preserves the tastes of her homeland, keeping Ukrainian family traditions alive in every jar.

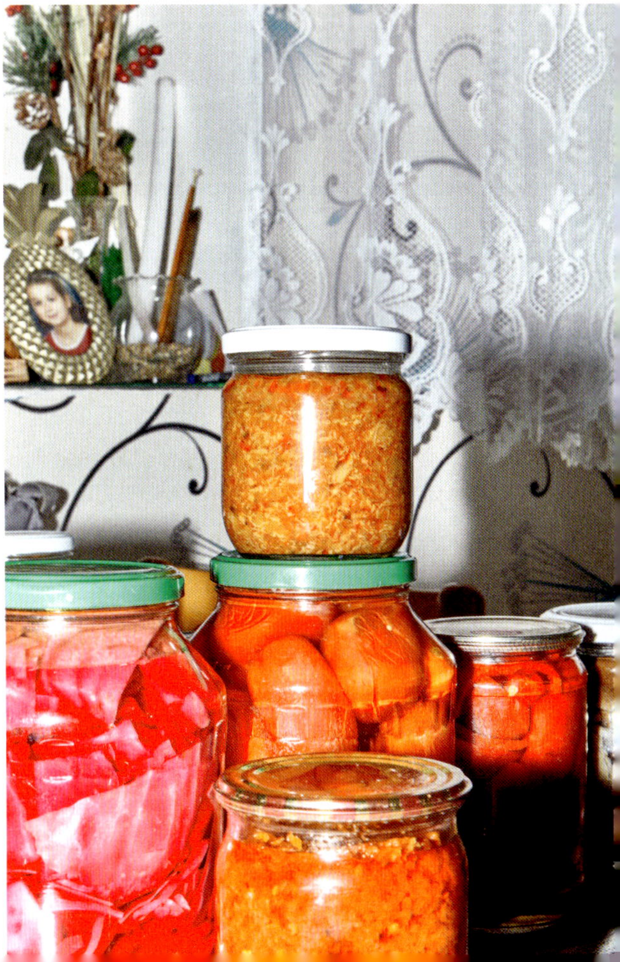

Friendly and warm-hearted, Marija comes from Koločava, a Ukrainian village on the southern edge of Sinevir National Park. She has been living in the Czech Republic for almost thirty years. What was meant to be a short adventure turned into a whole new life—she fell in love with the country, the people, and the landscape. Today, she works as a caregiver in a hospital for long-term patients.

Her great passion is canning. "My colleagues at work even gave me a canning pot for my birthday," she says enthusiastically. Her specialty is Mushroom Salad (see p. 182). "When fall comes, we head out into the forest to pick honey mushrooms. They start growing in September and thrive in the cooler weather around St. Wenceslas Day, on September 28. You can find them until late November, sometimes even into December. Raw honey mushrooms are actually mildly poisonous, but after cooking they're perfectly safe—and absolutely delicious!" she says, stroking her Yorkshire terrier, Max.

Mushroom Salad

For 5 or 6 canning jars (8 ounces / 300 ml each)

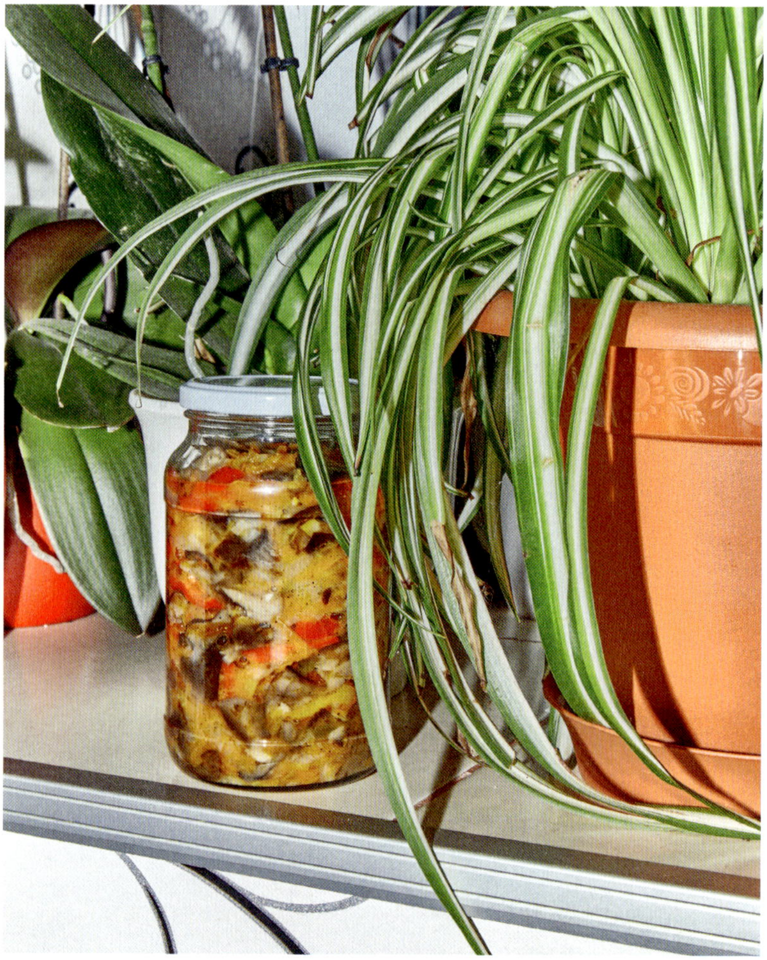

Ingredients

2 ¼ pounds (1 kg) honey mushrooms
1 pound 2 ounces (500 g) red bell peppers
1 pound 2 ounces (500 g) carrots
10 ½ ounces (300 g) onions
2 tablespoons sunflower oil
4 tablespoons Tomato Ketchup (see p. 126)
Salt
5 bay leaves
25 peppercorns

Bring the water to a boil in a saucepan. Trim and clean the mushrooms, wiping them with a cloth, if necessary, and boil for 15 minutes. Halve the peppers lengthwise, remove the white ribs and seeds, and wash. Now cut them into thin strips. Wash, peel, and shred (coarsely grate) the carrots. Peel and mince (very finely chop) the onions.

Drain the mushrooms, place them in cold water to shock them, and let drain in a strainer or sieve. Heat 1 tablespoon of the oil in a skillet or frying pan and sauté the onions. Add the shredded carrot and bell pepper strips and sauté for 5 minutes, stirring occasionally. Heat the remaining oil in a second skillet and fry the mushrooms for at least 20 minutes. Stir in the ketchup.

Add the sautéed vegetables to the mushrooms and season with salt. Put 1 bay leaf and 5 black peppercorns into each jar. Transfer the mushroom and vegetable mixture to the jars, close tightly, and process in a water bath. Place the jars upside down, let cool, and store in a cool, dark place. The mushroom salad should be matured for at least 1 to 2 weeks before use.

Tip This mushroom and vegetable salad goes well with skin-on boiled potatoes and chopped onions. It also makes a good accompaniment for grilled or roasted meat.

Sweet-and-Sour Pickled Beets

For 5 canning jars (16 ounces / 500 ml each)

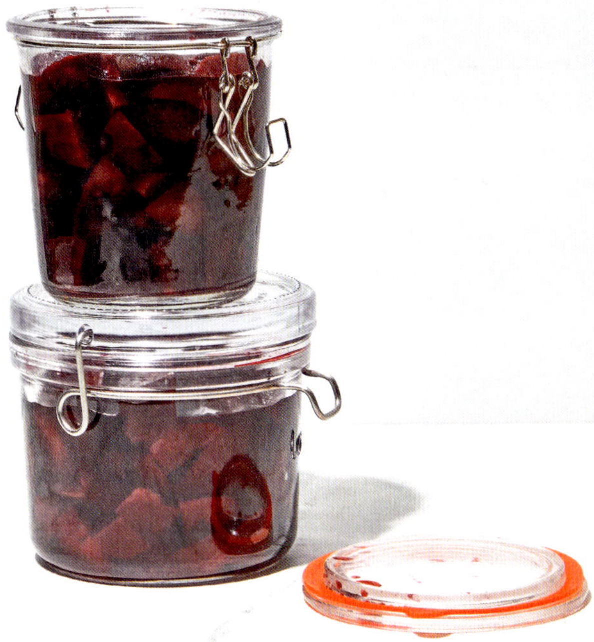

Ingredients

4 ½ to 6 ½ pounds (2–3 kg) of small, beets of equal size

4 ¼ cups (1 l) water

1 ½ cups (350 ml) distilled white vinegar

4 to 5 tablespoons granulated sugar

2 tablespoons salt

3 bay leaves

20 peppercorns

10 allspice berries

½ teaspoon fennel seeds or anise seeds (aniseed)

Wash and boil the unpeeled beets until firmly cooked. To test whether the beets are cooked through, prick them with a fork or a knife tip. They should be tender but still offer a little resistance. They will soften a little more once covered in hot pickling liquid. Drain, place in cold water to shock them, and let cool.

To make the pickling liquid, mix the water and vinegar in a saucepan and add the sugar, salt, bay leaves and spices. Bring to a boil, stirring occasionally, until the sugar and salt dissolve. Let boil for about 5 minutes, then remove from the heat.

Peel the beets, cut them into small dice or thinly slice, and transfer to sterilized canning jars. Pour over the hot liquid to cover the beets completely. Close the jars, process in a water bath, and let cool. Store in a cool and dark place.

Tip These sweet-and sour-pickled beets can be used to make Borscht (see p. 184) or Beet and Potato Salad (see p. 246), among others. They also make a good accompaniment for a skillet rice dish with meat and vegetables, and for salads with goat cheese.

Vegetarian Borscht

Serves 4

Ingredients

1 onion

3 cloves garlic

2 large carrots

4 large potatoes

2 tablespoons olive oil

3 tablespoons (50 g) tomato paste (puree)

2 bay leaves

5 allspice berries

Salt and freshly ground black pepper

6 ⅓ cups (1.5 l) vegetable broth (stock)

1 ⅔ cups (250 g) Sweet-and-Sour Pickled Beets (see p. 183)

1 cup (250 g) Sauerkraut (see p. 205)

1 tablespoon cane sugar

Sour cream and freshly chopped dill, to garnish (optional)

Peel and mince (very finely chop) the onion and garlic. Wash, peel, and cut the carrots and potatoes into small dice. Heat the oil in a pot and sauté the onions. Add the carrots and potatoes and sauté until golden. Add the garlic and cook for about 30 seconds, stirring continuously. Add the tomato paste and sauté until fragrant. Add the bay leaves and allspice berries, season with salt and pepper, and add the broth. Bring to a boil, then reduce the heat and let simmer for 15 to 20 minutes, until the vegetables are soft.

Drain the beets and add to the vegetables in the pot. Let simmer for 10 minutes. In the meantime, drain the sauerkraut and collect the liquid. Remove the bay leaves and allspice berries from the borscht and stir in the sauerkraut. Cook for another 5 minutes. Adjust the seasoning with sugar and the sauerkraut liquid.

Serve immediately, garnished with sour cream and chopped chives.

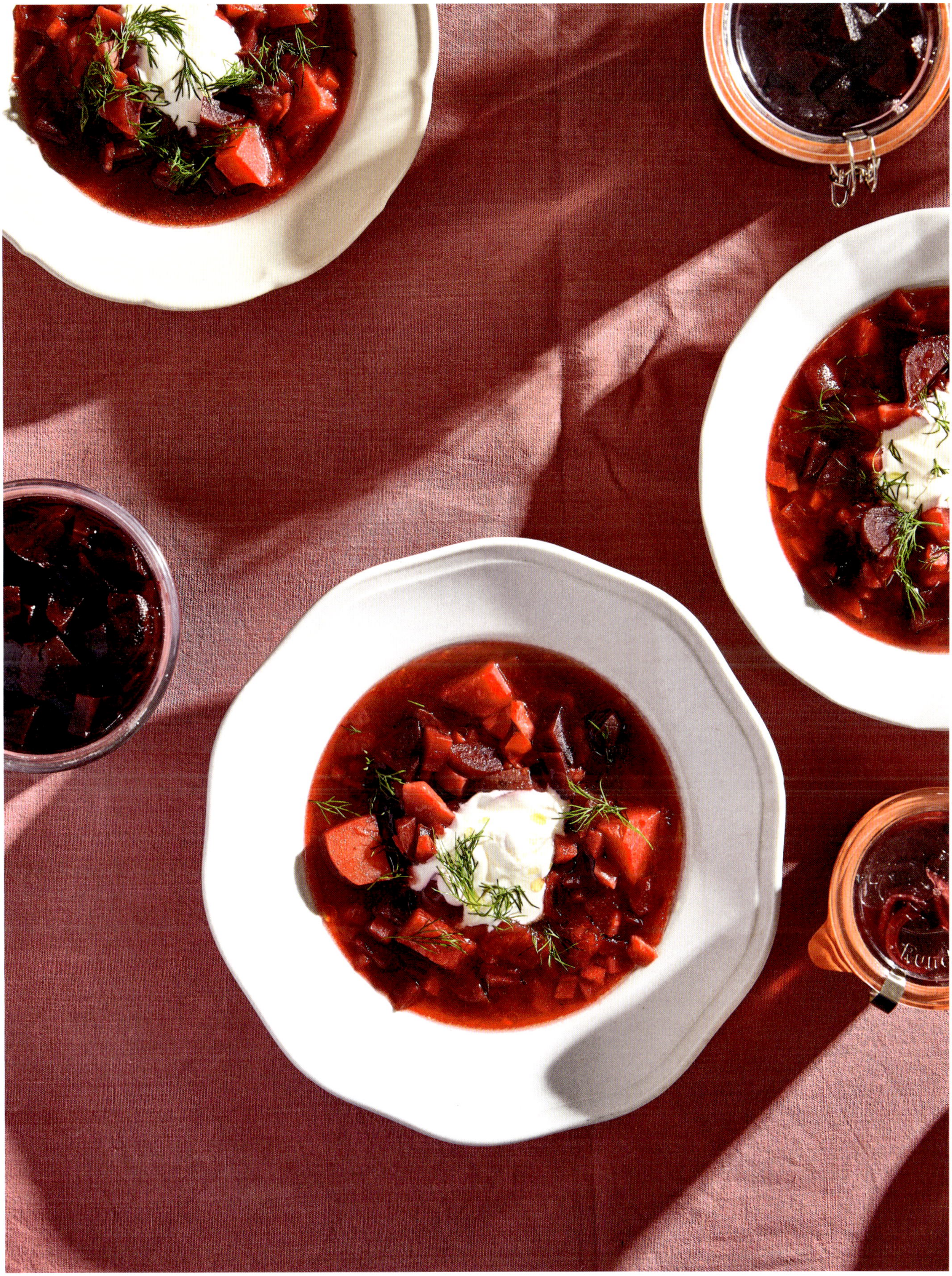

Pumpkin Puree

For 2 or 3 canning jars (8 ounces/350 ml each)

Ingredients

2 ¼-pounds (1 kg) red kuri (onion) squash

Preheat the oven to 325 °F top/bottom heat (160 °C/Gas Mark 3).

Wash and halve the squash and remove the stems. Using a spoon, scrape out the seeds, then peel the squash halves if necessary (see tips). Dice the squash and spread them over the baking sheet. Bake for at least 30 minutes, until soft.

Let the squash cool, then puree in a blender until smooth. If you want the puree to be very smooth, you can also push it through a strainer or sieve.

Transfer the puree to sterilized canning jars, close the lids tightly, and place them upside down. Use the pumpkin puree immediately or store in the refrigerator for up to 1 week. This puree can also be frozen for longer storage.

Tips Red kuri squash needs no peeling because the skin softens when baking. However, if the skin is discolored, scratched, or has any other irregularities, you should peel it before dicing.

Butternut squash also works great for making this purée; however, it always needs to be peeled before roasting because of its tough skin.

If the finished puree is too runny, transfer it to a bowl and refrigerate for a few hours. Then simply pour off the separated liquid.

This puree can be used to make a cream soup, a pasta sauce, or *bábovka* (see p. 188). It goes well with *lívance* (traditional Czech yeast pancakes) and you can also incorporate it into the dough for cinnamon rolls (buns) or the batter for a sponge cake or cheesecake.

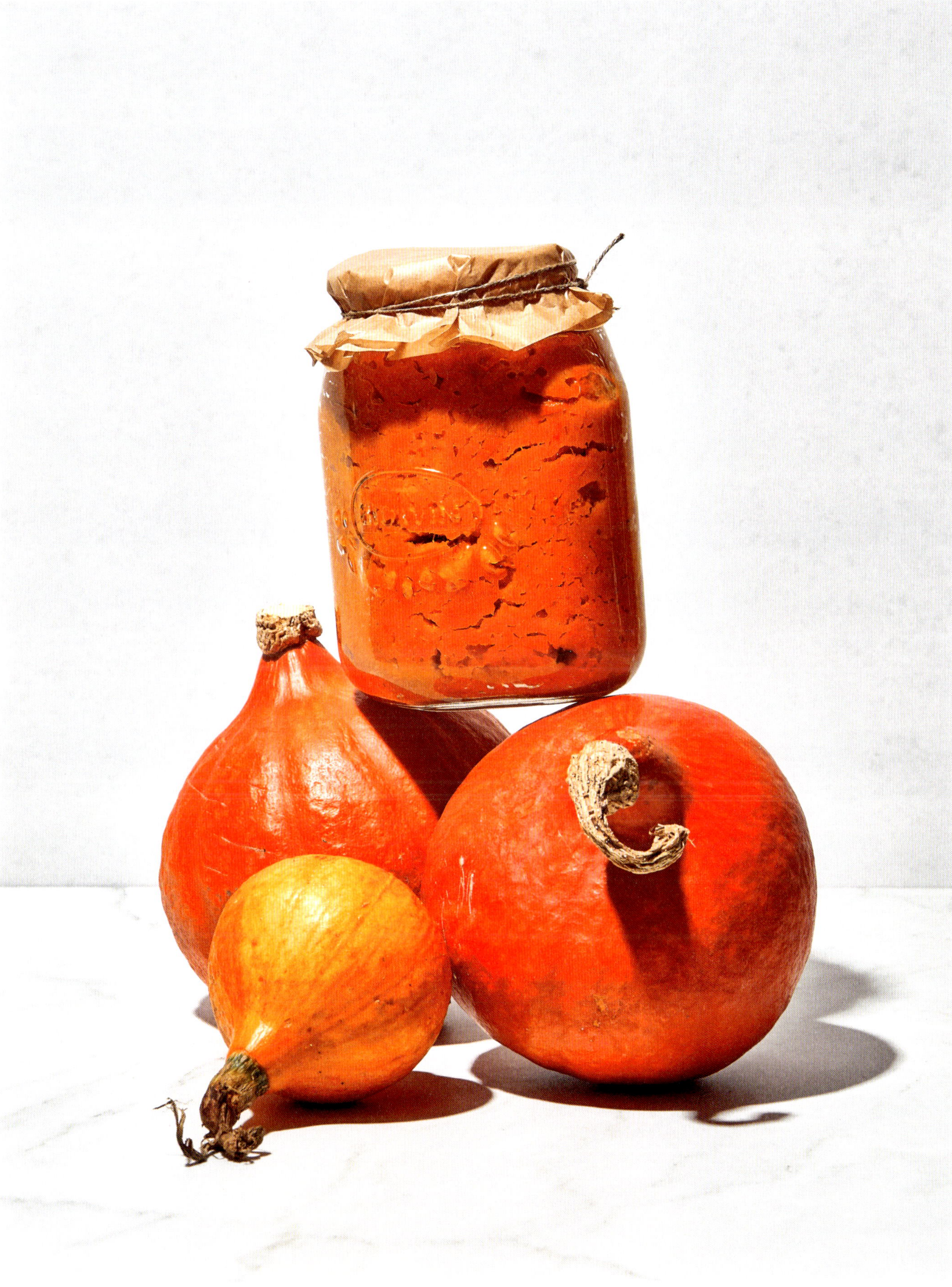

Marbled Cocoa and Pumpkin Bábovka

Makes 1 medium cake

Ingredients

¾ cup (180 g) unsalted butter, plus extra for greasing

Bread crumbs or crushed ladyfingers (sponge fingers) for lining

4 eggs

⅔ cup (130 g) cane sugar

1 organic orange

¾ cup (200 g) Pumpkin Puree (see p. 186)

2 ¼ cups (250 g) white spelt flour

2 ½ teaspoons (12 g) baking powder

1 pinch salt

1 teaspoon ground turmeric

1 pinch of ground cloves

2 tablespoons unsweetened cocoa powder

3 to 5 tablespoons milk

Preheat the oven to 340 °F top/bottom heat (170 °C/Gas Mark 3 ½). Grease a Bundt pan with butter and line it with bread crumbs or crushed ladyfingers (sponge fingers).

Melt the butter and let it cool to room temperature. Beat the eggs with the sugar until thick and pale. Wash the orange, finely grate the zest, and squeeze the juice. Gently fold the cooled melted butter, orange zest, orange juice, and pumpkin puree into the beaten eggs. Mix the spelt flour with the baking powder, salt, and spices and fold this mix into the batter. Mix well with a spatula until all the ingredients are incorporated and the batter is thick.

Pour half of the batter into another bowl and mix with the cocoa powder. Because this will make the batter a little thicker, carefully dilute it with a little milk until it has the same consistency as the pale batter.

Pour a portion of the cocoa batter into the prepared Bundt pan. Pour a portion of the pale batter over the top and repeat the process until the pan is filled with alternating batter layers. Bake for 45 to 50 minutes. Check that the cake is cooked by inserting a toothpick or bamboo skewer. If the toothpick comes out clean or only has a few crumbs sticking to it, the *bábovka* is done.

Remove the cake from the oven and let stand in the pan at room temperature for 5 to 10 minutes. Carefully invert the cake onto a wire rack and let cool completely. Cut the cake into slices and serve.

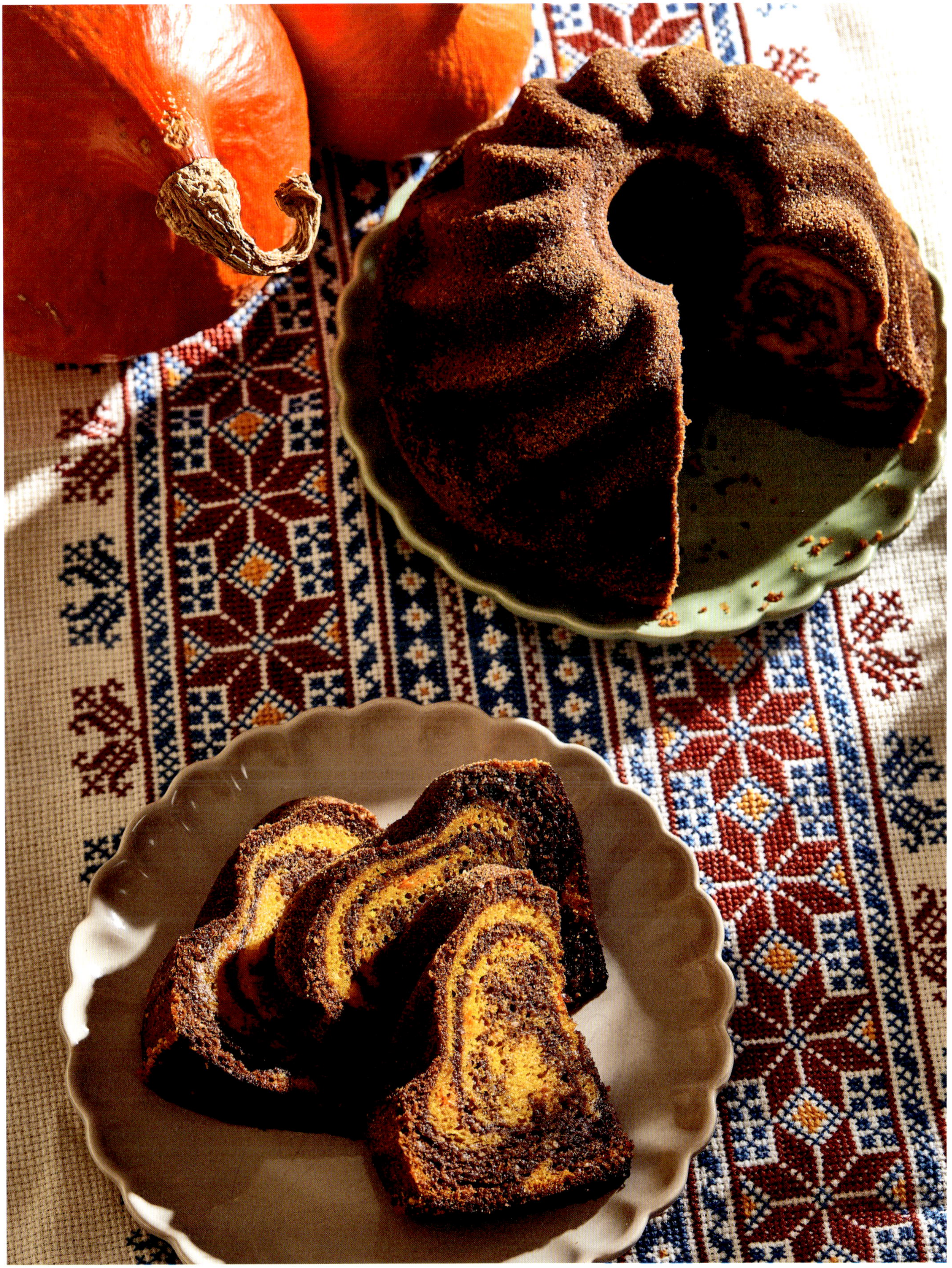

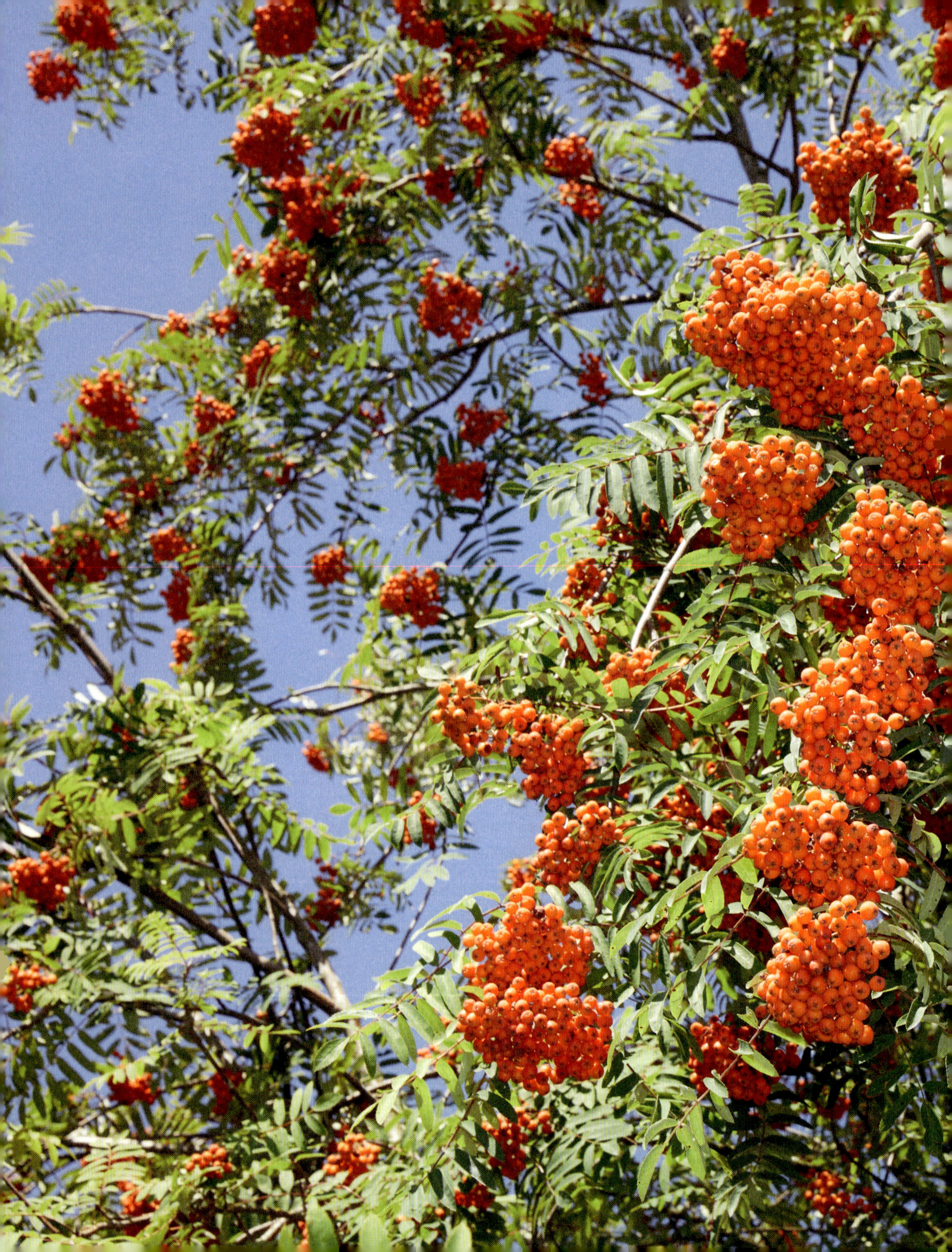

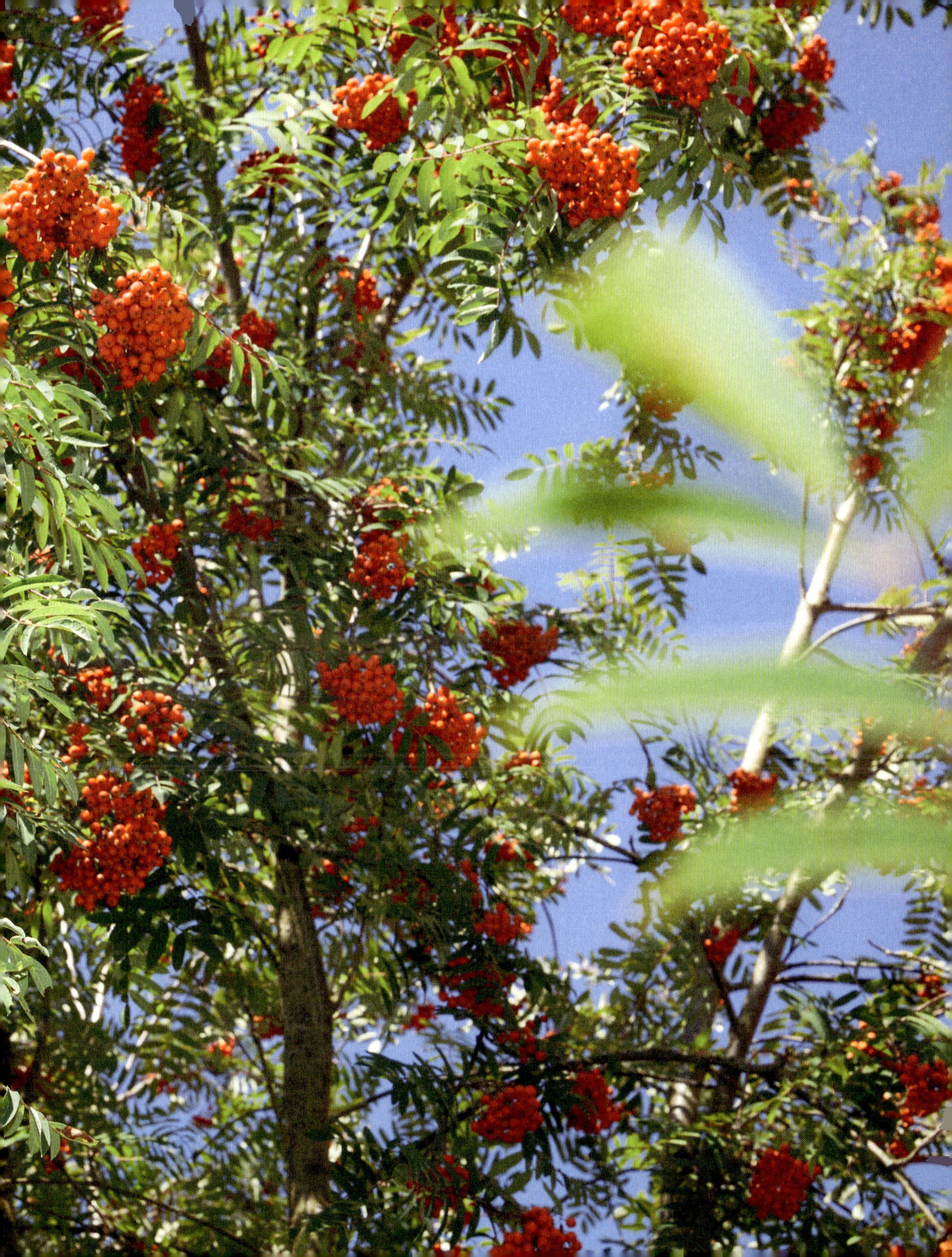

Rose Hip Jam

For 4 canning jars
(8 ounces / 250 ml each)

Ingredients

3 ¼ pounds (1.5 kg) rose hips

8 ½ cups (2 l) water

1 ½ cups (300 g) cane sugar

4 teaspoons (20 g) citric acid

½ teaspoon ground cinnamon

¼ teaspoon ground cloves or ground star anise

Wash the rose hips thoroughly, then trim off the stems and blossom ends. Put the rose hips into a saucepan and add the water, making sure to cover them completely. Bring to a boil briefly, then lower the heat. Cook for 20 to 50 minutes, until the rose hips are soft.

Puree the rose hips with the cooking water. Filter the puree through a fine-mesh strainer or sieve or through a cheesecloth (muslin) into a clean saucepan. Discard the seeds and hairs.

Add the sugar, citric acid, and spices to the puree and mix well. If the puree is too thick, dilute with a little hot water. Cook over medium heat, stirring occasionally, for about 15 minutes, until the jam thickens.

Transfer the hot jam to the sterilized canning jars, close the lids tightly, and place upside down. Let cool, then store in a cool, dark place.

Tips Very ripe rose hips picked after the first frost are the best for this jam. Cook less ripe fruit longer and add more sugar.

This rose hip jam is perfect for filling the traditional Czech Christmas cookies called *linecké cukroví*. You can also use it to make a delicious rose hip sauce to accompany roast wild boar.

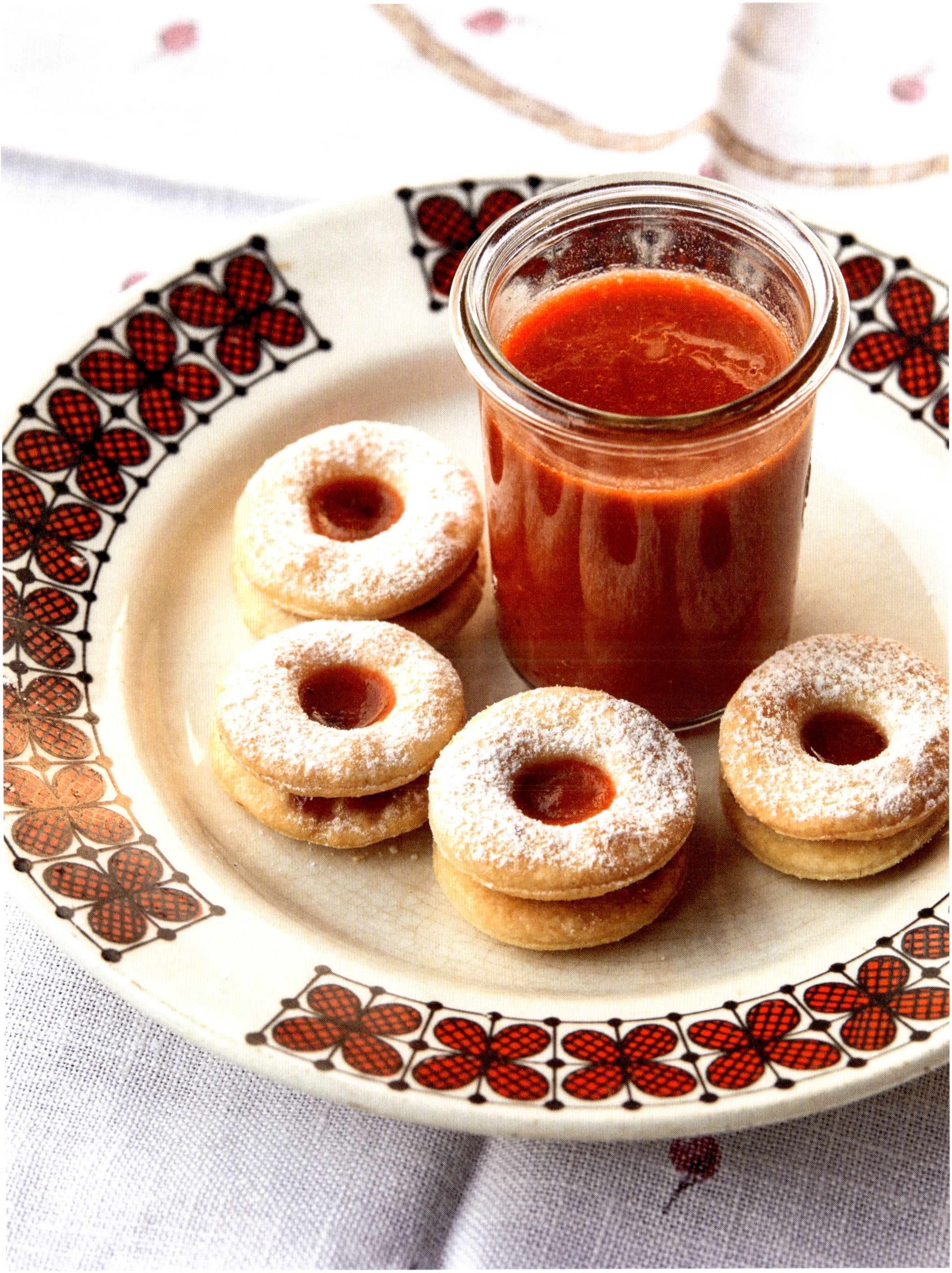

Sea Buckthorn Syrup

For 1 bottle (8 to 16 ounces / 500–750 ml)

Ingredients

Sea buckthorn berries

Granulated sugar

Carefully wash the berries in a strainer or sieve under cold running water and drain. Puree the fruit in a blender until very smooth and filter through a cheesecloth (muslin) or a fine-mesh strainer or sieve into a saucepan. You can also use a juicer for this step.

Measure out the juice obtained and then add the same amount of sugar. Warm the mixture slowly over low heat, stirring constantly until the sugar has dissolved. Remove from the heat immediately (the syrup must not boil).

Transfer the hot syrup to a sterilized bottle without filling it completely. Let the sea buckthorn syrup cool and seal tightly, then use immediately or store in the refrigerator. The pulp settles over time, so always shake the bottle well before use.

Tips Sea buckthorn syrup can either be drunk on its own in small servings (1 small shot glass or 2 tablespoons per day) or diluted with sparkling mineral water as desired. You can add ice and your favorite fresh herbs to the drink, such as mint or lemon balm.

Frozen sea buckthorn berries can also be used for this recipe. First defrost the fruit before juicing.

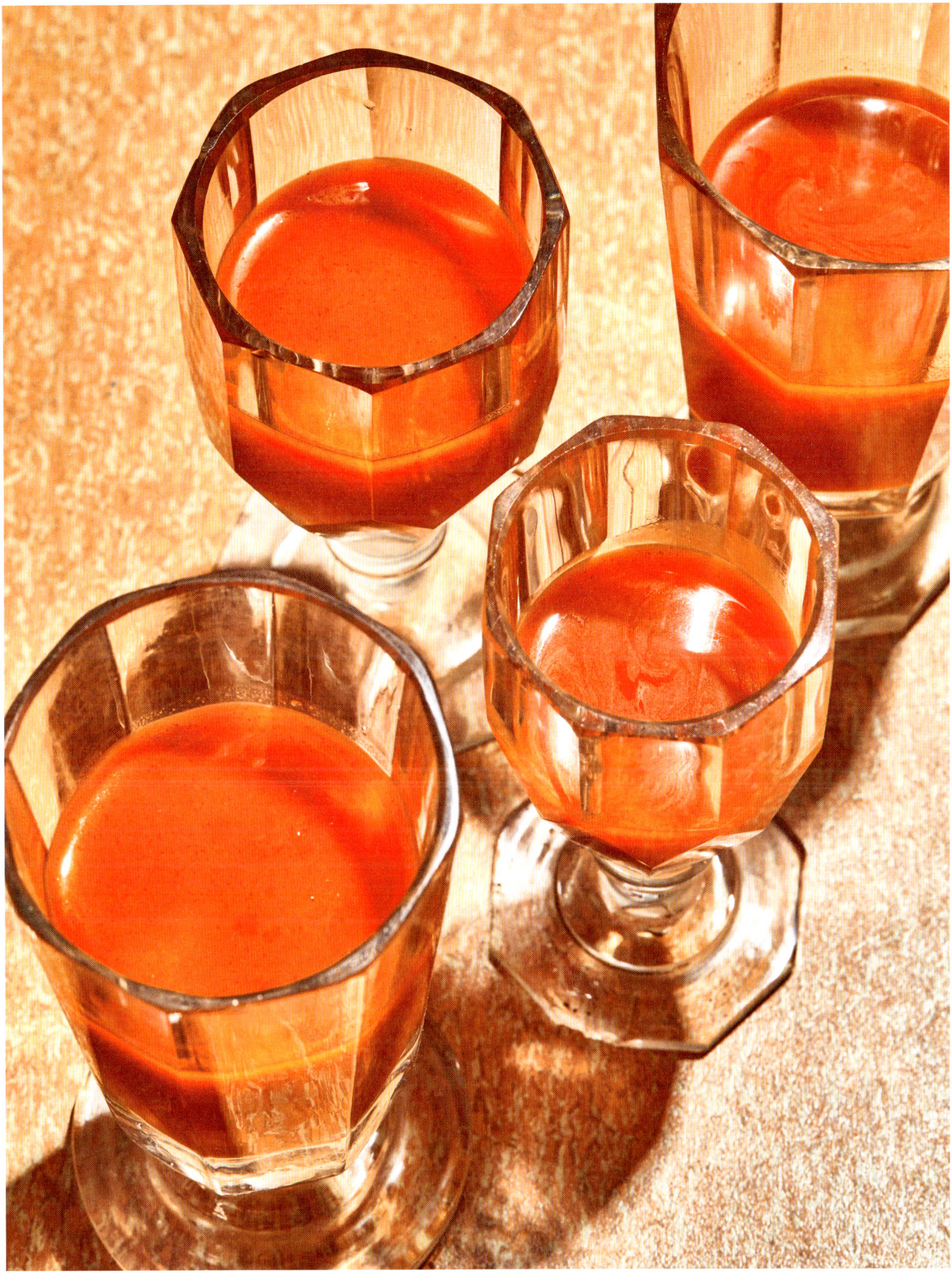

The Alchemy of Fermentation

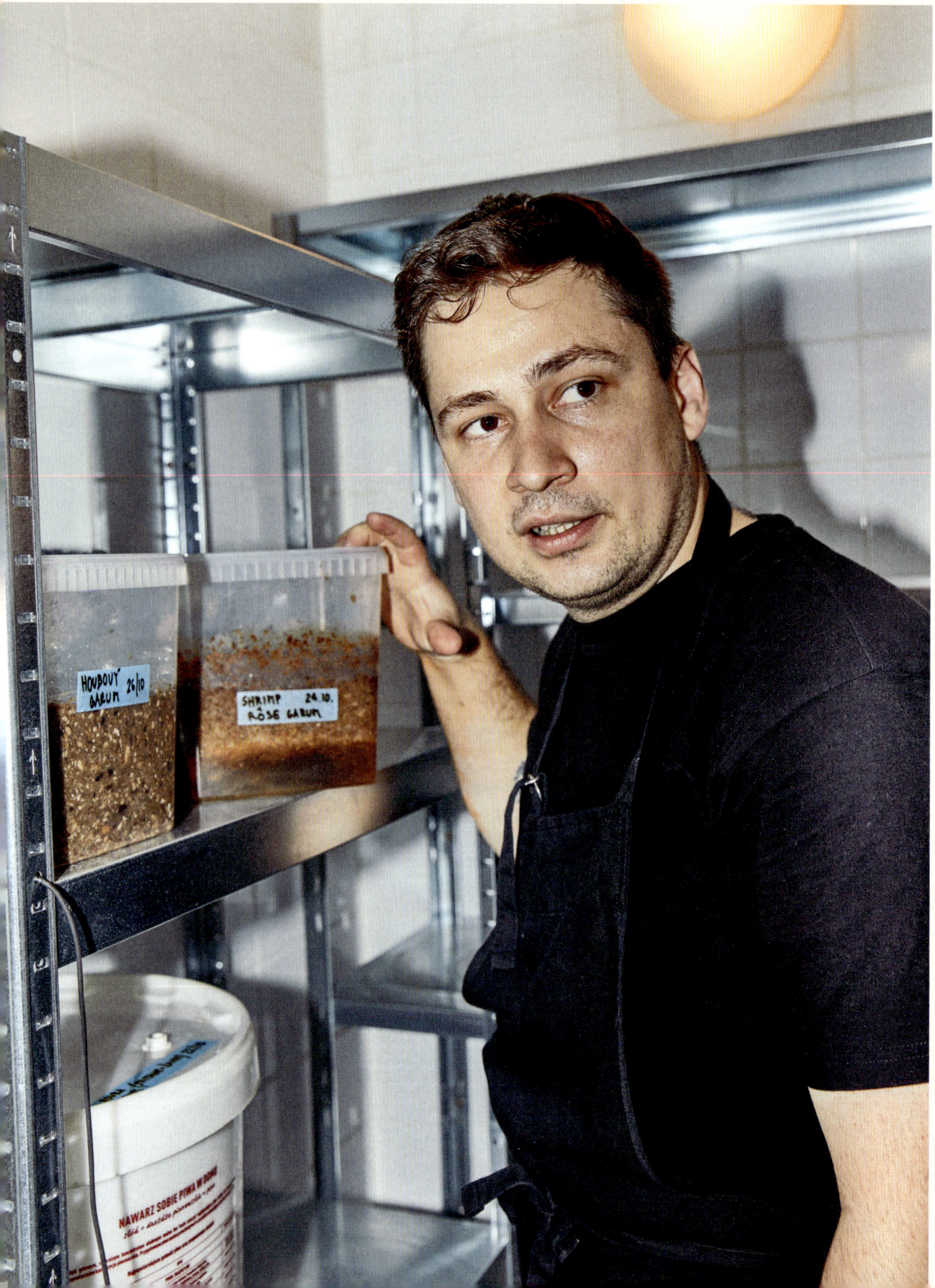

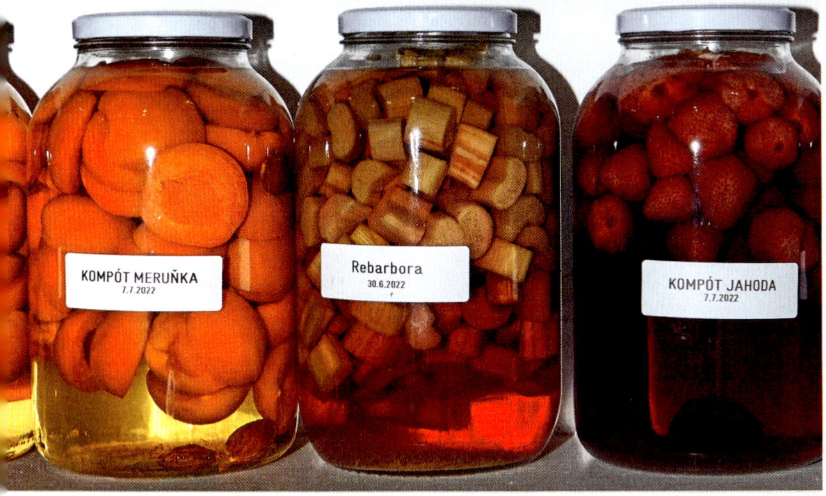

Guided by patience and curiosity, Erik Cehlár transforms ancient fermentation methods into modern delicacies that are both gut-friendly and temptingly flavorful.

Erik grew up in Slovakia, but he moved to Prague a few years ago to be with his girlfriend. His path into gastronomy was taken purely by chance. When he arrived in the Czech capital as a trained teacher and coach, he had to look for a part-time job to tide him over for a couple of months. He ended up helping out at the restaurant Eska, in the Karlín district, and what was meant to be a temporary job became the start of a new vocation.

"I started out with the basics, cleaning and chopping vegetables. One day a colleague didn't show up for a bistro shift, so I had to step in. Suddenly, I was serving breakfasts and brunches, and that was the moment I got hooked. From the bistro I moved on to the cold section and sides, and over time I worked my way up. I learned precision, patience and responsibility—the real craft of cooking," Erik recalls. At Eska, the kitchen team was already experimenting with lactic fermentation, and it was there, between jars of pickled vegetables and tibi lemonades, that his passion for fermentation finally took root.

After years in Karlín, Erik's curiosity for the wild world of fermentation brought him to Goodlok, a progressive beverage project and modern bistro that has the motto: "We want to drink well and have healthy gut." He now runs a full-scale fermentation lab on Prague's Jungmann Square. Alongside kombucha and *jun* (similar to kombucha but made with green tea and raw honey), he experiments constantly, creating new recipes and testing a variety of ingredients. He makes his own barley koji, plays with miso, and patiently lets black garlic age slowly for months.

His biggest hit these days is garum. "This special seasoning is a phenomenon in modern gastronomy, but the model comes from an ancient recipe. In Greece and Rome, garum was a prized commodity, a strong, umami-packed sauce produced for six to twelve months of controlled fermentation using fish entrails, bones, and heads. The process walks a fine line between proper fermentation and unwanted mold. Salt plays a key role, helping to control the autolytic process. Today, we also use koji to create garums from other ingredients, not just animal ones, such as mushrooms, for example, including shiitake grown right here in the Czech Republic," Erik explains.

Alongside home-made garum, or *garumko*, as Erik calls it, one constant in his kitchen is kimchi (see p. 199), the classic Korean superfood you can easily make at home. Compared to the exclusive ancient condiment, making this spicy, crunchy little salad packed with healthy bacteria—which often serves as a gateway to the world of fermentation—is an absolute breeze!

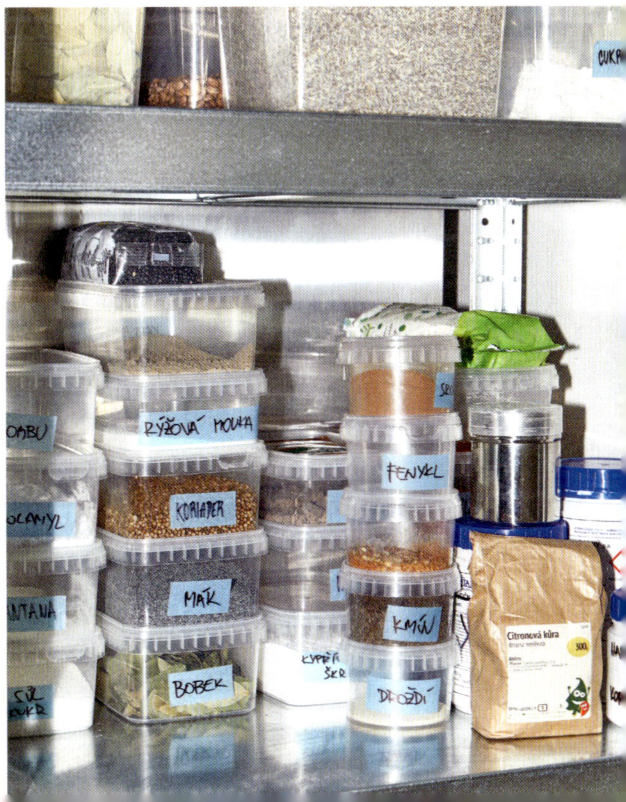

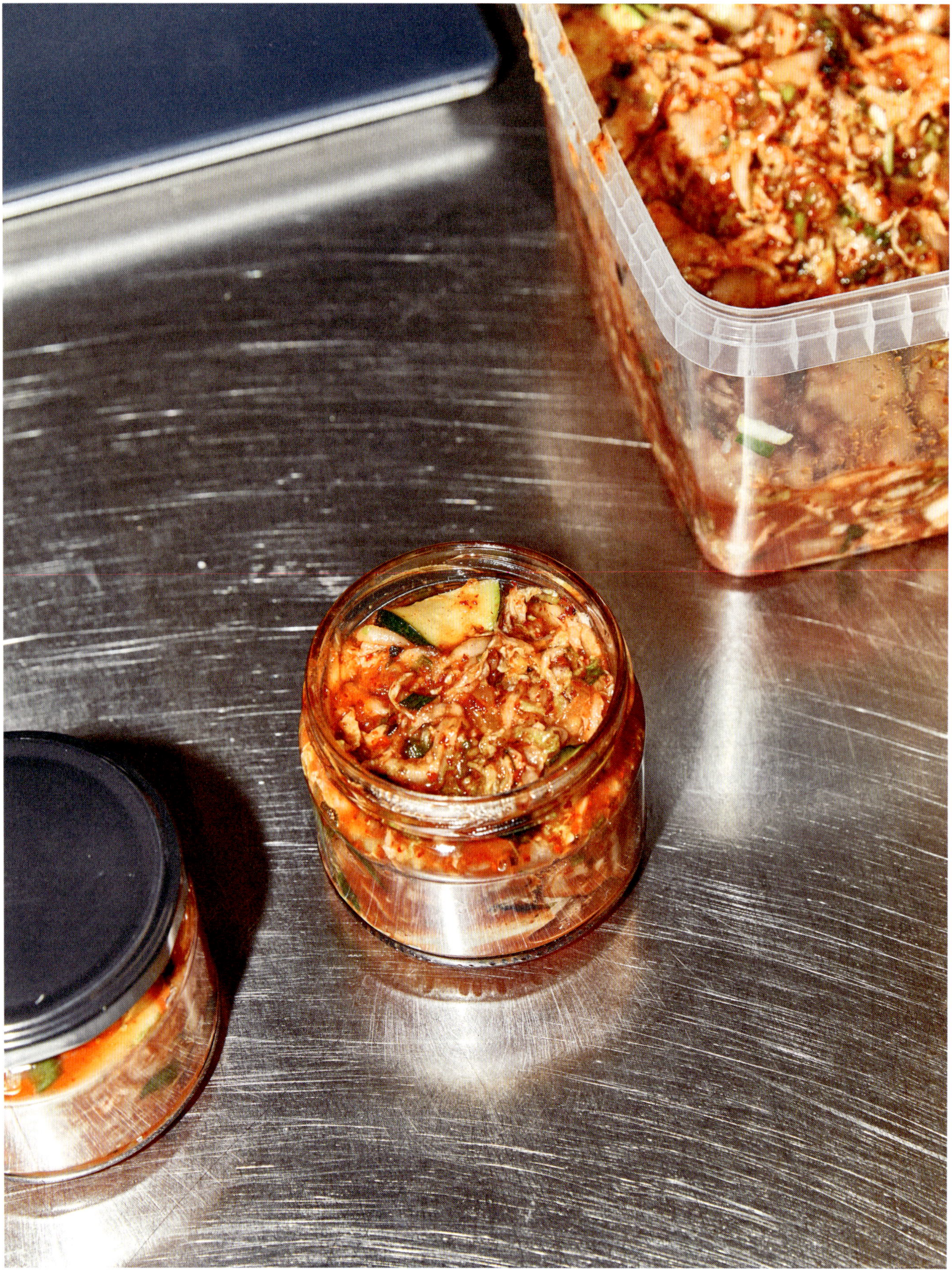

Kimchi

For 1 medium fermentation crock

Ingredients

3 ¼ pounds (1.5 kg) napa (Chinese) cabbage

4 ½ ounces (125 g) daikon (mooli) radish

4 ½ ounces (125 g) zucchini (courgette)

4 ½ ounces (125 g) scallions (spring onions)

1 small onion

3 cloves garlic

1 (1 ½-inch/4-cm) piece fresh ginger

1 apple

Salt

1 cup (250 ml) water

1 tablespoon rice flour

1 ½ teaspoons granulated sugar

½ cup (125 ml) fish sauce

2 ¼ ounces (63 g) Korean salted and fermented shrimp (saeujeot)

1 cup (250 g) Korean chili powder (gochugaru)

Remove the outer leaves from the cabbage and slice the rest into thin strips. Wash the daikon and zucchini thoroughly. Clean the scallions and trim off any wilted parts. Peel the onion. Cut the vegetables into thin rounds, strips, or rings. Peel and finely grate the garlic and ginger. Wash, peel, and core the apple, then coarsely grate.

Mix the vegetables with the garlic, ginger, and apple and weigh the mixture. Calculate 3 percent of the total weight and weigh out the same amount of salt. Mix the vegetables with the salt.

Put the water into a saucepan, add the rice flour and sugar, and stir with a whisk. Place over low heat, bring to a simmer, and cook to a paste with a porridgelike consistency. Remove from the heat and let cool completely. Stir the fish sauce, shrimp, and chili powder into the paste. Add the mixture to the salted vegetables, mix everything together well, and gently press it in with your hands. Let stand for about 1 hour; the vegetables will soften and release their liquid.

Drain and transfer the vegetables to a clean fermentation crock, collecting the liquid. Leave a space of 2 to 4 inches (5–10 cm) between the vegetables and the rim of the pot to allow foam to form on the surface. Add the liquid released by the vegetables. The kimchi should be completely covered by the liquid. If the vegetables float to the surface, use a sterilized fermenting weight to keep them in place.

Close the fermentation crock and let the kimchi ferment at room temperature for 3 to 4 days, tasting it from time to time. Once the flavor is to your liking and it has reached the desired level of sourness, transfer the jar to the refrigerator, where fermentation will slow down.

Use the kimchi immediately or let it mature in the refrigerator for a more intense flavor. This kimchi will be at its best after about 3 weeks. It will keep for several weeks refrigerated. Using a clean fork, press the vegetables down occasionally to keep them covered in the liquid.

Tips *Gochugaru* and *saeujeot,* are available at Korean grocery stores and online retailers. Fermented shrimp is an important source of umami; however, you can omit them if unavailable.

Wear disposable gloves when handling the vegetables and spicy seasoning paste, because contact can lead to allergic reactions and skin irritation. Be careful to avoid rubbing your eyes or touching your face when making the kimchi.

This kimchi can be enjoyed on its own or served as an accompaniment for other dishes. It is also great as a sandwich spread, served with fried noodles, or in Kimchi Fried Rice (see p. 238).

You can also divide the kimchi into smaller sterilized jars (16 ounces/750 ml each), closing them tightly.

Answering the Call of the Forest

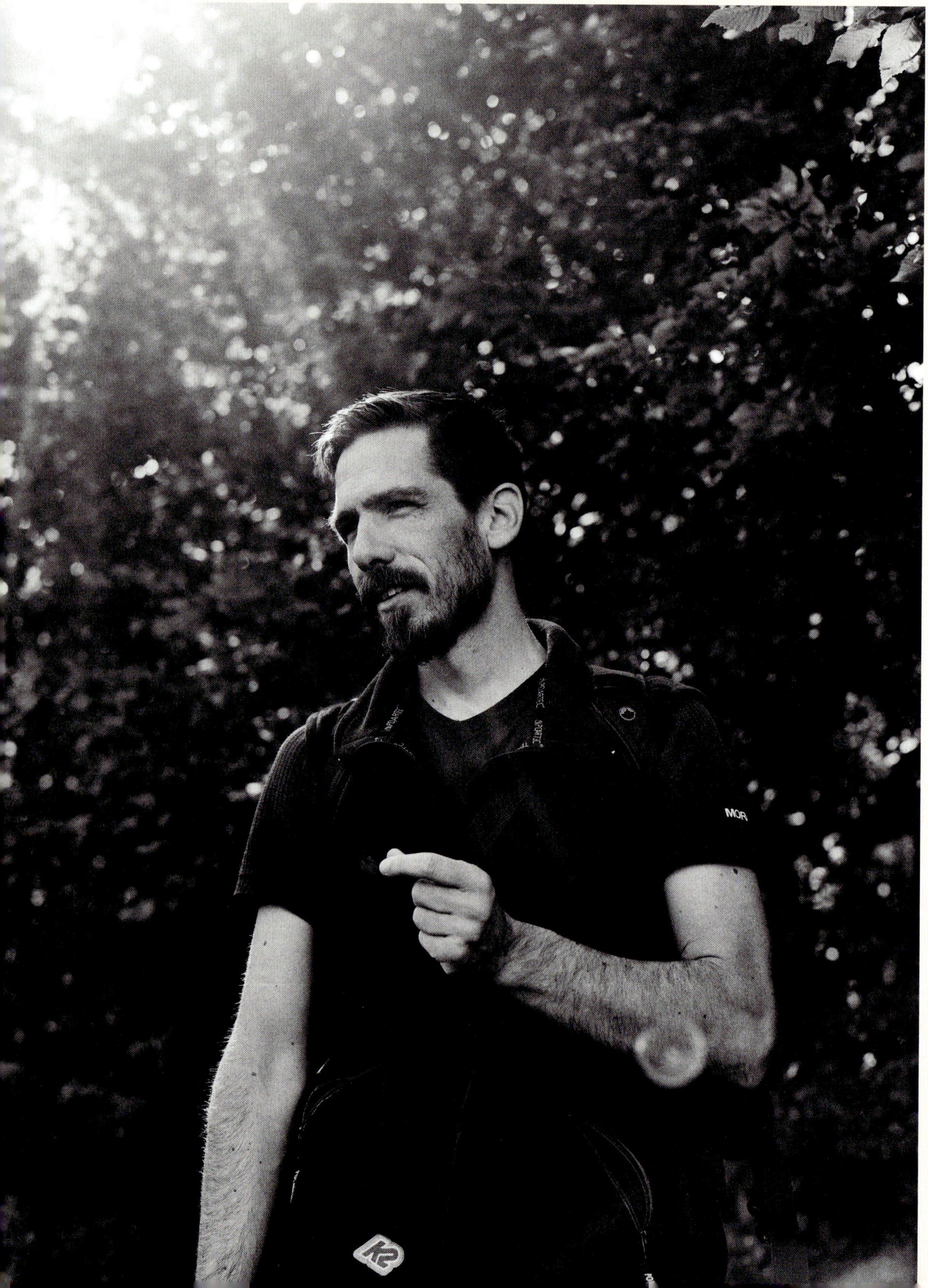

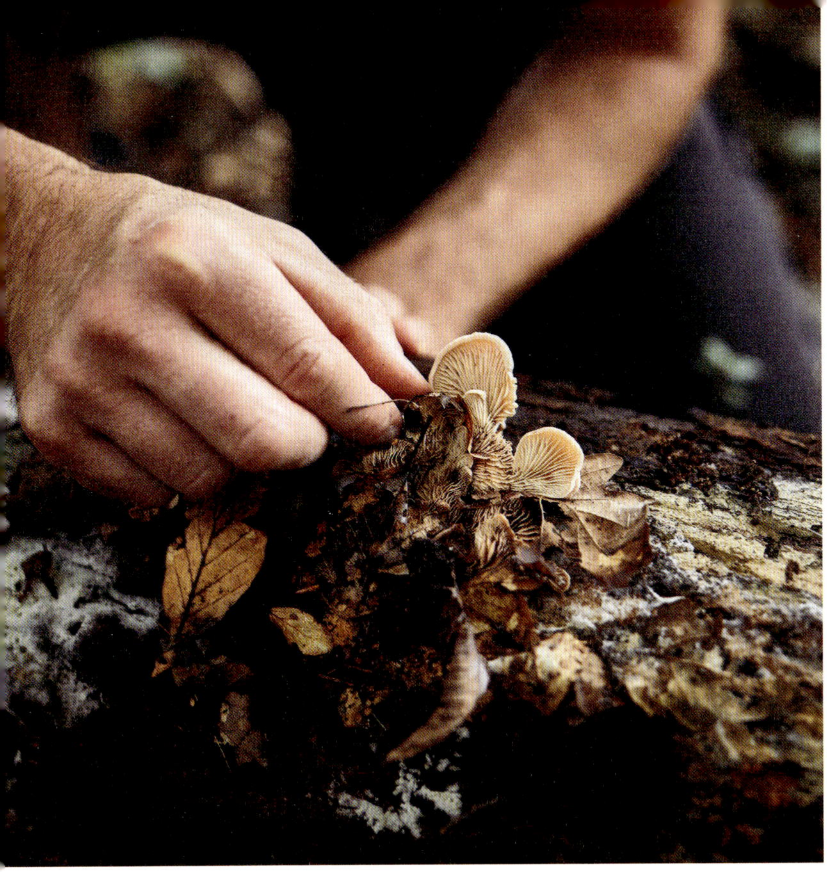

Leaving his office chair behind, mushroom hunter and fermentation enthusiast Vláďa Sojka has dedicated his life to forest adventures and culinary experiments.

Vláďa graduated from an economics-focused high school and then spent twenty years working as an IT technician in logistics. However, his real passion has always been mushroom picking, foraging, and food, and sooner or later it was bound to shape the next stage of his life.

His love of mushrooms and nature started early, sparked by his parents. As a child, he would walk through the forest with a basket, searching for rare mushroom species alongside his father. As an adult, he spent five years deepening his knowledge as a self-taught enthusiast before moving on to formal mycology lectures and more professional circles.

Today, he is able to identify hundreds of species and occasionally works with scientific institutions, but he still calls himself an amateur mycologist. His main mission, he says, is sharing knowledge with everyday mushroom pickers. He leads guided mushroom walks and runs a Facebook group called *Mykologická poradna* (*Mycological Counseling*). Currently, he most enjoys tracking the appearance of different mushroom species in the Křivoklát region and around the Český kras, hunting for rare finds and photographing them to share on his Instagram account @mushroomhunter.cz. He carries a small portable photo studio in his backpack and the shots are truly impressive!

In his free time, Vláďa is equally devoted to fermentation, both in theory and practice. He cofounded *Zkvašeno*, the most comprehensive Czech blog on food fermentation. One of his latest projects is cultivating kombucha cultures taken directly from wild environments. As a passionate "fermenter," he lectures widely, and his audiences includes both curious amateurs and gastronomy professionals. His online shop *Fermentárum* offers fermentation cultures, products, workshops, and books. Need miso, koji, a kombucha starter, or milk kefir grains? You know where to find them!

Vláďa Sojka loves to experiment. In his cellar, on one shelf, you'll find unusual types of miso paste alongside tempeh, vinegars of all kinds, umeboshi plums, and shoyu soy sauce. He aims to showcase the diversity of nature's bounty, often fermenting and pickling fruits that people typically pass by along country roads or at the edges of forests. In the fall, for example, he gathers sloes, which, after a long period of curing in salt, develop a flavor reminiscent of Mediterranean olives (see p. 202).

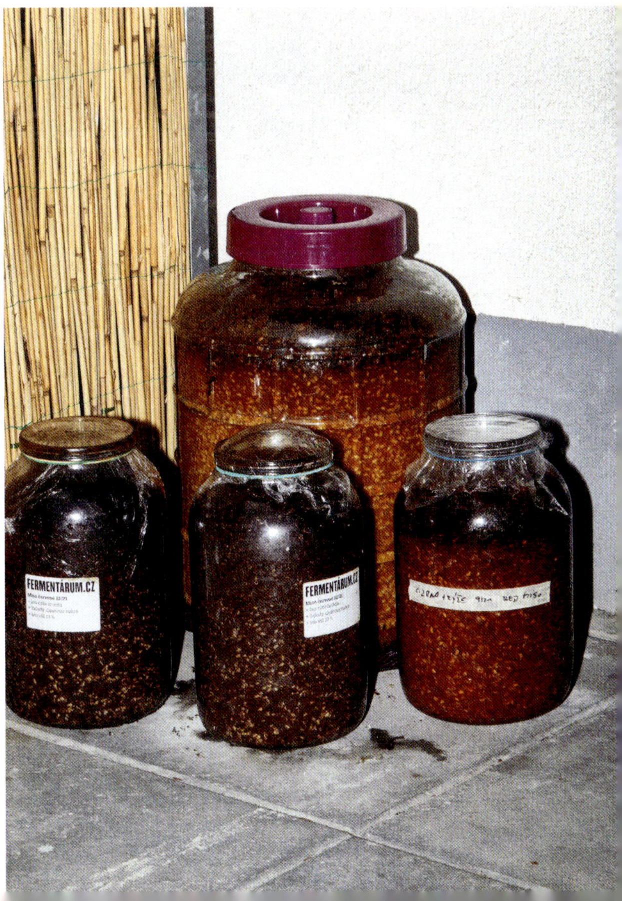

Salt-cured Sloe "Olives"

For 1 canning jars (8 ounces / 350 ml)

Ingredients

10 ½ ounces (300 g) sloes (blackthorn berries)

½ cup (150 g) salt

4 tablespoons olive oil

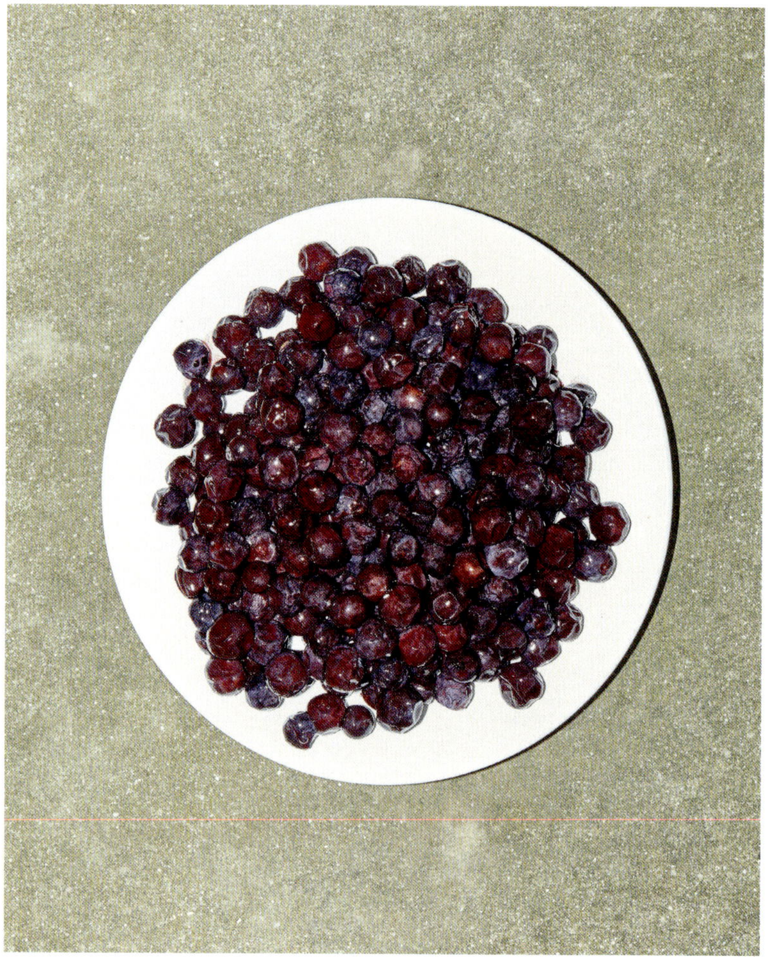

Wash the sloes and pat dry. Mix the berries with the salt and put them into a clean cloth bag (such as cotton). Hang the bag freely indoors for 3 to 4 weeks at room temperature. At least every second day, knead the berries a little with your hands through the bag, without touching them.

Rinse off the salt and transfer the cured sloes to a bowl. Drizzle with the olive oil and mix until all the berries are coated in oil. Transfer to a sterilized canning jar and seal tightly. Use the sloe "olives" immediately or store in a cool, dark place.

Tips Sloes are commonly believed to become sweet only with the first frost. However, sloes simply ripen late in November, when frost is already a possibility. For this recipe, you should pick sloes that are sweet but not yet too soft. This allows the berries to retain their firm texture even after curing in salt.

If you don't have a suitable cloth bag, you can also wrap the sloes in a cotton cloth or dishcloth (tea towel) and knot it tightly. The sloes can also be cured in a glass container.

You can use any pickled sloe juice that collects in the canning jar as you would an umeboshi vinegar to enhance dishes.

These "northern olives" are suited to dishes that typically contain real olives. The flavor is slightly different, more delicate.

Rowan Berry Compote

For 5 canning jars (8 ounces / 250 ml each)

Ingredients

4 ¼ cups (1 l) water

3 cups (600 g) granulated sugar

3 ¼ pounds (1.5 kg) rowan berries

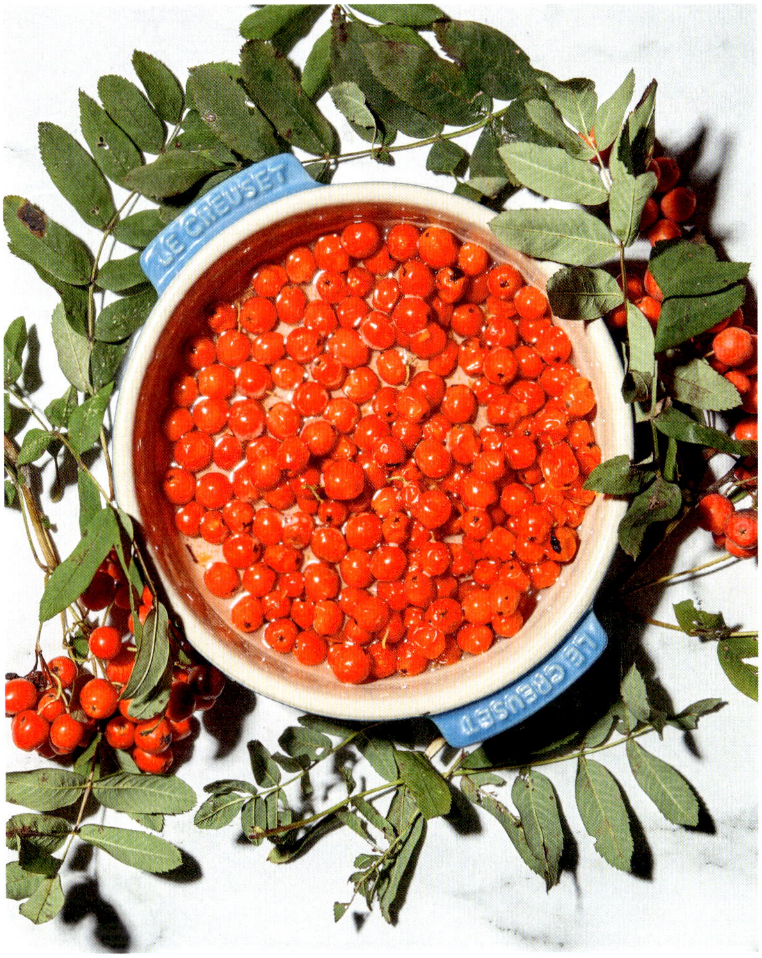

Mix the water and sugar in a saucepan, bring to a boil over medium heat, and let simmer, stirring occasionally, until the sugar dissolves.

Sort the rowan berries, remove any stems, and wash under cold running water. Carefully add the berries to the syrup and cook for about 15 minutes, until they turn glassy and soft. Be careful not to overcook the berries.

Transfer the berries to sterilized canning jars and pour over the hot syrup. Close the jars tightly, process in a water bath, and let cool. Store in a cool, dark place.

Tips Rowan berries are the fruit of the rowan tree, also known as the mountain ash tree. Only completely ripe, bright red berries should be used. They are best picked after the first frost, when they are sweeter.

Rowan berries picked before they are completely ripe can taste bitter and sour, although they lose their astringent taste if soaked overnight.

For even more aromatic berries, add 1 cinnamon stick, 2 or 3 cloves, and thinly sliced organic lemon zest.

This compote can be used in the same way as whole cranberry sauce, including *svíčková* (see p. 102), to enhance vegetables salads, and as an accompaniment for both grilled and roasted meat dishes and hard cheese. It also works well in desserts, such as cakes and ice cream sundaes.

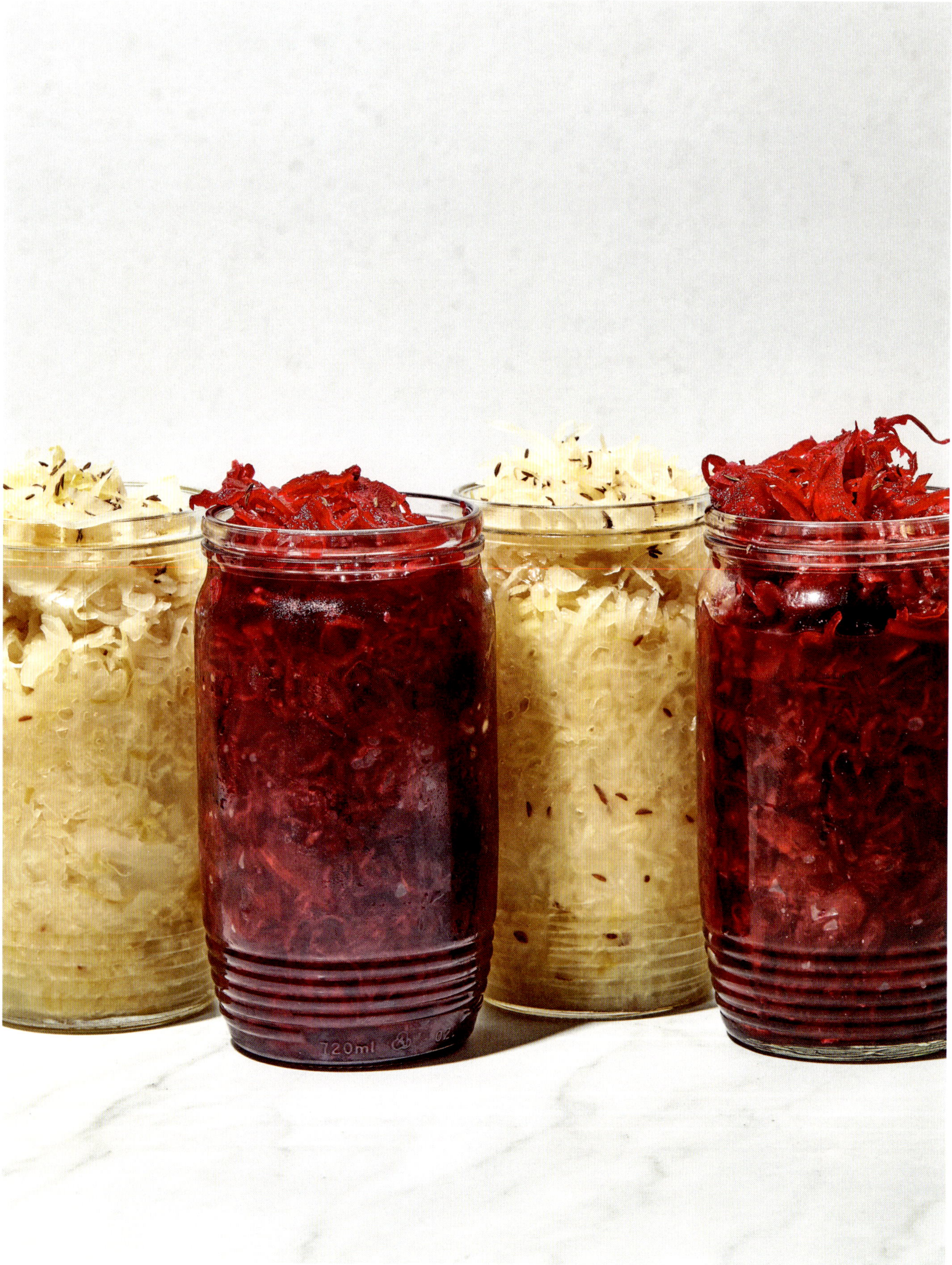

Sauerkraut

For 4 to 6 canning jars (25 ounces / 750 ml each)

Ingredients

2 large heads green, white, or red cabbage

1 ½ teaspoons (10 g) salt
for each 2 ¼ pounds (1 kg) of cabbage

1 tablespoon caraway seeds
for each 2 ¼ pounds (1 kg) of cabbage

Clean and trim the cabbages and remove any wilted outer leaves. Remove 4 large leaves and set aside. Quarter the cabbages and remove and discard the stem. Using a mandoline to slice the cabbage as finely as possible into a large bowl.

Weigh the sliced cabbage, then measure out 1 ½ teaspoons (10 g) salt and 1 tablespoon caraway seeds for every 2 ¼ pounds (1 kg) of cabbage. Sprinkle the cabbage with the salt and caraway seeds, mix well, and massage for at least 10 minutes with clean hands. Let rest for 2 hours, until the cabbage is soft and releases its juices.

Transfer the cabbage to a clean fermentation crock, filling it to 4 inches (10 cm) below the rim, and compact well. Collect the juices and add to the cabbage. The cabbage should always be covered with liquid as it ferments, otherwise mold can form on the surface. Cover the sliced cabbage with the reserved large cabbage leaves and weigh everything down with a sterilized fermentation weight. Close the fermentation crock and let the sauerkraut ferment at room temperature for 5 to 7 days.

Either leave the sauerkraut in the fermentation crock or transfer it to sterilized canning jars. Make sure that the cabbage does not come into contact with air, otherwise it may spoil. Add the juices, if required, weigh down the sauerkraut, and seal the jars tightly. Store the jars in the refrigerator or another cool, dark place. The sauerkraut can be used immediately if desired, however, it tastes best when aged for at least 1 month.

Tips If you want, you can season the sliced cabbage with anise, coriander seeds, mustard seeds, or fresh dill. It can also be flavored with thinly sliced onion, garlic, horseradish, or apple.

You may need to make a brine in case not enough juices are released by the cabbage. To do this, bring 1 cup (250 ml) water to a boil and let cool. Stir in 1 teaspoon salt and pour the liquid over the cabbage.

Rich in vitamin C, sauerkraut can be eaten on its own, but it also makes a great accompaniment for Saint Martin's Goose with *Lokše* (thin potato flatbreads, see p. 209), traditional roast or braised pork, and potato dumplings stuffed with smoked meat. Sauerkraut is also one of the main ingredients for borscht (see p. 184) and for Slovakian *kapustníky* (savory rolls filled with sauerkraut, see p. 206).

Kapustníky

Makes about 30 flatbreads

Ingredients

For the dough:

1 cup (250 ml) milk, plus extra as needed

1 (⅔-ounce/19 g) cake fresh yeast

⅓ cup (40 g) powdered (icing) sugar

¼ cup (50 g) lard, plus 1½ tablespoons (20 g) for brushing

4 cups (500 g) all-purpose (plain) flour or Italian "00" flour, plus extra for dusting

1 teaspoon salt

2 egg yolks

For the filling:

3½ ounces (100 g) bacon

1 teaspoon lard

2¼ cups (500 g) sauerkraut (see p. 205)

1 teaspoon crushed caraway seeds

1 teaspoon salt

¼ teaspoon freshly ground pepper

Gently heat the milk until lukewarm—do not let it boil. Pour half of the milk into a bowl, crumble in the yeast, and add 1 teaspoon of the sugar. Mix everything carefully. Cover the bowl with a clean cloth and let rise for 10 to 15 minutes. Melt the lard in a saucepan and let cool.

Sift the flour into a large bowl. Add the remaining sugar, the salt, mixture, remaining milk, cooled lard, and egg yolks. Using a wooden spoon or a stand mixer, gently mix to form a dough and knead for 10 minutes, until smooth and supple. It should easily come away from the sides of the bowl. If the dough is too wet, add a little flour. If it is too firm, add a little milk. Cover the bowl with a clean cloth and let rise in a warm place for 45 to 60 minutes, until doubled in volume.

In the meantime, to make the filling, cut the bacon into dice. Heat the lard in a skillet or frying pan, add the bacon, and fry until crispy. Drain the sauerkraut and squeeze out any remaining liquid. Add the sauerkraut to the skillet with the caraway seeds, salt, and pepper. Sauté, stirring occasionally, for 10 minutes. Remove from the heat and let cool slightly.

Shape the dough into small buns (6 ounces/170 g each). Flatten each bun with the palm of your hand and place 2 to 3 heaping tablespoons of filling in the center. Fold the dough over the filling and press the edges together to seal. Carefully roll out the filled dough pieces into ½ inch (1 cm) thick disks, 10 inches (25 cm) in diameter. Cut them into quarters or sixths.

Preheat the oven to 350 °F top/bottom heat (180 °C/Gas Mark 4). Arrange the buns on a baking sheet lined with parchment (baking) paper, cover with a clean cloth, and proof for 15 minutes. Brush with melted lard and bake for about 30 minutes, until golden. Or, heat a skillet and dry-fry the buns on both sides over low heat until golden, then brush with melted lard. Let cool completely and serve.

Tips Only have instant yeast at home? Go ahead and use it—just remember that you cannot substitute fresh yeast 1:1 with instant yeast. Instant yeast is 1.5 times stronger, so always use 1.5 times less! You also don't need to activate instant yeast in advance; simply sprinkle it over the flour and work it into the dough.

Before filling the dough with sauerkraut, you can also add 1 to 2 tablespoons of *bryndza* (Slovakian sheep milk cream cheese).

In some parts of eastern Slovakia, *kapustníky* are lightly sprinkled with powdered (icing) sugar before serving and enjoyed with hot tea.

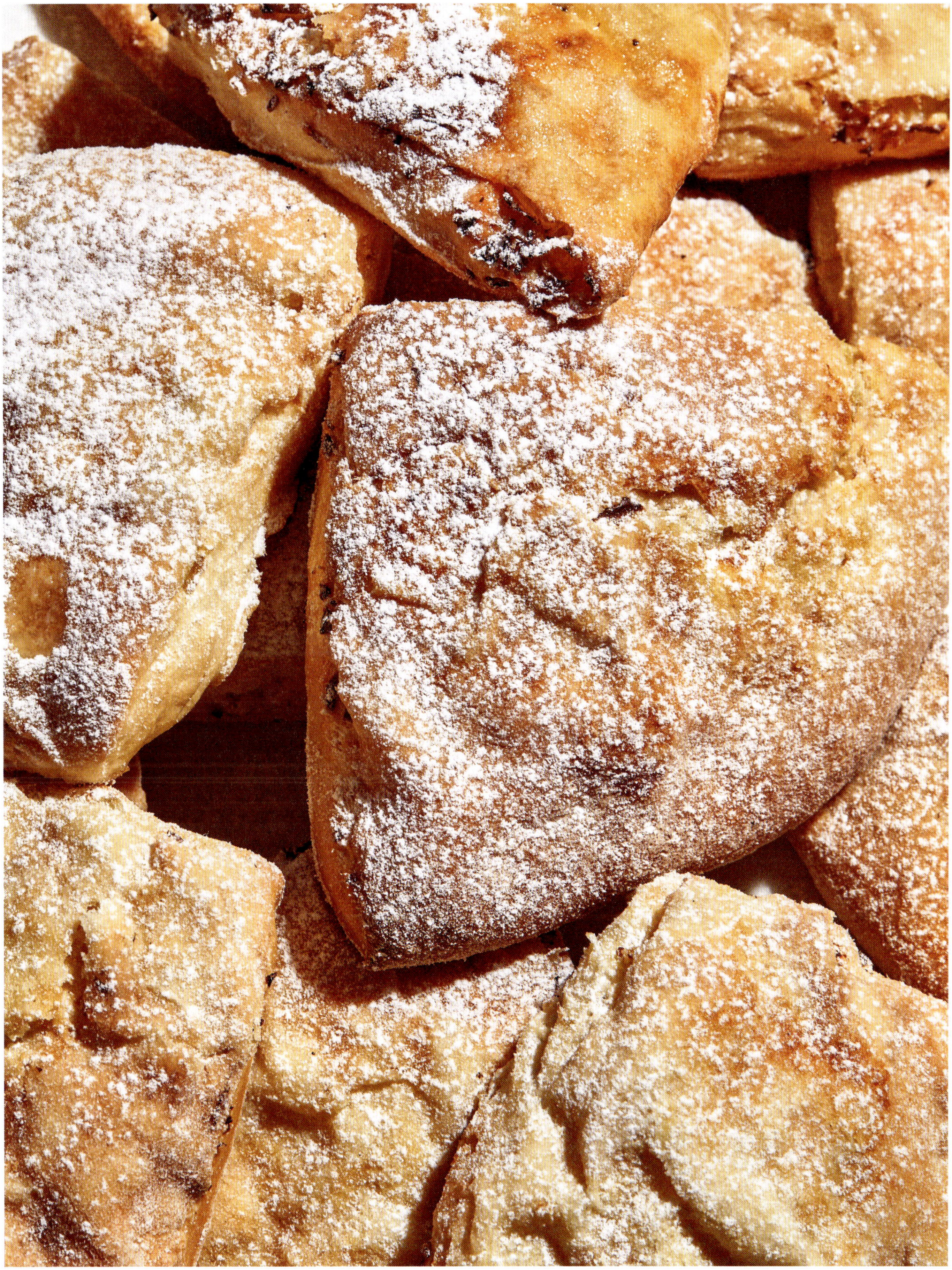

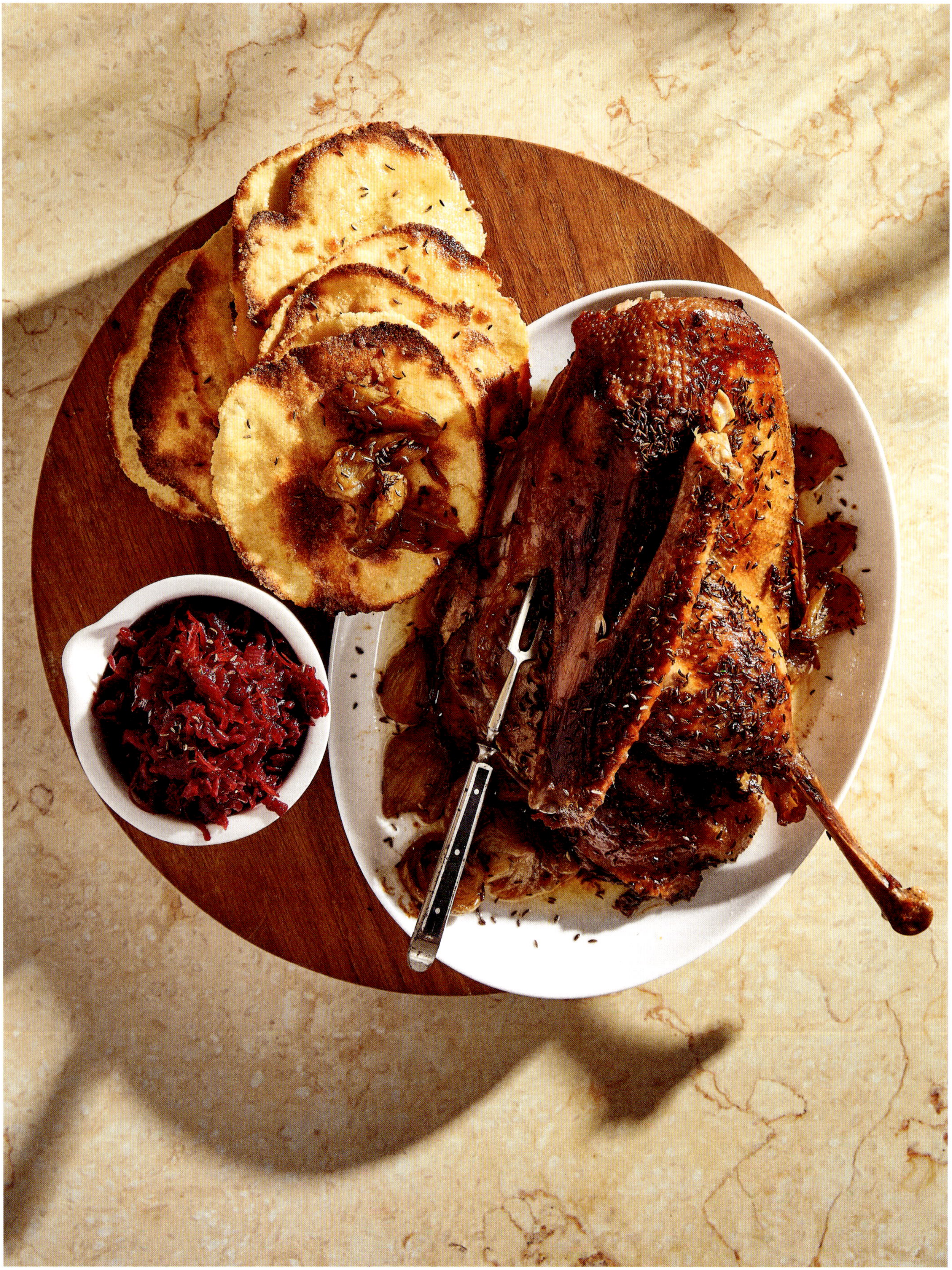

Saint Martin's Roast Goose with Lokše and Red Sauerkraut

Serves 2 to 4

Ingredients

For the roast goose:

½ goose, dressed for roasting

6 to 8 shallots

1 tablespoon salt

1 tablespoon caraway seeds

scant ½ cup (100 ml) water

For the red sauerkraut accompaniment:

3 ⅓ cups (750 g) Red Sauerkraut (see p. 205)

1 red onion

2 tablespoons goose fat

3 allspice berries

1 bay leaf

1 tablespoon all-purpose (plain) flour

4 to 5 tablespoons cane sugar

Salt and freshly ground black pepper

Remove the goose from the refrigerator at least 2 hours before roasting to come to room temperature. Preheat the oven to 350 °F top/bottom heat (180 °C/Gas Mark 4) and prepare a deep roasting pan.

Peel and halve the shallots and spread them evenly over the bottom of the pan. Wash the goose under cold water, pat dry with absorbent paper towels, and sprinkle all over with salt. Arrange the goose, skin side up, in the roasting pan. Sprinkle with the caraway seeds and add about scant ½ cup (100 ml) water.

Roast the goose for about 2 hours, until golden brown. The meat is done when it can easily be separated from the bone with a fork. Baste the goose with a little hot water every 20 minutes while roasting so that the fat under the skin comes out more easily. Skim off (and collect) any fat that escapes, so the meat roasts properly; it should not confit in its own fat. If the skin turns too dark, cover the goose with another roasting pan or aluminum foil.

In the meantime, to make the red sauerkraut accompaniment, drain the sauerkraut and collect the liquid. Peel and mince (very finely chop) the onion. Melt the goose fat in a saucepan over medium heat. Add the onion and sauté until golden. Add the sauerkraut, deglaze the pan with 2 to 3 tablespoons of the sauerkraut liquid, then add the allspice berries and bay leaf. Cover, reduce the heat to low, and let simmer for 20 to 30 minutes, until the sauerkraut is soft. Sprinkle over with the flour without stirring. Replace the lid on the pan and continue to simmer for 5 to 10 minutes. Remove the spices, stir, and adjust the seasoning with the sugar, salt, and pepper. Add a little more sauerkraut liquid if required. Cover with the lid and keep warm.

Finally, to make the potato flatbreads, finely grate the potatoes or press through a potato ricer into a large bowl. Add the flour and salt and knead with your hands to a smooth dough. If the dough is too sticky, add a little more flour. Divide the dough into roughly equal portions and roll out into thin disks on a floured work surface. Heat a cast iron skillet or frying pan and dry-fry the flatbreads, one at a time, on both sides. Dark bubbles should form on the surface. Flip the pancakes when they start to swell. Stack the finished pancakes on a plate and cover with a bowl to keep warm. Optionally, brush with a little goose fat. →

For the lokše (potato flatbreads):

2 ¼ pounds (1 kg) boiled potatoes, peeled and cooled

2 cups (250 g) all-purpose (plain) flour or Italian "00" flour, plus extra for dusting

½ teaspoon salt

Melted goose fat (optional)

Arrange the roast goose with the shallots on a serving platter and place in the turned-off but still warm oven. Skim off the excess fat from the juices remaining in the roasting pan. Transfer the drippings to a saucepan and reduce over high heat to a thick gravy. Drizzle the gravy over the goose or serve the gravy separately. Serve the goose accompanied with the red sauerkraut and the *lokše*.

Tips A young goose weighing about 6 ½ pounds (3 kg) is particularly suitable for this recipe. Its meat is more tender and cooks faster.

If you want to roast a whole goose, you should remove the giblets and cut off the neck and wing tips before salting. The organs (offal) and scraps can be used to make a stock to serve as a base for a soup or sauce. A whole goose should be roasted at 425 °F (220 °C/Gas Mark 7) for 20 to 30 minutes, and then at 350 °F (180 °C/Gas Mark 4) for 3 hours.

A frozen goose needs about 1 day to slowly defrost in the refrigerator.

You can also add 1 or 2 tart apples to the shallots in the roasting pan. Core and quarter the apples beforehand. If you are roasting a whole goose, you can also fill the belly cavity with smaller apples. They will caramelize as they roast and make a wonderful complement to the flavor of the shallots.

To make a traditional gravy for this roast goose, heat 1 tablespoon of the goose fat from the roasting pan in a saucepan and, using a whisk, mix with 1 tablespoon flour to make a roux. Stir in most of the drippings from the roasting pan and cook for 10 to 15 minutes, until the gravy thickens. If necessary, dilute with the remaining drippings.

Potato dumplings and bread dumplings are also suitable as accompaniments to replace the potato flatbreads, as are spaetzle, celery or pumpkin puree, gnocchi, or fresh bread.

Zucchini Kraut (see p. 117) also makes a delicious alternative to classic sauerkraut.

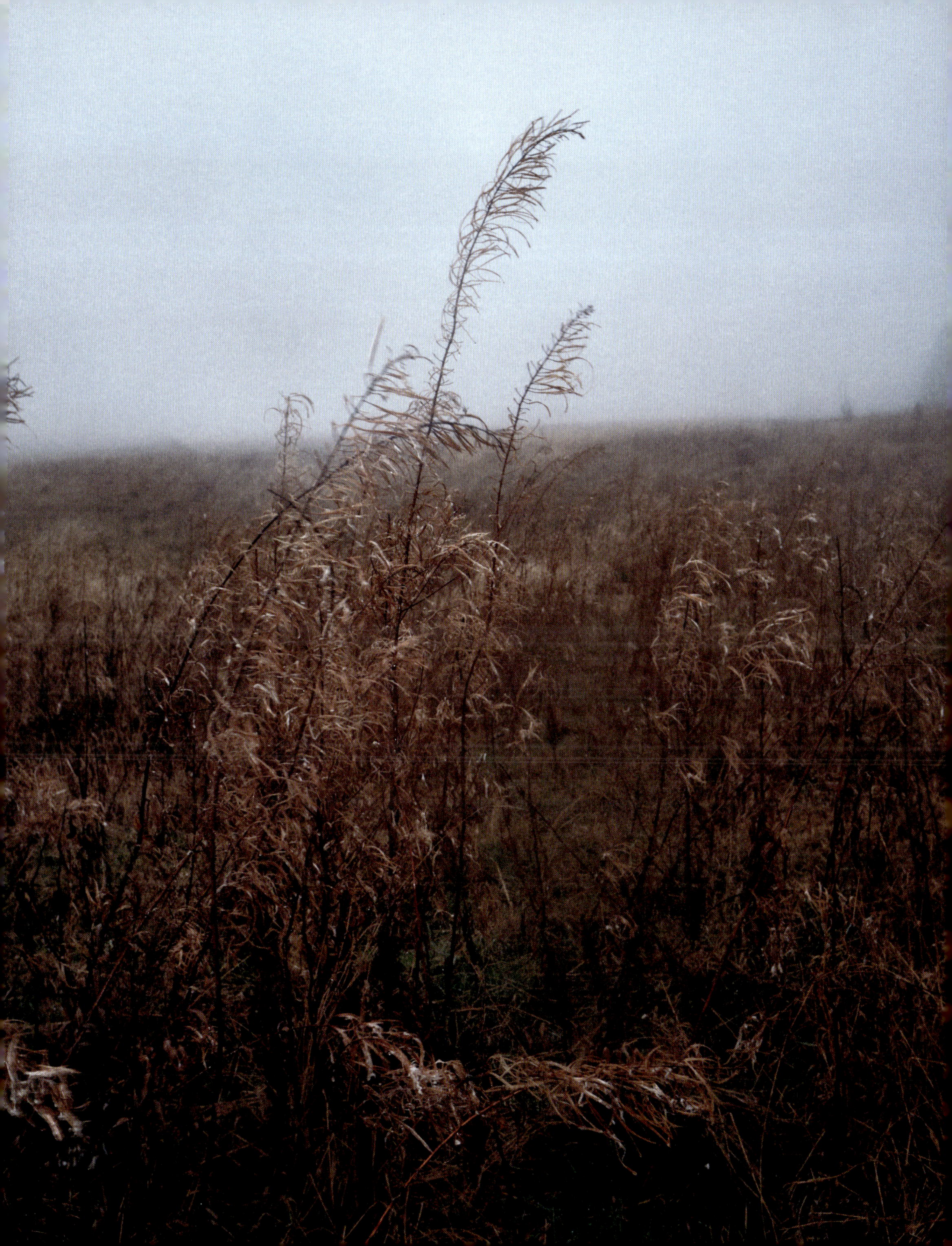

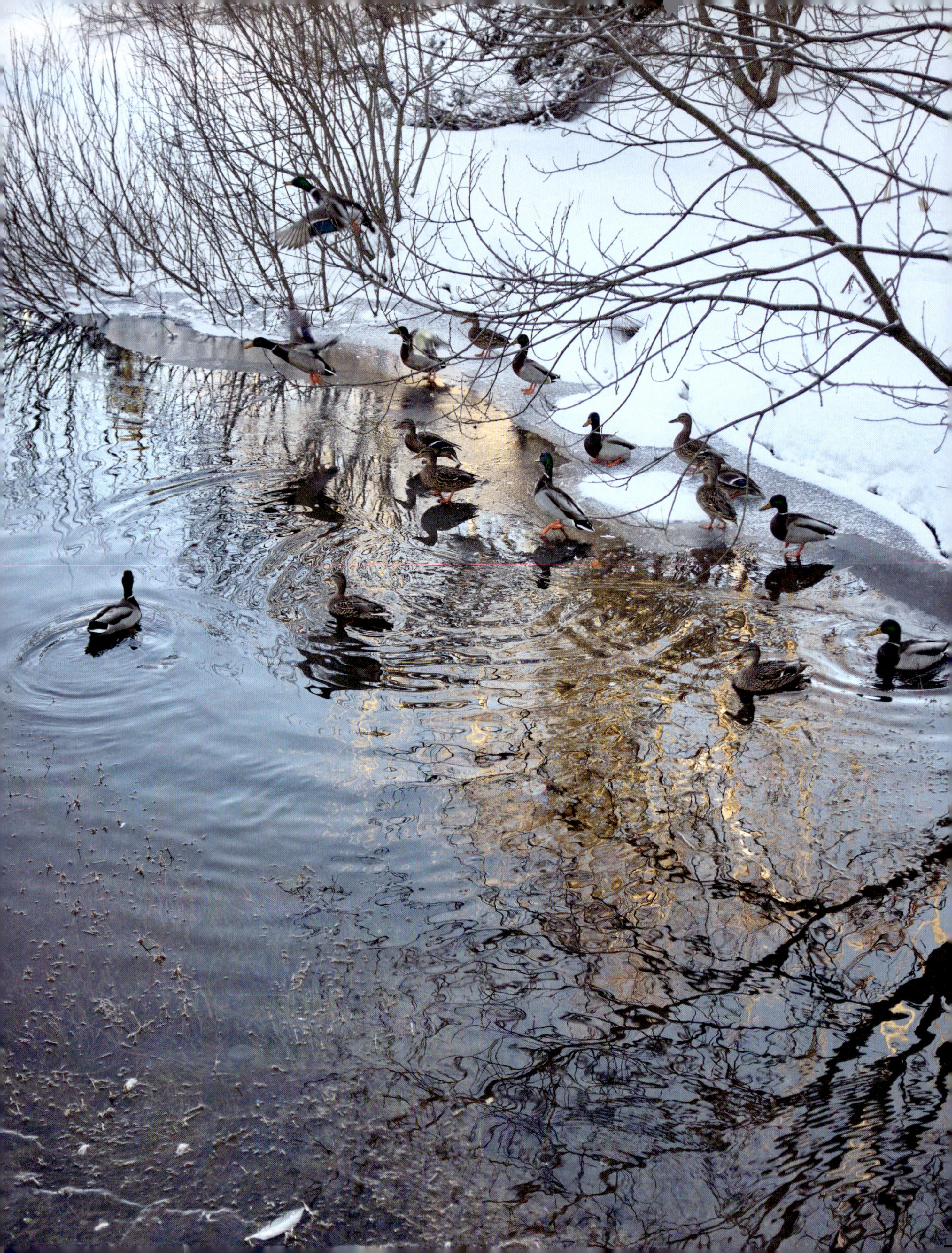

WINTER

Mráz kopřivu nespálí.

Frost does not burn the nettle.

Žurek—Sour Rye Soup

Serves 4 to 6

Ingredients

For the sourdough starter:

Scant 1 cup (200 ml) water

⅓ cup (50 g) dark rye flour or whole-grain rye flour

For the soup:

3 ½ ounces (100 g) slab bacon

1 (5-ounce/150-g) smoked pork sausage (such as Krakauer sausage, bauernwurst)

1 onion

1 large carrot

1 parsley root

3 potatoes

2 bay leaves

5 allspice berries

8 ½ cups (2 l) broth (stock)

Salt and freshly ground black pepper

2 to 3 cloves garlic

1 tablespoon dried marjoram

1 handful of Fermented Savoy Cabbage (see p. 227)

4 to 6 hard-boiled eggs, halved

Make the sourdough starter at least 3 days before use. To do this, bring the water to a boil in a saucepan and let cool completely. Put the flour into a large, clean canning jar (16 ounces/750 ml capacity), add the cooled water, and stir to a smooth slurry. Cover the jar with a clean cloth and let rest at room temperature for 3 days. The starter culture should have settled at the bottom of the jar and a liquid resulting from fermentation should have formed on top.

On the day, cut the bacon into small dice and the sausage into coin-size slices. Peel and mince (very finely chop) the onion. Peel the carrot, root parsley, and potatoes and cut them into small dice. Fry the diced bacon in a stockpot over low heat until the fat is rendered. Add the onion and sauté over medium heat until golden. Add the sausage slices, vegetables, bay leaves and allspice. Add the broth and season with salt and pepper. Cook over medium heat for 20 to 30 minutes, until the vegetables are tender but still slightly firm.

Mix the sourdough starter well to blend the solid part with the liquid until smooth, using an immersion stick blender, if necessary. Peel and crush the garlic. Remove the pot from the heat and gradually pour about three-quarters of the sourdough starter into the hot soup, stirring continousely. Add the garlic and marjoram. Return the pot to the heat and let simmer for 15 minutes. Taste the soup: *żurek* should taste pleasantly sour. Adjust the sourness by stirring in the remaining sourdough, if required—just don't forget that after adding the flour to the soup, it always needs to simmer for at least 10 minutes.

Remove the bay leaves and allspice berries from the soup and discard. Finally, coarsely chop the fermented cabbage and add to the soup. Adjust the seasoning with salt and pepper and serve in bowls with the eggs.

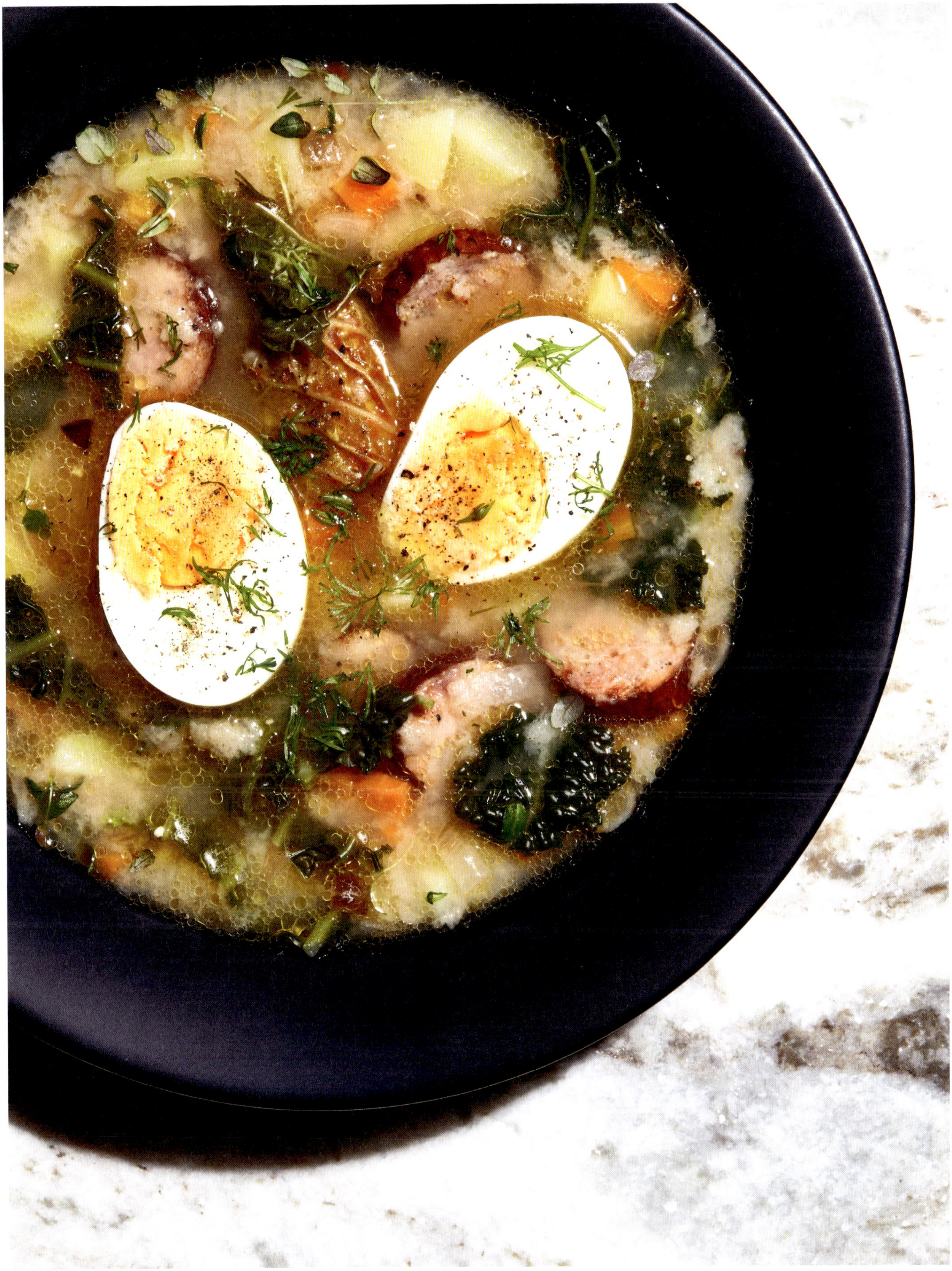

Quark Dumplings with Povidla Sauce

Serves 2 to 4

Ingredients

For the dough:

2 ½ cups (300 g) pastry,
pastry flour or all-purpose (plain) flour,
plus extra for dusting

2 eggs

1 pinch of salt

For the filling:

7 ounces (200 g) soft, creamy quark cheese

2 egg yolks

⅔ cup (80 g) powdered (icing) sugar

1 egg white

For the sauce:

3 ½ tablespoons (50 ml) dry red wine

⅓ cup (100 g) povidla (Plum Butter; see p. 144)

½ teaspoon ground cinnamon

¼ teaspoon freshly grated nutmeg

⅔ cup (100 g) poppy seeds, grounded

1 to 2 tablespoons powdered (icing) sugar

Mix the flour, eggs, and salt in a bowl, then knead by hand to a firm dough. Gather the dough into a ball and let rest in the refrigerator for at least 15 minutes.

In the meantime, make the filling. Mix the quark, egg yolks, and powdered (icing) sugar in a bowl until combined. Beat the egg white with a fork in a cup.

Place the dough on a lightly floured work surface and roll it out into a thin rectangle, then cut into about 2 ¾-inch (7-cm) squares. Place 1 teaspoon of quark filling in the center of each dough square. Brush the edges with beaten egg white and fold half of the square over the filling to form a triangle. Using your fingers or a fork, press the edges of the dough firmly together around the filling.

Bring water to a boil in a pot. In the meantime, to make the sauce, pour the wine into a saucepan and cook off the alcohol over medium heat for 5 minutes. Stir in the povidla with the spices and briefly simmer to heat the sauce, then remove from the heat. Once the water in the pot starts boiling, reduce the heat to medium. Carefully sprinkle in the dumplings and cook for 6 to 7 minutes.

Pour a little sauce onto each plate, arrange the dumplings on top, and serve dusted with ground poppy seeds and powdered (icing) sugar.

Tips You can also use a ravioli cutter to shape the dumplings. The quark dumplings can be served as a main course or in smaller portions as a dessert.

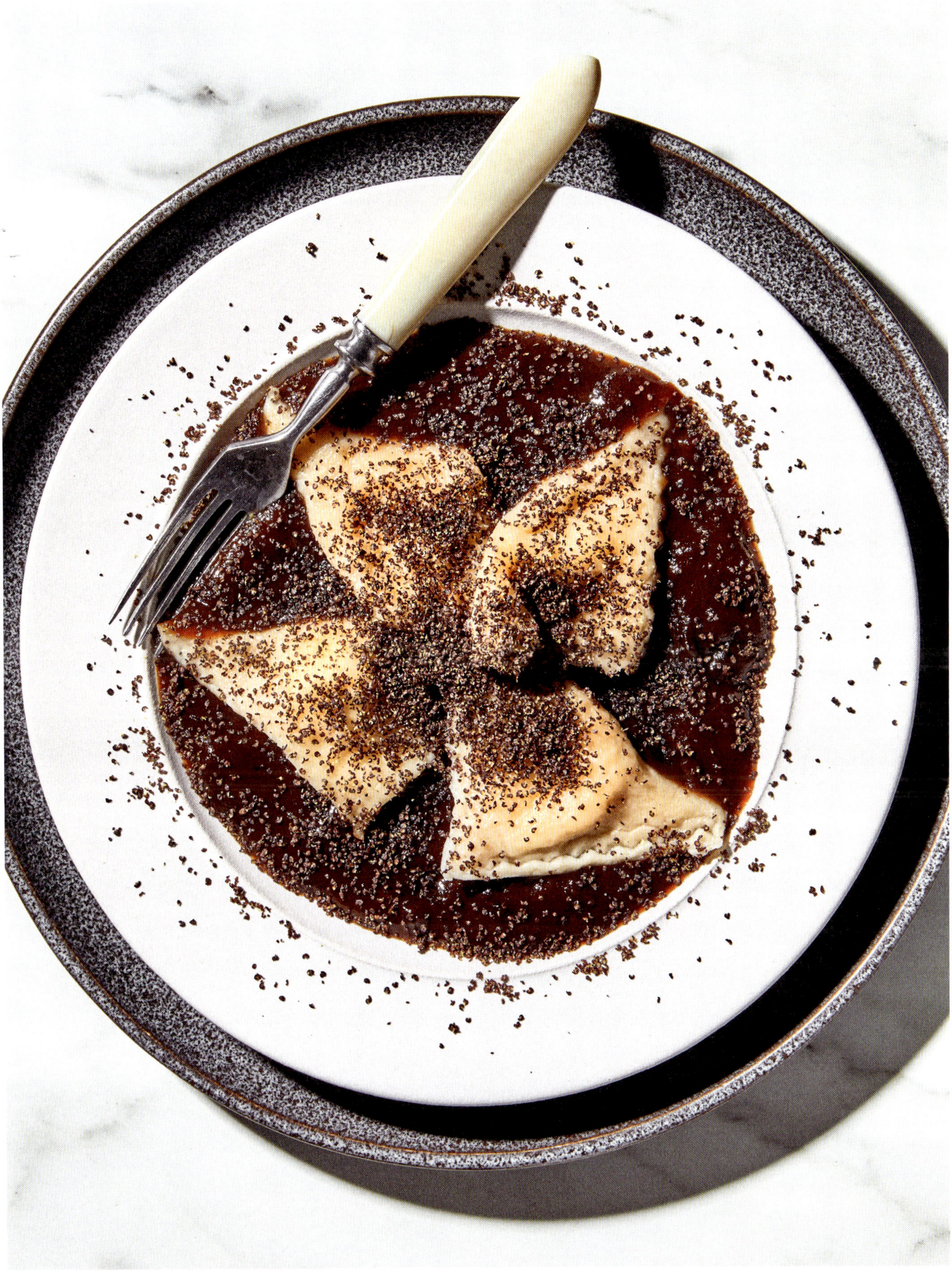

Creamy Jerusalem Artichoke Soup with Parsley Oil

Serves 4

Ingredients

10 ½ ounces (300 g) Jerusalem artichokes

1 large potato

2 shallots

2 tablespoons (30 g) unsalted butter

4 sprigs of fresh thyme

4 ¼ cups (1 l) vegetable broth (stock)

Salt and freshly ground black pepper

Juice of ½ lemon

4 tablespoons Parsley Oil (see p. 74)

Wash the Jerusalem artichokes and potato thoroughly, then peel and dice. Peel and mince (very finely chop) the shallots.

Melt the butter in a saucepan over medium heat and sauté the shallots. Add the diced Jerusalem artichokes and potato and sauté, stirring continuously, for about 3 minutes. Add the thyme and 3 cups (750 ml) of the broth, then season with salt and pepper. Stir and cover with a lid. Reduce the heat to low and let simmer for about 20 minutes, until the vegetables are soft.

Remove the thyme and puree the soup until creamy and smooth. Season the soup with salt, pepper, and lemon juice. If necessary, dilute with the remaining broth. Finally, divide the Jerusalem artichoke soup among bowls, drizzle with the parsley oil, and serve immediately.

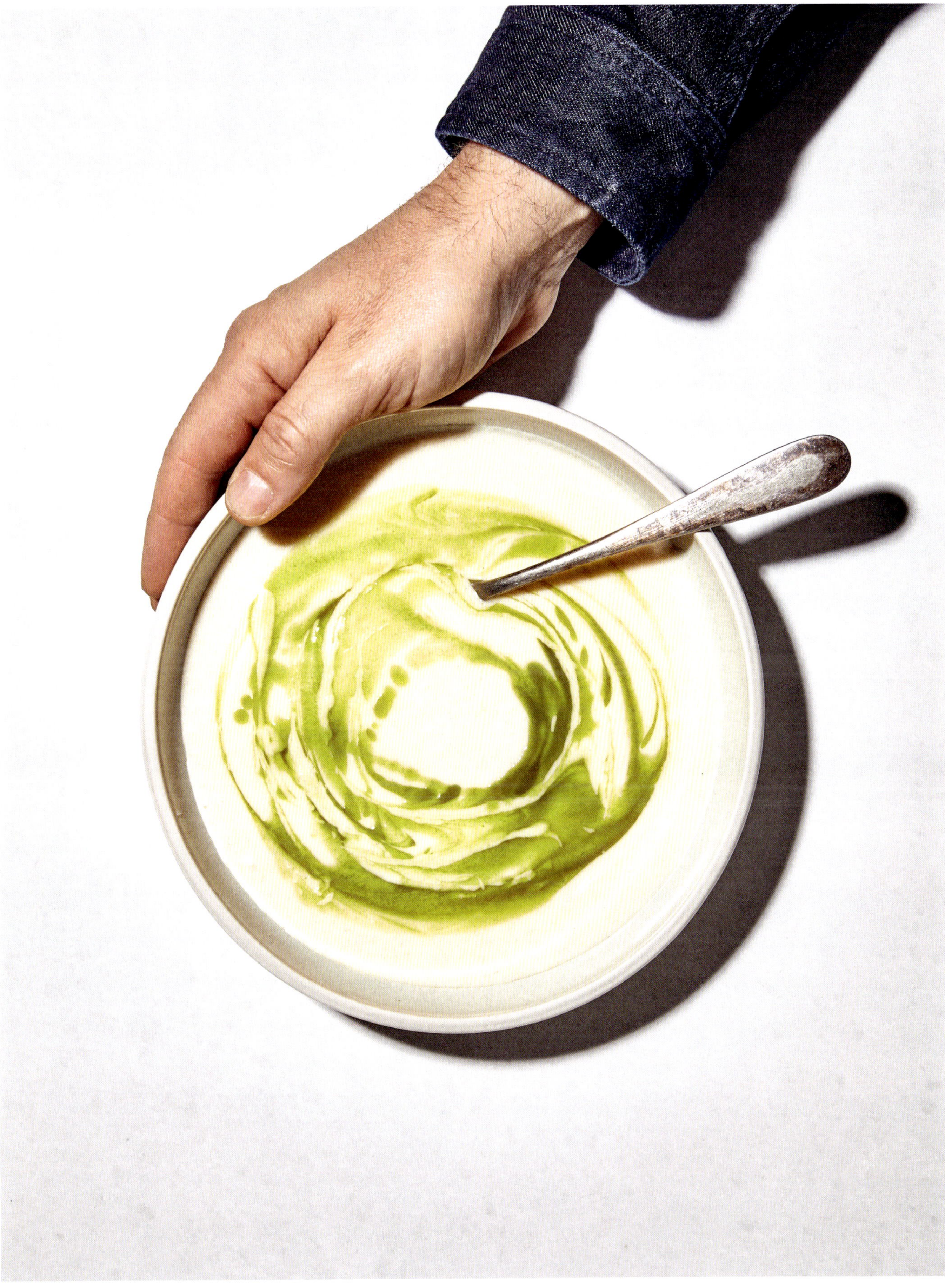

Pickled Bok Choy with Soy Sauce

For 2 or 3 canning jars (16 ounces / 750 ml each)

Ingredients

7 ¼ cups (1.75 l) water

4 tablespoons soy sauce (shoyu)

4 tablespoons rice vinegar

2 tablespoons honey

1 teaspoon salt

4 heads (1 ½ to 1 ¾ pounds / 700–800 g) bok choy (pak choi)

1 chili pepper

3 cloves garlic

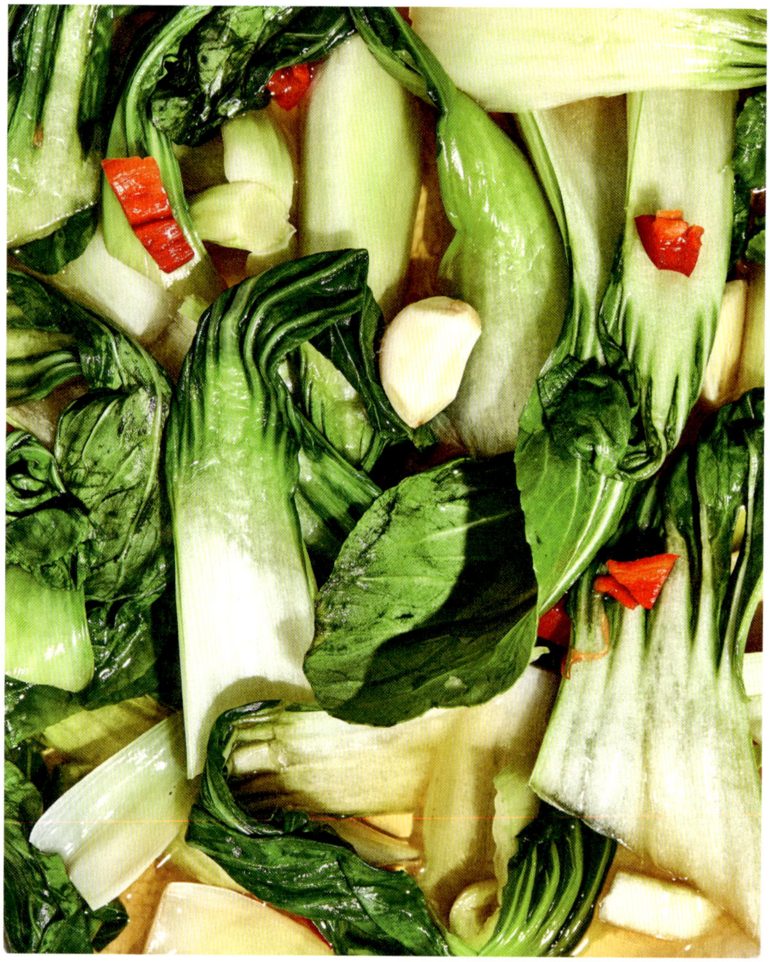

To make the pickling liquid, bring 3 cups (750 ml) of the water to a boil in a saucepan. Remove from the heat and stir in the soy sauce, vinegar, honey, and salt. Stir until the salt and honey dissolve completely. Let cool.

Bring the remaining 4 ¼ cups (1 l) of water to a boil in a second saucepan. Wash the bok choy, slice off the thick end of each head, and separate the leaves. Place a colander in the sink, add the bok choy leaves, and pour boiling water over them. Let drain and cool.

Wash the chili pepper, and if it's too hot, remove the seeds. Coarsely chop. Peel and coarsely chop the garlic. Transfer the bok choy to sterilized canning jars. Insert chili and garlic pieces between the leaves. Finally, pour over the cooled pickling liquid until everything is completely covered.

Close the lids tightly and refrigerate the pickled bok choy for 3 to 5 days before use. The vegetable will slightly change color while absorbing the flavors of all the ingredients.

Tip Pickled bok choy makes a good accompaniment for fish, meat, and fried dishes.

Pickled Spiced Celery Root

For 4 canning jars (16 ounces/500 ml each)

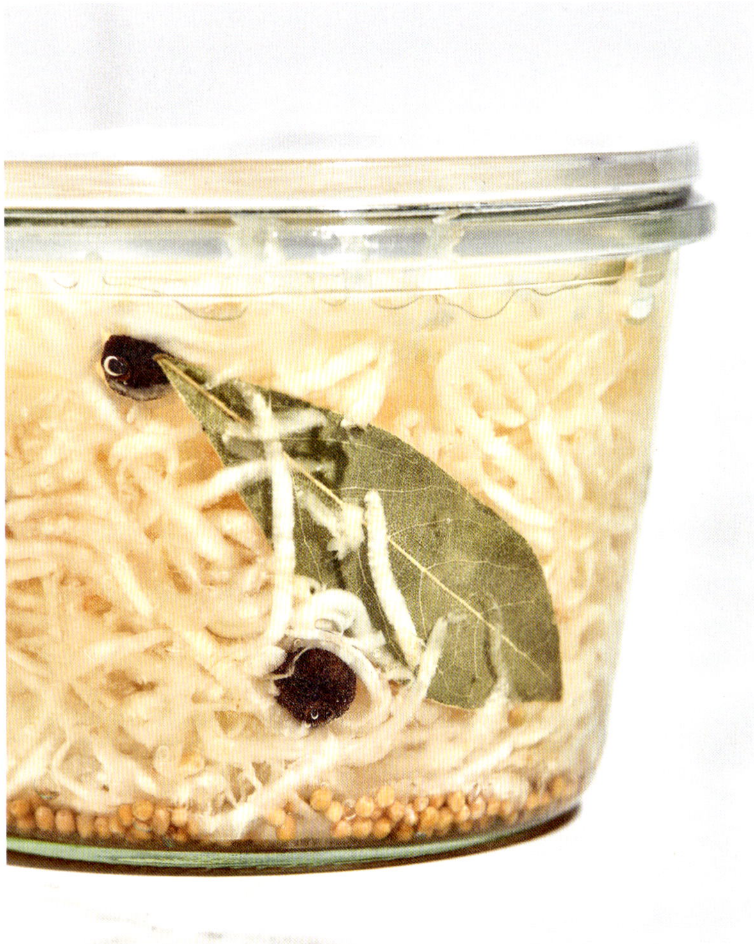

Ingredients

2 ¼ pounds (1 kg) celery root (celeriac)

3 ⅓ cups (800 ml) water

1 cup (250 ml) white wine vinegar

Scant ½ cup (100 ml) rice vinegar

⅓ cup (80 g) granulated sugar

1 tablespoon salt

4 bay leaves

1 teaspoon peppercorns

1 teaspoon allspice berries

1 tablespoon mustard seeds

Peel, wash, and coarsely grate the celery root or cut it into julienne strips. To make the pickling liquid, mix the water with both of the vinegars, the sugar, and salt in a pot. Bring to a boil, stirring occasionally, until the sugar and salt dissolve. Let boil for 3 minutes, then remove from the heat.

Arrange the celery root in layers in sterilized canning jars, adding the bay leaves and spices between the layers. Pour over the hot liquid and stir with a fork to remove any air bubbles. Finally, press the celery root down firmly. Carefully wipe the rims of the jars with a clean cloth, close the jars tightly, and place upside down. Let the pickled celery root cool and store in a cool, dark place. Pickle for at least 2 weeks before use.

Tip Pickled celery root is a good accompaniment for fatty dishes, such as broiled (grilled) or smoked meat and fish. It can also be used to make remoulade.

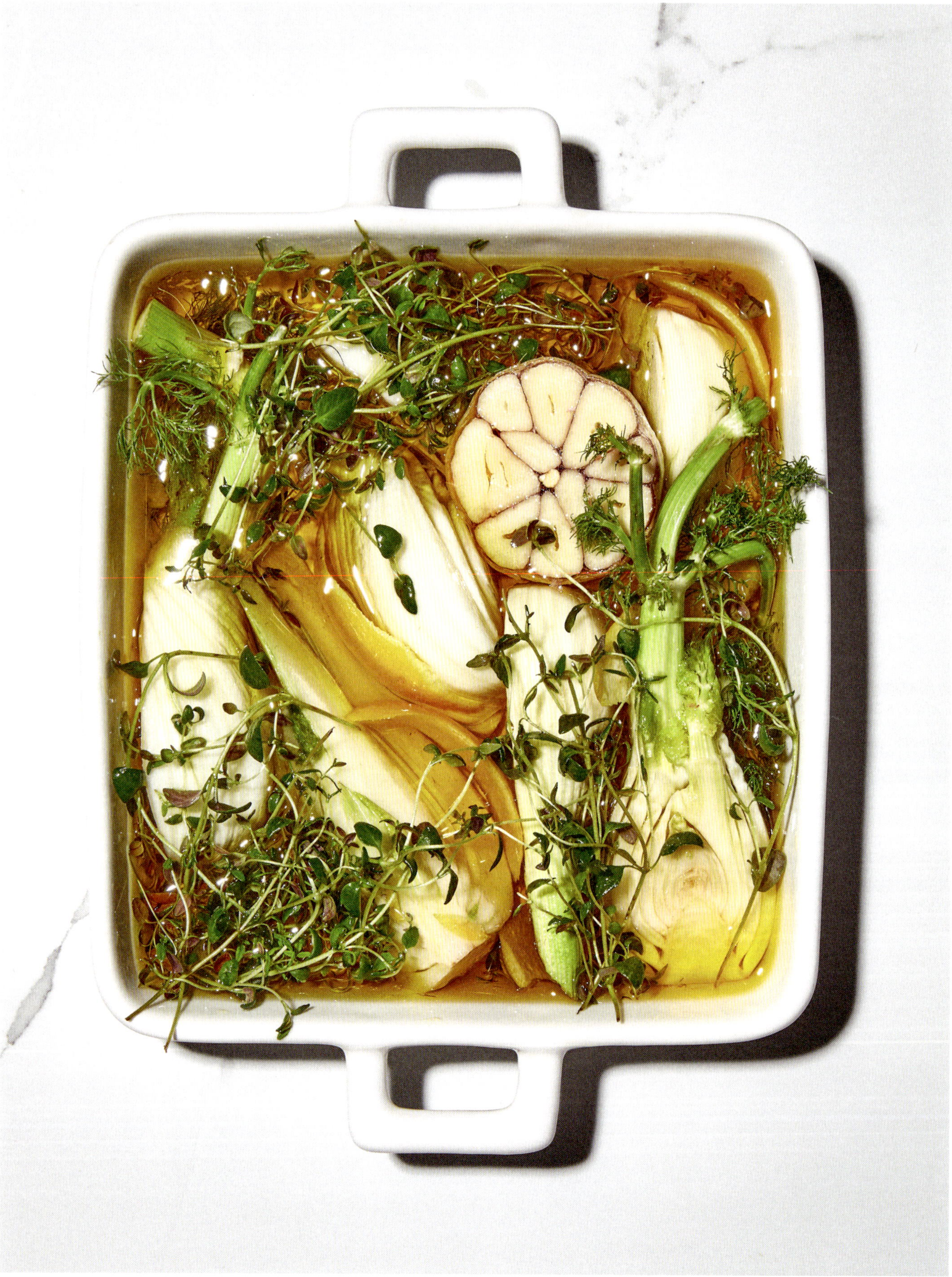

Fennel Confit

For 2 or 3 canning jars
(16 ounces / 750 ml each)

Ingredients

3 fennel bulbs

1 organic lemon

1 whole garlic head

2 tablespoons honey

1 tablespoon salt

Freshly ground pepper

4 sprigs of fresh thyme

2 to 3 cups (500–750 ml) olive oil

Preheat the oven to 340 °F top/bottom heat (160 °C/Gas Mark 3 ½). Wash and halve or quarter the fennel bulbs. Wash the lemon and using a vegetable peeler, remove wide strips of lemon zest. Cut the unpeeled garlic head in half widthwise.

Place the fennel in a small baking dish, drizzle with the honey, and season generously with the salt and pepper. Wash the thyme and shake dry. Add the lemon zest, garlic, and thyme to the fennel. Add enough olive oil to completely cover the contents of the baking dish. Put the baking dish into the oven and confit for about 1 hour, until the fennel is soft.

Let cool. Transfer the fennel confit to sterilized canning jars along with the lemon zest, garlic, and thyme. Add the oil from the baking dish. The contents of the jars should be completely covered in oil. Close the jars tightly and store in the refrigerator for up to 2 weeks.

Tips Fennel confit has a flavor reminiscent of pickled artichokes. It can be served as an appetizer, but it is also suitable as an accompaniment for a lot of dishes. It makes a delicious pizza topping and enlivens salads when cut into small pieces.

You can substitute sprigs of tarragon or 4 bay leaves for the thyme.

The remaining confit oil can be used to make pesto, salad dressings, marinades, and dips, as well as for pasta dishes and hummus.

The Renaissance of an Old Slavic Drink

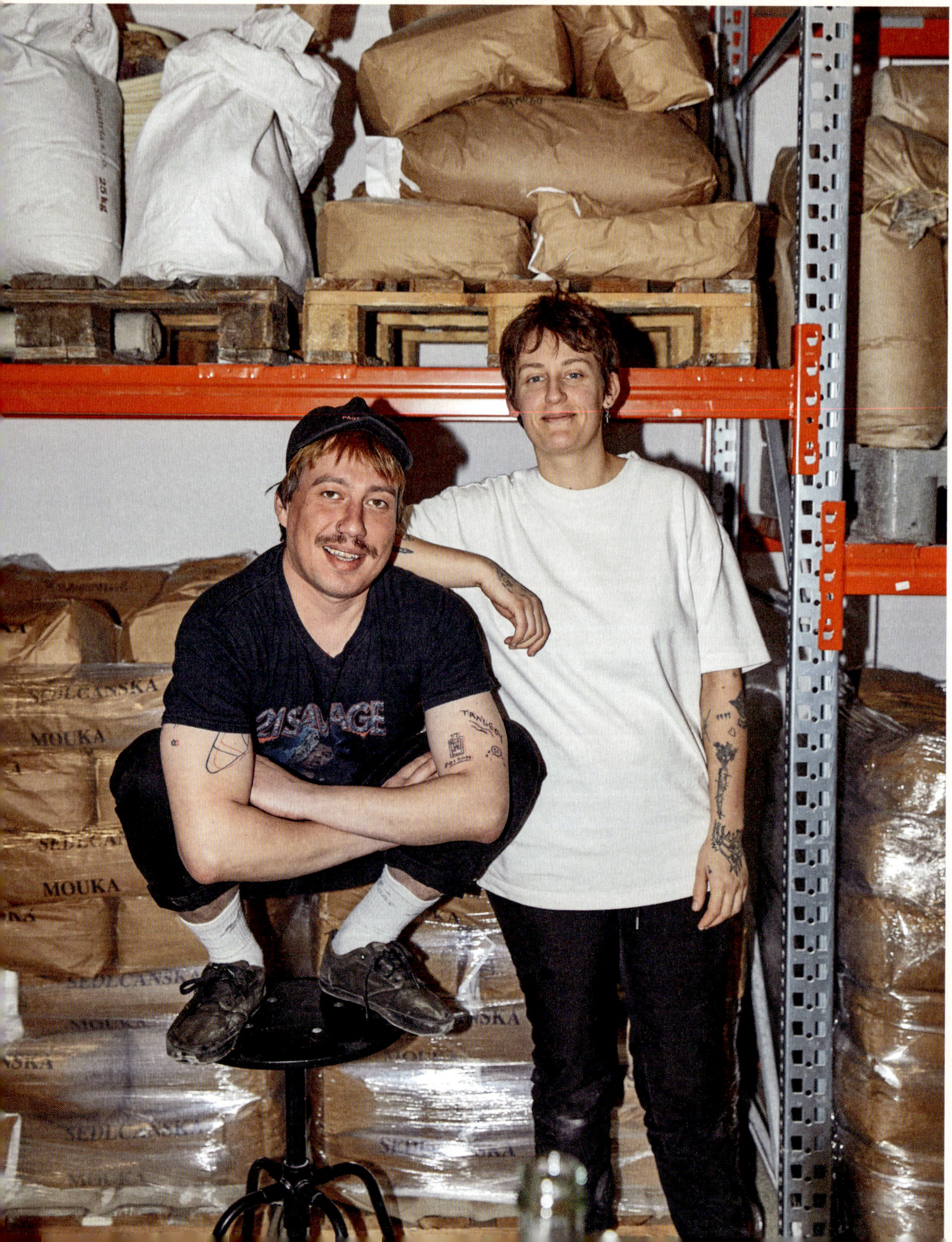

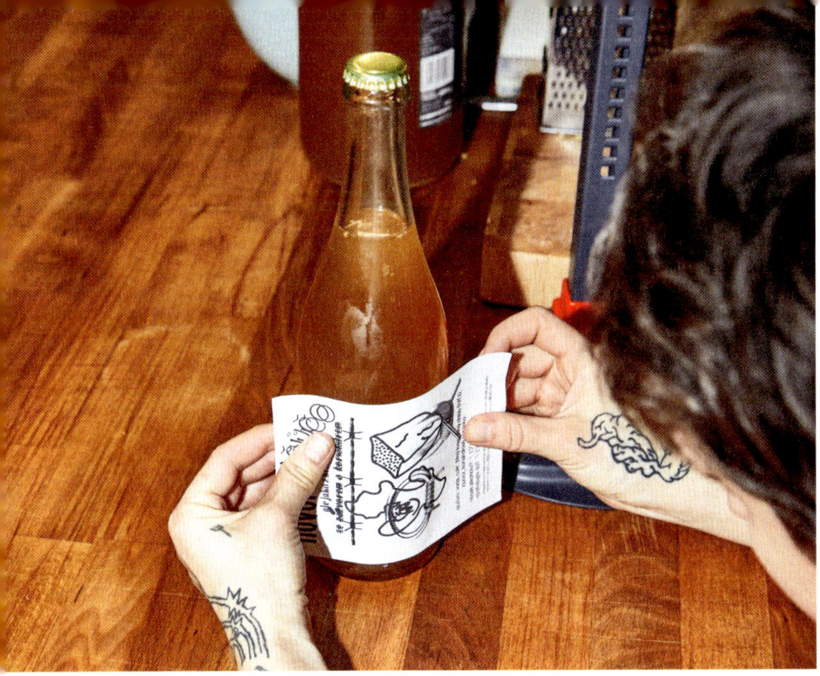

Kateřina Jakusová and Martin Kudrlička fear nothing in the kitchen—not even turning leftover sourdough loaves into scrumptious sparkling *kvass!*

Kateřina Jakusová grew up in Ostrava, but she moved to Prague with her family when she was fifteen. After finishing high school, she headed for Berlin. "I was drawn to cooking, but I didn't have any experience ... so I resolved the matter in the simplest way possible—I made some up for my résumé. Fake it until you make it!" she recalls with a grin. It worked. She landed a job at the well-known Berlin breakfast café *Silo*.

Those Berlin years gave her a crash course in cooking, and when she returned to Prague, she joined Eska in Karlín, a restaurant famed for its inventive use of local ingredients. It was here that Katka first discovered her love of preservation: canning, fermenting, pickling, and finding creative ways to make summer's bounty last through the winter. Work became play, and within five years she'd risen to assistant chef and even completed an internship at Noma, Copenhagen's world-renowned, three-Michelin-star restaurant.

From fine dining in Denmark, Kateřina's path led back to Prague's artisanal bakeries *Další kus* and *Alf & Bet*. There, she met Martin Kudrlička, and together they decided to bring back *kvass*, the ancient Slavic drink made from fermented bread. "Once, the bakery had piles of unsold loaves we hated throwing away," Martin says. "So we experimented; we're a little like those two clumsy DIY guys Pat and Mat, whom every Czech and Slovak remembers from that retro children's TV show, always tickering. But somehow, our experiments usually work. The *kvass* with ginger and coriander turned out amazing! It's the perfect New Year's Eve drink," they laugh (see p. 226).

Kateřina and Martin are proof that passion and a willingness to do things differently can lead to great things and success. Their shared experience in cooking and baking eventually steered both of them toward pizza. Martin moved south to České Budějovice, where he and his partner opened Pizza Paranormale, a playful restaurant devoted to Neapolitan-style pies, natural wine, and good cheer.

Kateřina, meanwhile, launched the pop-up Slice Slice Baby, which became so popular it turned into a permanent hip bistro in Prague's Holešovice district. With its laid-back vibe and friendly service, the place feels like a small family trattoria somewhere in Italy. "I'd call what we bake here neo-Neapolitan," Katka says. "It's traditional pizza from Naples, but with a modern twist. We add a little sourdough and olive oil to the dough, we play around with creative toppings, we make our own umami stardust, and we even serve dipping sauces for the leftover crusts. The Italians would probably crucify us for it!" she laughs as she slides another pizza into the oven.

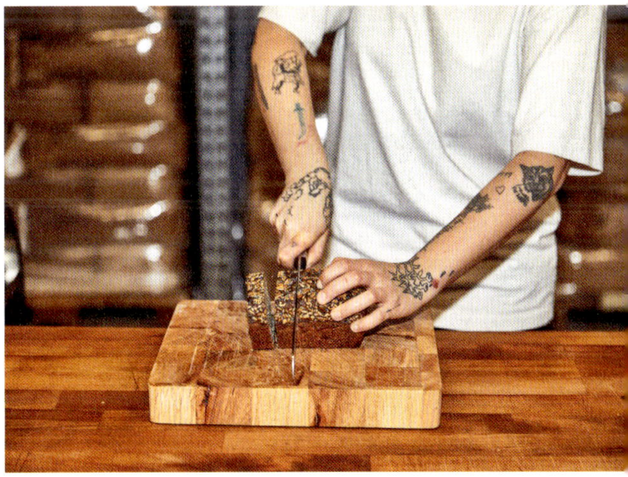

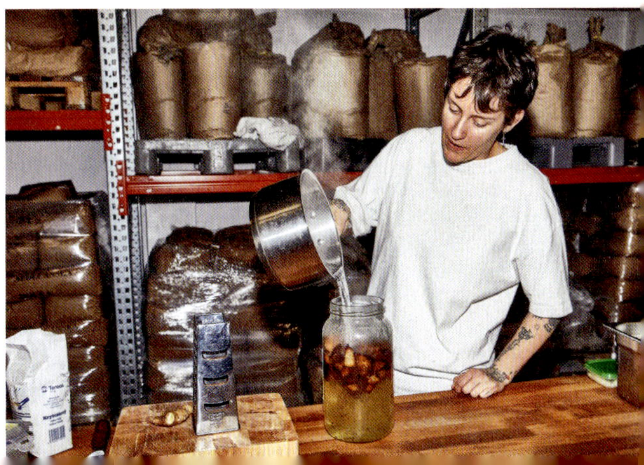

Kvass with Ginger and Coriander Seeds

For 1 large jars (64 ounces/3 l)

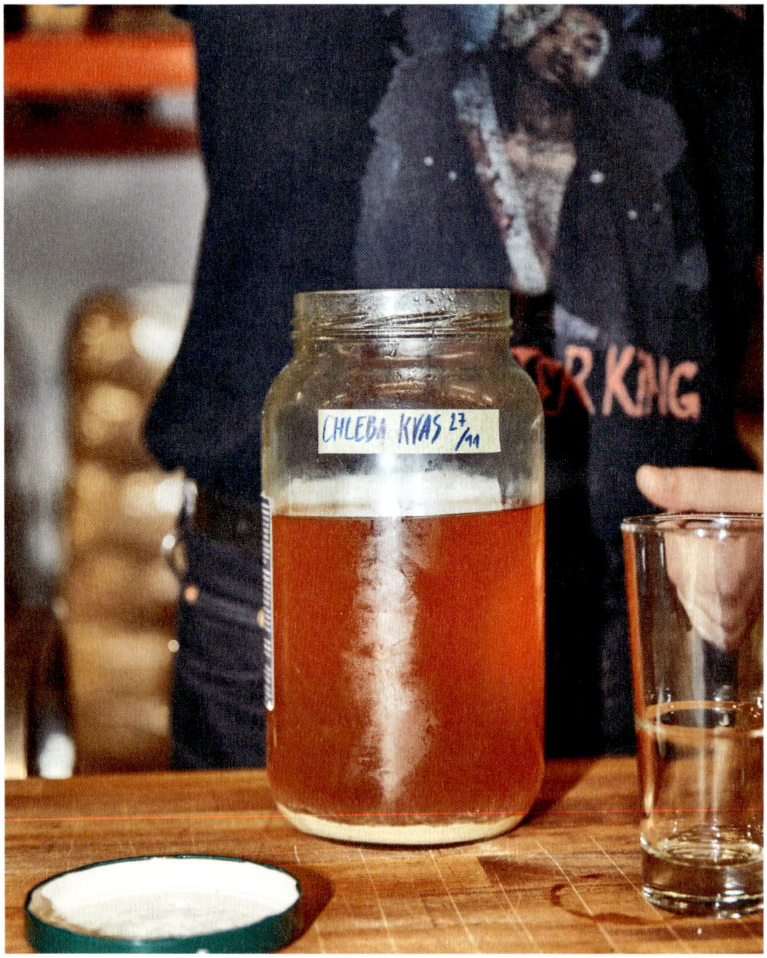

Ingredients

1 pound (450 g) rye bread, 2 or 3 days old

3 quarts (3 l) water

1 (2-inch/5-cm) piece fresh, unpeeled ginger

2 tablespoons coriander seeds

1 cup (200 g) granulated sugar

2 tablespoons sourdough starter

Preheat the oven to 340 °F (160 °C/Gas Mark 3½). Cut the bread into large cubes, place them on a baking sheet, and toast in the oven for 20 to 30 minutes, until dark brown. Meanwhile bring the water to a boil in a saucepan and let cool slightly.

Transfer the bread cubes to a clean wide-necked jar and pour over the hot water to cover them completely. If they float to the surface, use a sterilized fermenting weight to keep them in place. Cover the jar loosely with a lid. Let infuse in a dark place at room temperature (65 to 70 °F/18–21 °C) for at least 5 hours, preferably overnight.

Wash the ginger and coarsely grate it. Toast the coriander seeds in a dry skillet or frying pan. Strain the liquid from the soaked bread through a fine-mesh strainer or sieve into the sterilized jar. Squeeze the bread well with clean hands. Add the ginger, coriander seeds, sugar, and sourdough starter. Stir well, cover with a lid, and let ferment at room temperature for 2 to 3 days, until the mixture starts to bubble. Stir occasionally with a clean wooden spoon.

Drink immediately or store in the refrigerator (where the fermentation will slow down). The longer the *kvass* ferments, the less sweet it will taste.

Tips Sourdough starter is available from some bakeries (or ask a neighbour or a friend). It is also easy to make at home in 4 to 5 days. All you need is whole-grain rye flour and water. Or you can use 1 small (⅔-ounce/19 g) cake of fresh yeast, but the flavor of the *kvass* won't be as intense.

Different spices (star anise, cloves, cinnamon), herbs (mint, rosemary, basil), wild herbs (sweet woodruff), and fruit—whether fresh (berries, lemon) or dried (raisins)—are flavor enhancers. You can even use loose tea leaves to flavor your *kvass*. Experiment to your heart's content!

Fermented Savoy Cabbage with Garlic and Caraway Seeds

For 2 or 3 canning jars (16 ounce / 750 ml each)

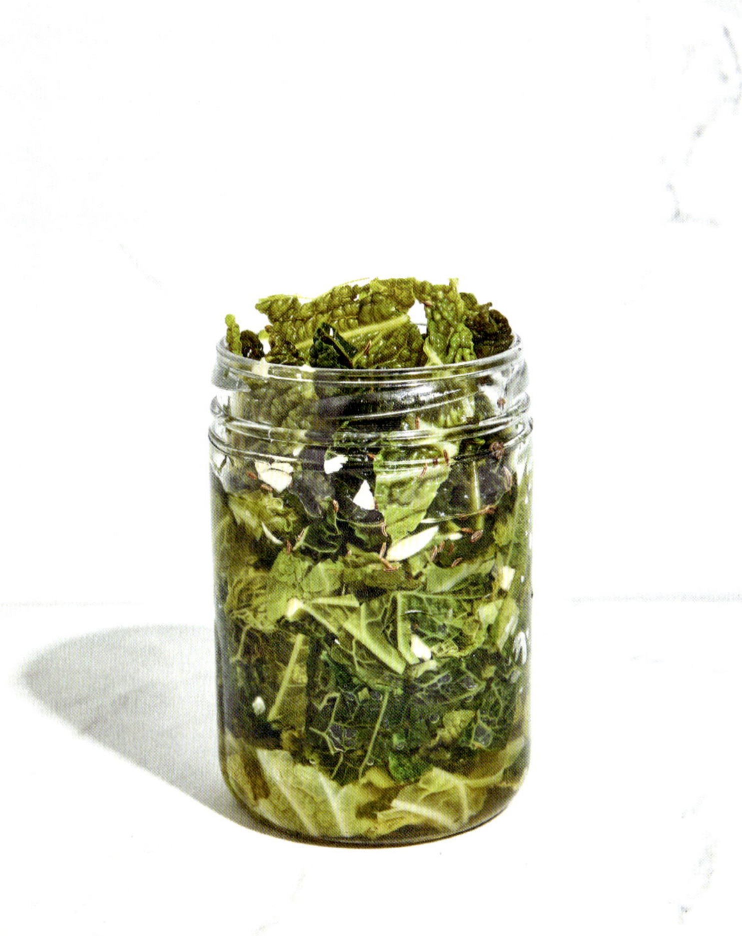

Ingredients

4 ¼ cups (1 l) water

1 tablespoon (20 g) salt

1 large head savoy cabbage

3 cloves garlic

1 tablespoon caraway seeds

To make the brine, bring the water to a boil in a saucepan and let cool completely. Add the salt and stir until dissolved.

To prepare the cabbage, remove the outer leaves. Divide the cabbage into individual leaves and cut out the ribs. Wash the cabbage leaves, tear them into pieces, and put them into a bowl. Peel and mince (very finely chop) the garlic and add to the cabbage. Sprinkle over the caraway seeds.

Press the cabbage down a little with clean hands and transfer to sterilized canning jars along with the garlic and caraway seeds. Fill the jars to about 2 inches (5 cm) below the rim. Press the cabbage down a little more inside the jars and pour over the brine, completely covering the leaves. If necessary, use a sterilized fermentation weight to keep them in place. Leave a space of about ¾ inch (2 cm) between the brine and the rim of the jar to allow room for the formation of foam on the surface of the liquid.

Place the lid loosely on the jars without closing tightly. Let the cabbage ferment in a dark place at room temperature (preferably 65 to 70 °F / 18–21 °C) for about 7 days. Remove the fermentation weight if using, close the lids tightly, and refrigerate. You can eat the fermented savoy cabbage immediately or store it in the refrigerator for several weeks. Always scoop it with a clean fork to prevent the vegetables from spoiling.

Tips You can use kale instead of savoy cabbage, or you can mix the two. Also, add fresh dill and thinly sliced carrots, if you want.

Enjoy this fermented savoy cabbage on its own or serve it with savory dishes. Like all fermented vegetables, fermented savoy cabbage is good for digestion.

Holubky—Stuffed Savoy Cabbage Rolls

Serves 4

Ingredients

1 savoy cabbage

1 onion

4 cloves garlic

1 pound 2 ounces (500 g) ground (minced) pork

8 ¾ ounces (250 g) ground (minced) beef

1 egg

3 tablespoons bread crumbs

1 teaspoon dried marjoram or oregano

½ teaspoon ground caraway seeds

Salt and freshly ground black pepper

2 tablespoons neutral vegetable oil

1 cup (250 g) canned diced tomatoes

3 cups (750 ml) Tomato Ketchup (see p. 126)

2 bay leaves

5 allspice berries

1 teaspoon granulated sugar

Cooked rice, to accompany (optional)

To prepare the cabbage, remove the outer leaves, then divide it into individual leaves. Note: Be careful not to tear the leaves. You will need 10 to 12 whole cabbage leaves. Peel and mince (very finely chop) the onion and garlic separately.

Bring a pot of water to a boil. In the meantime, mix the ground pork and beef and add half of the minced onion and garlic, the egg, and bread crumbs. Mix in the marjoram or oregano and caraway seeds and season generously with salt and pepper.

When the water comes to a boil, reduce the heat to medium and blanch the cabbage leaves for 1 to 2 minutes. Immediately put the leaves into ice water to shock them.

Heat the oil in a deep skillet or frying pan and sauté the remaining onion, then add the rest of the garlic and sauté for about 1 minute, until fragrant. Add the diced tomatoes and ketchup to the skillet, then the bay leaves and allspice berries. Stir in the sugar and season with salt and pepper. Mix everything together, reduce the heat to low-medium, and let simmer, stirring occasionally.

In the meantime, preheat the oven to 350 °F top/bottom heat (180 °C/Gas Mark 4). Cut the central rib out of each cooled cabbage leaf, leaving a notch halfway up the leaf. Moisten your hands with water. Gather a small portion of the ground meat filling into a cylinder and place in the middle of a cabbage leaf. Fold the sides of the leaf over the filling, then tightly roll up the meat toward the tip of the leaf to form a tight package. Arrange the stuffed cabbage rolls, seam side down, closely packed inside a baking dish or roasting pan.

Remove the bay leaves and allspice berries from the tomato sauce in the skillet. Pour the sauce over the cabbage rolls, cover with a lid or aluminum foil, and braise in the oven for about 20 minutes. Remove the lid or foil and bake in the oven for another 15 to 20 minutes.

Serve the stuffed savoy cabbage rolls with a little tomato sauce or accompany with cooked white rice.

Tips Green (white) cabbage or grape (vine) leaves can be used instead of savoy cabbage to make these rolls. Large nasturtium leaves are also suitable—they will give the dish a slightly spicy flavor.

In summer, use fresh ripe tomatoes instead of canned tomatoes for this recipe.

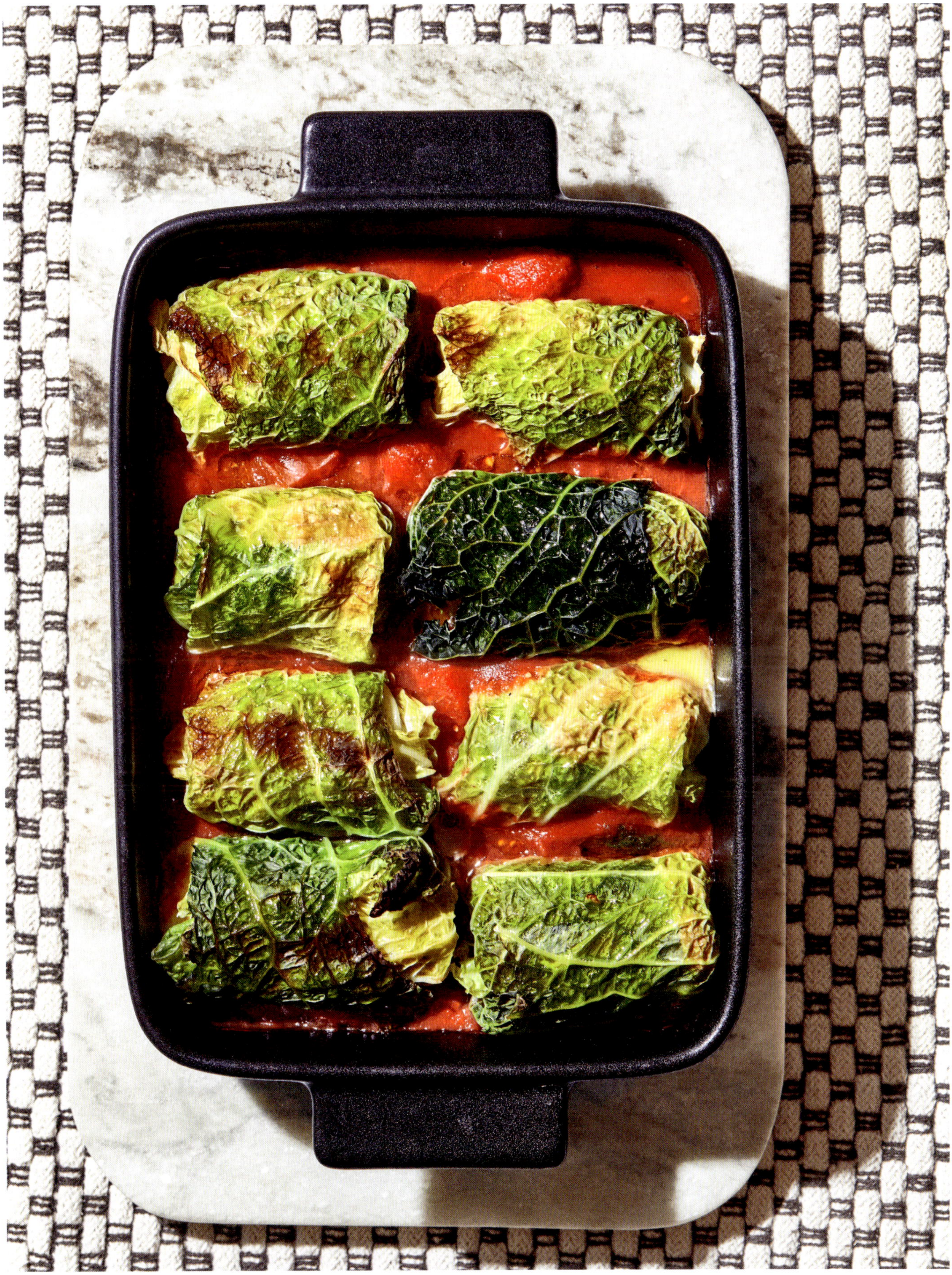

Punch Cake

Makes 1 rectangular cake
(12 by 8 inches / 30 × 20 cm)

Ingredients

For the pale sponge cake:

6 eggs

¾ cup plus 2½ tablespoons (180 g) granulated sugar

6 tablespoons water

1⅓ cups plus 2 tablespoons (180 g) semi-coarse flour (see tips)

1 pinch salt

For the pink sponge cake:

4 eggs

⅔ cup (120 g) granulated sugar

4 tablespoons water

1 cup (120 g) semi-coarse flour (see tips)

1 pinch salt

1 to 2 teaspoons red food coloring gel

For the soaking syrup:

⅔ cup (150 ml) water

⅔ cup (150 ml) raspberry syrup

Juice of 1 orange

Scant ½ cup (100 ml) rum

For the filling and icing:

¾ cup (250 g) Red Currant Jam (see p. 99)

Juice of ½ lemon

1 to 2 tablespoons raspberry syrup

1⅔ cups (200 g) powdered (icing) sugar

3 ounces (80 g) dark chocolate

Line 2 baking pans (12 by 8 inches / 30 × 20 cm) with parchment (baking) paper and preheat the oven to 340 °F top/bottom heat (170 °C/Gas Mark 3½).

To make the pale sponge, separate the eggs. In a deep mixing bowl, beat the egg whites to soft peaks, then add half of the sugar and continue beating to stiff peaks. In a large mixing bowl, mix the egg yolks with the remaining sugar and the water, then beat until the sugar dissolves and the mixture is thick, pale, and smooth. Fold in the sifted flour and salt, a little at a time. Finally, fold in the whipped egg whites. Divide the batter evenly between the two baking pans and smooth the surface with a spatula. Bake for about 12 to 14 minutes, until golden. Lift out the sponge sheets with the parchment paper and let cool completely.

Line one of the baking pans again with parchment (baking) paper. Make the batter for the pink sponge following the previous directions, coloring the batter with the food coloring before baking. (The batter should be an intense pink, because baking will make it fade.) Because this sponge layer is thicker than the two lighter ones, bake for 15 to 18 minutes. Remove the sponge as described above and let cool.

In the meantime, make the soaking syrup. In a saucepan, mix the water with the raspberry syrup and orange juice, bring to a boil, and let simmer for about 3 minutes. Remove from the heat and let cool. Stir in the rum.

Carefully remove the parchment paper from the cooled sponges. Spread the two pale sponge sheets with the red currant jam and drizzle the pink sponge layer evenly with half of the soaking syrup.

Place one pale sponge sheet on a serving plate with the jam-coated side facing up. Lay the pink sponge layer on top with the syrup-soaked side facing down. Drizzle the top of the pink layer with the remaining syrup, then place the second pale sponge sheet on top with the jam-coated side facing down. The result will be a three-layer cake with a pink sponge layer in the middle. Weigh the assembled cake down (for example, place a baking tray with a bag of flour on top) and refrigerate overnight.

To make the icing, gradually mix the lemon juice and syrup into the powdered (icing) sugar in a bowl until the icing turns pink and is a thick, but spreadable consistency. If the icing is too runny, add a little more powdered (icing) sugar. If it is too firm, dilute with a drop of lemon juice.

Ice the cake and refrigerate again for at least 30 minutes. Melt the chocolate in a double boiler (over a bain-marie) or in the microwave and, using a fork, drizzle it decoratively in thin lines over the icing. Refrigerate the cake for another 30 minutes until the icing and chocolate set.

Cut the cake into individual portions. Punch cake tastes best straight from the refrigerator.

Tips Use blood orange juice for an intense red color, or grapefruit juice if you prefer the syrup to be less sweet.

To replicate semi-coarse flour use a 1:1 mix of wheat semolina and a smooth flour, such as all-purpose (plain) flour, pastry or cake flour.

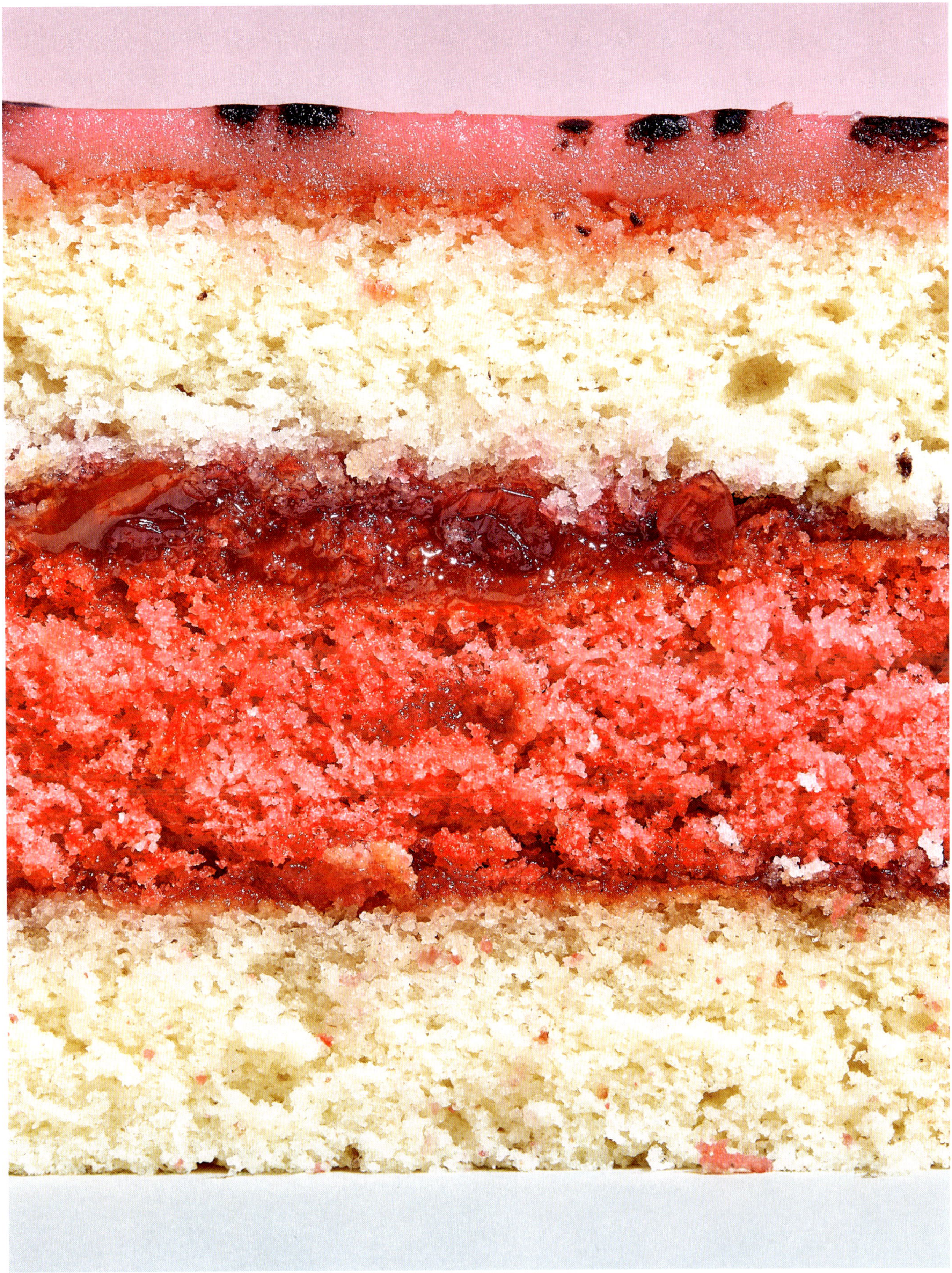

Brightening Winter with Preserved Lemons

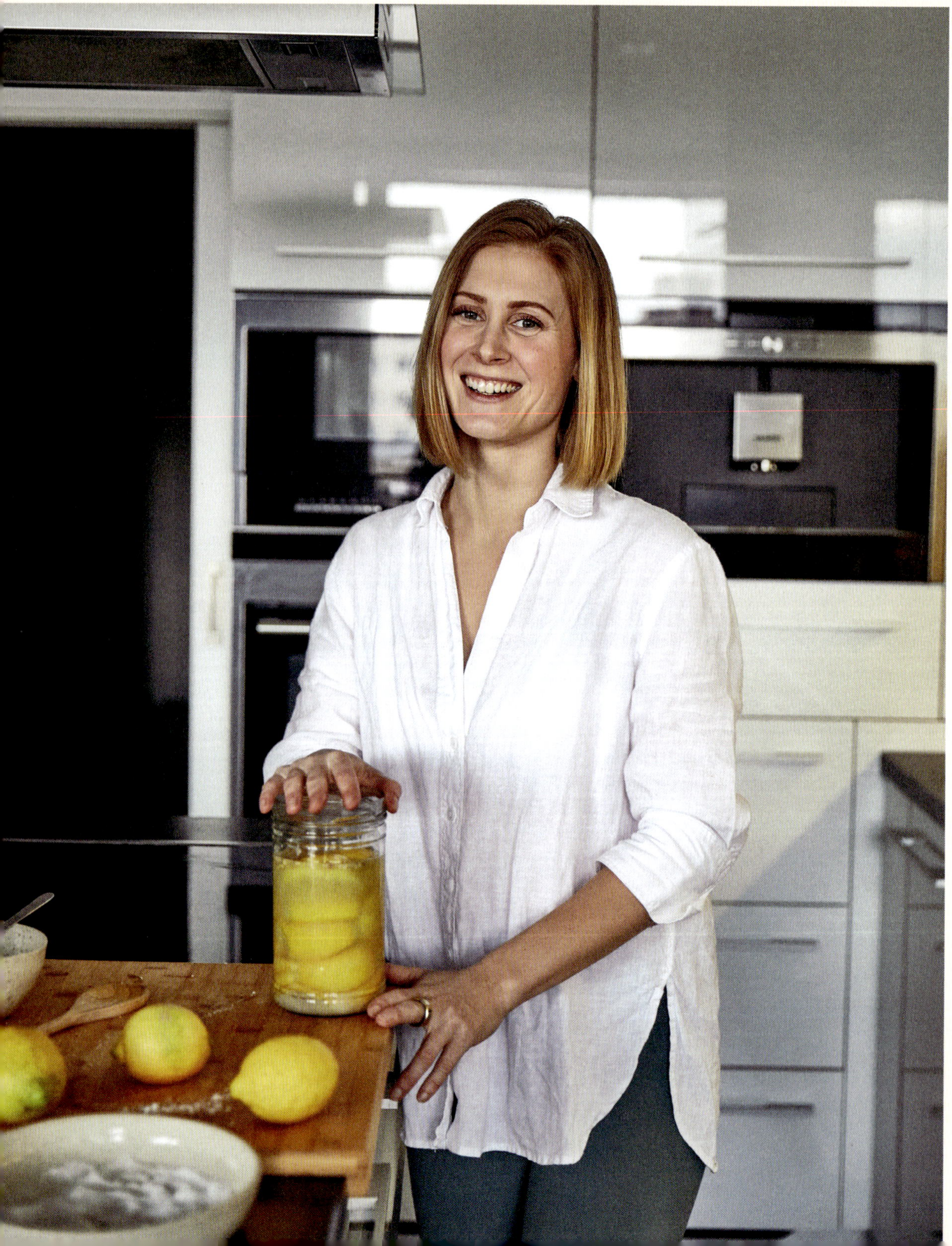

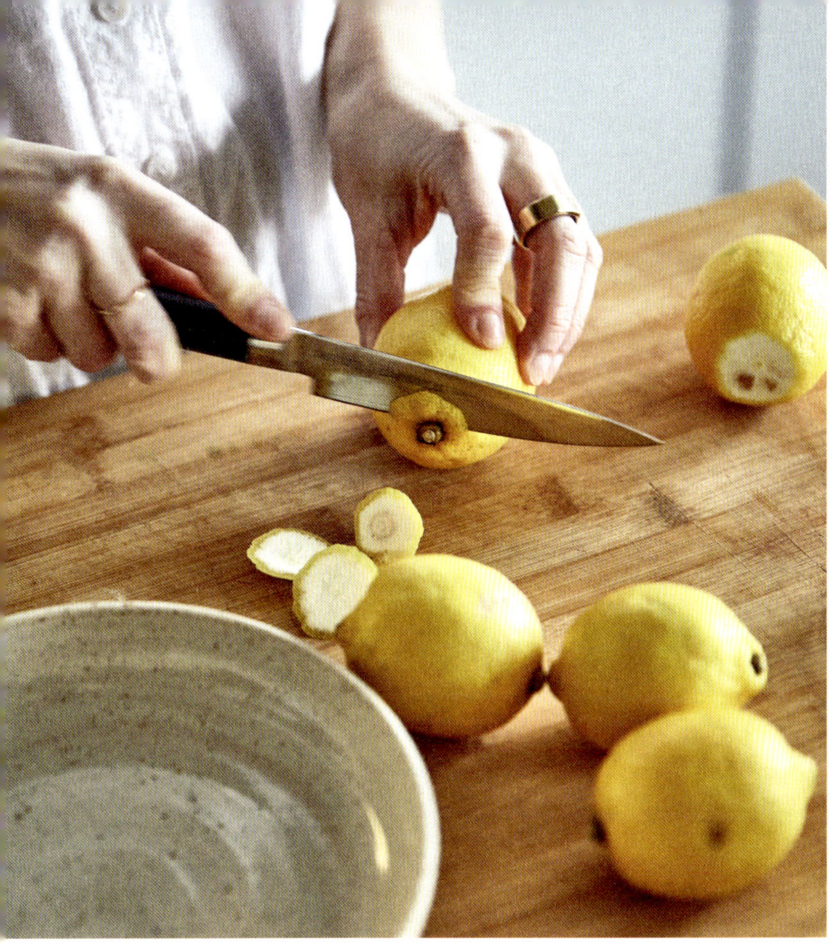

Michaela Luňáčková turns seasonal citrus into vibrant, a vitamin-rich preserved treasure, showing how simple fermentation can elevate cooking in the cold months.

Michaela Luňáčková is the founder of the platform *Yummy Paleo* and author of the book *Na celý život, Kniha plná opravdového jídla a zdraví* (*For Life: A Book Full of Real Food and Health*), born from her own search for better health. Her motivation came from years of living with eczema, exhaustion, histamine intolerance, and constant allergic reactions that left her struggling through each day.

It was so frustrating; I couldn't accept that I'd never again enjoy something as simple as an apple or a plum, or that I'd spend the rest of my life hunting for ointments to at least hide the same recurring problems."

The turning point came when she began exploring the link between nutrition, the immune system, and overall health. "My gut instinct told me there had to be a direct connection between what we eat and how our skin looks," she says. Michaela dove into research and experimented with different nutritional resets to learn what worked for her—and what didn't. Her energy returned, her skin cleared, and her health improved.

"I realized how essential it is to cook from basic, natural foods, to know how to put together a balanced plate, eat regularly, and prepare meals at home," she says. "I eat plenty of vegetables, good fats, and quality animal protein, and I'll have fruit when I feel like it, especially in summer. It's all about balance."

As a certified specialist in functional nutrition, Michaela also emphasizes the power of fermentation. "Fermented foods are natural probiotics," she explains. "They're rich in enzymes that support digestion and are packed with vitamins B, K2, C, and A. They strengthen the immune system, improve mineral absorption, regulate fat metabolism and appetite, and help restore a healthy gut microbiome and digestion." In winter, she ferments European citrus fruit (see p. 235).

Michaela believes in keeping things simple with local ingredients, seasonal variety, and real food. For more than a decade, she's been developing recipes and writing articles not just for people with autoimmune issues but for anyone who wants to eat consciously and feel better. She proves that cooking without flour, milk, sugar, or legumes (pulses) can still be colorful, satisfying, and delicious.

And as a mother, she keeps things practical and family friendly. "My goal is to share the principles of longevity—how to live a long, healthy life—based on science and experience," she says. "I want to show people that healthy food doesn't have to be dull. A thoughtful change in diet can do far more than give you prettier skin."

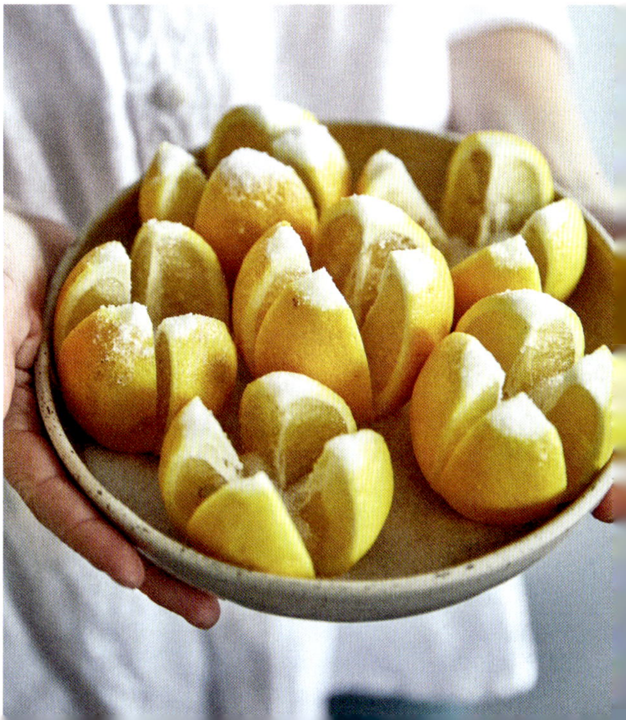

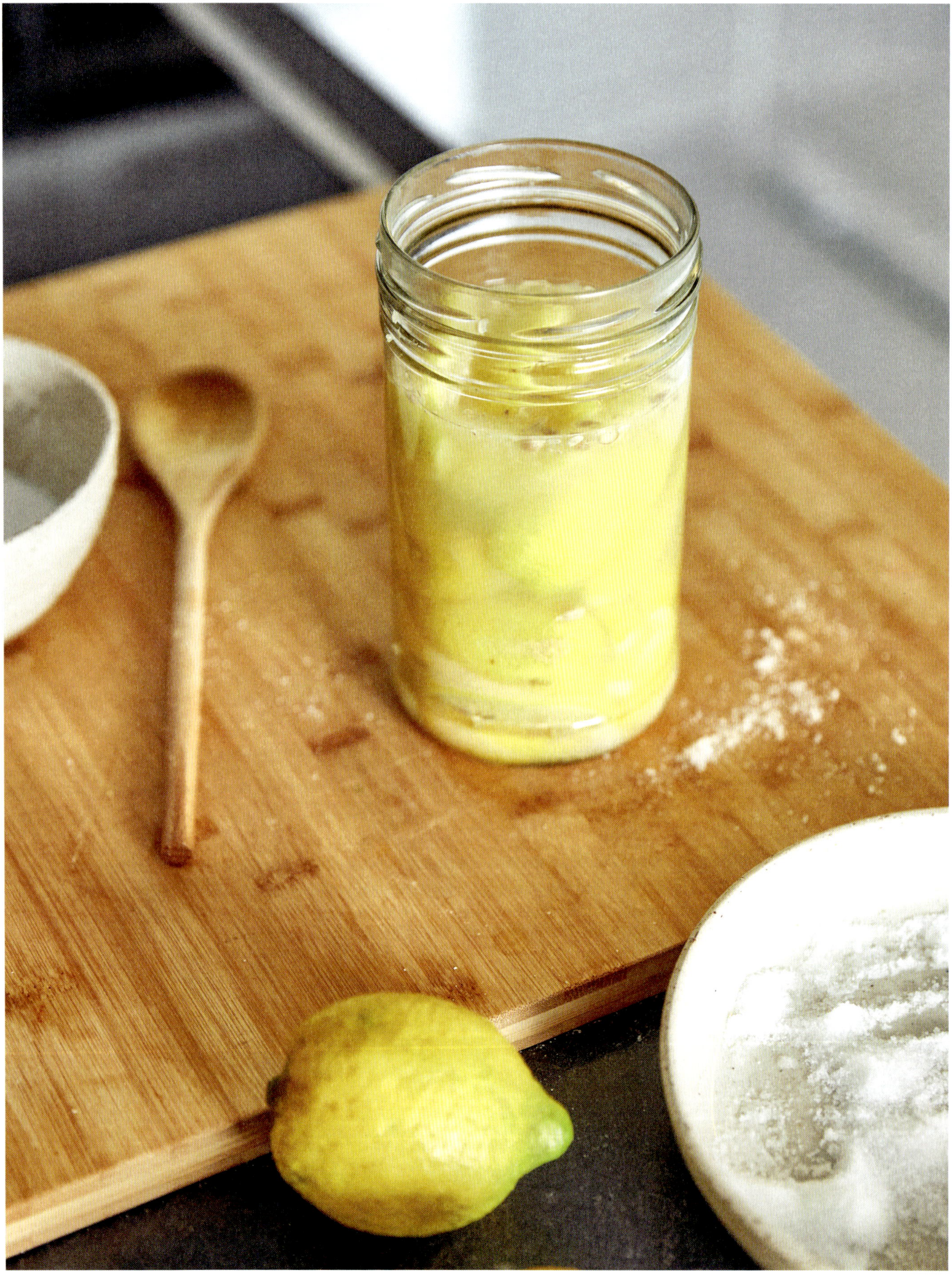

Salt Fermented Lemons

For 1 large canning jar (24 ounces / 750 ml)

Ingredients

4 organic lemons

About ½ cup (125 g) salt

Wash and dry the lemons. Slice off both ends of each lemon. Stand the lemons on one end and quarter lengthwise, cutting only three-quarters through so that the quarters remain joined. Sprinkle 1 heaping tablespoon of salt over the flesh of each lemon.

Spread about 2 tablespoons of salt over the bottom of a large canning jar with a wide opening. Put the lemons into the jar and compact them using a wooden spoon or pestle. Mash the lemons until a lot of juice is released and the fruit is completely covered with liquid. If the lemons float to the surface, use a sterilized fermentation weight to keep them in place.

Close the jar tightly and let the lemons ferment at room temperature (preferably 65 to 70 °F / 18 – 21 °C) for about 1 week. Open the jar, mash the lemons again, then close the jar again and refrigerate for at least 2 weeks. The preserved lemons will now be ready. They are not meant to be eaten on their own but are excellent for seasoning and enhancing a variety of dishes. To use, chop up the preserved lemons or squeeze them through a garlic press.

Tips You should use high-quality ingredients for preserving lemons, such as sea salt, Himalayan salt, or Guérande gray salt.

The soft, fine peel of preserved lemons has a pleasant salty and sour taste, making them suitable for using in dressings, homemade mayonnaise, oven-baked vegetables, and fresh salads. Preserved lemons also go well with meat, fish, and seafood, such as shrimp (prawns).

After the first week, the lemons can be flavored with red pepper (chili) flakes, fresh rosemary, or another favourite herb.

Finally, cut the salted lemons into small pieces and store in a sterilized screw-top jar in the refrigerator.

Orange Marmalade

For 6 or 7 canning jars (8 ounces / 300 ml each)

Ingredients

2 ¼ pounds (1 kg) organic oranges

Juice of 3 lemons

½ teaspoon salt

8 ½ cups (2 l) water

7 ½ cups (1.5 kg) granulated sugar

Wash the oranges thoroughly in hot water, dry, and slice off both ends of each one. Halve the oranges, squeeze the juice, and put the juice into a large pot. Add the lemon juice.

Using a small knife or a tablespoon, scrape out the remaining flesh and pith from the orange rinds. Wrap the pieces of flesh and pith together with the seeds in a clean cheesecloth (muslin) and shape into a pouch. Secure the pouch with a knot and place in the pot with the orange and lemon juice. Cut the remaining outer layer of orange rind into julienne strips and add them to the pot. Add the salt and water and cover the pot with a lid or clean cloth. Let infuse in a cool, dark place for 24 hours.

The next day, remove the pouch and squeeze well. Bring the mixture to a boil, then let simmer over low-medium heat for about 2 hours, until the pieces of orange rind soften. Add half of the sugar and stir until completely dissolved, then add the remaining sugar. Bring back to a boil and cook over higher heat for 15 to 20 minutes, until the marmalade thickens. The longer it cooks, the more the sugar will caramelize and the darker it will become. If foam forms on the surface, skim it off with a large spoon and discard.

Remove from the heat and let cool for 5 to 10 minutes. Transfer the marmalade to sterilized canning jars, close the lids tightly, and place upside down. When the marmalade has cooled completely, store in a cool, dark place. It will thicken a little more as it rests.

Tips Orange marmalade is perfect in winter, when European citrus fruit is in season. Orange marmalade is traditionally made from Seville oranges, a variety that is too bitter and has too many seeds to eat on its own.

This orange marmalade has a taste that is both bitter and sweet at the same time. Adjust the amount of sugar used according to your preference. Regardless, you will need at least 5 cups (1 kg) of sugar for the marmalade to thicken properly.

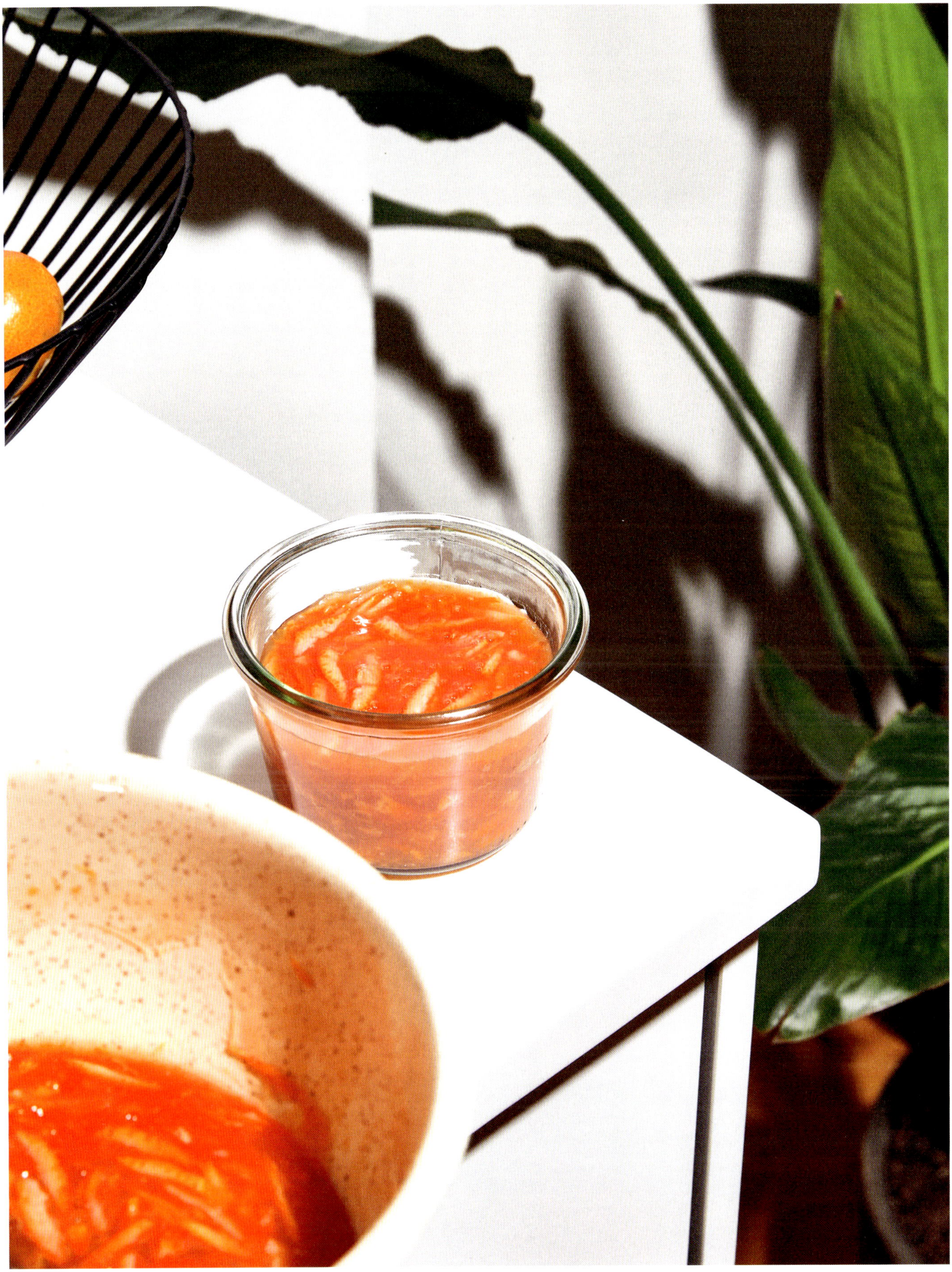

Kimchi Fried Rice

Serves 4

Ingredients

2 shallots

3 cloves garlic

1 (1¼-inch/3-cm) piece fresh ginger

1 cup (200 g) Kimchi (see p. 199)

3 tablespoons vegetable oil

1 teaspoon crushed red pepper (chili) flakes

2¾ cups (400 g) steamed rice

4 tablespoons soy sauce

½ cup to ⅔ cup (120–150 ml) kimchi juice

Salt and freshly ground black pepper

4 eggs

2 scallions (spring onions), green parts only

Peel the shallots, garlic, and ginger. Mince (very finely chop) the shallots, mince or crush the garlic through a garlic press, and grate the ginger. Cut the kimchi into small pieces, if necessary.

Heat 2 tablespoons of the vegetable oil in a deep skillet or frying pan. Sauté the shallots, then add the garlic and ginger and sauté briefly until fragrant. Add the red pepper flakes and toast over medium heat, stirring continuously, for about 10 seconds. Add the cold rice and kimchi and deglaze the skillet with soy sauce. Mix together well and let cook for 3 minutes. Add the kimchi juice and stir until evaporated. Season with salt and pepper, then remove the pan from the heat.

Heat the remaining oil in a large skillet and carefully crack in the eggs. Fry the eggs, sunny side up, over medium heat, for about 4 minutes. As soon as the whites are set and with the yolks still runny, remove from the heat. Wash and slice the scallions into thin rings.

Sprinkle the scallion rings over the kimchi fried rice and serve on plates, each topped with a fried egg.

Tips This recipe is perfect for using up leftover rice, up to a day old, from another meal, because it is drier and firmer than freshly cooked rice.

You are free to add your favorite ingredients, whether sautéed mushrooms, marinated tofu, crunchy green beans, blanched kale, pan-fried carrots, chopped peanuts, or cilantro; the possibilities are endless.

You can also sprinkle toasted sesame seeds or finely chopped nori seaweed over kimchi fried rice.

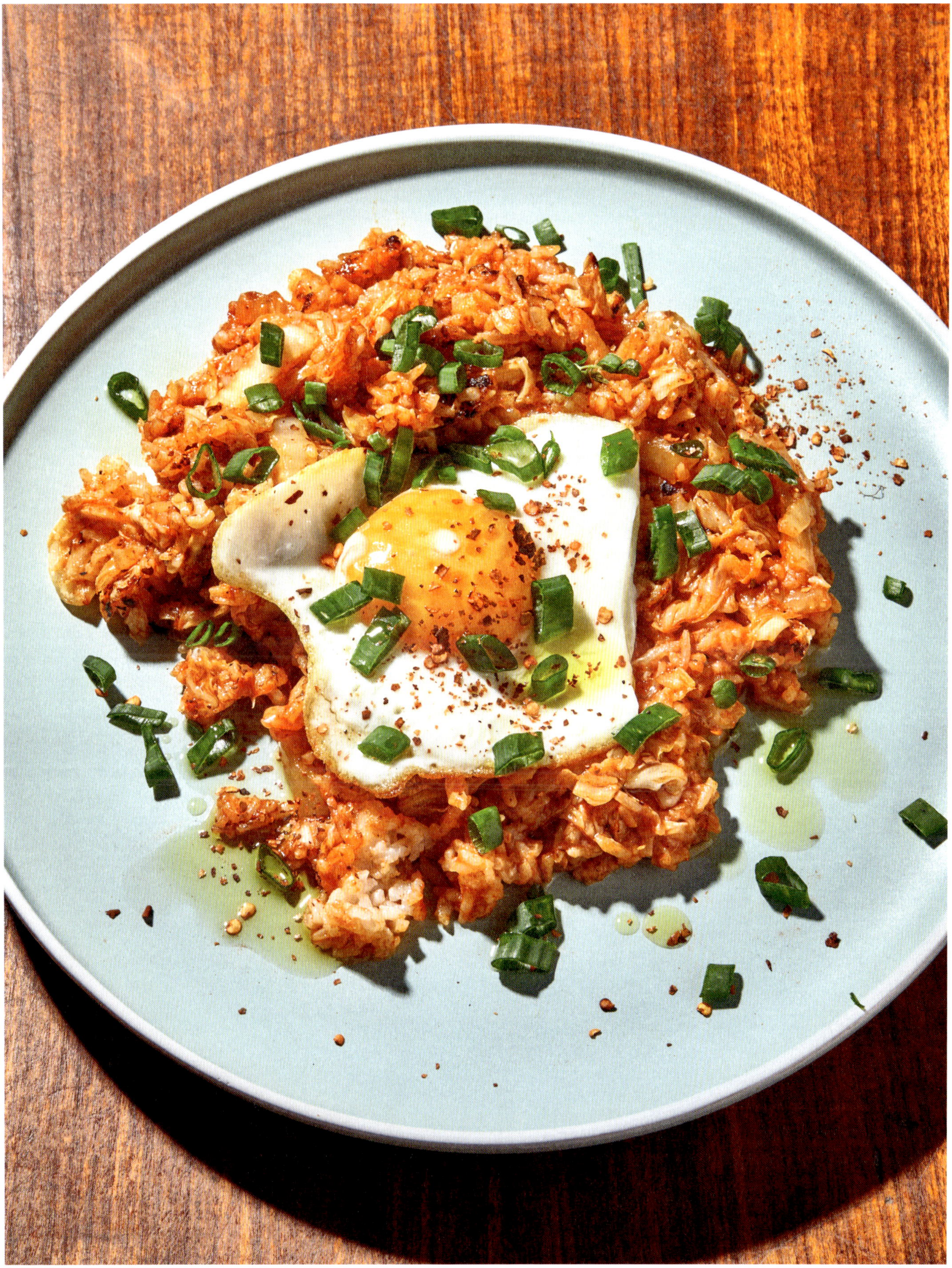

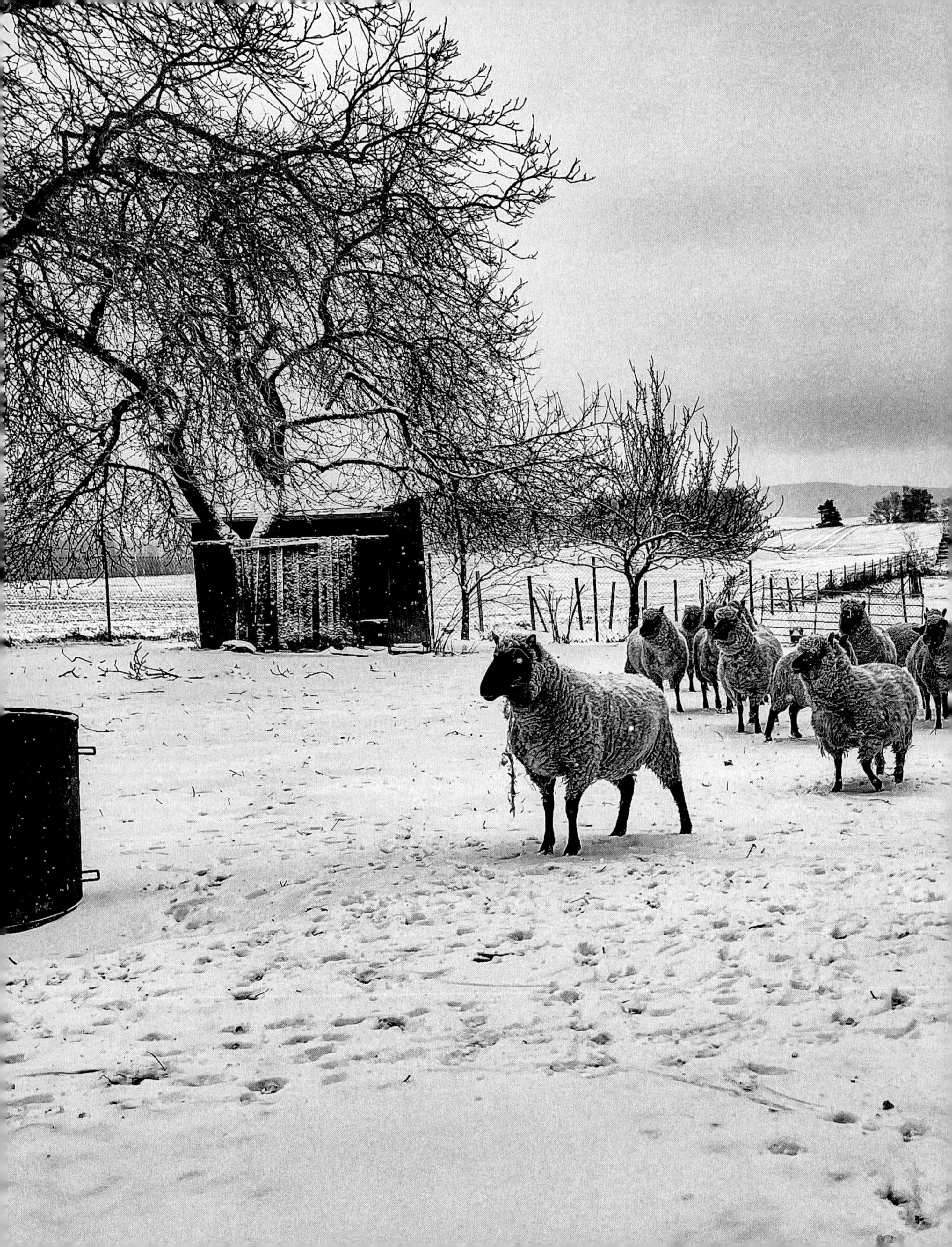

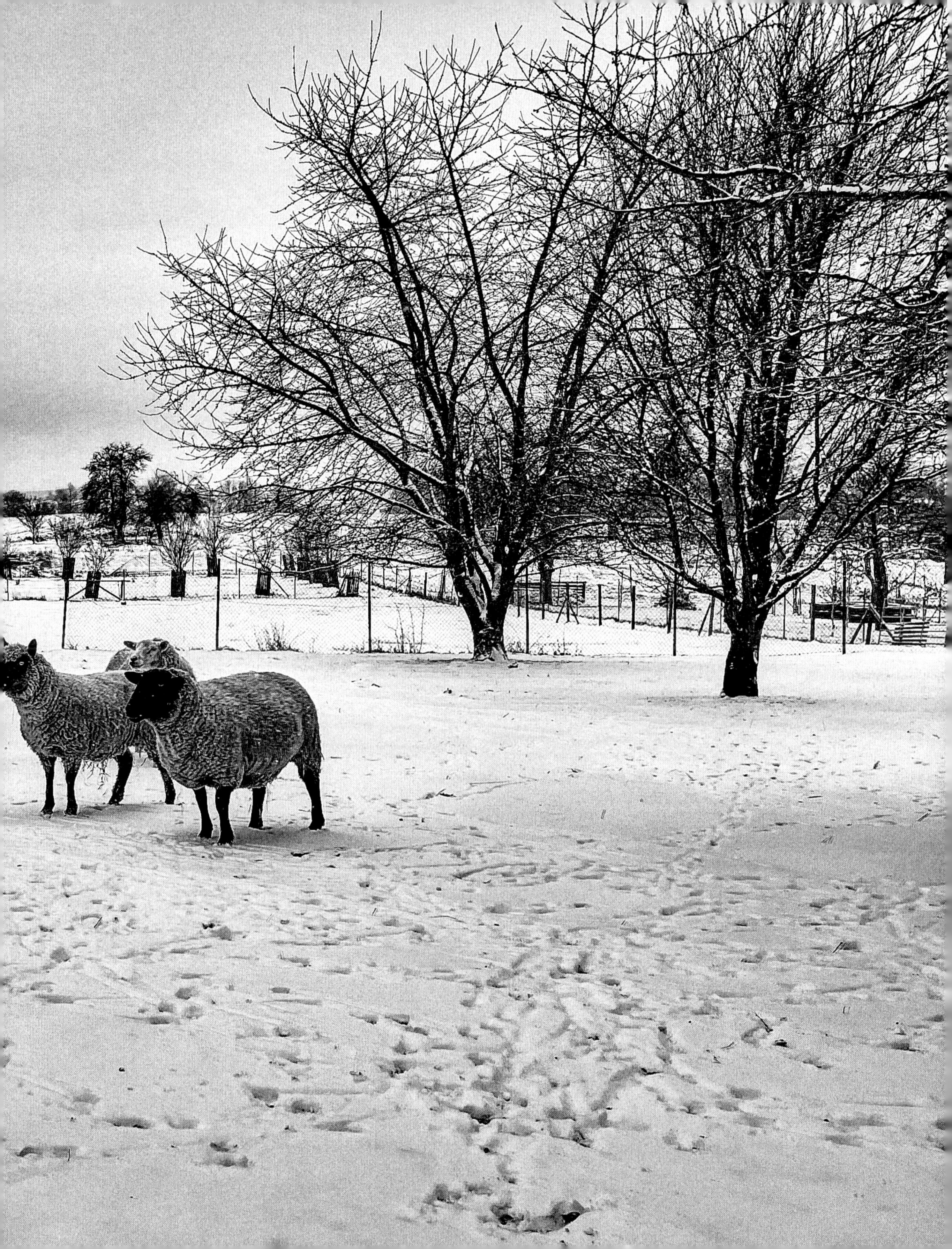

Time-Honored Natural Healing Power

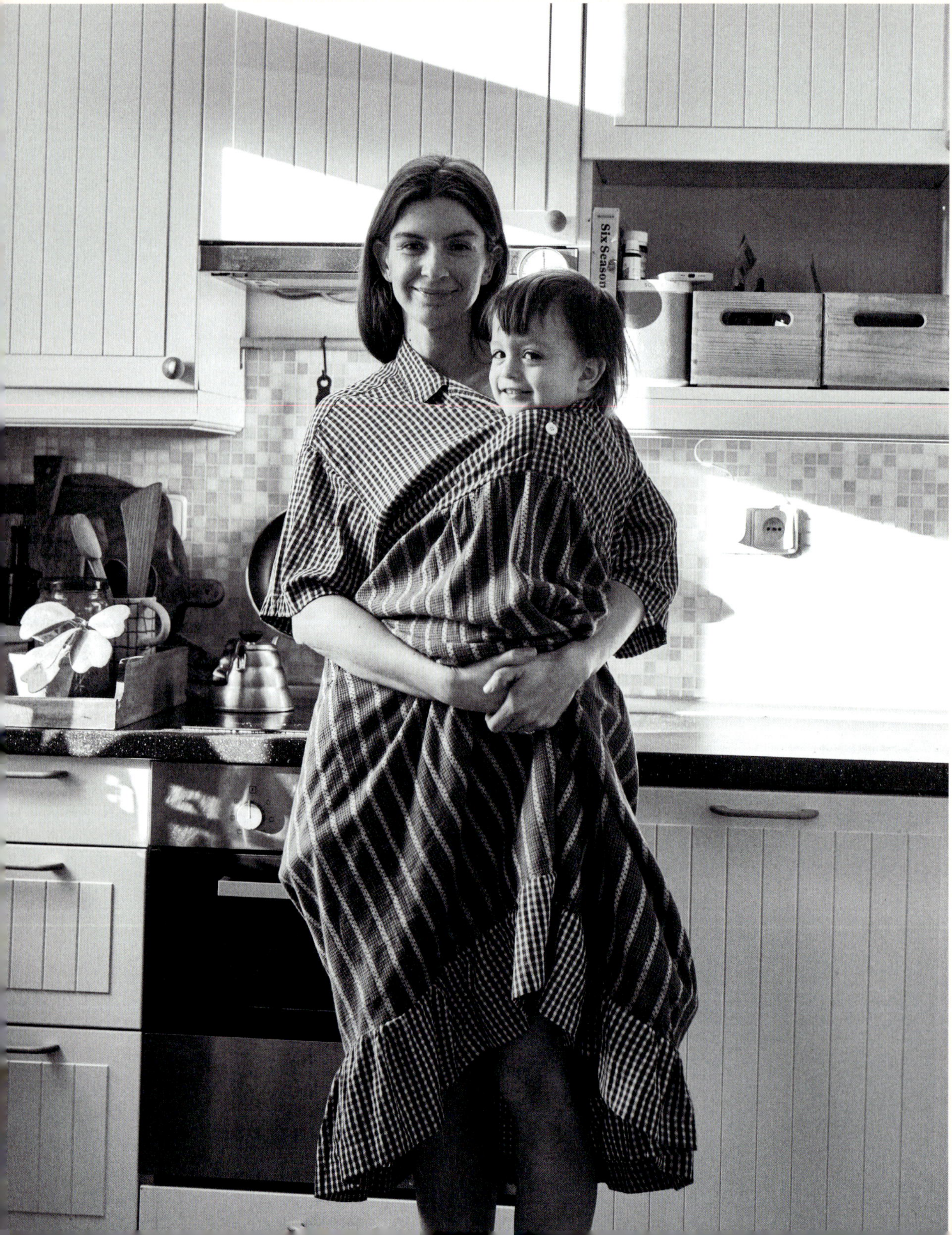

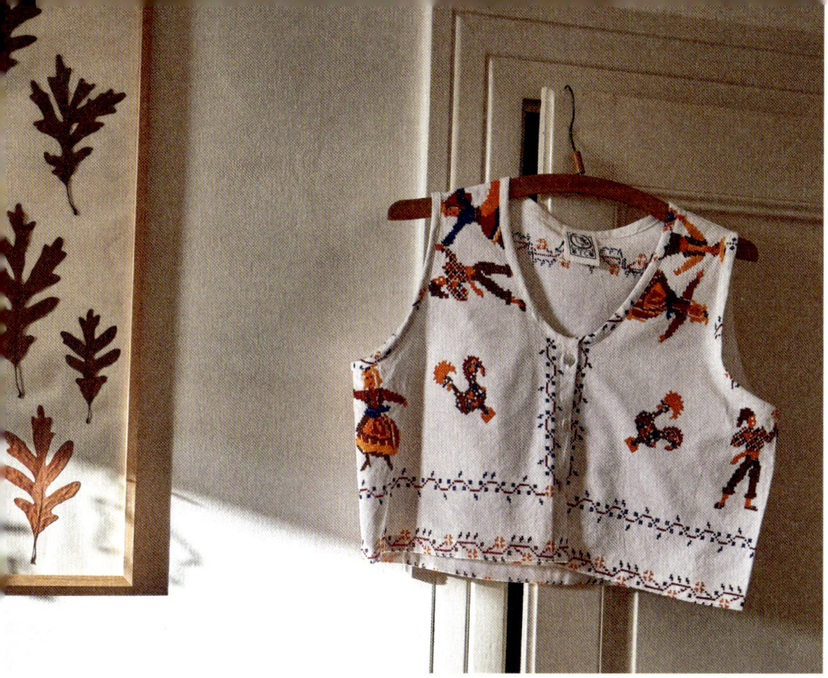

Each season, Zuzana Štefanides carefully stocks up on oxymel, a traditional herbal elixir that boosts immunity and tackles all winter colds.

Charismatic and effortlessly charming, Zuzana Štefanides is a Slovak wife, mother, and lover of all things vintage. When she and her family aren't roaming southern Europe for months in their caravan, they're at home in Prague's elegant Vinohrady district, enjoying life's slower rhythm. Creative to her core, Zuzana has always had a knack for bringing beauty into everyday life. Her passion is clothing—she ran a fashion blog for years—and, since she became interested in growing houseplants, she founded the green project *Pokojovky* with her friends. She's happiest browsing flea markets and bazaars. It was on one of her many thrift store (charity shop) trips that she began collecting old tablecloths, captivated by their quality and forgotten charm. One day she had an idea: why not sew clothes from them? That's how her original label, *Story of Tablecloth*, came to life.

From her Vinohrady apartment Zuzana transforms timeworn table linens into elegant shirts or dresses, each piece is unique, each one woven with a little piece of history. As she sews, she imagines the lives those fabrics once witnessed: family dinners, wedding feasts, the quiet poetry of ordinary days.

Beyond her love of craft, Zuzana is also an avid preserver who cans, freezes, and preserves whatever the season brings for the leaner months ahead. Each fall, and all through winter, she prepares *oxymel*, an ancient tonic known for its healing powers.

"*Oxymel* is a cure-all for flu and colds," she explains. "It's the first thing we reach for at home when we start to feel under the weather." She continues: "The word *oxymel* comes from Greek: *oxys* means 'sour,' and *meli* means 'honey.' No wonder, since its two main ingredients are vinegar and honey! The result is a sweet-and-sour, lightly fermented beverage infused with the flavor of whatever fruit and herbs are added." Zuzana insists there's no single "right" way to make *oxymel*, but there are a few golden rules:

- Use organic vinegar, ideally apple cider vinegar.
- Choose liquid honey—it mixes more easily. If your honey has crystallized, warm it gently in a water bath to about 97 °F (36 °C).
- If you prefer a tangier drink, simply use less honey.
- Let the *oxymel* infuse for about 20 days at a steady 50 to 54 °F (10–12 °C) in a cool place. Shake the closed jar regularly during fermentation.

Zuzana makes her *oxymel* from whatever she has on hand, whether leftovers from the refrigerator or fresh finds from the farmers' market. "What can you add to vinegar and honey?" she smiles. "Ginger, turmeric, horseradish, sea buckthorn, chokeberries, celery root, chili pepper, garlic, onion, rosemary, sage, cinnamon, pepper, elderberries, rose hips, spruce tips, plantain herb, fennel, nettles—anything you consider to be healing." And with that, she gives the jar another gentle shake, performing a little ritual of care that connects her to generations before her.

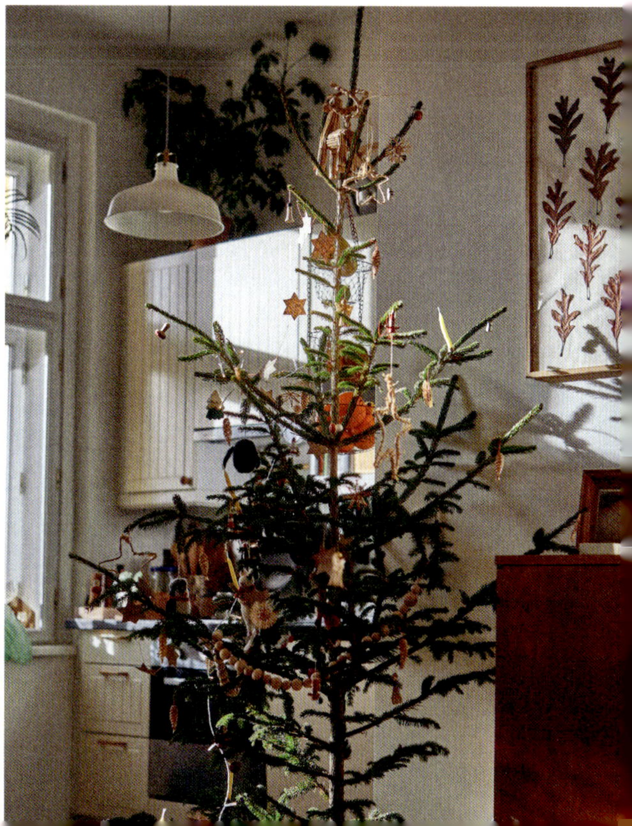

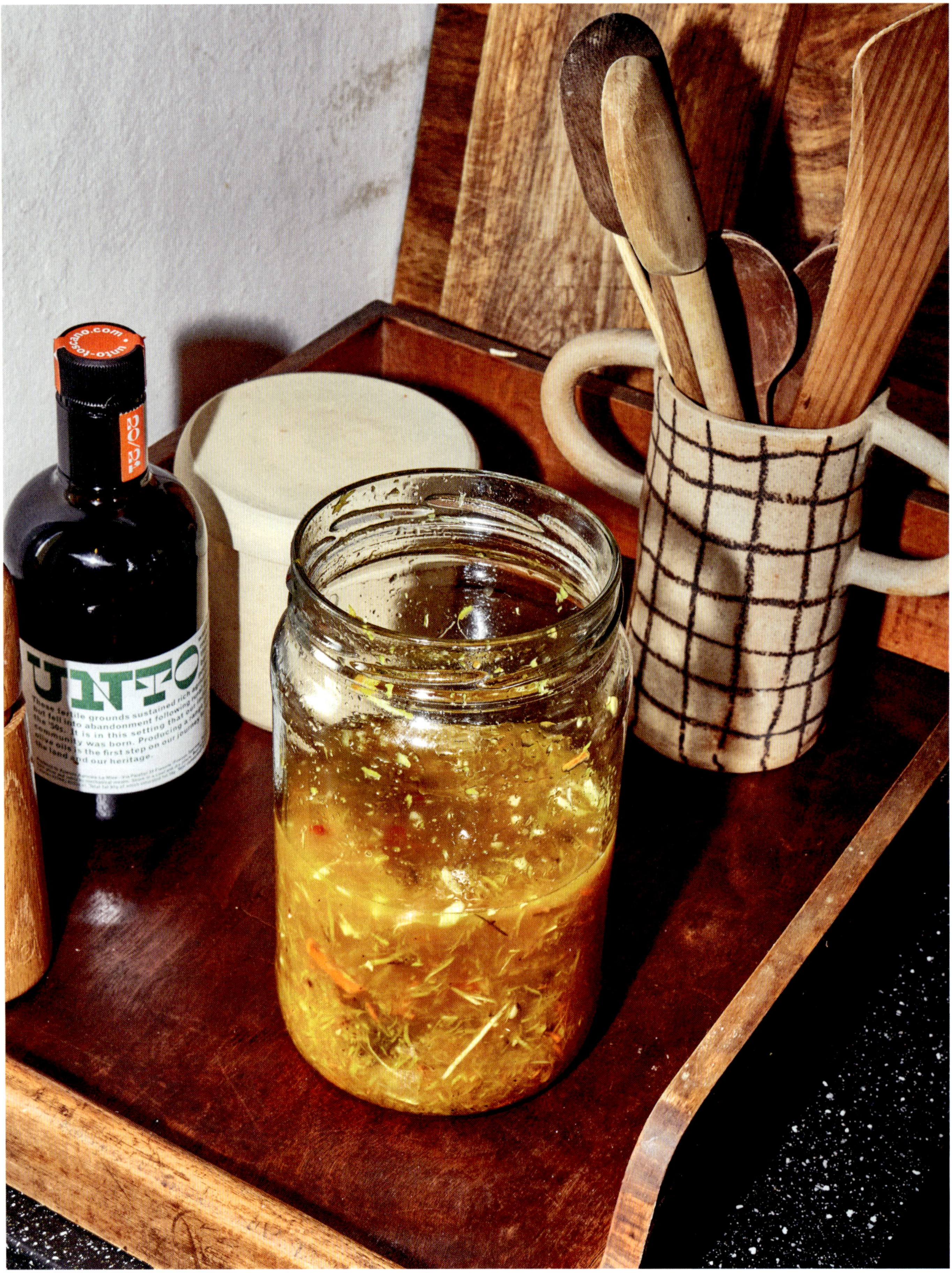
UNTO

Oxymel

For 1 large canning jar (25 ounces / 750 ml)

Ingredients

1 large red onion

3 cloves garlic

1 organic lemon

1 fresh chili pepper

2 to 4 sprigs of fresh thyme or rosemary

3 ½ ounces (100 g) fresh ginger

3 ½ ounces (100 g) fresh turmeric root

1 ¾ ounces (50 g) fresh horseradish root

2 tablespoons freshly ground pepper

About 1 ¾ cups (400 ml) apple cider vinegar

½ to scant 1 cup (170–200 g) honey

Peel and cut the onion into thin strips and peel and slice the garlic. Wash the lemon in hot water and cut without peeling into small dice. Wash the chili pepper and herbs and pat dry. Coarsely chop the chili and pluck the leaves from the herb sprigs. Peel and finely grate the ginger, turmeric, and horseradish. Transfer all the prepared ingredients to a sterilized canning jar and stir in the ground pepper.

Pour in enough vinegar to cover all of the contents of the jar. Close the jar tightly and place in a cool, dark place for between 3 weeks and 3 months. The longer *oxymel* is allowed to mature, the more intense and spicier it will taste. Shake the jar every day to better combine and distribute the ingredients.

Either filter the *oxymel* through a cheesecloth (muslin) into a sterilized bottle or blend and let rest in the closed jar for another week without stirring. To finish, add honey to the *oxymel* according to preference (as a rule, 1 part honey to 2 to 3 parts vinegar). The finished *oxymel* can be stored in the refrigerator for up to 6 months.

Tips A basement, cellar or cool hallway (50 to 54 °F / 10–12 °C) is recommended for storage. The *oxymel* must not be refrigerated as the cold temperature will stop the fermentation process.

As an immune-boosting tonic, take 1 tablespoon of *oxymel* a day in winter. In case of illness, you can increase the dose to 3 tablespoons a day.

Winter Beet and Potato Salad

Serves 4

Ingredients

1 pound 2 ounces (500 g) potatoes

10 ½ ounces (300 g) celery root (celeriac)

4 eggs, hard boiled

1 small red onion

½ cup (125 g) sour cream

½ cup (125 g) mayonnaise

2 tablespoons Dijon mustard

3 tablespoons Traditional Pickled Cucumbers juice (see p. 114)

1 handful freshly chopped dill, plus extra to serve

Salt and freshly ground black pepper

1 ⅓ cups (200 g) Sweet-and-Sour Pickled Beets (see p. 183)

Wash the unpeeled potatoes thoroughly and place in a pot of water. Cook over medium heat for 25 to 30 minutes. Peel and halve the celery root and add to the boiling potatoes in the last 15 minutes.

Drain the vegetables and let cool completely. Shell the eggs and rinse with cold water. Peel the potatoes. Cut the potatoes, celery root, and eggs into dice. Peel and mince (very finely chop) the onions. Put all the prepared salad ingredients into a large bowl. Add the sour cream, mayonnaise, mustard, pickled cucumber juice, and chopped dill. Season with plenty of salt and pepper and mix until combined. Drain the beets, add to the bowl, and gently mix.

Refrigerate the salad for at least 2 hours, preferably overnight. Taste again before serving and adjust the seasoning with mustard, pickled cucumber juice, salt, and pepper. Garnish with the minced dill and serve.

Tips You can replace the dill with parsley, celery leaves, or feathery fennel fronds. Add 1 or 2 tablespoons of grated Pickled Horseradish (see p. 264) for a pleasantly sharp, spicy note.

Diced apple will add freshness and juiciness to the salad.

Serve this salad for example on Christmas Eve with breaded fish and schnitzel. Finally, you can garnish the salad with hard-boiled egg quarters.

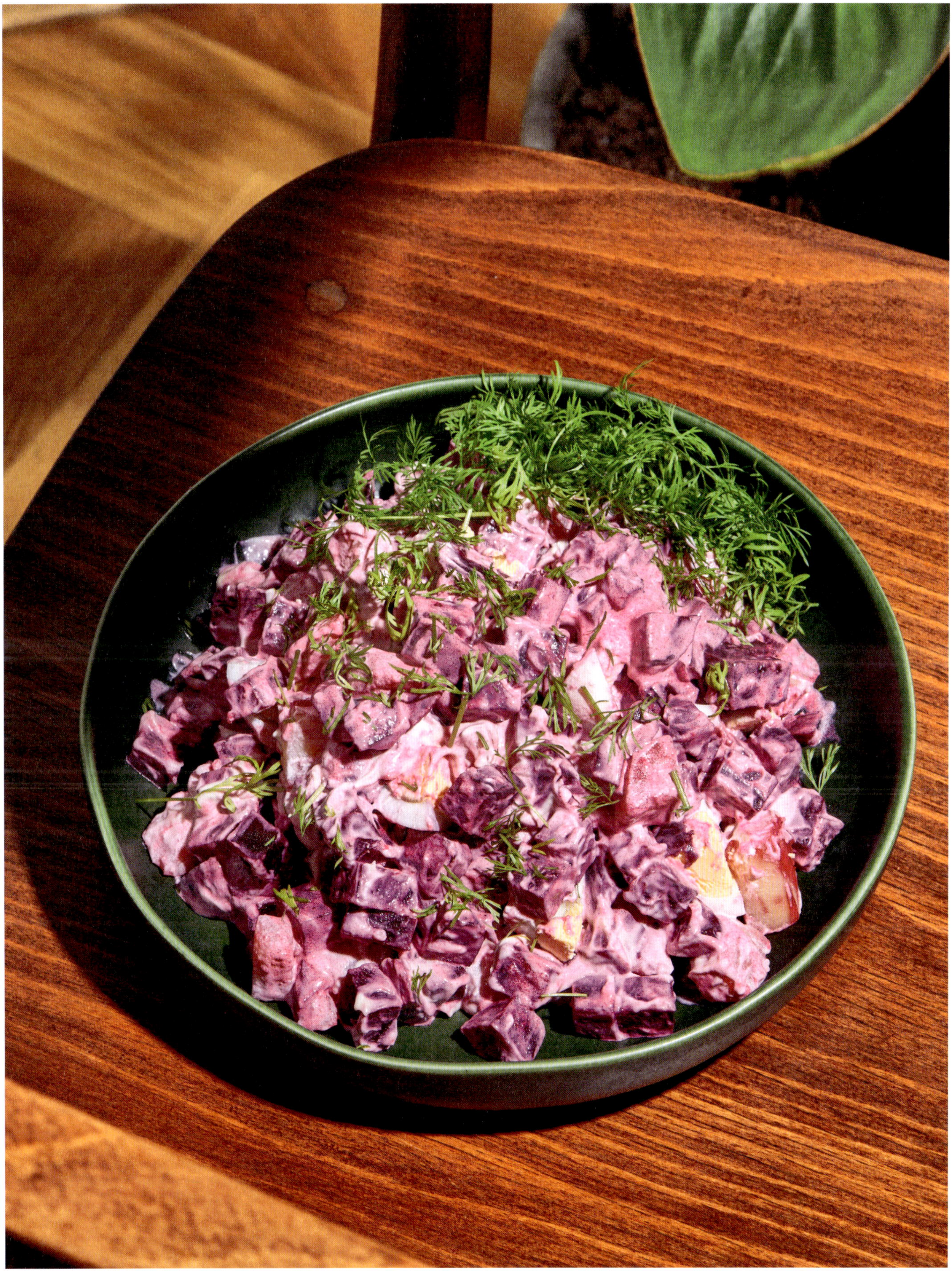

Huspenina—Homemade Pork Aspic

Serves 4 to 8

Ingredients

1 (1¾-pound/800 g) pork knuckle (hock), bone in and skin on

1 (1¾-pound/800 g) pig's foot (trotter)

1 onion

5 peppercorns

5 allspice berries

2 bay leaves

1 tablespoon salt

2 carrots

1 to 2 tablespoons distilled white vinegar

⅔ cup (100 g) frozen peas

1 tablespoon vegetable oil

Pickled Red Onions (see p. 176), to serve

Fresh sourdough bread, to serve

Using tweezers, remove any hairs remaining on the meat. Wash the pieces of meat and put them into a pot just large enough to hold them snugly. Cut off both ends of the onion and only peel off the top layer of skin. Halve the onion and add to the meat. Add the spices, bay leaves and salt and cover with cold water (½ to ¾ inch/1–2 cm over the meat). Cover the pot with a lid and bring to a boil. Reduce the heat to low and let it simmer for 2 hours 30 minutes to 3 hours, until the meat is tender and can easily be separated from the bone.

Peel, wash, and coarsely chop the carrots and add to the almost soft meat. Let simmer for 20 to 30 minutes, then stir in the vinegar and cook for another 3 minutes.

Remove 1 tablespoon of the broth from the pot, place it on a small plate, and let cool in the refrigerator. Carefully take the pieces of meat out of the broth in the pot and let cool. Blanch the frozen peas for 1 minute in hot water and drain.

Remove the meat from the bones and cut it into bite-size pieces. Carefully strain the cooled broth into a clean pot, making sure not to stir up the sediment at the bottom of the pot. Discard the sediment. Cut the cooked carrots into small dice and discard the onion and spices. Check on the aspic sample in the refrigerator; if it has set, then the broth has the correct consistency. If the sample has not set or has only partly set, cook the broth for at least another 30 minutes.

Season the broth with salt, if necessary, then stir in the meat pieces, diced carrots, and peas. Grease a smooth or ribbed loaf pan with the oil. Using a ladle, fill the pan with the aspic mixture. Let cool completely, then refrigerate overnight.

The next day, invert the aspic onto a plate and cut into thick slices. Serve accompanied with pickled red onions and their liquid, and fresh sourdough bread. Any leftover aspic will keep for 2 to 3 days in the refrigerator.

Tips Hindquarter pork knuckle works best with this recipe, because it contains more meat. Have your butcher cut the pork knuckle and pig's foot in half, which will allow the pieces to fit better in the pot and cook faster.

If you are worried that the aspic will not set properly, you can also stir gelatin into the broth.

Do you have problems unmolding the aspic? Simply dip the entire loaf pan into hot water for a few seconds.

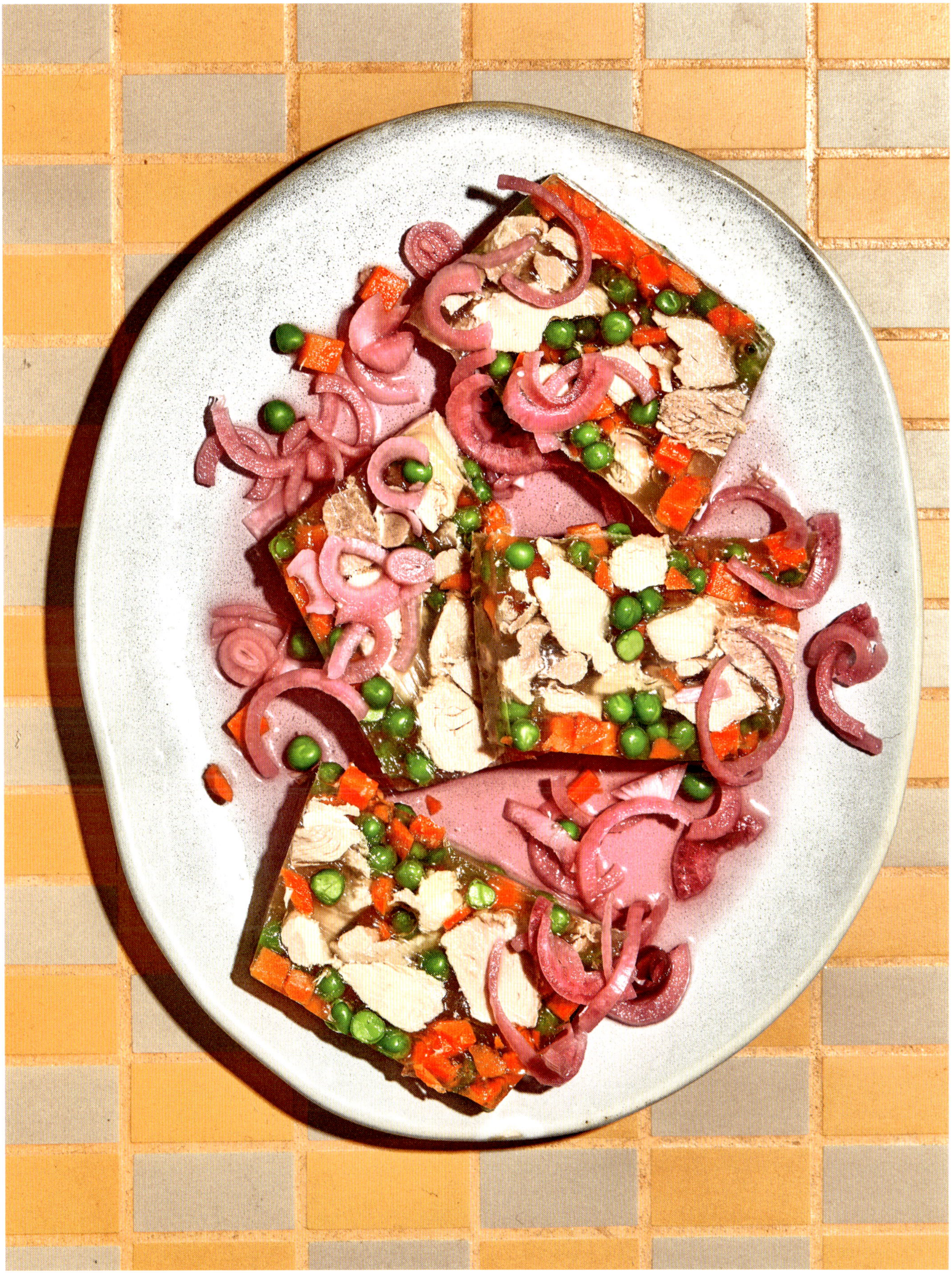

Breakfast Full of Sweet Memories

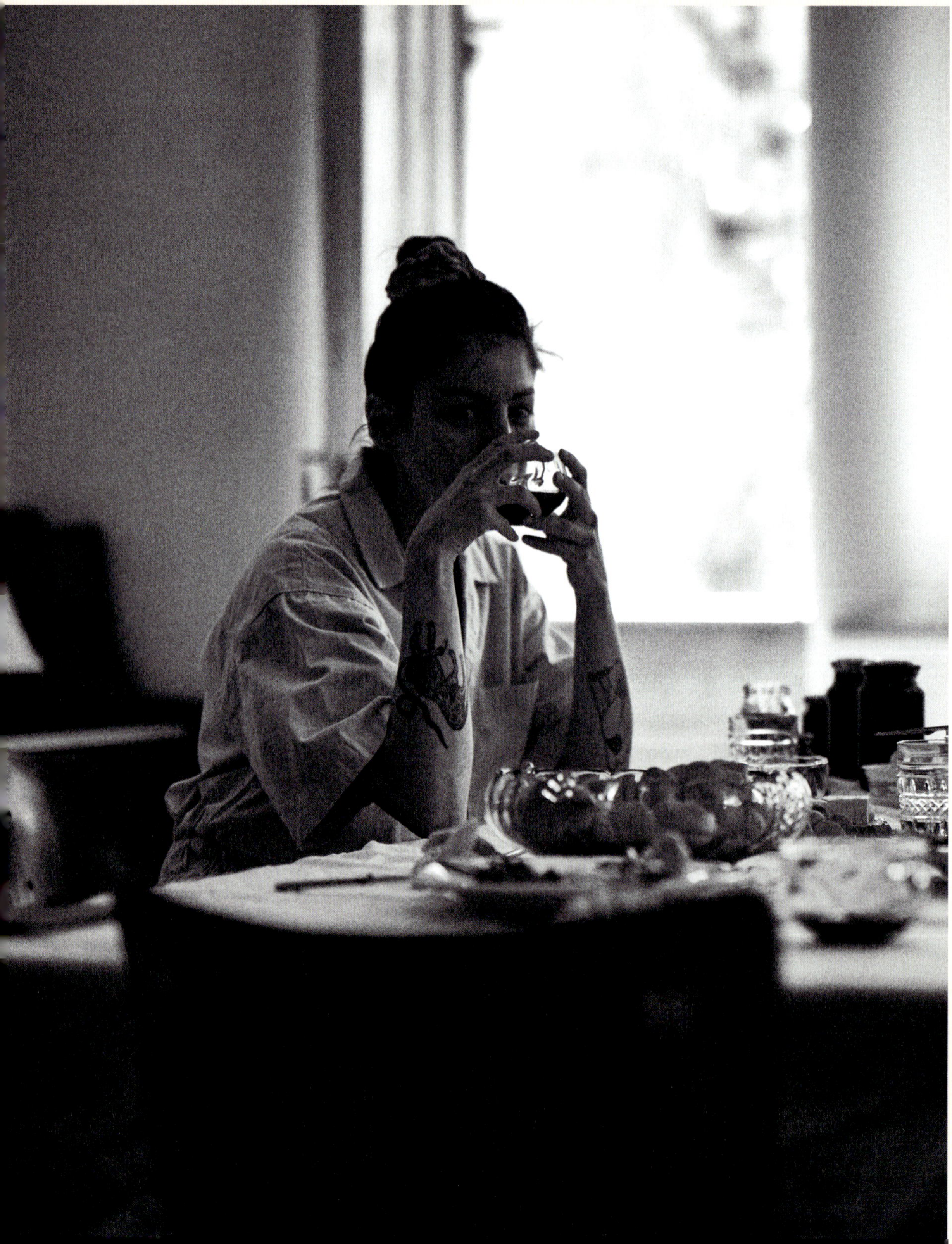

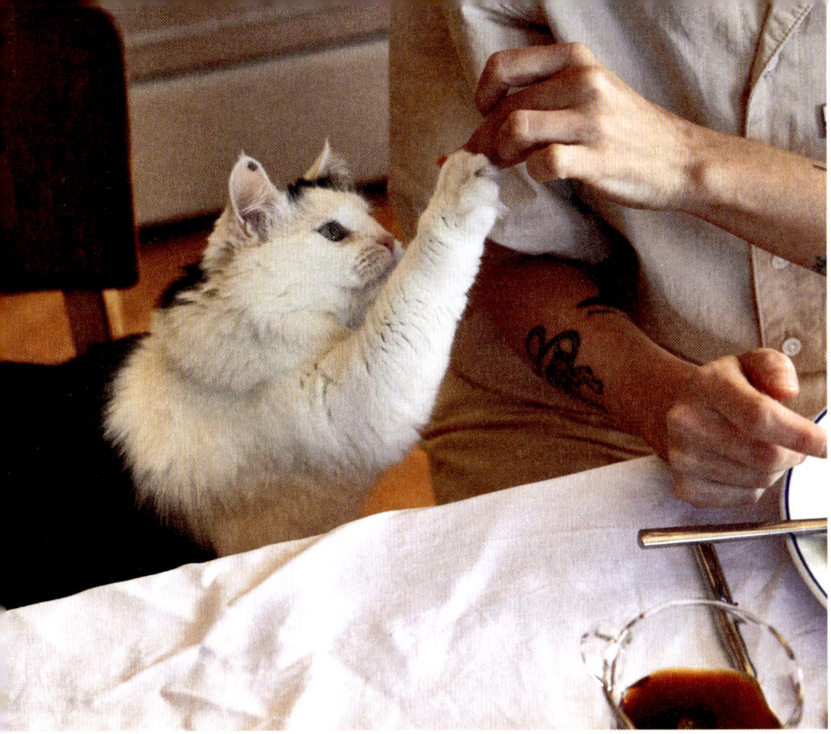

For Daniela Hannová, wild strawberry jam is more than a preserve—it's a weekend ritual, a little reminder of the pleasant things in life, and a taste of home.

Daniela Hannová, daughter of Marie Hannová (see p. 64), lives in Prague, where she works as a PR specialist. For the first thirty years or so of her life, her role in the family jam-making operation has mostly been limited to picking fruit. One of her strongest childhood memories is the feel of a string tied around her waist, with the attached basket growing heavier as the morning passed by at the family cottage.

Her mother ran a tight ship: raspberries and even Canadian blueberries had to *always* be picked with both hands. "It's the only efficient way," she'd say. Wild strawberries, however, followed their own rules. The family would spend hours bent low over the beds, picking patiently. For a single batch of jam, they needed at least a pound (half a kilo)—and with fruit that tiny, that meant a lot of time and a lot of passion. The work went on for as long as the short wild strawberry season would allow.

In recent years, Daniela has been making an effort to become more involved in the entire fruit-preserving process, from tending the garden beds to returning the clean jars to the cottage each year. Living in the city, she usually joins in only on weekends, while her mother spends almost the entire summer there, quietly keeping the rhythm of the garden.

Daniela's favorite jam, without a doubt, is wild strawberry—but she still gets frustrated while picking the fruit herself. The resulting taste, however, is priceless and worth every minute spent stooping in the garden! Spread thick on a buttered roll, it's become a staple of her long, lazy weekend breakfasts. She likes breakfast abundant and a little untidy, with everything on the table at once, flavors mingling, crumbs everywhere. That slight chaos, the stickiness of jam, the scent of coffee—they all remind her of those cottage mornings, eating bread with butter and jam out on the terrace overlooking the flower beds, or being right down by the garden, surrounded by plants. It's a small rebellion against a polished city life, and a nod to the earthy humor of the Pošumaví countryside.

Her cat, Soča, is never far from these breakfast feasts. She's especially fond of the smell of butter—not only the kind that melts beneath strawberry jam, but also the rich scent of the traditional Czech homemade rolls called *housky* that Daniela loves to bake (see p. 252).

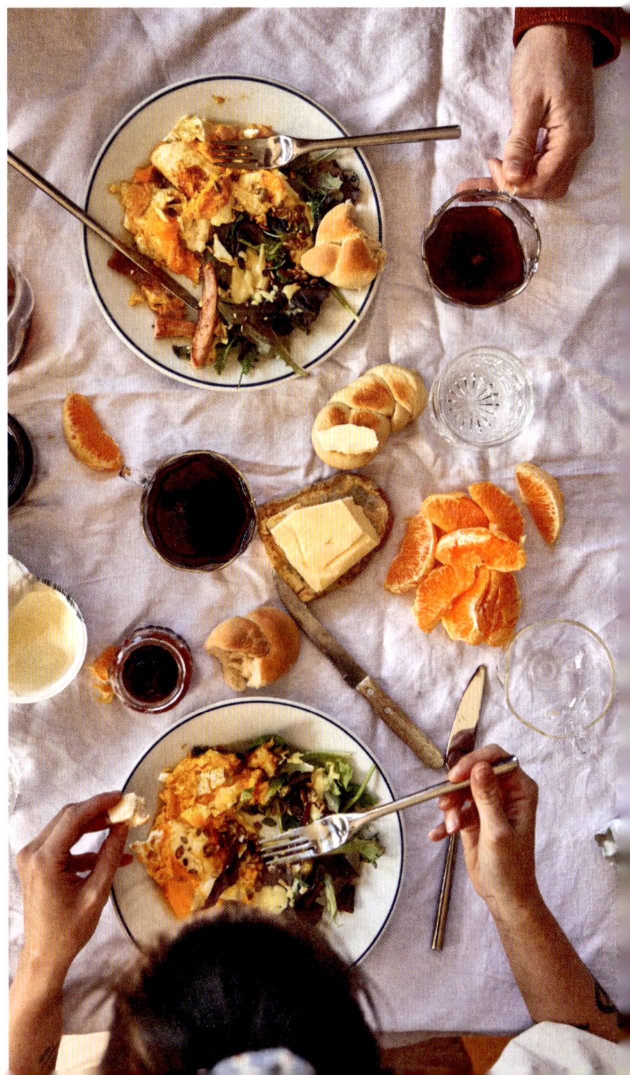

Housky—Braided Rolls

Makes about 15 rolls

Ingredients

1 cup plus 2 ½ tablespoons (275 ml) milk

1 small (⅔-ounce/19 g) cake fresh yeast

1 teaspoon granulated sugar

4 cups (500 g) pastry flour or all-purpose (plain) flour

1 ¾ teaspoons (11 g) salt

4 tablespoons (55 g) unsalted butter, softened

Water or beaten egg, for brushing

Caraway seeds or poppy seeds, for sprinkling

Gently heat the milk until lukewarm—do not let it boil. Pour half of the milk into a bowl, crumble in the yeast, and add the sugar and 1 teaspoon of the flour. Mix carefully, then cover with a clean cloth and let rise at room temperature for 10 to 15 minutes.

Sift the remaining flour into a large bowl and mix in the salt. Make a well in the flour, pour in the remaining milk, and add the softened butter and the activated yeast. Using a wooden spoon or in a stand mixer fitted with a dough hook, mix to a dough, then knead for about 10 minutes, until the dough is smooth and supple and easily comes away from the sides of the bowl. Cover the bowl with plastic wrap (clingfilm) or a clean cloth and let the dough rise in a warm place for about 1 hour, until doubled in volume.

Line 2 baking sheets with parchment (baking) paper. Knead the dough again and divide it into about 15 equal portions (about 2 ounces/50–60 g each). Roll each portion of dough into a 4 to 5-inch (25–30-cm) long strand. Make each roll by braiding a single strand as follows:

1. Lay the dough strand horizontally on the work surface. Bring the right end of the strand down and up over the center to create a loop. The top end of the strand should protrude over the horizontal part by ½ to ¾ inch (1–2 cm).
2. Place the left end of the strand through the loop on the right side without pulling on the dough.
3. Twist the bottom part of the loop to the right to form an eight.
4. Slide the end of the strand that is now on the upper right side, down into the lower part of the figure eight.
5. Gently pull the protruding end of the strand from the first step slightly outward and push it under the roll.

Arrange the braided rolls on the prepared baking sheets spaced well apart. Cover with a cloth and let proof for 30 minutes. In the meantime, preheat the oven to 450 °F top/bottom heat (230 °C/Gas Mark 7).

Brush the proofed rolls with water or beaten egg and sprinkle with caraway or poppy seeds. Bake for about 10 minutes, until golden. Let cool completely and serve.

Tips These *housky* taste best when fresh, served with butter and Wild Strawberry Jam (see p. 67), Apricot and Thyme Jam (see p. 119), or honey. They also make a accompaniment for savory dishes, such as salads.

Only have instant yeast at home? Go ahead and use it—just remember that you cannot substitute fresh yeast 1:1 with instant yeast. Instant yeast is 1.5 times stronger, so always use 1.5 times less! You also don't need to activate instant yeast in advance; simply sprinkle it over the flour and work it into the dough.

Brushing the rolls with a beaten egg before baking ensures a shiny crust and helps the seeds stick.

These rolls can also be frozen after they cool completely.

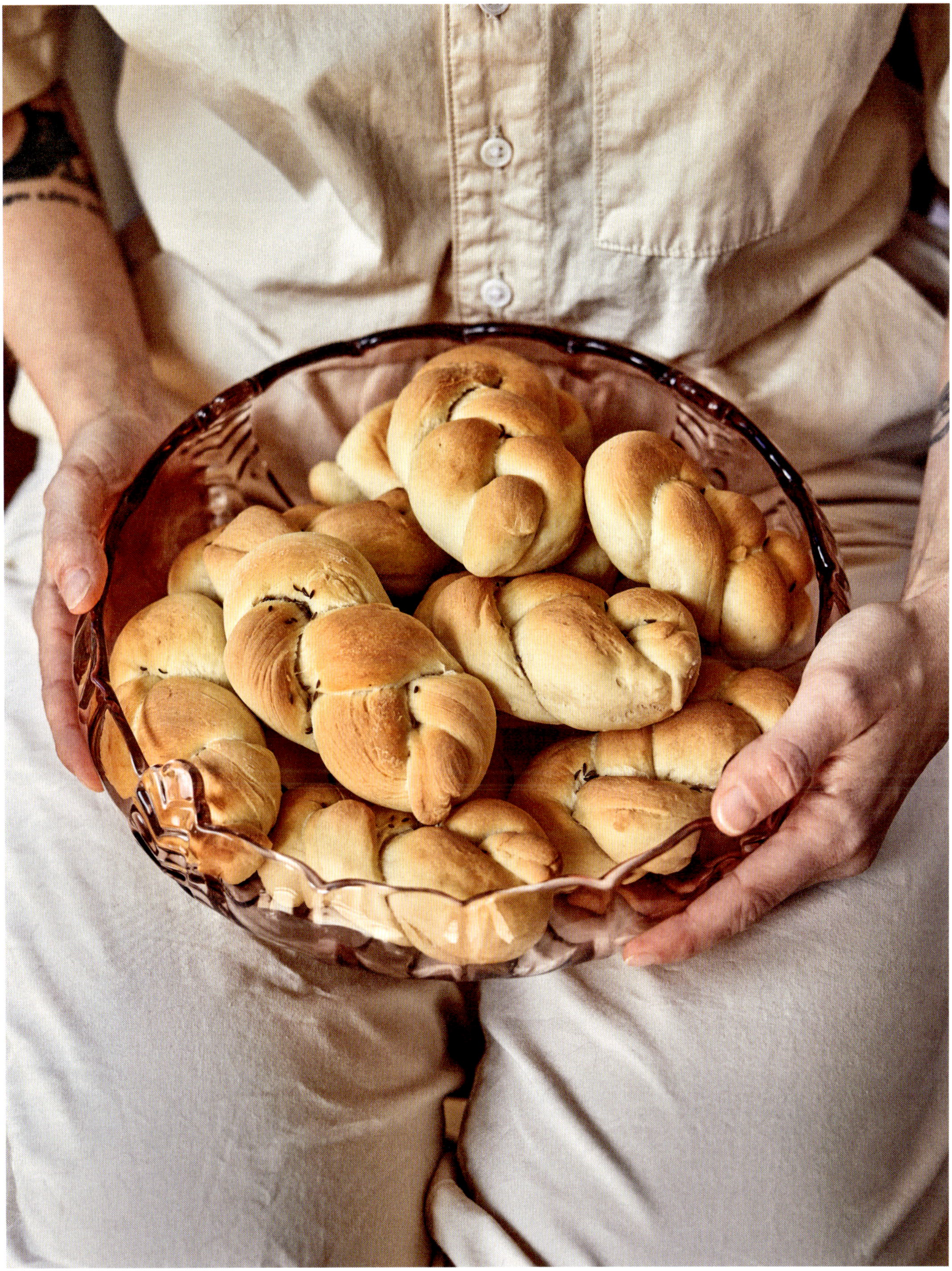

Lejoky—Old Czech Pancakes

Serves 4

Ingredients

About ⅔ cups (200 g) pastry flour or all-purpose (plain) flour

1 pinch salt

1 cup (250 ml) milk

1 cup (250 ml) water

1 egg

½ cup plus 1 tablespoon (125 g) unsalted butter

¾ cup (100 g) powdered (icing) sugar

Sift the flour into a bowl and add the salt, milk, water, and egg. Mix everything well with a whisk until the batter is lump-free. Let rest for at least 10 minutes. This batter should be slightly thinner than a conventional pancake batter. If it is too runny, thicken with a little flour, and if too thick, dilute with a little milk or water, then let rest for a few minutes.

Heat the butter in a saucepan and remove from the heat immediately. Heat a dry, preferably cast iron, skillet or frying pan, then using a ladle to add a scoop of the batter, cook small thin pancakes. Stack the finished pancakes on a plate, drizzling each with a little melted butter and dusting with a little powdered (icing) sugar. Serve warm.

Tip *Lejoky* are traditionally served with just butter and sugar, but you can also have them with your favorite preserves; for example, they taste great with a slightly tart Apricot and Thyme Jam (see p. 119).

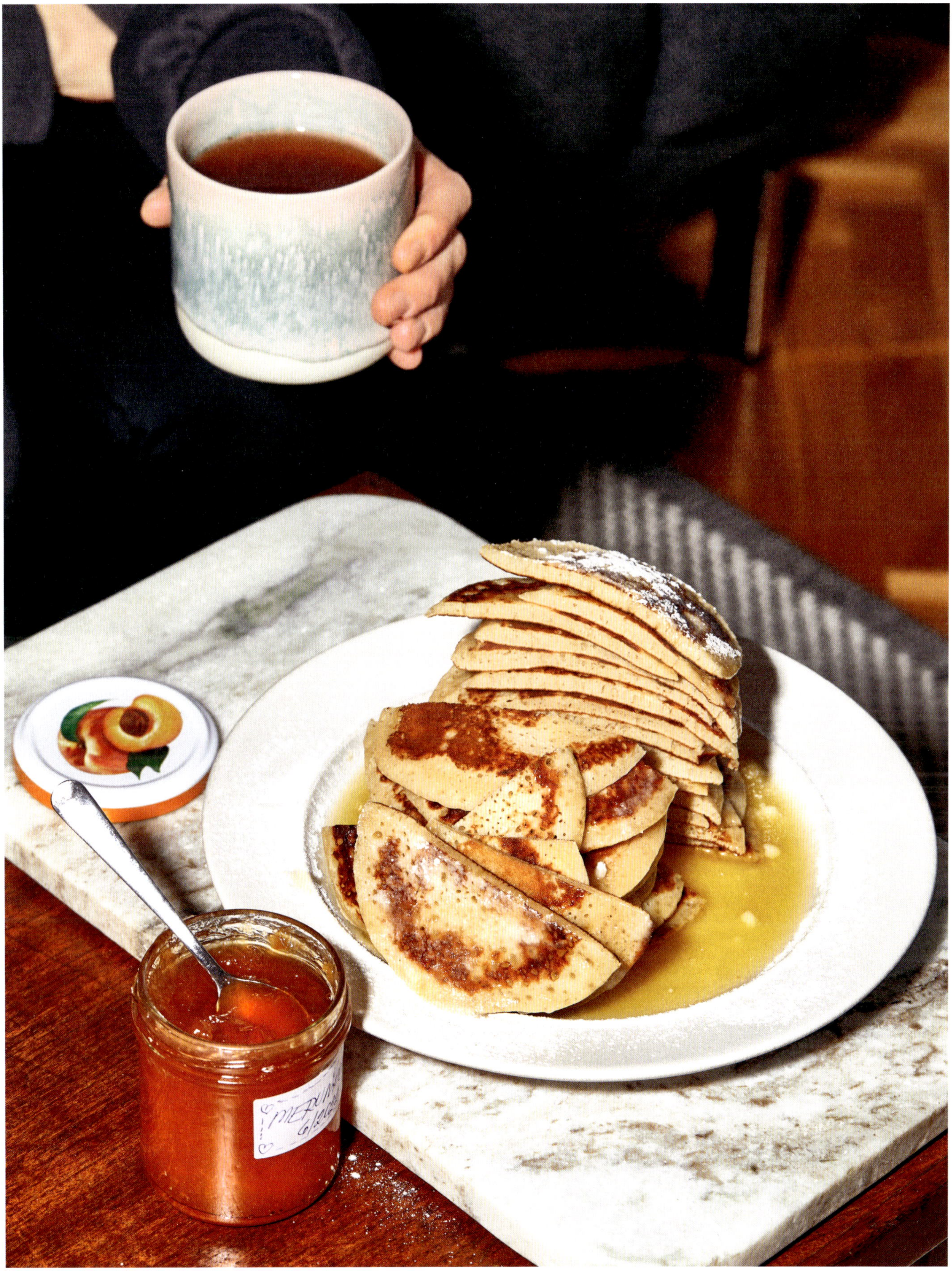

Smashed Potatoes with Chili Oil and Quark Dip

Serves 2 to 4

Ingredients

1½ pounds (700 g) small potatoes

1 teaspoon salt

4 teaspoons (20 ml) Chili Oil (see p. 133), plus extra for the dip

1 cup (250 g) soft, creamy quark (see also p. 15)

1 clove garlic

Salt and freshly ground black pepper

Wash the potatoes well, cleaning them with a vegetable brush, if necessary. Put the unpeeled potatoes into a pot and add enough water to cover them completely. Salt the water and bring to a boil. Parboil the potatoes over medium heat for about 15 minutes until they are half-cooked.

Preheat a convection (fan-assisted) oven to 450 °F (230 °C). Line a baking sheet with parchment (baking) paper. Drain the potatoes, let dry in the colander, and place on the baking sheet. Using the bottom of a mug, smash each potato flat and slightly brush with the chili oil. Bake for 10 to 15 minutes, until golden.

To make the dip, whisk the quark in a bowl until light and fluffy. Peel and mince (very finely chop) or crush the garlic clove through a garlic press and add to the whipped quark. Season with salt and pepper and mix well. Transfer the dip to a serving bowl and drizzle with chili oil.

Season the smashed potatoes with salt and a sprinkling of pepper and serve hot accompanied with the quark dip.

Tip You can also add minced fresh herbs of your choice to the dip, such as mint, dill, chives, or parsley. And why not try a combination of herbs?

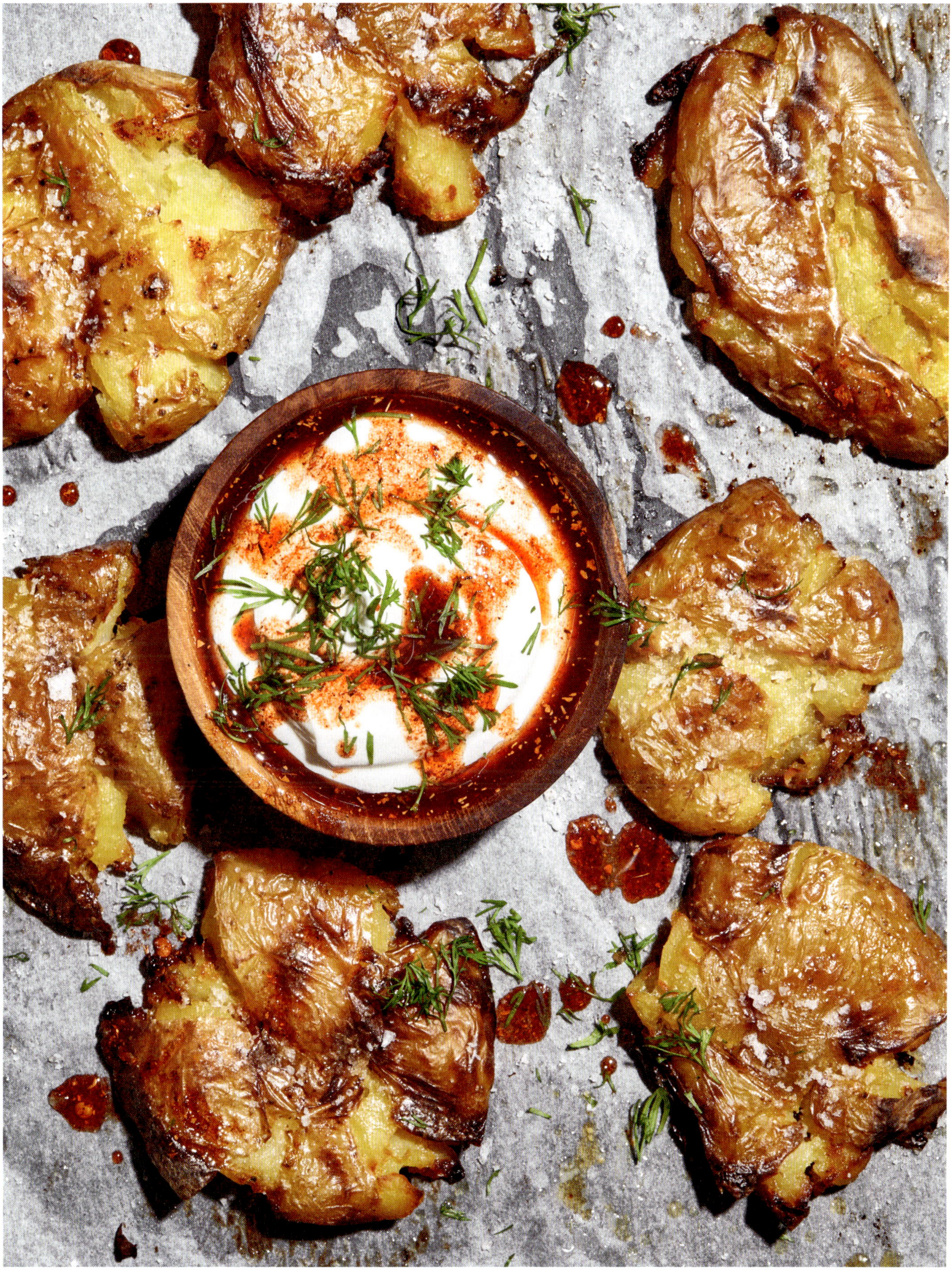

Španělské ptáčky—Czech Stuffed Beef Rolls

Serves 4

Ingredients

1 egg, hard boiled

2 large Traditional Pickled Cucumbers (see p. 114)

1 to 2 frankfurters (hot dogs)

4 slices bottom round steak

Salt and freshly ground black pepper

4 tablespoons medium-hot mustard

1 large onion

2 tablespoons lard

⅔ cup (150 ml) cold water

2 tablespoons all-purpose (plain) flour or Italian "00" flour

1 tablespoon cold unsalted butter

Steamed rice, to serve

Shell the egg, rinse it under cold water, and cut into quarters. Halve the pickled cucumbers, and cut the frankfurter(s) lengthwise into 4 equal sticks. Lightly tenderize the meat slices on both sides and season with salt and pepper. Spread one side of the meat with the mustard. Place a boiled egg quarter, half a cucumber, and a sausage stick on the bottom third of each mustard-coated meat slice. Roll up the meat slices and secure the rolls tightly with kitchen twine.

Preheat the oven to 350 °F top/bottom heat (180 °C/Gas Mark 4). Peel and mince (very finely chop) the onions. Heat the lard in a large roasting pan and sear the beef rolls on all sides over medium heat until browned. Remove the rolls. Sauté the onion in the roasting pan until golden. Return the beef rolls to the same roasting pan and add enough water to almost cover them. Cover the roasting pan with a lid and place in the oven. Cook the beef rolls for 1 hour 30 minutes to 2 hours, until the meat is tender.

In the meantime, make a slurry by thoroughly mixing 150 ml cold water with the flour in a mug. Let rest briefly.

Transfer the beef rolls to a plate and cover with aluminum foil to keep warm. Stir the slurry into the same roasting pan. Stir and let simmer over low heat for 20 to 30 minutes, until the flour cooks through and the gravy thickens. Using an immersion stick blender, blend the gravy until smooth. Finally, stir in the cold butter and season with salt and pepper. Return the beef rolls to the roasting pan and heat through in the gravy. Serve immediately with steamed rice.

Tips You can serve the *ptáčky* right after removing them from the oven, accompanied by the unthickened drippings. If you don't mind small pieces of roasted onion in the sauce, there's no need to blend it.

Arrange the rolls on plates and drizzle with lemon juice for more freshness.

Španělské ptáčky can also be served with a creamy sauce. In this case, make the sauce as described above and add ⅔ cup (150 ml) light (single) cream or whipping cream in the last 5 minutes of cooking. Serve with bread dumplings and Lingonberry-style Red Currants (see p. 105).

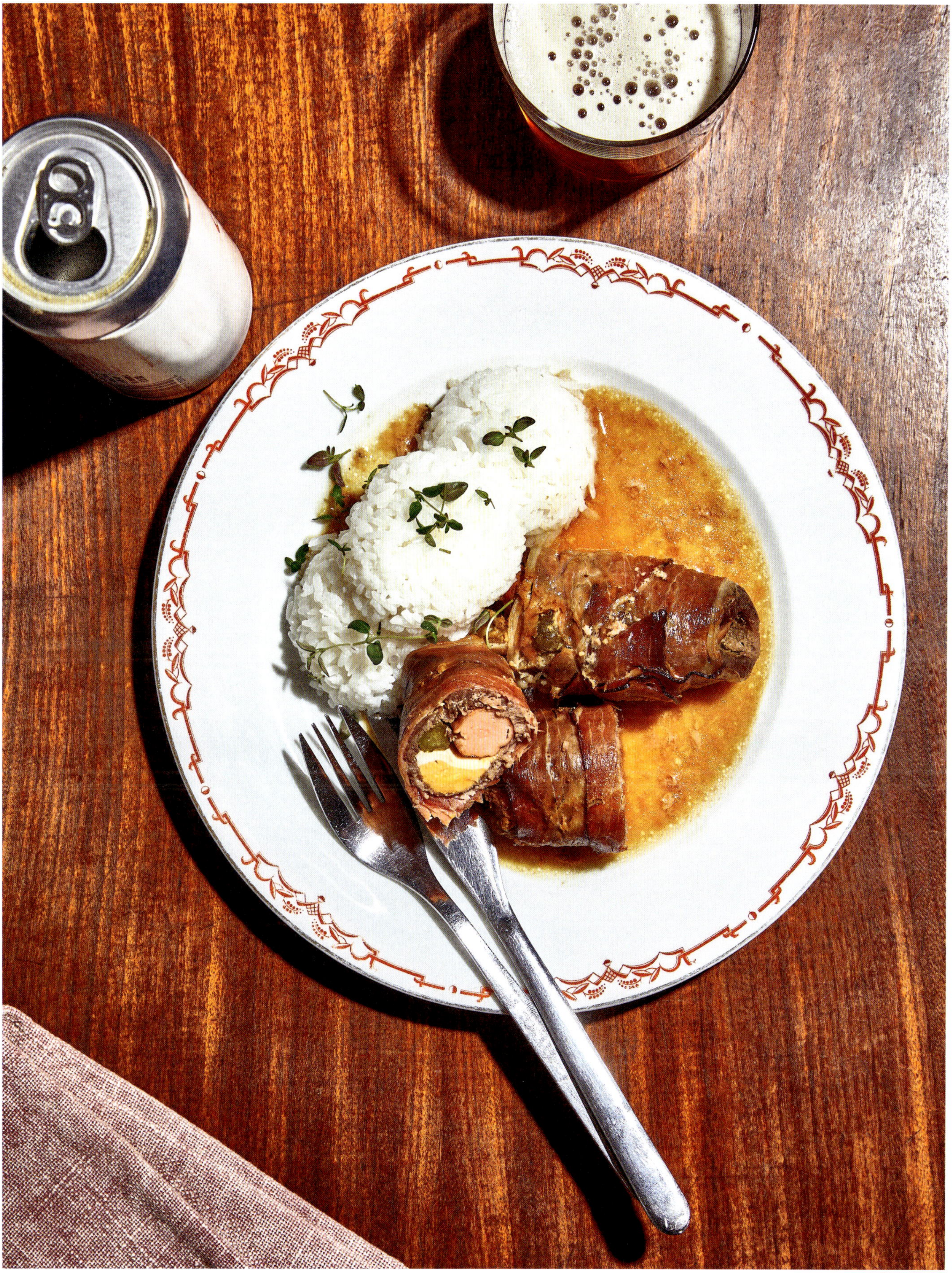

Pig Slaughter: A Czech Culinary Tradition and Social Event

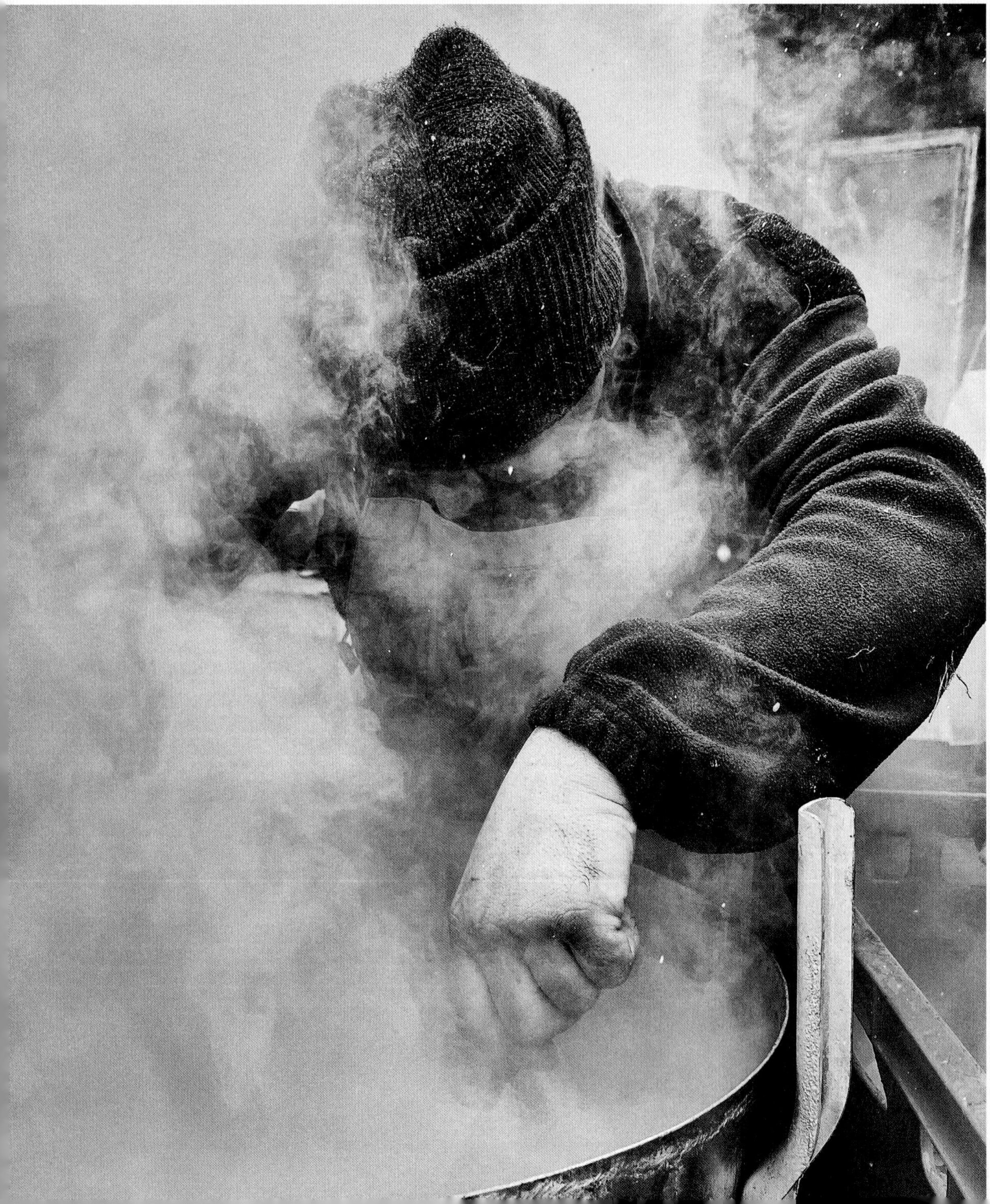

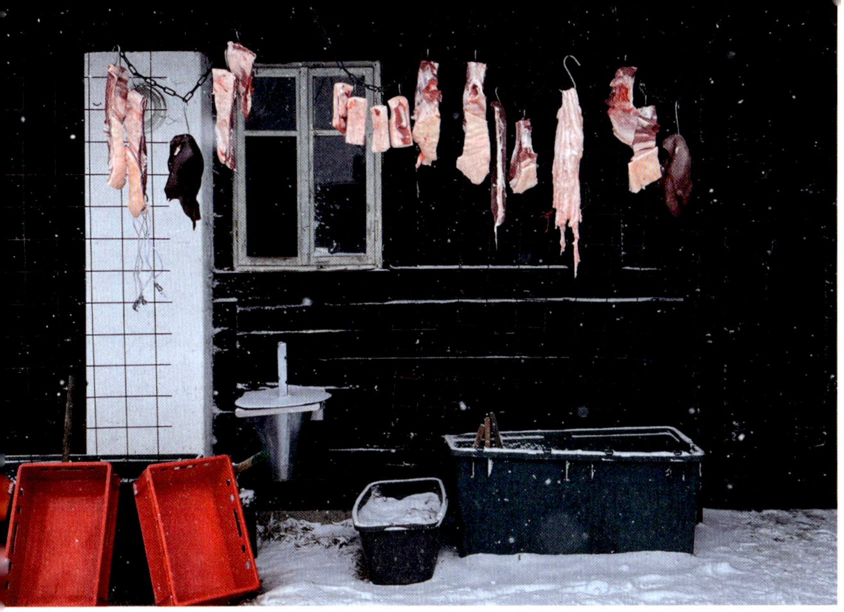

From blood soup to sweet baked goods, the Czech pig slaughter is a living ritual of shared labor, respect for the whole animal, and village camaraderie.

Home pig slaughter, known as *zabijačka*, is one of the oldest and most deeply rooted rural customs in Czech culture. It's more than a way of preparing food: It's a ceremony of community, gratitude, and abundance that has been handed down through the generations. Historically, it was one of the most important days of the year for any village household. Beyond the practical need to stock up on meat for the winter, it carried symbolic meaning, being a ritual that bound families and neighbors together through shared work and celebration.

The origins of Czech pig slaughtering date back to the Middle Ages, when pork began to appear more frequently on the tables of common people. Before industrial refrigeration, slaughtering could be done only in the cold months, when low temperatures naturally preserved meat and fat. It also spared families from the need to feed pigs through the long winter, when supplies were scarce. Slaughtering usually began around the Feast of St. Martin in November—a symbolic farewell to the bounty of fall—and continued through carnival season, the period of festivity between Advent and Lent. Fat Thursday (*Tučný čtvrtek*), marking the end of carnival, was the peak of the season; it was a day of feasting, dancing, and superstition, when you would eat and drink your fill to have strength for the year ahead. Many regions still observe these traditions today, each with its own local variations.

Unlike today's habit of buying anonymous, prepackaged meat from stores, the *zabijačka* provided a deeper understanding of where food came from. It was personal. The pig was raised at home, often named, well fed, and well cared for. Families knew the animal, and its death was treated with respect. Every part was used: meat, fat, blood, skin, entrails, and bones—nothing went to waste. This old ethic of respect for the whole animal feels strikingly modern today, echoing the "nose-to-tail" cooking movement.

The butchering and the feast that followed, carried a ritual tone, with a celebration of abundance, gratitude, labor, and the natural cycle of life. Everyone had a role: one person slaughtered, another rendered lard, a third seasoned sausage meat. The results were shared among all who helped and sent as gifts to family and friends. It's no wonder Czechs still say, with a wink, that "a pig has the most relatives." Delicacies still pile high on the tables at a traditional Czech pig slaughter today: *ovar* (boiled cuts from the head, tongue, neck, and shoulder), *mozeček* (brains with eggs), *prdelačka* (blood soup with groats), blood fried with onions, and *jitrnice* and *jelita* (white and black sausages). These savory dishes are accompanied by pickled horseradish, *vejmrda* (grated horseradish with apples), and mustard (see p. 264). And no Czech revelry is complete without something sweet, so there are *kolaches, boží milosti* (crisp, fried pastries dusted with sugar), strudels, and, of course, *koblihy* (see p. 106, 162, and 68).

Today, traditional home slaughtering is slowly disappearing. The decline of small farms, the year-round availability of pork, changing rural lifestyles, and growing interest in healthy eating have pushed *zabijačka* into retreat. Yet the spirit lives on: Restaurants now host "slaughter weeks," offering classic dishes throughout the year.

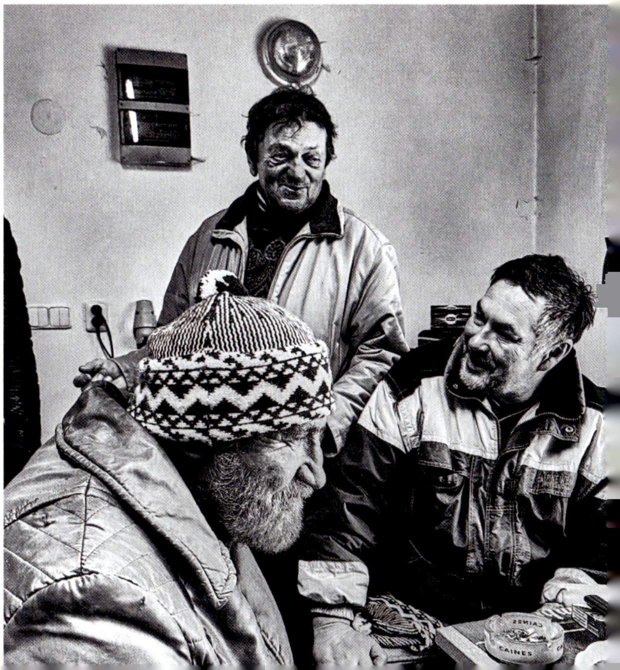

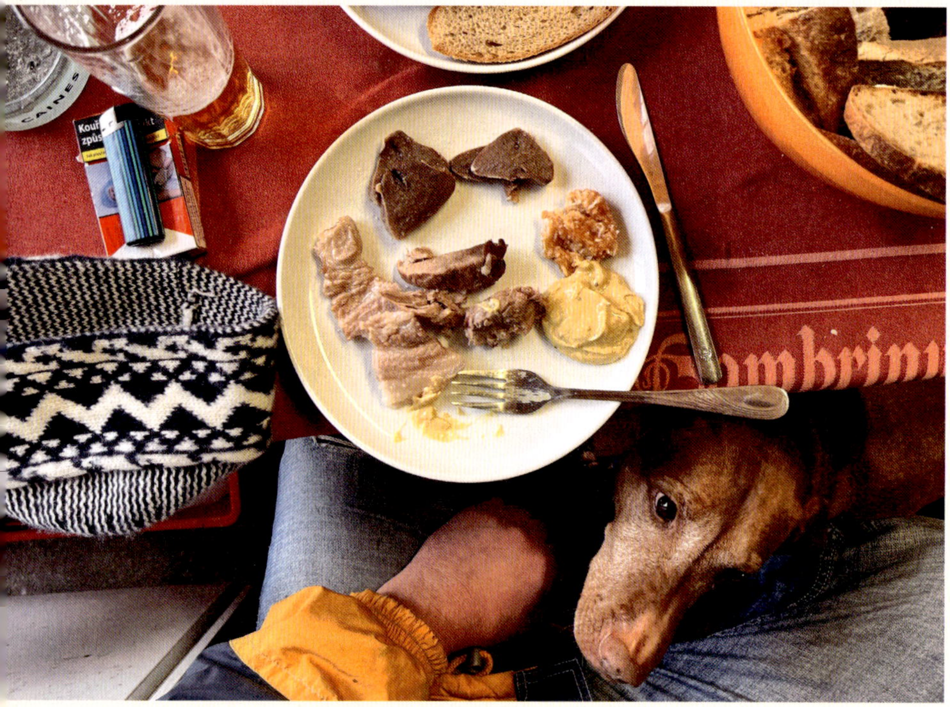

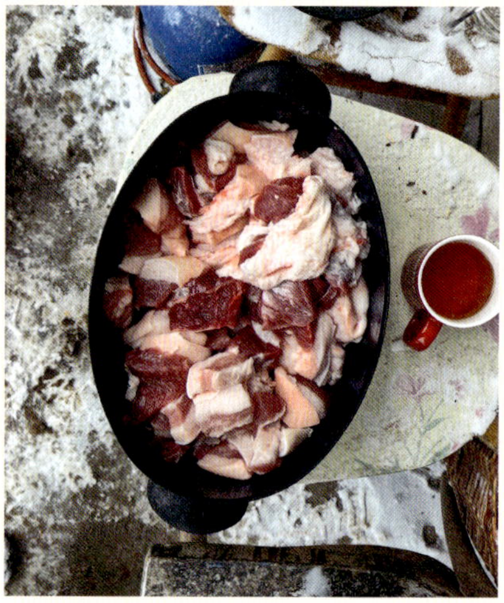

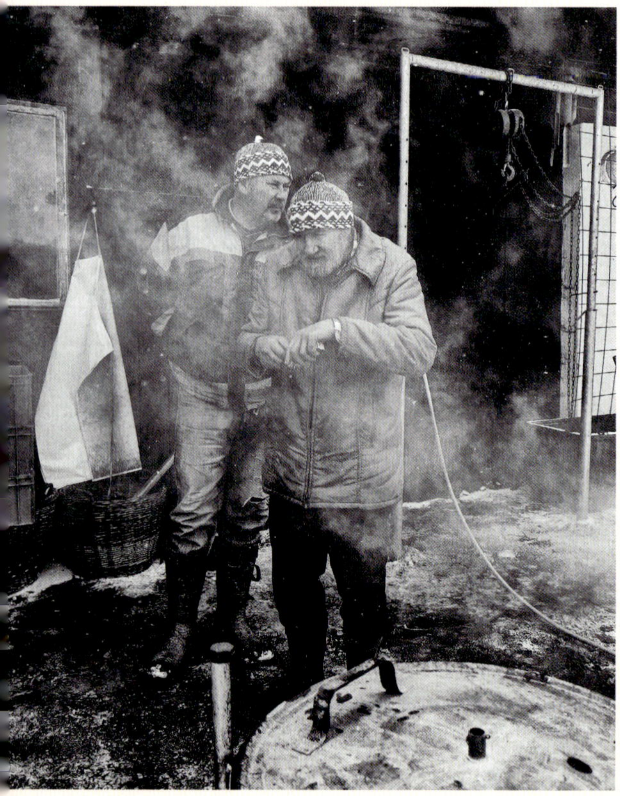

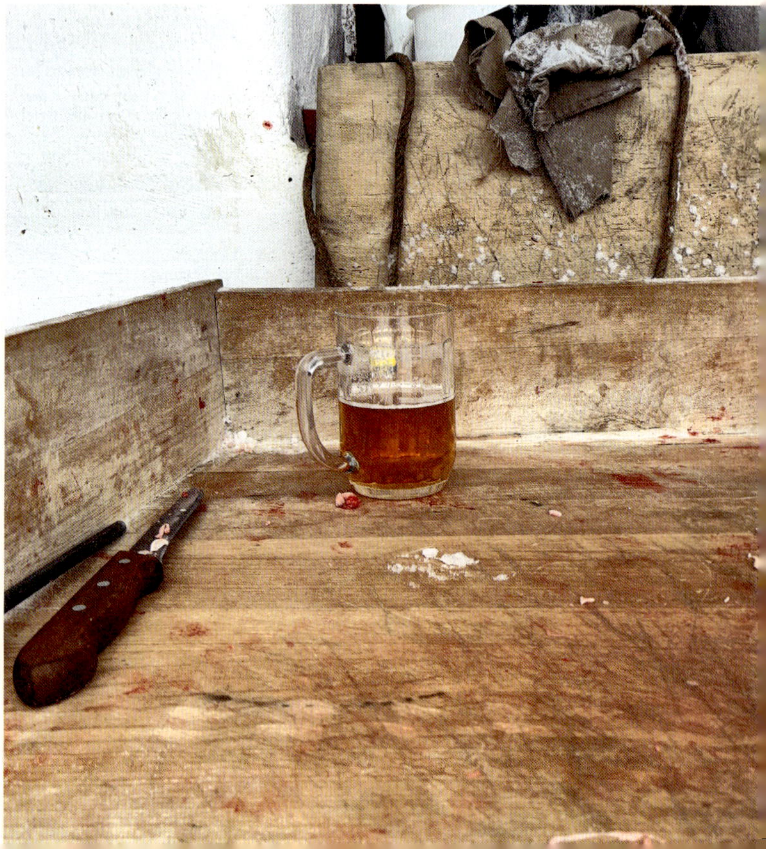

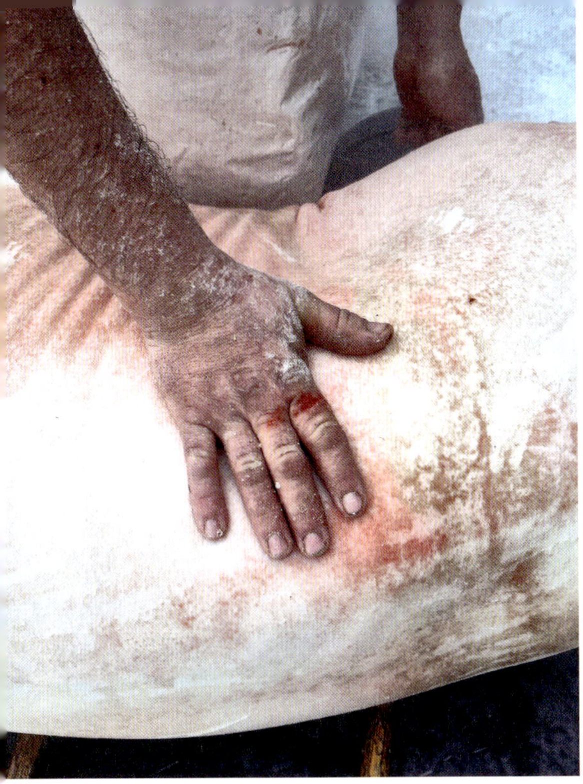

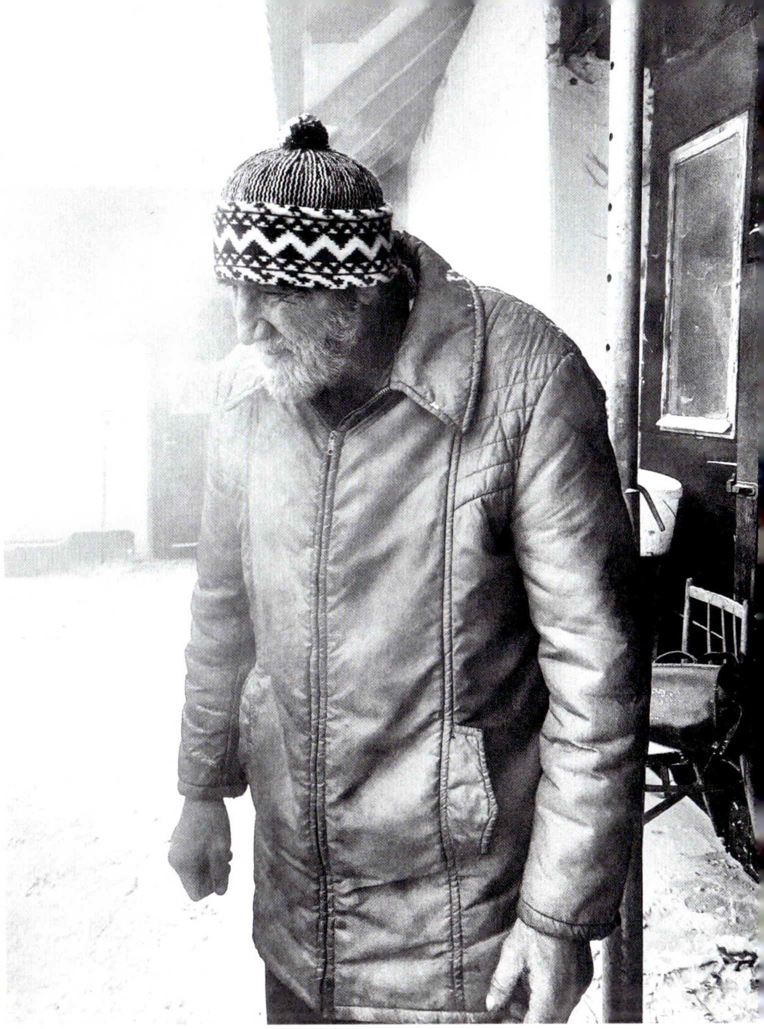

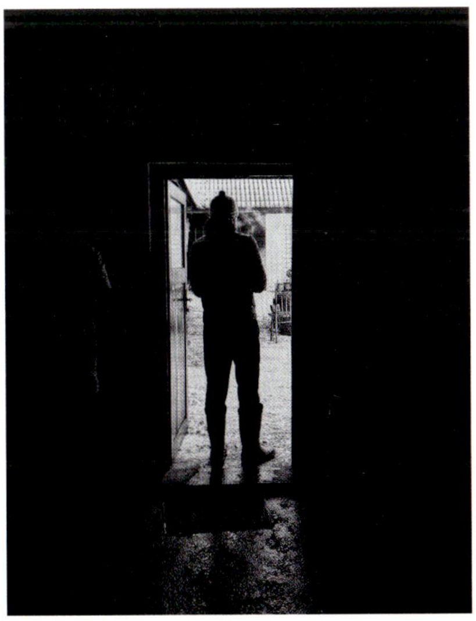

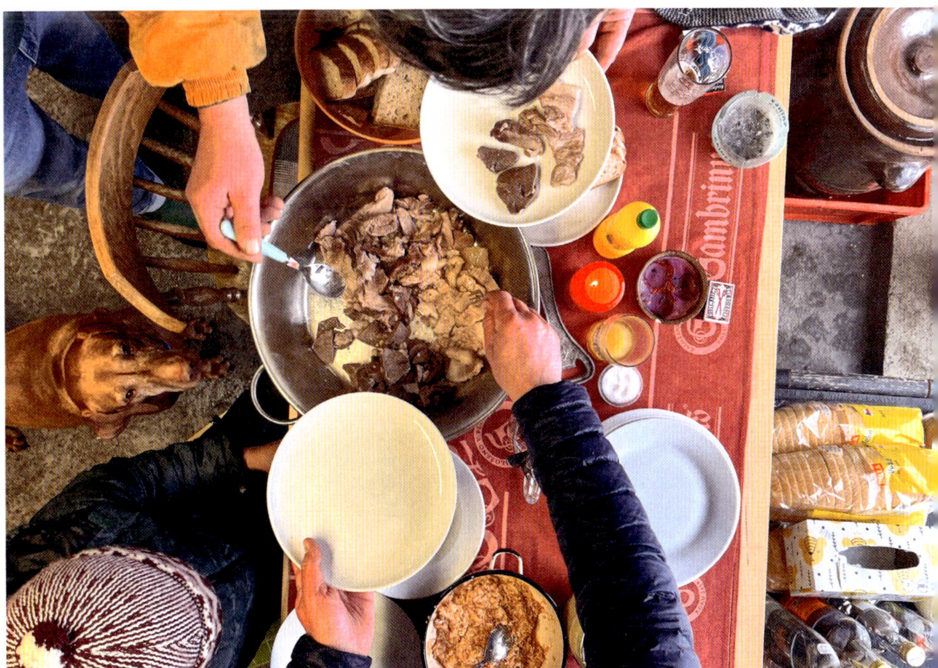

Pickled Horseradish

For 2 canning jars (8 ounces / 200 ml each)

Ingredients

Scant 1 cup (200 ml) water

2 tablespoon granulated sugar

1 teaspoon salt

10 ½ ounces (300 g) fresh horseradish root

3 ½ tablespoons (50 ml) distilled white vinegar

About ⅓ cup (80–100 ml) sunflower oil, plus extra if required

To make the pickling liquid, mix the water with the sugar and salt in a saucepan and simmer over medium heat, stirring occasionally, for 5 minutes, until the sugar and salt dissolve.

Trim and peel the horseradish, then grate it into a ceramic or glass bowl with the vinegar (the vinegar stops the horseradish from turning brown). Or pulse the sliced or chopped horseradish with the vinegar in a blender.

Pour half of the hot liquid over the horseradish, add the oil, and mix well. Add more hot liquid or oil if needed until the horseradish is glossy.

Transfer the horseradish to sterilized canning jars. Wipe the jar rims with a clean cloth. Close the jars tightly, place upside down, and let cool. Store in the refrigerator and consume within 1 week. If you want it to last the whole winter, briefly can the jars in a water bath.

Tips Homemade pickled horseradish is much more pungent than store bought! You'll probably shed some tears while preparing it, so brace yourself.

It makes a great base for creamy horseradish sauce. In this case, don't cook the horseradish for too long, otherwise it will lose its sharp taste. It should be stirred into the sauce only at the end.

Pickled horseradish makes a good accompaniment for traditional Czech pork feast delicacies, such as liver, blood or smoked sausages, and broiled (grilled) meat.

Vejmrda

For 2 canning jars (8 ounces / 200 ml each)

Ingredients

7 ounces (200 g) fresh horseradish root

3 apples

Juice of ½ lemon

2 tablespoons apple cider vinegar

2 to 3 tablespoons granulated sugar

2 large pinches of salt

Trim and peel the horseradish and wash the apples. Coarsely grate the horseradish and apples into a bowl and sprinkle with the lemon juice to stop the mixture from turning brown. Add the vinegar, sugar, and salt and mix well.

Cover the bowl with a plate and let the mixture infuse for at least 10 minutes. Adjust the seasoning with vinegar, sugar, and salt.

Transfer the apple horseradish mixture to sterilized canning jars and wipe the jar rims with a clean cloth. Close the lid tightly and refrigerate. If you want the apple horseradish conserve to last longer, you should briefly can the jars in a water bath. This will turn it slightly darker and softer and give it a milder taste.

Tip For a hotter version, add a little more horseradish. If you want the apple horseradish conserve to be a little sweeter, simply use more apples. Vejmrda can be used in the same way as Pickled Horseradish (see above).

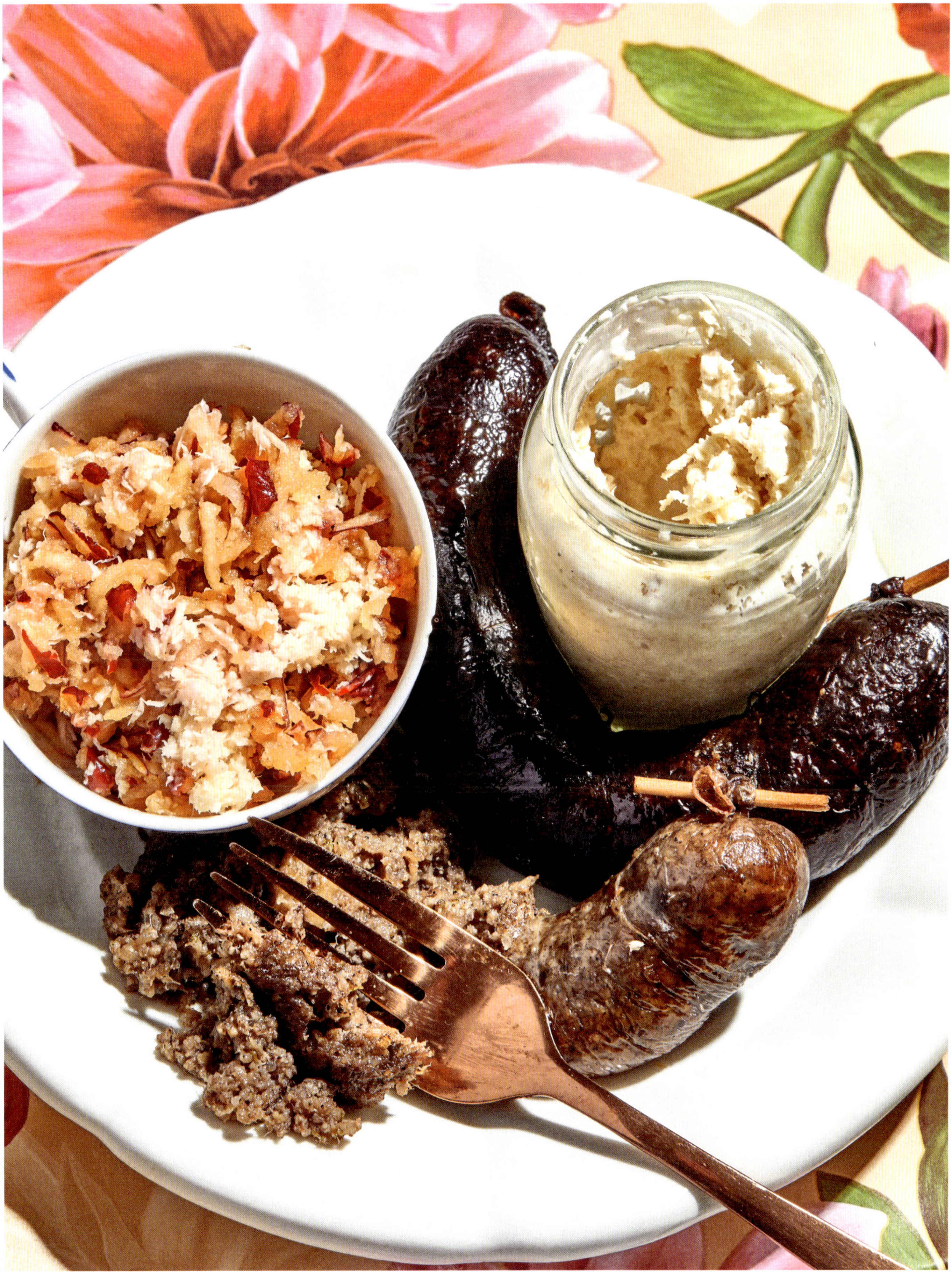

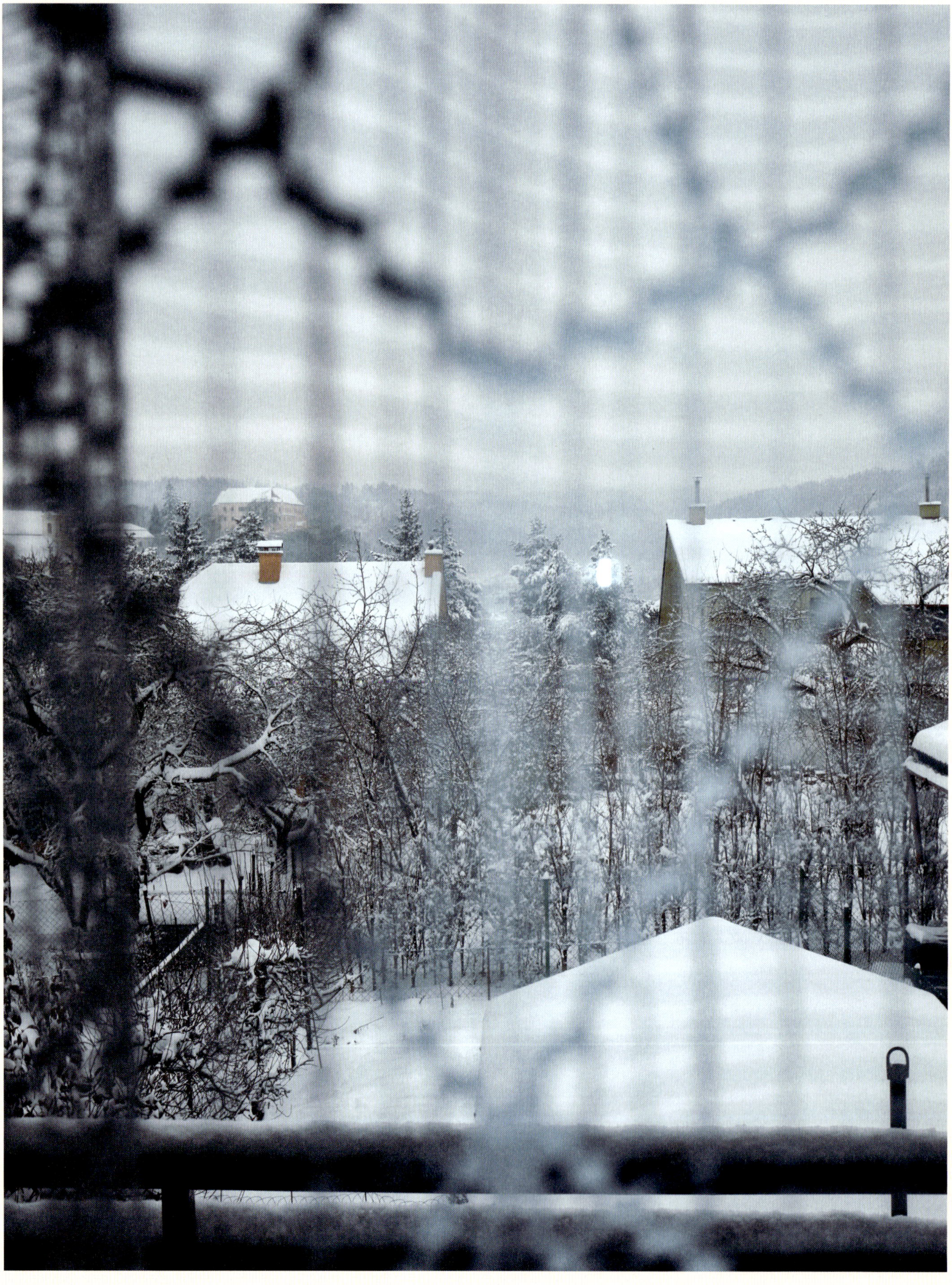

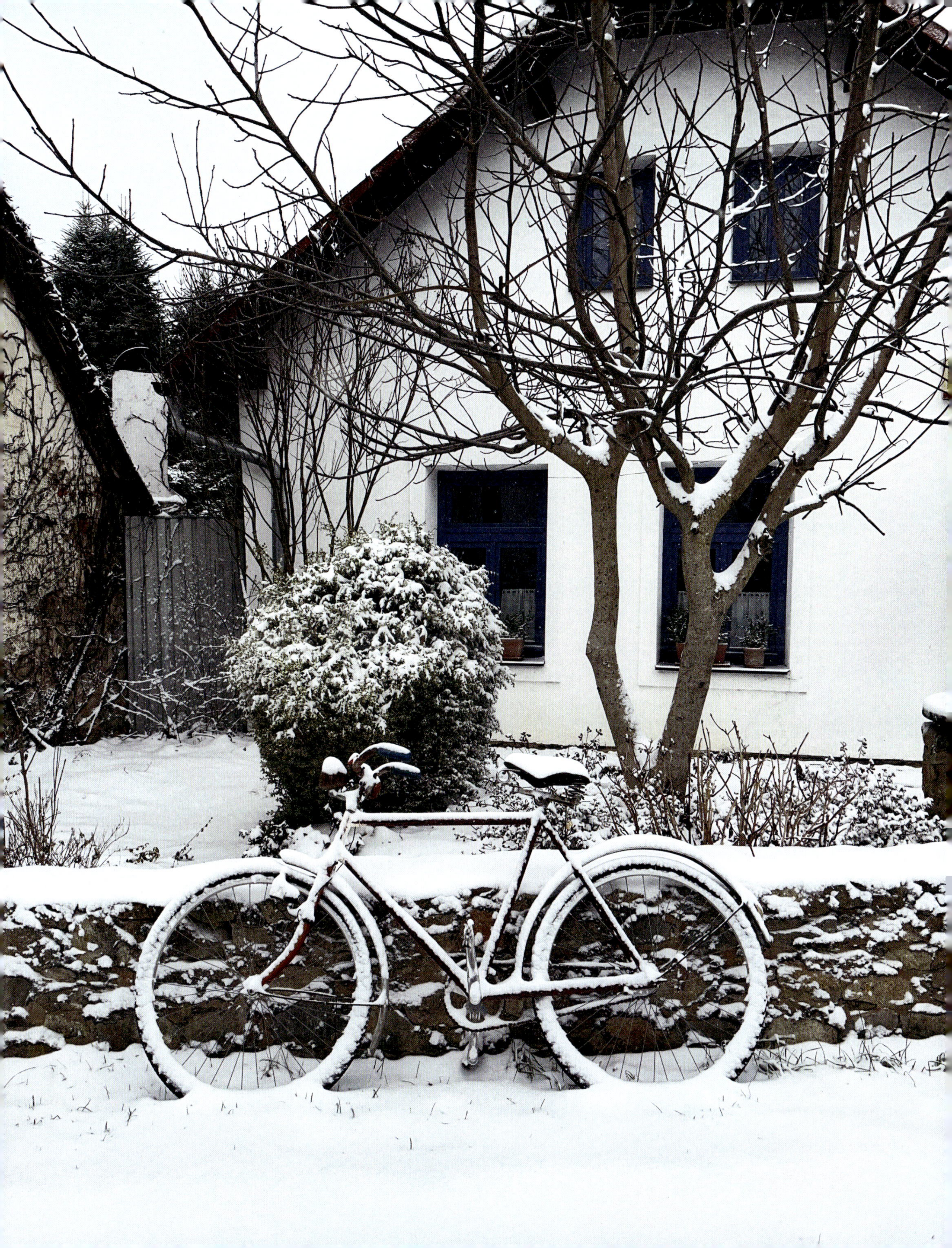

Common Canning Pitfalls and How to Avoid Them

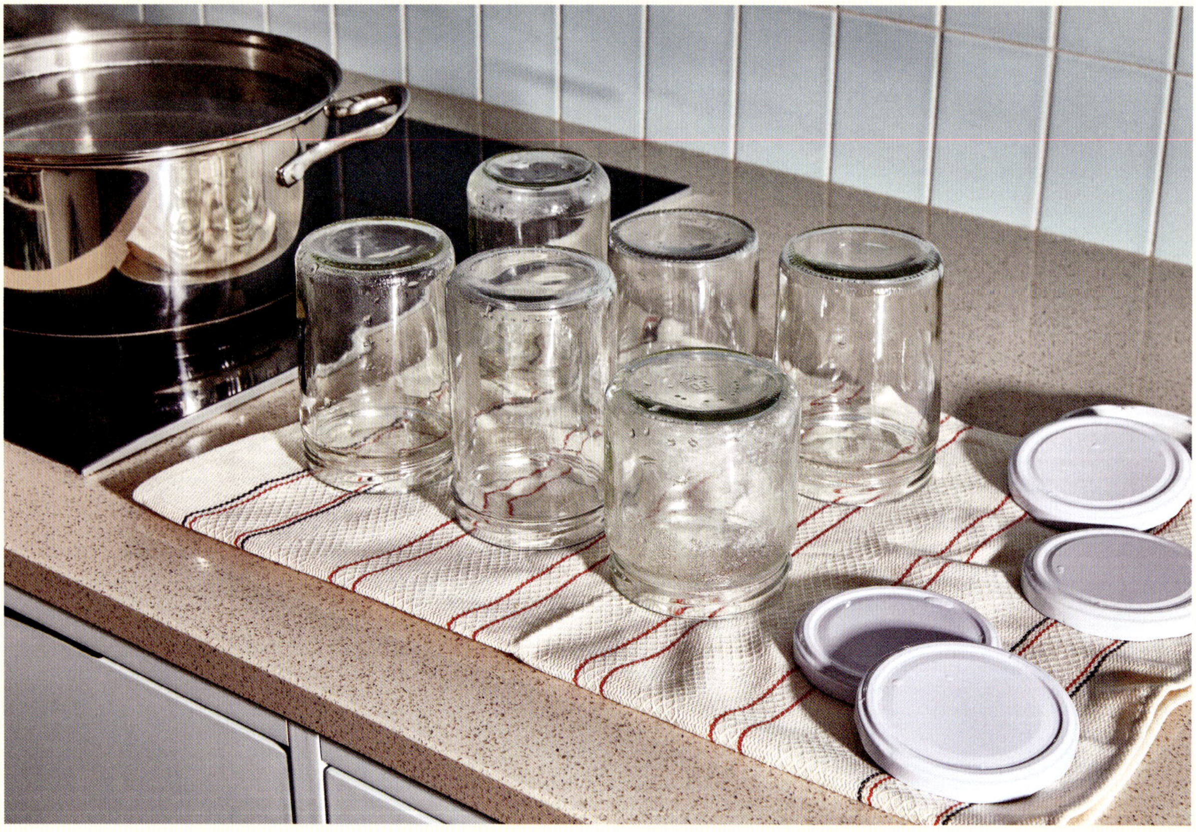

Homemade jams, fruity compotes, and spicy chutneys have long been some of the pleasures of everyday life. Canning is gaining in popularity, because it's sustainable, creative, and fun to do. But as with cooking or baking, not everything with canning always goes according to plan. However, with a little knowledge, typical mistakes can be avoided—and the result is guaranteed to be delicious. Which steps make the difference between successful preserves and a failed batch?

1. Cleanliness is everything

Rule number one: To ensure your preserves taste great and are safe to eat, cleanliness and sufficient heat treatment are essential. Jars with lids must always be thoroughly sterilized, and most fruit and vegetable products require heat processing. You can read how to do this on pages 10–11.

2. Sugar as a natural preservative

Sugar is not only a flavor carrier when canning but also acts as a natural preservative. A ratio of at least 2 ½ cups (500 g / 1 lb 2 oz) of sugar to 2 ¼ pounds (1 kg) of fruit or 4 ¼ cups (1 l) of syrup is recommended. If you use less sugar, store the jars in the refrigerator, which will keep the canned food fresh for about 2 weeks.

3. Lemon juice, an underestimated aid

Lemon juice or citric acid is also a useful helper. Both contribute to balanced flavor, vibrant color, better gelling, and a longer shelf life. Acidity also plays an important role in safety. A sufficiently acidic environment prevents the growth of dangerous bacteria, especially *Clostridium botulinum*, which can cause a serious illness known as botulism. Although botulism is very rare in homemade preserves, it's wise to minimize the risk in low-acid foods (such as mushrooms).

The juice of ½ lemon or 1 heaping teaspoon of citric acid is sufficient for 2 ¼ pounds (1 kg) of fruit or vegetables. Ideally, the acid should be added at the end of the cooking time to preserve the flavor. Vinegar or kombucha can also be used as natural preservatives. However, too much acid can impair gelling properties.

4. Uniform pieces for uniform results

Cut the fruit for preservation into even pieces of the same size. During sterilization, smaller pieces may soften more than desired. For the same reason, it's generally recommended to combine fruit and vegetables of similar firmness.

5. Fill jars correctly

Canning jars should always be filled to about ¾ inch (2 cm) below the rim. This will leave enough space for negative pressure and a secure closure. All ingredients should also be completely covered with liquid—otherwise they risk unsightly discoloration and even spoilage.

6. Clean rims ensure durability

Splashes on the rim of a jar during filling may hinder the lid from creating an airtight seal. Therefore, always wipe the edge with a clean dishcloth (tea towel). Even better, use a filling funnel to save time and nerves.

7. Close the lid properly

Screw the lids on securely, but don't overtighten them. Heating the jars creates pressure that must be able to escape. If a lid is on too tightly, no vacuum can form during cooling, meaning that the jar will leak. Leftovers that fill only half a jar should be stored in the refrigerator after cooling and used up as quickly as possible.

8. The classic gelling test

How to tell if your jam has the right consistency? Briefly chill a saucer in the freezer, add a spoonful of hot jam, and wait for a short time. If it sets and is no longer runny, the consistency is perfect. With a little experience, you will soon be able to recognize when it is ready directly in the pot—the jam will form wrinkles when stirred that disappear slowly.

9. Every minute counts

Excessive heating destroys not only vitamins but also taste and texture. For this reason, a kitchen timer is a good friend to have when canning. If the fruit or vegetables are already covered with hot syrup or a pickling liquid, sterilization time can often be reduced by a few minutes.

10. If something goes wrong, it is best to discard

Does the preserve smell off, bubble, appear cloudy, have mold on the surface, a bulging lid, or hiss when opened? If you have any doubts about the quality of the preserve or whether the sterilization was done properly, discard the contents to be safe. Never consume or taste suspicious preserves! Even a small amount of contaminated food can cause serious poisoning.

INDEX / COLLECTION OF RECIPES

GOD IS A PICKLE

Recipes and Stories for Preserving the Seasons
A Culinary Journey Through the Czech Republic

This book was edited and designed by gestalten.

Edited by Iris Hempelmann and François-Luc Giraldeau

Written by Šárka Otevřel Camrdová

Photography by Marek Bartoš

Translated from Czech into English by Booklab GmbH

Editorial management by Friederike Christoph

Design & Layout by Melanie Ullrich

Production management by Martin Bretschneider

Typefaces by Christian Jánský (Victor Serif)
and David Jonathan Ross (Roslindale)

Printed by Optimal Media GmbH, Röbel

Made in Germany

Published by gestalten, Berlin 2026

ISBN 978-3-96704-209-2

1st printing, 2026

With deep thanks to everyone who made this book possible, especially:

Czech editor: Kristina Šemberová
Food stylist: Petra Frýdlová
Photography production: Snack & Friends, snackandfriends.com
Initial Design Concept: Lucie Bajgartová
Idea for Book Title: Jumping Jacks

For more information and to order books, please visit www.gestalten.com

Die Gestalten Verlag GmbH & Co. KG
Mariannenstrasse 9–10
10999 Berlin, Germany
hello@gestalten.com

Bibliographic information published by the Deutsche Nationalbibliothek

The Deutsche Nationalbibliothek lists this publication in the Deutsche Nationalbibliografie; detailed bibliographic data is available online at www.dnb.de

This book was printed on paper certified according to the standards of the FSC®.

FSC www.fsc.org MIX Paper | Supporting responsible forestry FSC® C108521

Disclaimer: Readers should follow the safety guidelines and warnings provided throughout the book. The authors and publisher expressly disclaim responsibility for any adverse effects that may result from the application or misapplication of the information contained herein.